On the Edge of Paradise
A. C. BENSON: THE DIARIST

A History of Wellington College

Godliness and Good Learning
Four Studies on a Victorian Ideal

The Parting of Friends
*A Study of the Wilberforces
and Henry Manning*

Two Classes of Men
*Platonism and English Romantic
Thought*

On the Edge of Paradise

A. C. BENSON: THE DIARIST

David Newsome

JOHN MURRAY

© David Newsome 1980

First published 1980
by John Murray (Publishers) Ltd
50 Albemarle Street, London W1X 4BD

Filmset by Keyspools Ltd, Golborne, Lancs.
Printed in Great Britain by Fakenham Press Limited, London & Fakenham

British Library Cataloguing in Publication Data

Newsome, David
On the edge of paradise.
1. Benson, A C – Biography 2. Authors, English
– 19th century – Biography 3. Authors, English
– 20th century – Biography
I. Title
828′,8′09   PR4099.B5

ISBN 0-7195-3690-1

To
WALTER HAMILTON
with deepest gratitude

It is so strange to be always, as I seem to be, on
the edge of Paradise and never quite finding the way in.
(July 1910)

You are not in the least like the children of Archbishops.
(Gertrude Bell to A. C. Benson, 1911)

A rhetorician without passion, a quietist without peace.
(A. C. Benson on himself, 13 August 1917)

CONTENTS

ILLUSTRATIONS

Illustration credits: Magdalene College, Cambridge, 1, 2, 8, 10, 11, 17, 18, 19, 20; Nicholas Mosley, 4; Sir John Barnes, 7; Sir Rupert Hart-Davis, 12; Royal Geographical Society, 13; Beatrice Brocklebank, 15; George Rylands, 16.

ACKNOWLEDGEMENTS

My chief debt of gratitude is undoubtedly to the Master and Fellows of Magdalene College, Cambridge, for allowing me the fullest possible use, for the purpose of publication, of the whole of the vast Benson collection in the Old Library at Magdalene College. In particular, I should like to thank Dr Walter Hamilton, who was Master of Magdalene at the time that the invitation was extended to me to undertake this work. He has also read through the whole of my typescript, making many valuable suggestions and corrections. I am also grateful to Mr Robert Latham (Pepys Librarian) and Mr D. Pepys-Whitely for their help and advice to me on the occasions of my visits to the Old Library in search of further material and photographs. The greatest possible encouragement has been given to me by those who knew Arthur Benson personally and who corresponded frequently with him. Of these, I should especially like to thank Mr George Rylands of King's College (who also has read the book in typescript) and the Rt. Rev. David Loveday, who loaned me many letters. The Rt. Rev. and Rt. Hon. Lord Ramsey of Canterbury has also shown very kind interest and sent me a copy of his father's private recollections of A.C.B. at Magdalene, where they were colleagues for so many years. Sir John Barnes and Mrs Beatrice Brocklebank kindly offered me letters and photographs. I am indebted to Sir Rupert Hart-Davis for a copy of the drawing of Hugh Walpole as a young man. At Christ's Hospital, two successive librarians – Mrs O. M. Peto and Mr N. M. Plumley – have kindly consented to act as custodians of the huge crate of Benson diaries, on loan to me from Magdalene. I had generous help from my daughter, Mrs Louise Winchcombe, in indexing the diaries; and from Mr John Granger and my youngest daughter, Cordelia, in compiling the index to the book itself. As ever, Mr John Murray has taken the closest personal interest in the progress of the book; and Mr Roger Hudson, who has been most directly concerned with its production, has been a wonderful support throughout. I am very grateful.

PREFACE

The dead are free to reveal their innermost secrets. More questionable, however, is their freedom to reveal the secrets of others. When Arthur Benson left instructions that his diaries should be locked away for fifty years after his death (17 June 1925), he was well aware that susceptibilities could be offended by the publication of certain of the confidences that came his way as well as by the frankness of his private comments. He was not, however, a very old man when he died, and he counted a number of young men among his closest friends. It is not therefore surprising that some of his circle should have survived long enough to learn something of the private thoughts that he harboured during the periods when they knew him well, although it is to be hoped that none of them will have cause to take offence. Indeed, his kindness and affection towards the young were such that it is highly unlikely that they should wish to be other than charitable towards him.

For those who never knew him personally, some of his statements and opinions (especially when he was commenting upon eminent personages) might seem gratuitous, ungenerous, even unfair. It is to be remembered, however, that the opinions recorded are intensely subjective; and many of the statements, being in the main the record of private conversations, are quite incapable of verification. If, then, I have inadvertently caused any hurt to others by faithfully transcribing Arthur Benson's words, I apologise sincerely. Certainly there has been no wish or intention to cause the slightest offence to anyone.

DAVID NEWSOME

THE MAN AND HIS DIARIES

I want prejudice, preference, humanity, humour, malice,
salinity, a hundred little spices, in my dish.   (May, 1903)

I confess to feeling the most minute and detailed interest in
the smallest matters connected with other people's lives and
idiosyncrasies.   (*From a College Window*)

The diaries of Arthur Christopher Benson comprise one of the most
extensive and detailed private records of a man's thoughts and
observations of his times that has ever been preserved. In all they run to
one hundred and eighty volumes and provide (with the single exception
of four blank years during a period of mental breakdown) a continuous
chronicle from the summer of 1897, when Arthur Benson was thirty-five
and a housemaster at Eton College, until his death, as Master of
Magdalene College, Cambridge, in June 1925 at the age of sixty-three.
The whole record amounts to more than four million words.

Why, it may be asked, does a man take the trouble to write a diary –
especially a diary of such substance as this? He may feel that his life is so
important that he owes it to posterity to record his actions and
impressions day by day; or that the times in which he is living, and the
events he is privileged to witness, are so momentous that – granted the
faculty of accurate observation and a fluent pen – he must take upon
himself the task of chronicler. He may write in order to justify a
controversial life or a much-abused career; he may be so introspective
and self-absorbed that he can only get to grips with his doubts and
dilemmas through the medium of a *journal intime*. Or, quite simply, he
may so enjoy the exercise of writing that his diary becomes a sort of
personal indulgence – the satisfaction of some compulsive craving for
self-analysis and self-expression.

Of all these possible answers, probably the last comes nearest to the
truth. Something must happen, of course, to supply the impetus. With
Arthur Benson, it was undoubtedly the reading, during the early summer
of 1897, of Francis Warre Cornish's edition of the *Letters and Journals of*

I

The Man and his Diaries

William Johnson Cory – one of the most inspiring, and certainly one of the most controversial, figures in Eton's history; the ardent lover of youth who, as an Eton master, had converted the relationship between master and pupil into a sort of romance, and who had been compelled to leave Eton 'under a cloud' during the Head Mastership of J. J. Hornby. On 23 August 1897, Arthur Benson wrote: 'I never had the courage to begin this sort of Diary before, but W.J. inspires me. I shall be glad if I can keep it up. I used to think I should not be long-lived, and felt ominously. Now I wd. give much to have kept one. It is the answer to all people like myself who want to write and cannot.'

This last observation seems curiously wide of the mark when it is recalled that Arthur Benson had already published three volumes of poems and four prose works besides (three of which he admittedly viewed with different degrees of dissatisfaction); that he was at the time engaged in writing the massive two-volume biography of his father, who had died as Archbishop of Canterbury in October of the previous year; and that in the course of the next twenty-eight years nearly fifty more volumes were to be added to his list of published works. Nevertheless the diary entries did not flag for an instant. They became more detailed and wide-ranging, if anything. As his reputation as a writer became more secure, so the diary came to fill another personal need: the need, as he put it, 'to get some of the venom out of my system'; to indulge his passion for minute observation and irreverent description of the quirks and foibles of both his critics and his friends (his friends, perhaps, most of all); to write what he could never say in public, partly for fear of giving offence and partly because the image which he created for himself as a writer (serene, sagacious, charitable, confiding – like one who lies 'on a sofa looking at the sunset with melancholy eyes') was so totally at variance with the *moqueur* and *convive*, which was the side of his nature most evident and most congenial to his friends. And as the dichotomy between the two personalities became more marked, with Arthur Benson's rising success with a reading public which he shunned socially, so the diary came to be more and more preoccupied with the problem of his own identity, posing the ultimate questions – 'Who am I?' – 'What does it all mean?'

These were certainly questions which taxed those nearest and dearest to Arthur himself. His brother Fred (the novelist, E. F. Benson) described Arthur's personality as 'self-contradictory', there being 'no connecting point of contact between the two sides of his nature'. On the one hand there was the brother he knew and whose company he enjoyed –

'the most humorous and entertaining of companions, appreciative and incisively critical'; on the other was the fatally fluent, avuncular philosopher-and-friend of an essentially second-rate reading public, whose appetite for his facile homilies on the beauty of life, and the thread of gold as 'the fibre of limitless hope that runs through our darkest dreams', seemed virtually insatiable. Fred conceded that Arthur enjoyed feeding these hungry sheep, and fulfilled something in himself by doing so, quite apart from the considerable material rewards that success brought him. But his real genius and charm lay in his capacity as a 'tête-a-tête' conversationalist, where his mordant wit and amazing memory for detail could have full play. This was the authentic personality, as opposed to his idealised self, and the world might have to wait until the publication of his diaries before the image could be corrected.

Percy Lubbock, the only other person to read the whole of Arthur's diaries before they were locked away in their huge, specially-constructed crate for their fifty-year confinement, came to a similar conclusion. He had reason to know Arthur Benson better than most. Their friendship dated from his becoming Arthur's House Captain in September 1897, and from that time until Arthur's death he became his most constant, if not his closest, companion. Often enough he would take Arthur to task for writing books unworthy of his gifts. He was disturbed, however, by finding that in the philosophy that he preached Arthur was more sincere than he had ever supposed, and that much of his self-criticism and introspection arose from his sense of the gulf that separated the actual from the idealised self. This led Lubbock to warn future readers of the diary against taking the self-portrait too seriously. Those who knew and loved him 'have the look of him by heart – sitting low in his chair, ruddy and bulky and rough-haired, twitching his cigarette with restless fingers, throwing back his head with his enjoyable, infectious laugh; and this is a sight to be recalled again and again and lingered over, now that he is gone, and now that we are faced by a portrait of him, in his diary, wherein his true likeness is at many a point missed entirely. Introspective as he was often believed to be, absorbed in contemplation of his own peculiarities, in fact he never knew himself well enough to record himself aright. Here is one thing, the geniality of his presence, which he failed to see as others always saw it.'

Accuracy, and the capacity to enthral, are perhaps the two chief requirements in a great diarist. That the record abounds in circumstances and descriptions of interest is without doubt. After all, Arthur Benson's diary, as all great diaries should be, is as much about other people as it is about himself. In himself, he is an interesting figure rather than a person of great historical consequence. This is not to say that much was not expected of him. He was the eldest surviving son of Edward White Benson, Archbishop of Canterbury. His mother was the sister of one of the most revered scholars in Cambridge – the moral philosopher, Henry Sidgwick. Lord Halifax, in August 1905, congratulating Arthur on his book *The Isles of Sunset*, stated that he thought the Benson family, taken together, absorbed 'all the talents of a generation'. Hard, indeed, it was to live up to expectations such as this, and from time to time Arthur was haunted by the fear that, given his excellent start in life, 'I ought to have done better.' In the end, he had every cause for satisfaction. All his ambitions were realised one by one – a fortune from his writing, even though his works (with the exception perhaps of 'Land of Hope and Glory') have hardly stood the test of time and his reading public was not exactly the audience he would have chosen; a decoration for the uncongenial work which he undertook in editing Queen Victoria's letters; distinction and a definite responsibility in the Mastership of Magdalene, in which capacity he accomplished his longfelt desire to raise and embellish the College to a greater extent than any other figure in its long history.

More significantly, however, Arthur Benson's career placed him at various stages of his life within the most eminent and influential circles of late Victorian and Edwardian England. There was the ecclesiastical circle that centred upon Lambeth, in many ways his natural and domestic milieu, not only because he was his father's son but also because of his enduring friendship with Archbishop Randall Davidson. There were the propinquent circles of Eton College and Windsor Castle, in both of which Arthur found a place – as of right and by natural inclination at Eton, where he had been King's Scholar, master and housemaster, and by chance or good fortune at Windsor, through his remarkable facility in producing hymns, odes and verses for special occasions which elevated him for a while to the position of a sort of unofficial poet laureate. Literary success, and friendship with figures like Henry James and Edmund Gosse, brought him into the not altogether congenial world of London letters and a place in the Royal Society of Literature. Finally, his personal fame and social gifts (rather than any notable scholarly accomplishment) led him into the inner circles of influence and university politics at Cambridge. It was from these circles that Arthur's friendships were drawn; and it was upon the members of these circles, major or minor, lovable, unpleasing or grotesque, that he focused his 'microscopic eye'.

He was, indeed, ideally placed by circumstance, temperament and natural gifts to portray the dramas and antics which entrée to these circles allowed him to witness. Although his place within them was never questioned, he had a natural reluctance ever to commit himself entirely to any institution and always preferred to observe rather than to become involved. As Percy Lubbock once told him, he 'held nothing sacred'. His gifts were essentially spectatorial, and he chose for himself a position on the fringe of wherever action was taking place – on the periphery, or – as he expressed it himself, 'on the edge of life; on the green margin – and have as much or as little as I choose'. This gave him the ideal vantage-point for observation. Furthermore, his love of the absurd and his lively imagination enabled him to extract the maximum of drama, pathos and humour out of every situation that he described, and these he rendered the more graphic by his incomparable facility for memorising physical detail.

Percy Lubbock's *caveat* about over-reliance on Arthur's accuracy must, however, still be borne in mind. From time to time in the text of the diaries, Lubbock has ventured himself to make certain emendations and corrections. On one occasion (an account of an episode, which he himself had related to Arthur, illustrating the extravagance of Bernard Berenson), Lubbock has written in pencil: 'Accurate in spirit but not in detail'. There are, indeed, good grounds for questioning the accuracy of the record in certain respects. Often the diary was written up hurriedly, sometimes after a gap of several days. It is doubtful whether Arthur ever checked what he had written subsequently, and there are many instances of repetitions of events and conversations, sometimes on successive days.

Inaccuracy – Arthur once said – was a Benson family failing. Fred was by far the worst, and would shamelessly improve upon any circumstance or occasion he was relating for the sake of a good story. 'In my own case it is partly memory which is weak, and partly imagination which is strong.' Actually he did himself less than justice here. Inaccuracy was certainly a fault for which he took others to task – notably Oscar Browning, who shuffles with that 'curious sidling motion of his big frame' through the pages of the diary off and on. He had, Arthur once wrote, 'an infinite capacity for not taking trouble', and he recorded gleefully the occasion of 'O.B.'s' editing a manuscript journal of Thomas Cook for a historical society, when he set an amanuensis on to the tedious task of copying out the original, which he made no effort to check. Two hundred and twenty blunders were discovered in the first few pages.

> O.B.'s idea of editing had been apparently to cross out anything he didn't understand. One event happened in 1702, but O.B. thought the Old Style was being employed and altered it to 1703. Presently 'the Monarch' and '*his* schemes' were mentioned [William III]. O.B. altered 'his' to 'her' for Queen Anne.

When there was remonstration, O.B. replied: 'Why, my dear fellow, they only gave me £100 for it.'

Arthur Benson's own recollection of physical details, as has been said earlier, was amazingly accurate. His description of natural scenes and of people, of events which he had witnessed, are authentic to the minutest particular. Where he is open to question is in those areas where all diarists must be to some extent suspect. He occasionally recounts gossip as fact; he indulges in rhetorical embellishment of stories told to him and of conversations recalled. Sometimes pique and anger lead him into writing more than he means to say by way of condemnation, more even than he actually feels. There are bound to be inaccuracies. But this does not invalidate the authenticity of his impressions, both general and particular. As Arthur himself put it in his preface to his book of biographical studies, *Memories and Friends*: these sketches 'make no claim to be complete or even necessarily *true* impressions, but they are *my* impressions, faithfully recorded.'

* * * * *

Did he, however, present a true picture of himself? He certainly envisaged that his diaries would be read by posterity. 'I wonder whether anyone will ever read this', he wrote in 1905, 'and wonder if I am posing all the time.' He expressed the hope, later, that some future reader would endeavour to retrace some of the walks he described; and – in the midst of the first crippling depression recounted in the diary (January 1909) – he wrote: 'If any record is ever made of my poor life, I have *no objection* to any of this seeing the light. It won't hurt me, and it may give some little comfort to others who suffer.'

How frank and unrestrained Arthur Benson could be in his judgements, both of himself and of others, will be seen in the pages that follow. But there were limits which he freely acknowledged. In March 1903, he wrote as follows:

> I reflect that, intimate in some ways as this diary is, there are at least *two*

thoughts, often with me, that greatly affect my life, to which I never allude here. I suppose people's ideas of privacy differ very much. Some people's minds are like a wide park, with a high wall and lodges – no one but callers admitted – the house in woods. Some are like suburban villas on the street. I don't think my sense of privacy is very general – but it is very strong about one or two things – and I have a carefully locked and guarded strong room. Anyone might think they could get a good picture of my life from these pages; but it is not so.

A year later, Arthur could still reflect, 'What an odd book this diary is! So full now – and so very *nearly* the whole truth. Just not, of course. But I think nearer than most diaries, except Pepys.' Occasionally he would tantalise the reader with some deliberately enigmatic remark. 'If I could but write this all out at length, with names and details and places, what an extraordinarily interesting entry it would be! but of course I cannot. ...' With Hugh Walpole in September 1905, he records a happening over lunch: 'Saw a strange thing happen – a door opened – of which I must not say more'. Sometimes he is implicit when he could have been explicit. There are undoubted cases of *suppressio veri*; on the other hand, he appears to eschew *suggestio falsi*. As Ruskin had said of *Praeterita* – on certain matters 'I have told them all it is good for them to know.'

This is only to be expected. But as the record advanced so it became more and more a *journal intime*, and the strongroom came to be rather less carefully guarded. It remains to be answered, however, whether he came, in the course of his emotional and spiritual wrestlings, to solve the problem of his true identity and supply a faithful picture of himself. He certainly tried to be realistic about his faults, although he would tend to overstate them and thereby diminish the effectiveness of the self-criticism. In September 1902 he reflected on the ways in which the diary had helped him to see the weaknesses of his own character:

It is an old theory of mine that if one *suspects* oneself, however slightly, of a fault, it is pretty sure to be there – and what is more to be flagrantly obvious to other people. Well, I know pretty well what my faults are – I am pretentious, sensitive, unsympathetic, indolent, self-indulgent, weak-minded, liking rewards better than deserving, self-absorbed, ambitious, sceptical. I have on the other hand got some humour, intellectual dexterity, interest in character, a strong sense of beauty, tolerance, kindliness. But my virtues won't wash. I write this with my eyes open. But *it is He that hath made us* – and perhaps He is making me better though I do not see it.

Hugh Walpole, meeting Arthur after a long estrangement only a month before he died, made the shrewd, if unkind, observation that the faults which Arthur was prepared shamefacedly to concede were really only faults that could be interpreted as virtues. Certainly it is better to be sceptical than intellectually rigid, and pretentious rather than unkind. One can admit to being self-absorbed while never allowing that one lacks a sense of humour. Nevertheless Arthur was genuinely self-critical and recognised, at least theoretically, that 'the faults that really disgust one in other people are the faults one has oneself'. After a walk with Oliffe Richmond in Cambridge in May 1907, he sums up his companion as 'a confirmed and charming egotist. He is so handsome and lively and pleasant that his charm hides the bareness and hardness of his nature. But he looks upon everything as simply ministering to himself; and though I think this is probably my own fault too, it seems very ugly when one sees it in another.'

He was very conscious of his tendency to over-react (why is it – he once mused – that 'one dislikes the things one dislikes so much more than one likes the things one likes?'); and would occasionally laugh at his own sour grapes ('not very profound, all this!', he wrote after a pompous disquisition on the unworthiness of ambition, prompted by the news of Walter Raleigh's knighthood). After dismissing Bishop Macrorie as 'vain, perverse and self-satisfied', he conceded (somewhat unusually, it must be admitted) that 'one ought not to judge people without knowing them better'. Perhaps in one area only was Arthur consistently blind to a fault, and at the same time unreasonably critical of the same attitude in others, and this was in his resentment to criticism from his friends. Arthur Benson valued his independence highly; and one of the first lessons that had to be learnt by anyone who would belong to his circle of intimates was the phrase from Aristophanes – 'Don't make your house in my mind'. He might be intimately confiding (another favourite phrase was the passage from Theocritus, 'Be partner of my dreams as of my fishing'), and he expected confidences in return. But any attempt to be dogmatic, to impose one's views, to 'hustle' him out of his routine and chosen way of life was deeply resented. 'I do *hate* the infallible attitude', he wrote towards the end of his life. 'I could talk politics all evening to Ld. Balfour, with whom I disagree, and not be nettled; and I couldn't talk for 5 mins. to Salter, with whom I agree, without being nettled. It is the manner of holding opinions and the sense of finality of one's own judgment which maddens me.'

'I am incapable of resentment unless there is an obvious *intention* to hurt', he once wrote. Alas, this is not true. Almost all the quarrels, imagined enmities and alienations that took place in his life came about from Arthur's sensitivity either to opposition or to criticism rarely, if ever, intended to cause him hurt. And unfortunately, as Percy Lubbock rightly observed, 'he did not . . . consider the independence of others as carefully as he defended his own.' Circumstances would – often enough – prove him wrong; but he could not learn from experience. There is therefore more than a touch of the hypocritical when he takes Frank Salter to task for rebuking him on his habit of so freely criticising his friends: 'I confess I don't see the point of shutting one's eyes to faults in people one loves. If one can only love them by pretending to ignore faults, it's a poor business. I wish them different just as I wish myself different.'

If Arthur did not freely admit his shortcomings here, at least the diary does nothing to disguise them. The same can probably be said of the self-contradictory nature of his personality. All the facets of his character are displayed abundantly, and what one has to remember in attempting to resolve the contradictions is that while we are all perhaps more than one person – our idealised self as well as our actual self – the contrast becomes the more confusing when the subject has to bear the additional burden of manic depression. As is well known, all the Benson family – to a greater or lesser extent – suffered from this condition. Arthur was incapacitated by what he himself described as a sort of 'neuralgia of the soul' twice during his professional career. Throughout his first breakdown, between 1907 and 1910, the diary is written up with scarcely a gap. During the second, between 1917 and 1923, considerable detail is given of the breakdown itself and the re-emergence into active life and buoyant spirits. When the manic depressive is down, he is totally down. His norm of life becomes abject wretchedness and the feeling of abandonment. All the sights, sounds and senses which gave him pleasure become a sort of torment to him. They not only fail to answer to his needs; they serve as a mocking reminder of some former happiness of which he can no longer be a part. They intensify the sense of infirmity and loss. Conversely, when the black cloud has been dispelled, the sense of the joy and beauty of life returns with an added intensity, and depression vanishes as if it had never been; therefore no lessons can be learnt from it; only a fierce joy in the experience of release.

Two characteristics, essential to an understanding of Arthur Benson's personality, arise from this. The first is the recognition of the transitoriness of the sublime – the sweet can become bitter, and the bitter sweet. Hence the compulsion to describe the fleeting moment of joy,

9

somehow to freeze it into words to make it permanent. It is not therefore surprising that the idealised self of a man prone to manic depression should be the interpreter of the simple in nature, the philosopher of serenity, and that his prayer should truly and sincerely be that he might grow in the wisdom of 'quiet things, reading, music, sitting in the sun, breathing the air and watching the sky', aspiring to the love of 'simple pleasures, the talk of simple people, homely offices, gentle words, the singing of birds, the sound of leaves and streams'.

The second characteristic is the realisation that he had to learn to cultivate a social manner which could disguise his switch of moods. This was partly a lack of assurance. He felt more secure in a world which depended purely upon his power of observation and literary expression. He could never believe that he was a brilliant *convive*, a seemingly relaxed and natural conversationalist, mainly because he was so self-conscious; he had too often to put on an act; his social discourse had to be studied; writing came so easily to him. 'My feeling in society', he wrote in May 1903, 'is that of the walrus – with a ponderous sadness, conscious of ponderosity, and yet unable to be lighter.' Ten years later, when accused by Frank Salter of cultivating a pose in his books, of diffusing 'a mild kind religious sort of atmosphere, while in real life I was brisk, profane, worldly etc . . .', he admitted the two sides of his personality. 'My books represent my lonely thoughts and moods. . . . In ordinary intercourse I am different. . . . But the books are much more real than the talker.' He sensed, too, that he was not the only literary figure to dwell in two worlds, to have a solitary self and a social self. He suspected it of Leslie Stephen, after reading F. W. Maitland's 'great biography', which brought out the contradictory qualities of arrogance, sentimentalism and heroism. It was even more evident in A. E. Housman. 'His two public characters', he wrote in November 1912 'are passionate and rather macabre verse (Shropshire Lad) and very incisive criticism. In ordinary life he is a prim old-maidish, rather second rate, rather tired, rather querulous, person.'

Housman was 'old-maidish' in ordinary life. With Arthur Benson, it was the exact opposite. *The Times* described him in 1914 as a 'voluble old maid' in his writings. Arthur agreed – up to a point. Books 'always make me put on my company manners!', he admitted, conceding that his published works revealed a certain affectation in style, largely absent from the writing in his diaries. But the fact remained: 'such humour and levity as I have is the result of conversational excitement, just a shield which I hold up . . ., but alone I am observant and melancholy. . . . It's a curious duality – outward sensitiveness and inner hardness.' It was the judgement on himself that he adhered to all his life.

*   *   *   *   *

In September 1903, Arthur – during a visit to London – took lunch at Hatchett's restaurant (an unusual occurrence for him). It was 'in an underground room, with the whisper of Piccadilly above. The room so contrived that I saw myself in a series of mirrors, in pairs – apparently side by side – all over the room, in every corner – and moreover dim avenues of myself into the dark recesses of dimly-lit halls – a ludicrous sensation.'

This might be taken as a sort of allegory of what his diaries represent. Other characters abound in it; but they are all as seen by the writer. They appear only as they relate to him or cross his path. If Arthur Benson's life-story were told purely through the pages of his diary, without any comment or analysis, the picture would be too subjective for a definitive biography. This was something that Arthur perceived himself in writing his study of Henry Sidgwick in *Leaves of the Tree*. 'It seems at first sight that to let a man tell his own life-story by diaries and letters is the nearest you can get to the truth of him. But in the case of hard brain-workers, especially if they have a strain of sadness in their temperament, the self-made record is not really the truest portrait.'

Arthur Benson says much about himself in a mood of introspection. He writes copiously about other people, observing them minutely and irreverently from the green margin, which was his chosen path to walk. When one places the subject and his objects into perspective, when one links the observer with the observed, then the crucial problem of life – of anyone's life – comes into focus: the problem of personal relationships. As will be seen from the study that follows, all Arthur Benson's problems – his lack of security, his various experiments in changing his occupation and his environment, his quest for the ideal of friendship, the agonies of his dark moods and the fitful joys of the blessed moments, his attempts to enunciate a philosophy of the serene life in his books – all arise from his inability to find the right answer to the question 'Who am I – in relation to *others*?'. The mirrors in Hatchett's restaurant are really an image or allegory of self-absorption – again, an infirmity that Arthur frankly conceded in all members of the Benson family, except perhaps his mother.

In this respect Arthur paid the penalty for his own natural gifts, suffered from the defects of his own virtues. Nature had made of him a consummate observer and spectator; a natural diarist, in fact. But if one stands on the fringe of life in order to observe it, one cannot become part of the scene one observes. This was Arthur's predicament in his relations with every institution he served. He could be *in* a circle, but not *of* it. Tragically this refusal to belong to any circle, group or institution extended to a psychological inhibition from close intimacy with any other person. He was frightened of love (much as he might feel its need) because love made demands and limited one's independence. If to gain a perfect loving relationship is to experience such Paradise as may be a man's to attain, then such a gift could not be his. He must stand – to use his own phrase – 'on the edge of Paradise', knowing where it lay but incapable of finding any way in.

This is the continuing theme of Arthur Benson's life. And it is interesting to note that it is what he would have wanted somebody to extract from all the mass of personal material that he left for posterity to peruse. He wanted his diaries to be read; but he did not want his life to be recorded purely in his own words. Furthermore, he wished to be critically assessed. 'I, personally, could not conceive desiring to be romantically depicted', he once wrote. 'If my life were to be portrayed at all, I should desire my faults, failings and absurdities to be accurately recorded.'

He knew he had failings. He knew he had missed, maybe, the most precious thing in life. But if his virtues were deficient, so was there virtue in his defects. Two months before he died, he described the ideal subject for biography in the following terms: those who 'have not displayed high technical accomplishment in any field. Such men and women have inspired deep emotions, have loved intensely, have cast a glow upon the lives of a large circle, have said delicate, sympathetic, perceptive and suggestive things, have given meaning and joy to life, have radiated interest and charm.'

This is very near to a description of his idealised self, the man he wanted to be thought to be. His diary reveals many other facets of a complex character, some more pathetic, some less winning, some which undoubtedly enhance the subject's charm. Even so, it is interesting to observe how very closely that description of the ideal subject for biography approximates, in terms of his acknowledged personal influence upon his contemporaries, to Arthur Benson himself.

Chapter One

CHILDREN OF THE ARCHBISHOP

> It is strange to sit beneath the portraits of papa and Uncle Henry – and rather sad too. I had a good start; I ought to have done better.   (October 1909)

> We talked very frankly about the difficulty of being sons of famous men, and how it overshadowed one by inevitable comparisons.
>   (Conversing with Sir Philip Burne-Jones, August 1912)

When Mary Benson heard in July 1903 that her youngest son, Hugh, had decided not to renew his Mirfield vows and to put himself immediately under instruction for the Church of Rome, she remarked to Arthur 'half pathetically and half humorously that someone . . . had said to her that her children might cause her pain and vexation, but she *would never be dull*'. That might seem almost an understatement. Of her six children, two died young (her eldest son, Martin, from meningitis as a Scholar of Winchester in 1878, and her eldest daughter, Nelly, from diphtheria followed by heart failure at the age of twenty-seven in 1890); Arthur became famous in ways that will be seen, while causing acute anxiety in his domestic circle through his propensity to nervous illness; Maggie had the deepest and most original mind, studying philosophy and researching into Egyptology, but fell under the shadow of mental derangement in 1907 from which she never recovered; Fred became a society novelist and wit, and moved away from the ecclesiastical and intellectual ethos of the Benson household into a smart and moneyed set; and, finally, Hugh – volatile, perverse and with all the love of life and enthusiasm of the child that refuses to grow up – became a Monsignor and burnt himself out through his ceaseless activity as a missioner, novelist and preacher, dying from heart failure in 1914.

There is no shortage of material about life in the Benson household. It is possible that no family in history has written so prolifically about itself. Both Arthur and Fred produced four books of family reminiscence apiece; and Arthur intruded articles and essays about members of the family and his own upbringing in at least nine other books besides. So

13

fascinating a household was it; so dominant a character was their eminent father; so many and so distinguished were the guests and visitors, whether at Wellington, Lincoln, Truro or Lambeth, that material for dramatic situations, tragic or comic, and for rich biographical vignettes was always close at hand. Writing, anyway, was the natural outlet for those of the children who lived long enough to indulge it, and the family trait of self-absorption also doubtless provided relish for their subject. 'The Benson mind', Arthur once wrote, 'naturally thinks that anything which concerns itself is of the nature of a national crisis and a local convulsion. It is all lit up in a kind of golden glory, and the actors have tongues of fire on their heads.'

A *Benson* characteristic, he says; not a Sidgwick one. It was more typical of his father than of his mother. Both the Bensons and the Sidgwicks came from Yorkshire stock, who had settled for different reasons in the Midlands. Edward White Benson's start in life was to learn the lessons of thrustful self-improvement in order to eradicate the disaster of his own father's early bankruptcy and death. He did so through the scholarly influence of James Prince Lee (Chief Master of King Edward's, Birmingham) and his close friendship at Cambridge with two other Birmingham boys, Brooke Foss Westcott and Joseph Barber Lightfoot, eventually securing for himself the highest honours at Trinity College, Cambridge. While a master at Rugby he had lodged with the Sidgwick family and had decided, almost at once, to offer his hand in marriage to the youngest daughter of that intellectual household when Mary (or 'Minnie') was only twelve. Their engagement was not made official until her seventeenth birthday. They married a year later, when Benson swept her off, together with the Sidgwick family nurse, Beth (Elizabeth Cooper), to the newly-founded Wellington College, over whose fortunes he was to preside as Master for the next fourteen years.

In one sense it was a natural union. Edward White Benson and Mary Sidgwick's widowed mother (Mary Crofts) were cousins. They came from the same social and intellectual background. In another sense, it was very far from being natural, because temperamentally Benson and his young bride were poles apart. The husband was masterful, demanding, passionate, ambitious. Mary Sidgwick had the combined charms of her three brilliant brothers (William, Henry and Arthur, all of whom became dons at either Oxford or Cambridge) – gaiety, light-heartedness, tenderness and sympathy. She married before she had had any life of her own, feeling totally inadequate to the demands imposed upon her, fearful of her husband's severity and cut off from her natural companions. But she was dutiful and generous, and tried to please. She learnt so well to conceal her true feelings (her sense of incompatability, her need for intimacy with members of her own sex, even her loss of faith for a period, after they had left Wellington for the Chancery at Lincoln) that Benson became more and more dependent upon her for his own security, especially through the black depressions which dogged his career, even though preferment came to take him from the Chancellorship of Lincoln Cathedral to become first Bishop of Truro in 1877 and Archbishop of Canterbury in 1883.

It was much later that her children came to realise the true situation of their parents' married life. Fred and Arthur discussed the matter together in August 1923, when they had both read the pathetic journals found amongst their mother's papers after her death in June 1918. 'She was afraid of papa (I don't wonder)', Arthur wrote, 'and it must have been terrible to have been so near him and his constant displeasure. The wonder is that he did so much. ... In fact this little record changes my whole view of their relations. It seems to me now that they were two very vivid and splendid people – but utterly antagonistic in temperament, and probably ought never to have married. Hers by far the finer nature, with *casual* faults. His the intense nature, with the faults of ambition, self-will, domination – not a big heart, and sentimental rather than loving. She intellectual, far-ranging, critical, intensely loving.' Then again: 'We [A.C.B. and E.F.B.] wondered if they had ever *really* loved. Certainly I never remember their seeking each other's company or wanting to be alone together.'

All the Benson children adored their mother. She was 'one of the greatest blessings of my life', Arthur freely acknowledged. As children 'our relations ... were perfect. We trusted her, we turned to her for everything; she was the gayest and liveliest, as well as the most perceptive of companions. We were entirely at ease with her, and yet obeyed her promptly and gladly.' With their father, however, it was a very different matter. It was not that he punished them. It would almost have been better if he had. If they offended, his displeasure lay heavily upon them like some dark and brooding cloud. They had failed to live up to his expectations, and he sorrowed for them visibly. They could not relax with him. Every opportunity to point a moral or to make the improving remark was assiduously taken, so that conversation was always strained. He seemed unable to communicate the love which he undoubtedly felt.

Arthur came to see this in time and to appreciate the pathos of the situation. Long after his father's death, he discovered that all their letters as children had been lovingly preserved by him. 'Strange that Papa should have treasured these', he wrote, 'and yet not given us the impression that he cared like that for us. In those days he seemed to me more censorious than affectionate. How *can* children understand that they are loved, unless it is shown them plainly? Yet all my recollections of those days are of constant vigilance and self-repression, for fear Papa should be vexed. I never said what I thought, but what I thought he would like me to say. And all the while behind the scenes he was keeping our scraps, with tender little inscriptions and records of dates etc.' Both the father and his children hungered for affection, but neither could find a way of expressing it. 'He had no "little language" like Swift. And he rather repressed it in others.' The children were proud of their father; they basked in the glory and the spectacle of his power and ascendancy. But always there was strain. Even when Arthur was a young man, and his father Archbishop, the tension remained. On holiday together, with Benson travelling incognito, there could be no light relief. Arthur recalled staying with him at The Bell in Gloucester:

> He had no sense of comfort, and we sate miserably in a poky inn drawing-room with three frozen females – and then we had prayers in his bedroom – said vespers, I think, at great length, the chambermaid coming in in the middle, a grief to me. Papa always felt the need for *economy* at an inn – had a small bottle of claret, out of which we each had one glass and then it was corked up for the next night. He would have *liked* to be comfortable, but didn't know how, I think – his fear of waste was so strong.

In the first book Arthur ever published (in 1886) – a somewhat ill-judged compound of autobiography and fantasy, called *Memoirs of Arthur Hamilton*, written under the pseudonym 'Christopher Carr' – he gives a description of Arthur Hamilton's father which is unmistakably drawn from his own experience: a man desperate for affection, but feared and disliked by his children (not dissimilar to the father of 'Hugh Neville' in *Beside Still Waters*, another barely-disguised autobiography published in 1907). An incident is described in which 'Arthur Hamilton' is moved to write the words 'I hate papa' on a piece of paper and to bury it somewhere in the garden. That such a piece of paper was actually buried in the garden of the old Master's Lodge at Wellington, one can have little doubt. Arthur came in due course to write the official biography of his father after his death in 1896, and perhaps for the first time truly appreciated just how eminent and effective an ecclesiastical statesman, diocesan Bishop and Archbishop he had been. He was, as it were, converted to the realisation of his undoubted greatness by having to research and to write his life. At the same time he became more poignantly aware of his father's own need and craving for love. So to all Arthur's emotions about his father there came to be added a strong sense of guilt. He should have filled more effectively the terrible vacuum caused by the death of Martin, his father's favourite son. He had not done so. He had allowed himself to hate, or at the very least to be indifferent, when he should have loved.

It is not surprising, therefore, that this sense of guilt returned time and time again to nag him in his dreams. Arthur shared with his father the ability to recall – and to record – with extraordinary vividness his equally extraordinary dreams – fantastic, absurd, sometimes macabre, sometimes hilarious. In all some four hundred dreams are described in the diary, often in considerable and graphic detail. His father frequently appeared in them, especially in the years following his death, when Arthur was working on his biography and discovering aspects of his character and achievements of which he had barely been conscious as a child and a young man. On 11 October 1902, he wrote in his diary on the sixth anniversary of his father's death: 'It seems sometimes *years* since he died ... as if he spoke and looked out of a bright cloud in the past. ... Sometimes it seems yesterday. His grave, commanding, exacting, loving presence is often with me; and I often dream of him, I am thankful to say.' Sometimes the dream-image was the old censorious one – reproving Arthur for biting his nails, rebuking him for being sulky and ungracious, or just being maddeningly unreasonable. At other times he would appear in improbable situations – digging the garden of a suburban house; dressed in a khaki cassock and grumbling about his obligation to read *The Times* daily 'on the chance of finding one fact for my commentary on the Romans'; appearing as if transfigured with a 'shining youthful countenance' about him. But the most significant dreams of all were those in which father and son were pictured as reconciled, either because they discovered in their dream-situation that they could express their love for each other without embarrassment or awkwardness – the father being represented as embracing Arthur tenderly or fondling him in a way which caused no resentment – or they have become partners in some secret and ludicrous enterprise from which the rest of the world has been excluded. In a dream of February 1916, Arthur discovers that when his father shuts himself away, he is actually playing with toys, in a dark and secret place under the stairs, dressed in his purple cassock. When Arthur catches him in his furtive employment, 'Papa nodded and giggled; then he said, "But now that you have found me out, you must run down here as often as you can, and we will have a good game at something – You don't know what fun it is".'

The most extraordinary dream of all in which his father figured occurred in November 1901. It is worth reproducing in full:

> I was sitting in a kind of saloon-carriage by the side of a lake. The rail on which my carriage stood went round the lake; the other dipped into it. I saw the metals going down into the clear water, and the waves lapping on the pebbles. I heard a noise; and at the top of a little heathery hill behind – the place was a moor – appeared a huge engine, like a traction engine, coming down at a *furious* pace, like a dragon upon me. I saw the blue gleaming metal of which it was made; it flung out cataracts of black smoke, but I was not afraid. It dashed into the water by me, running on the submerged metals drawing a train of red trucks, empty, and simply tore across the lake, throwing off the water in huge jets over it, the smoke struggling through the foam, and disappeared with its train of trucks over a low hill. Then I was in a marble-paved hall, belonging, I knew, to some university, with rather a cross portress at a table in the centre. I could see the dim reflection of ourselves in the floor as we moved about. Then I was in a garden, playing with some children, an odd game played with golf balls and wooden spades: John Sarum in a brown Norfolk jacket. The garden was neglected and rather provincial, but jasmine grew profusely. In running to pitch a ball I saw an odd stone in a garden bed, a piece of crystal, which I took up, and, rubbing off the dirt, found it a statuette of a girl riding on a mule, loaded with grapes. I looked up and saw that E.W.B. had joined the game, in his cassock. I took it to him, and he smiled and touched it, and said 'You shall yet return and bring your grapes with you.' Then he kissed me, and I felt the slight roughness of his cheek as I used to do as a child; then he blessed me very solemnly. The dream faded.

Always the cassock; usually the kiss; often the exchange of some absurdly esoteric remark, which father vouchsafes to son. He was there in his dreams; it was inconceivable that he was not still somewhere actively employed, and surveying Arthur's progress and doings gravely from afar. 'He loved me – I loved him not.' Could he redress that lack of appreciation in the past by what he achieved in the future? He could never take Martin's place; never fulfil what he might have aspired to. The consciousness of his father's pleasure or displeasure lived with Arthur all his life. Whatever he accomplished, or whatever he shirked in the way of posts or responsibilities that might have been his with greater effort, his conscience had to wrestle with the nagging question – was he, would he ever be, a son worthy of the Archbishop?

*   *   *   *   *

'The one thing I have not had in my life which I should have valued', Arthur wrote in August 1901, 'is the ancestral connection with *one* place. I have spent all my life in tearing up roots.' If there was one place which stirred in him the feeling of returning home, where he truly belonged, where memories were unclouded by any sense of bitterness or insecurity, it was Wellington College in Berkshire, where he spent the first eleven years of his life. He was born at 6.30 p.m. on 24 April 1862 in the house by the main entrance, looking over to the avenue of rhododendrons and the lake, which served as the Master's residence until the building of ampler premises in the Gothic style in 1865. His first memories were of the day-nursery in the old Lodge – its 'pleasant smell ... when the gas was lit (it had a twisted tube) and the table laid for tea by the fire', the strange pictures pasted on the wall, which took on curious expressions as dusk came on, especially an owl with wicked eyes which needed to be propitiated; a tiny walled garden outside, with a disturbing stone carving in the shrubbery, like a disembodied head with an 'insupportably fearful' face.

'Looking back, it always seemed to be summer in those days.' There were comfortable people, like his mother and Beth, who accepted you as you were. Beth, in those days, was 'a little, light-footed, wiry Yorkshire woman' (although nearly thirty years before she had entered William Sidgwick's service, walking ten miles from Barnsley with her mother on a hot July day, to begin seventy-seven years of service with the Benson and Sidgwick families). She was totally predictable; her stories (which were few and rather sorrowful) never deviated in the telling in either word or expression; her love and devotion were always instinctively felt; she never scolded, she never fretted, she was seemingly never tired; she claimed nothing for herself. There was the security and companionship of a large family – close-knit in the sense of enjoying each other's company and rallying to each other's defence, while not being in the least dependent on any one of the group for their pleasures and pastimes. Martin, the eldest son, was something of a being apart. He alone, in those days, seemed to be relatively at ease with his father, although Nelly developed the same capacity as she grew older and stepped into Martin's place after his untimely death. Arthur could recall mutual adventures with

19

Martin – their terror at being accosted by an old tramp in hussar uniform, when Arthur ran away in the certainty that Martin was being kidnapped; playing on Brighton beach together in 1869 and searching for the shells of Pholas. But their relationship was not a close one. 'He lived a very self-centred life as a boy', Arthur recalled, 'and I often used to feel that he admitted no one inside the fence. He was very contemptuous, too, of my want of knowledge, feeble memory, flaccid interest; and at times, as if in a mood of regret, intensely affectionate, generally in *absence*. What a strange relation the relation of brothers is – a kind of compulsory friendship!'

The greatest personality was Nelly. She was like Arthur in her possession 'of the microscopic eye of the minute philosopher', delighting in other people's oddities, but unlike him in her marked preference for people rather than for places. She tended to be the organiser of their games, forming secret societies, devising plays with Maggie for their dolls, one being overheard by Arthur, who had concealed himself in a cupboard, only to give himself away by bursting into laughter at the improbable line – 'How sweet is the affection of these innocent babes!'

Wonders and absurdities there were in plenty for children to marvel and giggle at in the comings and goings of the Master's Lodge of a famous public school (as there were to be also in a Cathedral Close and in a Bishop's Palace). There were deferential persons, quaking at the prospect of seeing their father; there were self-important Governors, with some of whom – the Premier, Lord Derby, for instance, the Duke of Wellington and John Walter of *The Times* – their father seemed oddly and uncharacteristically ill at ease. There were the various aunts and uncles and friends of the family – the extraordinary Aunt Etty (Henrietta Crofts, Mrs Sidgwick's sister), who dressed in purple silk and had a voice like a man's; the fascinatingly ugly Dr Lightfoot, and their father's brother Christopher, an invalid who moved about in a wheeled chair and had to be carried upstairs by his valet. 'This was regarded as a pleasant variety on ordinary ways of life', Arthur recalled. 'No thought of compassion or sympathy ever entered my head; I fancied rather that he chose to be like that.' And on one day, the routine of the household was totally disrupted for the visit of a severe little woman in black, whom everybody spoke to in awed tones (except Beth, who addressed her firmly as 'My Majesty') until Martin broke out laughing at her bonnet and was rewarded (as Arthur was too) by a solemn kiss from a pair of royal lips.

But it was the surroundings of Wellington that bound Arthur's heart to it for the rest of his life: Yateley Hall with its park-like fields, walled garden and dark lake surrounded by woods; Eversley Rectory, and walks there on Sundays in the holidays to visit the most unconventional parson in the Church of England – Charles Kingsley, whom all the children adored; even Broadmoor, the criminal lunatic asylum, set away on a hill surrounded by pine-trees and heather; close by, amidst the pine-woods and the sandy rides, a place of romance called 'the honeywoman's cottage' which 'used to smell so sharp and fragrant from the box-hedges, and the wood fire . . . the "eternal calm", the great spruce avenue, where I first felt the stirrings of poetry, at the sound of the rustling wood and the sweet name'.

Years later, Arthur would admit to his far greater happiness in middle-age than in the times of his youth. He meant by that his sharpened sense of beauty, his emancipation from the shyness of youth, the terror of committing solecisms with the eyes of adults upon him, the release from being *in statu pupillari*. There was, however, a special freedom of childhood which he associated with Wellington alone – the freedom to wander, to discover, to look for oneself, to be deliciously independent. His account of his childhood in *Beside Still Waters* shows just how much certain crucial features of his character were formed and nurtured in these surroundings: how little personal relations mattered to him in those days; how much his love was given to purely inanimate things; how his regret at leaving home was not so much the severance from people whom he loved, but the thought of all his precious haunts – 'the stream passing slowly through its deep pools, the bee-hive in the little birch avenue beginning to wake to life, and that he should not be there to go his accustomed rounds, and explore all the minute events of his dear domain'. He would seek for little assurances of permanence by accumulating small treasures and planting them away in some secret place (what he would call a 'fetish'). He cultivated his powers of observation 'of a hundred curious and delicate things', and thereby chose for himself the path that he would always thereafter seek to walk – going 'his solitary way, looking, looking. . .'

Whenever, subsequently, his travels took him within sight or scent of that particular corner of Berkshire – the combination of pine-woods, rhododendrons and Bagshot sand – he would find himself suffused with a sort of 'heart-hunger, the thrill of my native land. The heather breaking into crimson bloom, the delicate sword-grass that grows under the firs, the white light on the bracken deep in the wood, the scented air – all brings me straight back to childhood.' On one day in August 1902, cycling through Ascot, he decided to go out of his way to Hartford Bridge Flats, where years ago he and Martin had seen a hare caught screaming by the ears.

> I halted near the top, turned round – and then I caught my breath in earnest. There was Well. Coll., with its two flanking towers and the slender fleche – Edgbarrow and Ambarrow, Sandhurst Church, Broadmoor, a great red splash on the hill – Sandhurst Lodge and the Farm, past which we used to walk to Yateley – on the edge of the sloping wood above it that gave me my first sense of poetry – to look into the hot wood with its humming flies and wonder where it went to. There it all lay, in a kind of glory, with the sombre fir-clad hills all round – besprinkled, alas, with red gables of new houses – it gives me a strange yearning, a heart-hunger for I do not quite know what. ... I felt somehow as if all the old life was going on quietly there, and I with my holland-cased fishing rod trotting thro' the meadows to Yateley. The pool of the mill there, with the old wooden footbridge and the alders is as real to me as anything that I see – and yet when I went there the other day it was all gone.

He compared his sense of vision and perspective as a child. 'I often retrace these fields in dreams. But the odd thing is that I have no sort of recollection of *wide views* as a child. I suppose one's eyes were always looking *close*, for small things – the acquisitive love of little treasures etc., and though I have many little mental vignettes, they are all of small definite things – copses, pools, sandpits, trees – I don't suppose one enjoyed or cared for a wide view. One's horizon was small and also possibly where I now look *over* hedges etc., I then looked *into* them.'

Three years later, he pondered over the same problem – how memory tended to magnify the size and distance of the scenes of one's childhood. The walks one used to take: 'What a little way we used to go! ... Why must everything change and hurry onwards? Why must we grow old and dull? What lies behind it all? Where are Nellie and Martin and Papa? Do they remember and love the old days? The strange thing is that in thinking of it all, I seem always to have been *alone*. I suppose I was very self-absorbed as a child: and I think my love of *places*, of woods, and heather and streams was stronger than my love of people.'

In this he truly recognised how much the child was father of the man.

*   *   *   *   *

In 1872, at the age of ten, Arthur joined Martin at Temple Grove, an old-established boarding-school for boys at Mortlake, where under the stern but scholarly guidance of O. C. Waterfield, entrance was secured to the leading public schools of the land. Thence Martin went to Winchester in 1874, Arthur to Eton in the same year, and Fred to Marlborough in 1879. 'I hated the place', Arthur said subsequently, 'and said good-bye to it with joy.' There was no obvious cause for his misery. He was not subjected to bullying, although he could recall the occasional unpleasant incident happening to other boys. He was never chastised by Waterfield, although he witnessed several executions and decided that the course of prudence was regular hard work and to keep as far as possible out of Waterfield's way. He did not encounter anything smutty or sordid, avoiding even 'to my loss and hurt' the first opportunity of a romantic friendship offered to him by 'a gentle-looking creature, Raikes-Currie by name,' who 'made shy overtures of friendship to me in the course of a walk, and even showed me a poem beginning "In the dark halls of Fotheringay", which seemed to me a work of amazing genius'.

Arthur kept himself to himself. It was not for the want of pleasant and stimulating contemporaries – Lord Grey of Falloden, Lord Dungarvan, Roundell Palmer and M. R. James (later Provost of King's and of Eton). 'My one idea', Arthur wrote, 'was to seclude myself utterly and entirely from relations with other boys'; and he regarded with horror his father's suggestion that he might invite a friend to stay in the holidays. Home was his private sanctum. He endured school; he re-entered his own world of mystery and romance in the holidays; and the two should never mingle. The few moments of pleasure that Temple Grove gave him were characteristic incidents – being fussed over when ill, in the sick-bay at the top of the house, presided over by a former maid of the Bensons called Louisa, where he would indulge his spectatorial tastes by looking out of the window, watching a grocer's shop across the road and the performance of setting out the wares; or when he discovered a loose paling in the playground fence and looked through to discover an enchanted spot beyond: 'a quiet place, the tail of a neglected shrubbery', seemingly unvisited, with overgrown laurels and tall elms, and in a glade thick with periwinkles, three tiny grave-mounds, 'the graves, I have since reflected, of dogs, but which I at the time supposed to be the graves of children. I gazed with a singular sense of mystery, and strange dream-pictures rose instinctively in my mind, weaving themselves over the solitary and romantic spot.'

In retrospect, he rather regretted the picture he could recall of himself as a boy: 'fond of my own designs, glad to be left alone', making an absurd fuss and bursting into tears over any situation when he would be forced to be dependent on somebody else, as when he visited the Wordsworth household at the Bishop of Lincoln's Palace at Riseholme in 1869, because he knew that he would not be able to button his collar without help. 'I was a very worthless creature – charming, I dare say, and friendly enough, with vague ideas of beauty, but utterly adrift and quite despicable!'

He had been at Temple Grove for only one year when the family left Wellington for Lincoln on his father's appointment as Chancellor of the Cathedral. It marked a change in all their lives. For the first time the children saw their father in a relatively subordinate position, as he served his four-year apprenticeship for the episcopate; for Mary Benson, for the first time since her marriage, she could begin, if only in small ways, to live a life of her own and seek the female companionship that her nature craved for, especially at a time of deep and incommunicable spiritual doubts. And Arthur discovered one of the great loves of his life – the Cathedral, and the life of ceremony, liturgy, ancient customs and antiquated offices of which it formed the focal point. 'I feel *at home* in a cathedral as nowhere else', he wrote in later life. 'I am sure, if there is any metempsychosis, that I was once a monk – or, say, a secular Canon.' Everything about the canonical life entranced him – 'the haven of the Cathedral close, to walk in ecclesiastical processions, to preach and write'.

It seemed, at this stage, that that could well be his future. For the present, there was the whole mysterious world of the Cathedral to explore; the fascination of living in a genuinely medieval house; the fun of observing a whole pageant of absurd and quaint cathedral dignitaries: the Dean (J. W. Blakesley), austere, abstracted, a churchman and scholar of the old school, walking with curious constraint behind his verger, 'moving only from the hips, his body held rigidly, and slightly stooping'; Bishop Mackenzie, the Subdean, who composed anthems, conducting them in his episcopal robes, 'his genial face illumined with the sweet pride of authorship'; Archdeacon Kaye, a prim, precise man who accompanied all his remarks 'with a constant succession of little bows, like a pigeon patrolling a lawn'. When, in 1911, it was suggested to Kaye that, having reached the age of 85, he might feel it right to retire, he demurred on the grounds that he was only too conscious that his sense of responsibility was increasing every day. Arthur commented in his diary: 'It was strong enough, when I remember him nearly 40 years ago, to be numbing and paralysing! He did nothing whatever that I am aware of, but preach impossible sermons, sit in his study, and advocate caution.'

Arthur loved the Lincoln phase of his life. 'The Chancery of Lincoln is connected in my mind with no tragic or even sorrowful event whatever, and suggests no painful reminiscence.' Exploration with his father's master-key certainly provided dramas. On one occasion, traversing the nave clerestory on a narrow stone ledge without any railings, Martin lost his nerve half-way across and Arthur had to talk and guide him back, not daring for one moment to look down at the drop below. All the children would make a secret journey to the great bell-chamber of the central tower, on the first day of the school holidays, just before noon, to wait for the moment when Great Tom would sound the hour, preceded by four hammer-strokes on the lesser bells, and to see which of them would flee for the refuge of the staircase (where actually the reverberation was worse) before the thunderous crash of Great Tom himself.

Many times they visited Riseholme where Christopher Wordsworth and his family lived. The friendship between the two families had been of long standing. The relationship between the Bishop and Edward White Benson had developed into one of filial love. Elizabeth Wordsworth, his brilliant daughter who was to become first Principal of Lady Margaret Hall, Oxford, had – Arthur hints – strong feelings for his father also. He did not know of the correspondence which passed between them, but had noticed her evident jealousy at the attentions which his father paid to her sister, Priscilla, when they were on holiday together some years before. The relationship was even further complicated by the strong attachment of Mary Benson to Elizabeth. To the children, however, Riseholme meant a three-mile excursion out of the city to an estate of romantic grandeur, with a lake where they could row and fish, 'looking out for the great mottled pike that used to lie basking among the weeds as we glided overhead'. On one such outing, Arthur nearly met his death by drowning, but was rescued in the nick of time by the gardener. On another visit to Riseholme he was moved to commit a totally motiveless and nonsensical theft – a hideously ugly enamel brooch from a washstand, which he subsequently filled with toothpowder and tried to burn on the fire for fear of it being discovered.

None of the children wanted to move to Truro when the episcopal summons came from Lord Beaconsfield during the Christmas holidays of 1876. There was no official residence at first. While the arrangements were negotiated for the acquisition of Kenwyn Vicarage (later called 'Lis

Escop'), the family lived first in a villa in Porthgwidden, and then for a short while with a local Truro solicitor who happened to be Mayor that year. But Truro had delights of its own. Lis Escop was a superbly situated house, facing south, high above Truro, looking over two valleys, spanned by great railway viaducts, beyond which lay the estuary, 'a creek of wide mud-flats at low tide, at high tide a sleeping lake'.

By this time Arthur was a young Etonian of fifteen, tall for his age, very fair-haired, powerfully built and handsome. And it was at Truro that he began to make enduring and formative friendships. This was a time, as he himself recalled, 'of opening youth and feeling and such resolutions as I ever indulged in – ardent ecclesiasticism; and the pleasure of finding myself capable of inspiring friendship and not quite such a fool as I had up till then believed myself to be'. The first, and most adored, of these new friends was Arthur Mason, Benson's chaplain and Diocesan Missioner, who had joined the new Bishop, from a Wellington mastership and a Fellowship at Trinity College, Cambridge, with an ardour for the pioneering work ahead of them equal to Benson's own. He was striking to look at, fresh-faced yet firm of feature, with a sparkling intellect and a transparently emotional nature to go with it. He was caressing and affectionate in friendship without either self-consciousness or sentimentality. And both Arthur and his father loved him. In later years, Arthur could never think of him 'without a glow of the heart – and, alas, alas, without some tears of the mind. ... There was something so beautiful and intense about his youth. I can never be thankful enough for his kindness to me. How much I remember those expeditions with him in his huge Corsican cloak and the little purple book of poetry he used to read from in his grave thrilling voice.'

After Arthur Mason, in order of affection, came John Reeve, curate-in-charge of Kenwyn, again uninhibitedly emotional, brisk and undaunted, full of laughter and delighting in his mission; a man who 'flung his heart about in handfuls', and somehow swept up everybody with him. Then came Francis Carter and G. H. S. Walpole (father of the novelist, Hugh, and later Bishop of Edinburgh), with both of whom Arthur maintained a friendship until the end of his life. The main spiritual influence upon him, however, came from none of these men, but from a more occasional visitor to Truro, whom Benson had appointed his examining chaplain, G. H. Wilkinson, Rector of St Peter's, Eaton Square. Wilkinson was to be Benson's successor in the see, and brought about in the older and senior man a transformation in his spirituality which amounted almost (in Arthur's words) to a transfiguration. It is impossible to describe how it was achieved, although it happened in a matter of days, as it is impossible to define Wilkinson's own spirituality and religious convictions which cut across all the traditions. He was a mystic by nature, an Evangelical by tradition, and a devotee of Catholic usages and symbolism. He spoke a different language of intensity from anyone either father or son had met before.

In February 1878 tragedy struck the Benson household in the sudden death of Martin, who fell victim to meningitis while away at school. He had parted from his father and the family at the garden gate of Kenwyn, sad at returning to Winchester before the start of Arthur's term. No one had an inkling of what was to come. When Arthur was told the news at Eton, he went off alone and sat with his head in his hands, not understanding why he did not feel the blow more acutely. But his father was almost paralysed by the shock. All his hopes had been wrapped up in his eldest son; all the love which he wanted to express to his children was somehow focused on the only one of them with whom he felt he could truly relax. And it was he who was taken. In a state of desperation and dereliction, Benson turned to Wilkinson for help and strength.

For Arthur, Wilkinson was to provide the only personal spiritual influence that he could accept unreservedly and uncritically. As he grew older, and early thoughts of taking Orders gradually receded, he was to count among his friends and acquaintances men who had had no such reservations and who rose to high positions within the Church. Arthur showed respect for their convictions, but his independent spirit refused direction or counsel from any of them. Wilkinson alone could speak directly to his needs and conscience. It had been so from the first moment they had spoken privately together in the garden at Lis Escop, after which Wilkinson followed Arthur to his room and asked him to kneel while he prayed with him and blessed him. In the greatest spiritual and emotional crisis of his life, which was to occur in his last years at Cambridge, it was to Wilkinson, and to him alone, that Arthur went to pour out his heart.

*   *   *   *   *

It is curious that Arthur, who wrote so much about his family and about the personalities who influenced his life, actually vouchsafes so little information about his career as an Eton schoolboy. He was not miserable there in the sense of his wretchedness at his exile in Temple Grove. When he entered College as a King's Scholar in September 1874, the experience was rather one of emancipation. Every society has its rules and customs, and many of them petty and pointless, but at least at Eton the customs were hallowed by antiquity. It was more like the fascination of the protocol of the cathedral close than the pent-up frustration at the whims of some omnipresent autocrat. The masters let you be, provided you somehow did your stint of work; and they exercised no direct disciplinary role, except for the Lower Master in your early years (Francis Durnford until 1877, followed by J. L. Joynes). The Master in College (Broadbent) presided at prayers and was consulted on matters of business, but left the discipline in the hands of Sixth Form. This could be wayward and sometimes harsh, but one rapidly learnt how not to stand out and be unduly noticed; otherwise 'one found out by the light of nature what one might do and what one might not'.

It helped if one had a sympathetic and kindly fagmaster, and here Arthur was lucky. After one term he became fag to Reginald Smith (later his publisher, as senior partner of the house of Smith, Elder and Co.). Smith had himself suffered vilely at the hands of his own fagmaster (Sir E. C. Perry), and was determined that Arthur should never experience such miseries. He therefore treated him with paternal kindness and courtesy, helping him (not always correctly) with his work, allowing him the refuge of his study from the noise of Long Chamber, and showing indulgence to him even when he poached his eggs in a kettle full of coffee. There were menial duties, as servitor, to discharge in College hall (holding back the long gown-sleeves of senior boys as they carved at table), but Arthur found the duties 'amusing' rather than otherwise, even when rebuked by Herbert Ryle for dirty hands and unkempt hair. The other important personal contact was his tutor, to whose pupil-room he regularly went for 'private business', and in G. E. Marindin, Arthur found a kindly and easy-going mentor whom he frankly acknowledged to have been far too indulgent to second-rate work. He was insufficiently critical and 'not the tutor I ought to have had'.

The real contrast with Temple Grove was the freedom to roam, and the long hours during which one was permitted to do relatively what one pleased: a three-hour space on each of the three half-holidays in the week, and only a few compulsory games; whole holidays on saints' days and certain anniversaries; and the freedon of the castle grounds, Windsor Park and the surrounding countryside, even Windsor High Street, to while away the hours. On his very first Sunday, Arthur – typically –

planted a 'fetish', 'a white stone carefully inscribed with the date' in a hole in a tree. Long Chamber was more constraining, but it was not the place of notoriety in the 1870s that memoirs and histories have made of it in the days of Keate. Only once did Arthur recall being bullied: by Russell Macnaghten (brother of Hugh, Arthur's contemporary), the memories flooding back to him on meeting him in 1914 – 'a tiresome, egotistical, foolish boy. He used to bully me in old days, and [I] remember his ricking my neck and how I dissolved in tears.' W. R. Inge (later Dean of St Paul's), he recalled, was given a tougher time, being 'eccentric and passionate' – great handicaps in a youngster at boarding-school, if too obviously exhibited – and, indeed, it was in the company of Inge that Arthur received his only recorded caning, from a member of Sixth Form, a 'gentle caning' for 'making a small bonfire of old blotting-paper, which filled the place with smoke'.

One of the compulsory constraints was on one's friendships and companions in the early years. The accepted convention was that friendships with boys from other houses, or in College beyond your Election, were suspect and firmly discouraged. This unwritten rule became less obligatory as one established seniority; and when one reached the eminent status of the First Hundred, all such strictures disappeared. Arthur's own Election provided him with several long-lasting friends – Willy Boyle, whom he had known slightly from Wellington days, when he lived at Sandhurst Rectory, and Marcus Dimsdale, both of whom accompanied him to King's; Remington White Thomson, later a colleague as an Eton master; and – the closest friend of all – Herbert Tatham, again a future Eton colleague, the companion of countless holidays, a man (and boy) exactly suited to Arthur's tastes: easy-going, good-natured, unambitious, and with a congenially disrespectful wit.

So Arthur adapted himself to Eton, without conceding, until his last two years, that he was really happy there. 'I was not consciously happy in those days', he wrote; 'but, looking back, I see that there was a freshness and an élan about it all.' He disliked the cult of athleticism, only once attending the cricket match at Lord's, and then detesting it; but being strong and bulky, he found he could get by, and even reach a certain distinction both in football and in athletics. His own predilections ran counter to the popular enthusiasms. He disliked rowing; he loved looking at and sketching old buildings; he developed a fascination for the Chapel music, and became something of an authority on the Anglican double-chant, finding congenial companions who shared his tastes, if not his opinions, in Monty James and Hugh Childers.

None of these friendships was a romantic attachment. But with the onset of adolescence came inevitably the heightened awareness of physical beauty and the craving for a close emotional bond which, at first, naturally enough, he could but dimly understand. The feeling was really awakened by his passionate love for a much older boy, Cecil Spring-Rice. Arthur described his feelings, years later, in his diary:

> I adored him at a distance when I was at Eton. I was 15 and he I suppose 18. His room was opposite mine and I admired the artistic quality of all he had. Then his pale abstracted face, aquiline nose, mobile and scornful underlip were beautiful. He was not very popular then. I remember him walking rapidly and alone into school talking to himself. I remember admiring his small hands which seemed like real continuations of his arms, not like rude additions! But I never spoke to him till the blissful day when I had gone to Henley, and tired of heat and noise, made my way to the station to return. He got into the same carriage and told me ghost stories. I hoped it would lead to acquaintance later but it did not. He was aloof and satirical then.

Before long he found himself exciting the interest of older boys. The first to make overtures was a sixteen-year-old called Vassall (later Father Vassall-Philips of the Redemptorists). 'He was an idle, talkative, sentimental boy, who took a great fancy to me and was very kind to me; and the mildly sentimental did me nothing but good. It was very odd how some of us little boys used to hang about with the big boys, Vassall, Burrows (Bishop of Chichester in later years), Tatham (M.T.), Stephen, Lowry (later Headmaster of Tonbridge) etc. – sit in their rooms, talk to them.' If he had been the housemaster, he would never have allowed it, he admitted. On the other hand, there was no corruption that he knew of, 'though there was much filthy talk among my own contemporaries'. Only once was he in real danger of seduction, though he did not realise it at the time. There was a very elegant boy called Pott, the son of Archdeacon Pott, who mixed with a bad crowd of whom he became 'an evil plaything', and eventually was obliged to leave Eton. One evening he invited Arthur, urgently and persistently, to accompany him into Lower Passage, where they were alone. He would not explain what he wanted, but kept stopping, waiting and listening. In the end he slipped away and nothing happened. 'I have often felt', Arthur wrote subsequently, 'that I was in some danger that night – though he made no suggestion and said not a word of evil. But I feel no doubt that there was something in his mind, and that only what we call an accident thwarted it.'

Then Arthur came to experience a different kind of love, in the development of a romantic and longer-lasting attachment to a boy of the same standing as himself and more nearly of the same age. The friendship is described in *Beside Still Waters*, but without identification: a wholesome relationship, exciting 'a depth of sacred emotion, too sacred to be spoken of to any one, even to be expressed to himself'. It transformed him as a person; it gave to life a sharpened savour; it made him realise for the first time in his life 'that it was indeed possible to hold something dearer than oneself', breaking once and for all 'the dumb isolation in which he had hitherto lived', opening 'for him the door of a larger and finer life, and his soul, endowed with a new elasticity, seemed to leap, to run, to climb, with a freshness and vigour that he had never before so much as guessed at'.

Who was this friend who gave to Arthur his first sensation of genuine love? Was it the boy whom he, later in the same book, describes as his companion on a sublime summer's day, bathing together in an enchanted place by a weir, recalling years later the memory of 'the delicious freshness of the turf under his naked feet, and the sun-warmed heat of the wooden beams of the wharf'? They had walked back to Eton arm in arm, the one saying to the other: 'Let us remember today', the compact being acknowledged by a smile and a nod, which brought them together into the charmed circle of mutual content, security and love. One such day is recalled in the diary in the company of Charles Wood, who died young, and who was his companion at a water-party in Goring Pool; a day with 'one of the sweetest creatures that ever lived and died – how we ate and drank and talked and sang – even then, with all his look of health he showed langour, I remember'. It could well have been Hugh Macnaghten, with whom Arthur became 'absolutely inseparable' (as he told Geoffrey Madan many years later). 'There was always something fierce and jealous about Hugh's affection. It was like a bird, an eagle perhaps, which when it had finished picking one's bones might fly away.'

The more likely identification of the unnamed friend is Harry Cust, a boy of singular brilliance and promise, slightly older than Arthur but in the same division and who overlapped with him at Cambridge; he was to ruin his subsequent career in politics by a life of hopeless indulgence. He was the subject of Arthur's poem *Utrumque nostrum*, recalling the intimacy of their feeling. A later sight of him, as a dissipated politician, attending Eton Chapel, caused Arthur to recall his earlier feelings: 'But, oh dear me, my heart beats no longer at the sight of him, as it would have

31

long ago. He is nothing but a crumpled rose-leaf, a singed gnat. . . . How art thou fallen from heaven, O Lucifer, son of the morning! I don't think there was *anyone* so entirely brilliant, on whom we laid our money so certainly as H.C.' In their relationship at Eton as boys, he was 'a great butterfly – while I was nothing but a big moth'.

This experience of love, coming when it did, marked the transition of Arthur's Eton life from good-humoured tolerance to the blissful enjoyment of his last two years. Genius departed with the going of personalities like Cecil Spring-Rice and J. K. Stephen (Curzon was not regarded as a genius – a pathetic failure to solicit Russell Macnaghten had excited derision and there was a general suspicion that he had cribbed in the Newcastle). Gradually Arthur and his friends took their place, passing successively through the divisions of Austen Leigh and Edmond Warre, thence to the First Hundred (in E. D. Stone's division), and finally to Hornby himself. Arthur became President of the Literary Society (on one memorable occasion having to entertain Ruskin as a guest speaker) and was elected to Pop. The circle of friends enlarged – St Clair Donaldson, Cecil Hugesson, Stanley Leathes, Monty James. They were themselves, for those beneath them, lords of creation to be watched with envy mulling beer after supper on a Sunday night, imitating Hornby or Austen-Leigh; taking the liberties that went with seniority, breaking bounds (with Harry Cust and Monty James) one June night after a meeting of the Shakespeare Society to listen to the Guards' Band playing 'The Lost Chord' to Queen Victoria at dinner in the Castle, and laughing at the rebuke when apprehended at midnight as they returned from Sheeps' Bridge. And so, in 1881, the leave-taking, with every circumstance of emotion – only to meet, most of them, again at King's in October; driving away in the carriage packed with boxes and trunks, 'ascending the bridge by the beloved playing-fields, with its lawns and elms, the gliding river and the castle towering up behind'. A few tears – but no remorse. 'I was only grateful and fond and sad at leaving so untroubled and delightful a piece of life behind me.'

*   *   *   *   *

October came, finding Arthur settling into rooms in the old Chetwynd buildings of King's, and taking stock of a small community of some sixty undergraduates, the majority of whom were old Eton friends. In most respects both the society and its way of life were highly congenial to him. Perhaps the least congenial part was the Classical Tripos, for which he read without great enthusiasm, never proceeding beyond Part One and eventually gaining a 'modest' place within the First Class. 'I was starved intellectually by the meagre academical system', he wrote in later years, deriving no lasting love for classical literature, a very imperfect understanding of philosophy, and managing to gain respectable honours mainly through wide, if desultory, reading and a familiarity with the Classics generally rather than any deep knowledge of the texts. He acknowledged no marked scholarly influence upon him by way of lectures or supervisions. His main contact with dons appears to have been either with the King's tutors – G. W. Prothero and J. E. C. Welldon – or with former Eton figures, like Oscar Browning, whose 'Sunday evenings' had by 1881 begun to degenerate into somewhat tedious, personal, self-centred soliloquies, pale reminders of the *art de salon* which had rendered him so dangerous and undesirable an influence in the eyes of both Hornby and Warre.

Prothero was never a friend. Arthur found him a mixture of 'a cold heart and an affectionate manner', ineffective as a tutor and positively unhelpful and unsympathetic when he most needed his support. Welldon, however, became a friend for life. After dining with him in his rooms on 5 May 1882, Arthur described him as 'orthodox, genial and positive – possessed of every possible advantage of strength, bodily and mental – perhaps deficient in grace of either'. Both aspects of the man fascinated him more and more as they maintained their relations through adult life, meeting on reading parties when Welldon was Headmaster of Harrow, or having intermittent tête-à-têtes in London or Manchester after his unhappy experience as Bishop of Calcutta. From time to time, family connections and friendships brought Arthur into the company of eminent Cambridge figures. One such was Brooke Foss Westcott, Regius Professor of Divinity and Fellow of King's, cordial, intense, with an embarrassingly shrinking personal modesty, whom Arthur would meet in his informal conversazione on Sunday afternoons at which tea was served – 'strong, uncompromising College tea'; or even sometimes on holiday with the Benson family, such as the occasion when they all went to Normandy together, and Arthur noted with amusement the Professor's total inability to relax, as he joined in at a cockshy which had been set up on the beach, and threw stones at it 'with a deadly intentness, far harder and quicker than anyone else'.

There was Arthur Verrall, who had been his father's favourite and most brilliant pupil, described in 1882 as 'the prince of emenders, a scientific scholar, the cleverest and most original talker I have ever yet heard'. Henry Bradshaw, University Librarian, an old family friend, was a Fellow of King's, drawing round him a circle of friends over whom he exercised an influence 'stronger', as Arthur put it, 'than the influence of any man in Cambridge'. It was a personal magnetism difficult to define, for Bradshaw himself was a complex character; erudite, yet curiously indolent and fastidious, romantic and affectionate, yet incisive and unsentimental – in some ways the ideal mentor and counsellor in times of trouble, because he gave direct advice from a loving heart, as Arthur himself was to discover during his own personal crisis in his last two years at Cambridge.

Occasionally he would visit Henry Sidgwick at Hillside, but not perhaps as often as he would have wished. The few encounters were always memorable because Sidgwick had the gift of bringing out the best in every guest he entertained; but his own radiant sincerity, which had caused him to resign his Trinity fellowship as he came to abandon all dogmatic faith, made him reluctant to exercise any personal influence over Arthur which could possibly cause offence to his father, who in 1883 had become Archbishop of Canterbury. As Sidgwick's nephew, Arthur was privileged to meet the brilliant and passionate Frederic Myers, and was entertained by him for lunch at Leckhampton House in 1883. There were certain advantages in being the son of a famous father, Arthur conceded. People wanted to meet you – Matthew Arnold, for instance, when he came up to Cambridge at the height of his fame to receive an honorary degree. But there were also expectations; and in his first year, Arthur was perfectly happy to involve himself in all the occupations and pursuits that would gain him immediate acceptance and eventual advancement.

He rowed for King's, although he eschewed the follies and vulgarities of out-and-out athleticism. He joined the Union; and while he never spoke at a debate, he was put up for the Union Committee, battling for the vacant place with Austen Chamberlain. He was a member of the Pitt Club; he took part in two Greek plays (in the *Ajax* with J. K. Stephen, and playing the High Priest in the *Birds*). More significantly, he secured election to the Chit-Chat Club (a prestigious society for the reading of weekly papers), succeeding Arthur Clough as Secretary but failing to gain entrée to the most coveted and exclusive of all Cambridge intellectual circles, the Apostles, chiefly because it was supposed that its notorious free-thinking might endanger his ultimate prospects within the

Church. 'The *sceptical* test was the one applied', Arthur reflected. 'I suppose I swallowed too much to be accepted.' He joined the Cambridge Browning Society, and found himself elected Secretary after delivering an allegedly brilliant paper on *Waring*. Having attained office, he apparently allowed the Society to die through his failure to summon any further meetings, possibly because he was invited *ex officio* to meet Robert Browning at a breakfast party organised by Sidney Colvin and found him so ordinary and undistinguished a man in private converse – no more than a good-natured bourgeois – that he lost all further enthusiasm for perpetuating his name and works.

Of his undergraduate circle, J. K. Stephen was undoubtedly the luminary. Arthur had fallen under the spell of this attractive, brilliant, perverse and unconventional boy (Leslie Stephen's nephew) while at Eton, where he had been the natural foil to Cecil Spring-Rice in the exchange of disrespectful witticisms and sophisticated literary judgements, striking awe in the hearts of the younger guests at O.B.'s Sunday evening parties. At Cambridge he came into his own. There was every opportunity for his love of the absurd and the incongruous; there was every sort of arena in which he could display his skilful irony and subtle wit, gaining all the most coveted honours and enchanting dons and undergraduates alike. Everything came so easily to him; and yet there was a strange melancholia within him that somehow held him back from the intimacies that he craved for and made him difficult really to get to know. Arthur saw much of him in his first year. He became a member of his informal club (the T.A.F. or 'Twice a Fortnight'); he would stroll with him often at night down to the bridge over the Cam, discovering something of the deeper perplexities that underlay the superficial brilliance.

When J. K. Stephen went down (in 1882), Arthur inherited his rooms – a large set on the ground floor of Gibbs's Building, on the staircase next to the Chapel. He moved to the top floor in his final year, and Monty James succeeded him. The circle of friends had now enlarged. In addition to his Eton contemporaries, Willy Boyle, Marcus Dimsdale and Hugh Childers, there was Goldsworthy Lowes Dickinson (who beat Arthur for the Chancellor's English Medal); Harry Goodhart and Harry Cust from Trinity; two colourful personalities who were to make their names at the Bar and in journalism, Jerry Harman and Leo Maxse; and – in 1883 – his future Eton colleague and lifelong friend, Lionel Ford, together with Walter Headlam, the most brilliant Greek scholar of his generation.

These are names redolent of a golden age; and the memoirs of many of these figures, including several biographical sketches written by Arthur himself, which are amongst the best essays he ever wrote, suggest an era of exhilarating intellectual vitality, carefree companionship and unbounded promise. The spirit of emancipation was abroad, as if late Victorian England was selfconsciously freeing itself from fetters that had bound its forbears, rejecting their assumptions, rising confidently above the aridity of their debates, looking to new disciplines, seeking new repositories of truth, shaking off old inhibitions, alert to the challenges of reconstruction – in politics, social reform, whole new territories of the mind – which an earlier generation had either failed to recognise or from which they had averted their eyes. This was not just the arrogant judgement of self-important youth. Historians of later Victorian Cambridge have recognised a peculiar richness in the decades when the influence of Sidgwick was paramount, a heroic quality, imbibed by the best of his pupils, and giving to the period from 1870 to about 1900 a unique spirit of honest enquiry and social responsibility which would make way in time for the more frivolous superficiality of the Edwardian age.

This was not Arthur Benson's true world, although he lived for a time in it and was deeply influenced by certain currents of its intellectual tide. He was never much interested in politics; his innate conservatism predisposed him always to stand for ancient ways; and, in his last year, moved him (uncharacteristically) to adopt an active role within the internal politics of King's in defence of its Eton exclusiveness against the attacks of Nathaniel Wedd and an ex-Oppidan, J. J. Withers, with whose reforming zeal he was totally out of sympathy. As Henry Sidgwick commented, having read Arthur's first efforts at fictitious autobiography in 1886: 'It is a curious performance. . . . One point in it that struck me was the complete absence of the *socialistic* enthusiasm which I have always regarded as the main current of new feeling among thoughtful young men during the last few years here. . . . It might have been written in the last century, so far as the relations of rich and poor are concerned.'

Nevertheless 'thoughtful' he became – indeed, deeply and agonisingly introspective, as, in the autumn of 1882, two events precipitated the first crippling depression of his life. Percy Lubbock has described the experience as 'a crisis of emotion and religion'. Arthur himself always subsequently referred to it as 'my great misfortune', 'the greatest and most sudden blow that ever befell me – which influenced my life incomparably more than anything before or since'. It was certainly sudden. Whatever it was that befell him was associated with a particular date – 9 November 1882 – which became, years later when he had embarked upon a regular diary, an anniversary of woe: 'my great anniversary' which 'made its mark like nothing else in my whole life'. On that day, and through that night, he experienced a crisis of dereliction so intense that, years afterwards, the rooms that he had made so unmistakably his own, with the Blake-like designs and the mysterious mottoes and the memories of J.K.S., became tainted with the recollection of the darkest hours he had ever known.

What happened? Two versions of a 'great misfortune' befalling the undergraduate career of 'Arthur Hamilton' (in the fictitious 'Memoir' published by Arthur in 1886) and of the unnamed hero (a 'distant cousin') of *The House of Quiet*, published in 1904, provide the answer, at least in general terms. Set beside later allusions in the diary, enigmatic and oblique as many of them are, both versions appear to refer to Arthur Benson's actual predicament, although it has not been possible to reconstruct the precise sequence of events. Both aspects of the crisis reflect the mood, the life-style and the intellectual ethos of Cambridge of the 1880's.

This was agnostic Cambridge. The great figures of the 1870's and 1880's were the free-thinkers and the sceptics. Where thirty years before the future leaders of the Church had met in eager debate and high idealism, now future politicians, social reformers and advocates of free enquiry had taken over their positions with a confidence and sense of vision no less eager or idealistic. In Oxford, T. H. Green could guide Paget, Gore and Scott Holland towards a new theology of in-carnationalism, which linked the theology of the Tractarians with the teaching of Hegel and presented a dynamic social philosophy within the framework of Christian belief. The corresponding influence of Sidgwick in Cambridge was quite the reverse. The great Christian teachers of late Victorian Cambridge – Westcott, Lightfoot and Hort – could not command the personal sway of Green and the younger ardent incarnationalists of Oxford; nor could they rival Sidgwick or Seeley in speaking to the hearts of men like Jebb, Maitland, Myers, Henry Jackson, the Balfour brothers and – after them – the intellectual élite of the 1880's into which circle Arthur Benson came to be drawn. Until that moment, religion had been something one accepted as part of the inevitable framework of domestic and institutional life. Arthur had neither questioned it nor found that it answered to his inner needs in any other sense than a vaguely emotional or sentimental experience. It was part of the air he breathed. He simply accepted it. It appealed to his love of order, antiquity and ceremonial.

At Cambridge, however, he was forced to concede that Christianity might have to be defended. Harry Goodhart at Trinity had done his best to unsettle him, and to remove the one obstacle that stood in his way for election to the Apostles. He felt unable to consult his father, who would never have understood and would have been bitterly hurt. The Archbishop had objected to his accepting an invitation from a friend to go up to London to see an Irving play and to meet the great man himself afterwards for fear of his being seduced into undesirable theatrical company. Arthur had meekly, if grudgingly, obeyed. He could never have faced a confrontation on a deeper issue. He therefore shrugged it off; refused to be drawn into sceptical debate; and in this matter, as in so many others, he backed away from the centre of controversy and took up the infinitely more comfortable posture of non-commitment, choosing to remain on the fringe.

Then came the Cambridge Mission. As he describes the impact in *The House of Quiet*, the circumstances were these. The day had started like any other Sunday in term: a dreary morning service in chapel; a Sunday walk with a friend in the afternoon; coffee after Hall. For a joke, the group of friends decided to go to the Corn Exchange to listen in at a Revivalist meeting. To begin with, it fulfilled all Arthur's love of the absurd – an unctuous and bilious-looking man playing a ridiculous harmonium, the congregation encouraged to sing to get itself into the mood. Then – the Evangelist himself, at first so ordinary and unimpressive, not even eccentric enough to laugh at. And then what he said. ... One could not but listen, and something began to drive home. After that, every word became compulsive, and a terrible self-revelation became plain. The words 'burnt into my soul. He seemed to me to prove the secrets of my innermost heart.' Members of the audience, even the cynical and carefree who had come to mock, began responding to the preacher's invitation to join him on the platform. Arthur himself got up; but he moved against the press of the others, stumbling into the night, returning dazed and sickened to the privacy of his rooms. He slept only fitfully, waking in the middle of the night to the consciousness of self-hatred and abandonment. It was the prelude to weeks of agonising depression, bordering on madness. He sought to escape by relentless academic work, all to no avail. He consulted an eminent Roman Catholic priest, and received a hard remonstrance. He tried to pray. Eventually he made his way to the one person who seemed to be able to see lovingly into his soul, and through his gentle guidance, and the assurance that he was by no means the first to suffer so, he was nursed back into sanity, although he could never entirely heal the wounds.

That this was an actual experience there can be no doubt. Certain details have been distorted. 9 November 1882 fell on a Thursday, for instance, not a Sunday. A later diary entry (at the end of August 1907, when Arthur was again suffering from depression) confirms, however, the general authenticity of the episode. 'I was fully as bad as this in 1882', he wrote, 'at the time of the Cambridge Mission, worse, I think. But then I had had a bad shock.' Other references suggest that he went for a short period to the mental hospital at Fulbourn. From the description of his spiritual director, it is certain that he sought the help of G. H. Wilkinson at St. Peter's, Eaton Square; and the Roman Catholic to whom he had written was undoubtedly John Henry Newman. Any possible confusion about this incident arises from the fact that it appears to have been coincidental with a second, and rather different, emotional crisis, the circumstances of which are impossible to recover in specific detail.

Again, part of the explanation, or at least the background, lies in the flavour and life-style of late Victorian Cambridge. Much will be said hereafter of the *mores* of an earlier age with regard to romantic friendship within exclusively male communities, a phenomenon so normal and respected throughout the period covered by this book that the greatest care must be taken to avoid slick and dismissive judgements. Every age creates and nourishes its own prudery. In the nineteenth century, the normality of both men and women forming highly emotional relationships with those of their own sex, of the same age or sometimes older or younger, as the case might be, was neither questioned as necessarily unwholesome nor felt to inhibit the same relationship with the opposite sex, leading to perfectly happy marriage. Sexual relationship outside the marriage-bond was most definitely deplored; and so sacrosanct was the bond in social convention that demonstrative friendship between those of the same sex was regarded as natural and acceptable, while overt exchanges of affection and endearment between a man and a woman might seem an offence against decency. Doubtless there was much ignorance and naivety in the general unawareness or lack of recognition of the depth and range of the sexual urge. Some of this was priggishness – a deep desire *not* to know. It is curious, however, and to some extent ironical, that the permissiveness of the late twentieth century has tended to create a different sort of prudery: a fear of being labelled, arising from the popularisation of Freudian psychology and the propensity to a facile use of clinical sexual terms. The twentieth century has become perhaps too knowing about such matters; the Victorian and the Edwardian ages were perhaps not knowing enough. Be that as it may, much of what follows has the period flavour of uninhibited male relationships which makes of the Cambridge of the 1880s almost a forgotten world in the university life of today.

In 1886, under the pseudonym Christopher Carr, Arthur published the book which he subsequently regretted ever allowing to see the light of day. He realised that 'Arthur Hamilton', whose *Memoir* the book purported to be, was too easily identifiable as himself. He made somewhat jejune attempts to disguise the background. Hamilton was a Wykehamist, not an Etonian; his father was a retired Army officer not an Archbishop; he went to Trinity, not to King's. But the character of his hero was undoubtedly a self-portrait, and the events of his early life were, with the exception of some not very subtle inversions of subject and object, well-remembered episodes in Arthur Benson's own childhood and youth. Thus Arthur Hamilton's career at Cambridge is vitiated by the experience of some 'great misfortune' which scars him for life. The date is 8 November 1872, and the event is recorded in his diary for 9 November 1872 in the single entry 'Salvum me fac, Dme'. It is suggested that the explanation might be the effect upon Hamilton of a Revivalist meeting that he attended, but this is dismissed as being 'merely fortuitous'. Whatever it was that scarred Arthur Hamilton for life, it went deeper than a transient, if direct, appeal to his religious susceptibilities. The true reason, investigation was to show, was the collapse of a deeply intense emotional relationship with a younger man. It had started at Winchester; and there it developed into a mutual love of sublime intensity; a friendship 'above all other loves, noble, refining, true; passion at white heat without taint, confidence of so intimate a kind as cannot even exist between husband and wife, trust such as cannot be shadowed'. Arthur Hamilton precedes his friend to Trinity; but when the other joins him, three years later, it is clear that he has been led astray by a bad set at school. He falls into a similarly corrupt group at Cambridge, and on the fateful day of revelation, the whole truth comes out. Hamilton had been deluded and betrayed. 'The other's was an unworthy and brutal nature, utterly corrupted at bottom.' He writes in his diary: 'Moral wounds never heal.' He meditates suicide. 'I believe I lie on the brink of insanity.'

How much of this was true? More particularly, if there was such a friendship in Arthur Benson's life, who was the friend? There are certainly grounds for supposing that however deeply the experience of the Cambridge Mission had afflicted him, this was not the sole cause of the breakdown that he eventually suffered. But no confidence can be placed in any of the details in the *Memoir* to assist identification. For example, in the *Memoir*, an episode in Arthur Hamilton's school life is recorded as follows:

> A sixth-form boy took a fancy to me, and let me sit in his room, and helped me in my work. The night before he left the school I was sitting there, and just before I went away, being rather overcome with regretful sentiments, he caught hold of me by the arm and said, among other things, 'And now that I am going away, and shall probably never see you again, I don't believe you care one bit.' I don't know how I came to do it ... because I was never demonstrative, but I bent down and kissed him on the cheek, and then blushed up to my ears. He let me go at once; he was very astonished, and I think not a little pleased; but it was certainly a curious incident.

Such an incident took place in Arthur Benson's life, but in entirely different circumstances. Fortuitously it is recorded in a diary entry for August 1902 (on the day of Edward VII's coronation) as a 'flash-back' on hearing the news of the death from appendicitis of Arthur Webster, the only son of the Lord Chief Justice. Arthur wrote as follows:

> I cannot forget how the ugly affectionate little boy, as he then was, came to Braemore. I was then feeble and ill, I remember. He took very much to me, and I played with him and talked to him. They were going off in the early morning and said good-bye overnight. I was standing by the fire in one of the drawing-rooms alone. He shook hands – looked round the room – and then with a sudden impulse came close up to me, put his arms round my neck and kissed me. It moved me very much at the time. He darted away and I have never seen him since, but have always felt affection for him.

This happened on one of the many occasions when the Benson family were staying with Sir John Fowler for the shooting at his Scottish estate at Braemore. The Websters and the Bensons were friends (Arthur Webster's father being then Attorney-General). It cannot be dated precisely, but it appears to have taken place between Arthur's breakdown at Cambridge and his writing of the Arthur Hamilton *Memoir*. He has used an incident fresh in his mind, altered the circumstances entirely and inverted the characters.

The retrospective references in the diaries to intense emotional friendships during Arthur's Cambridge career are few. In his first year, he formed a romantic attachment, which was very short-lived, with Arthur Somervell, an exact contemporary at King's who was later to earn distinction in the world of music. Arthur recalled him as a 'pretty, sensitive boy' with 'dark eyes, pink complexion and curly hair. . . . Such a feminine and pious genius'. The pressure in this friendship came from Somervell. Arthur felt that he treated him ill. 'To this day I cannot say why. We sate up talking one night very affectionately and intimately about many things – he took my hand, I remember, in his own, speaking about religion. He was a very sweet-natured youth, demonstrative and affectionate. I had seen much of him and had got much attached to him. The following day he went away for a few days, during which time I conceived an unreasoning dislike of him – quite inexplicable to me – I remember his return, how he hastened in, how I rebuffed him. "You don't turn round, you don't get up, you don't speak to me – What has happened?" What indeed!'

He was again the object of adoration as an undergraduate from Dalton, later Canon of Windsor, whose best man Arthur became. It was Dalton, he alleged, who did his best (with his father's aid) to deter him from the prospect of one of the very few female romances of his life – with Dalton's future sister-in-law, in fact, Miss Erna Thomas (later, as Mrs Sparrow, one of his most insistent female correspondents). They met on holiday in 1884. 'Oddly enough', he subsequently recalled, 'if it hadn't been for two chance remarks, from Dalton and E.W.B. about the mistake of early marriage, I could have been in love with her, if I had stayed a few days longer with them.'

What other claimants remain? He had had an intense friendship with Harry Cust at Eton, and his career at Trinity (not King's) overlapped with Arthur's, and they had several friends in common. For a while, the intensity of their friendship was renewed, certainly until 1883, a year later than the experience of the Cambridge Mission. A later diary entry, however, recalling an episode sometime in 1883, is suggestive of an impending fall from grace. The Cust family lived in a stately home at Cockayne Hatley; and Arthur spent a fortnight there with Harry when only he and his two sisters were at home. 'About 6 in the morning in the glimmering dusk, I woke. There was a boisterous wind and I heard the rooks cawing. I found Harry seated on my bed in a dressing-gown. He could not sleep.' They had been talking late into the night and Harry wanted to continue 'as before, half-humorously, half-mournfully. We spent a day or two there mostly strolling about and he told me (I thought) all his heart. What a splendid creature I thought him, and what a great man I knew he would become. And now? In broken health, heir to a peerage, with a taste for drink and a dark story behind his marriage; yet he is the best company in the world; and sometimes, as lately, makes a good speech.'

This was written in 1903. Their friendship undoubtedly collapsed. Cust became the 'bright Apollo' who had 'fallen'. As he grew older, he showed all the signs of the dissipated life – 'tipsy, obscene, useless'. If the emotional friendship which dissolved into ruin was his intimacy with Harry Cust, the 'great misfortune' divides into two separate events. The religious crisis came in November 1882, undoubtedly inducing intense depression. The emotional wounding came at least a year later, a fact which would fit more closely with the time-scale as described in the *Memoirs of Arthur Hamilton*. It seems at the very least highly probable that some collapse of an intense personal relationship left a deep wound, holding Arthur back from committing himself wholeheartedly in love to another person ever again. It is clear, too, that the depression never really lifted until his undergraduate career was over.

Only one of all the diaries he preserved covers jottings about his life and his moods prior to 1897. One or two of these refer back to Cambridge. On 16 February 1885, he records: 'For more than two years ... I think it is not an exaggeration to say that I have not had one happy day.' So it was that a Cambridge career that had started with such promise, with his contemporaries expecting so much, ended with this dismal summary of what he had achieved:

> In 1881 went up to King's – my great misfortune in Nov. 1882. I have often thought I was nearly out of my mind – and have certainly never quite recovered it. Idleness and moody religion followed. Got a First in Classics, 1884 June. ... Went back to King's and read enough theology to very nearly wreck my religion. To Eton, Jan. 1885.

Chapter Two

THE PRECARIOUS TRADE

It's a precarious trade, and depends much on calm nerves.
(24 September 1897)

I feel rather weary of this bright, vivid sociable place.... I
want to live on the edge of life: on the green margin.... My
life lies outside the life of these swells.   (3/4 June 1902)

The only idea which Arthur Benson had somewhat vaguely entertained
about a future career was the likelihood – sooner or later – of his
proceeding to Orders. The combination of his spiritual crisis at
Cambridge and the unedifying experience of a few months' study of
theology, in the hope that his doubts might become resolved, impressed
upon him the futility of taking any further steps in that direction, at least
for the time being. He never really seriously considered the question
again. At any rate, the invitation from Dr Warre to join the Eton staff in
January 1885 offered a breathing-space during which time he could
explore other possibilities. As it turned out, he stayed at Eton for twenty
years; and although he could never quite believe that teaching and the
guidance of the young came naturally to him, he acquired in time
sufficient reputation, affection and respect as a Housemaster to be very
seriously considered for the Headmastership of Eton when Warre retired
in 1905.

When he arrived at Eton, however, in his new capacity he felt neither
particularly committed nor in the least bit confident of success. At the age
of twenty-two, he reflected, Gladstone had embarked upon his
parliamentary career, while 'I was ... just a big, shy schoolboy, with some
second-rate friends, with no ideas about anything, except a liking for boys,
a wish to teach classics, and a desire to write feebly imaginative books.'
His only teaching experience had been as instructor, for a short while, of a
little class in a Cambridge Sunday School, and he therefore viewed with
trepidation the confrontation with his fourth-form division of over forty
boys 'in the unpartitioned end of Lower School'. His lodgings were at
Baldwin's Shore, a quaintly gabled house facing Barne's pool, only a
single room deep, which he was to share with Edward Lyttelton for

44

nearly four years. He liked his rooms; he rapidly sensed too the feeling of home-coming. He met again several old friends – Ralph Inge, Herbert Tatham and (within a year) Hugh Macnaghten. In his first week he experienced the salutary sensation of facing a class with one's lesson insufficiently prepared (a Geography period in which his ignorance of Asia was embarrassingly demonstrated); he 'sent down a boy for cribbing, and felt a brute when the lad burst into tears. Thereafter his early experiences went unrecorded, because the pressure of duties and the social round frustrated a first and somewhat stilted attempt to keep a regular chronicle of his doings.

Such entries as this single early diary contains – spasmodic, descriptive of thoughts and states of mind rather than of events during his first twelve years on the staff – suggest that Arthur's depressions lingered on for several years. This may, however, be a false impression gained from a volume in which he only wrote when his mind was clouded by anxious and inexplicable dreams or gripped by a mood of introspection. The records and the reminiscences of others present a different picture. Within a year his pupil-room was full. He was inundated with requests from parents to register their sons for his boarding-house long before that responsibility was to come his way. He seems also to have been an exceptionally popular colleague, making close friendships not only with those of his own seniority but also with much older men, in particular Francis Warre Cornish (the Vice-Provost), H. E. Luxmoore and A. C. Ainger, whom he had of course known as a boy. He became such an outspoken critic of public-school athleticism in later years that it is something of a surprise to discover that he took a full part in games, especially football, until an accident to his knee in 1889 put a stop to his playing days, freeing him for the more congenial employment of walking and cycling with friends. He certainly looked a footballer: tall, bulky, very strongly built, towering above the acknowledged athletes in the school, even cutting the Lytteltons down to size; and he made a daunting partner to J. E. K. Studd as full-back for the O.E.'s, Studd being a muscular Christian of unrelenting ferocity whose practice on the football-field, Arthur recalled, was to knock 'everyone down with a consciousness of rectitude, not kicking them in one place, but hitting them all over, and leaving them on the ground like a broken egg'.

Yet for a while he was fidgety and unsettled. He competed for a King's Fellowship in 1888 on the basis of a hastily-compiled book on Archbishop Laud. Prothero was scathing in his criticism, and Arthur had to admit that his scholarship was seriously deficient. 'If important works had to be consulted and I found them dull, I said frankly that they were unreadable. . . . I did not verify names or dates. I copied freely from other authors. The contemptuous reception of the book did me nothing but good.' At the time, however, he was so hurt by the rebuff that he revoked a codicil in his will leaving five hundred pounds to King's, and swore that he would never return to Cambridge until he was invited to receive the degree of LL.D.

To make matters worse, home had ceased to be the anchorage which he had always counted upon. There was practically no home life at Lambeth; dignity and magnificence in plenty, state dinners and great garden-parties 'with the court full of carriages and a stream of guests moving about the garden and house'. The result was 'we were never alone'. There was the refuge of Addington, thirteen miles away, where – with its great woods, parks and gardens – the Archbishop and his family could live in the style of a *grand seigneur*. His father loved Addington but could never find repose there. 'Away from the stir of London life, and with more leisure to think, he used to feel the stress of the great problems with which he was confronted, and his own fancied inadequacy to deal with them.'

> Yet the house is inseparably connected with him in my memories [Arthur wrote]. I can see him with his cloak and soft hat, pacing up and down on a sunny, frosty morning in the garden terrace, looking up at the great cedars which he loved. I can see him dressed for riding, feeding the horses with bread and sugar at the door, or strolling on a Sunday with his canvas bag of broken crusts for the swans on the pool, and a *Christian Year* in his hand, which he would read aloud to the party, sitting on a heathery bank in the wood. Most clearly of all, I can see him in his purple cassock after evening chapel, sitting down to write endless letters till one or two in the morning, looking up with a smile as we came to say good-night, twitching the glasses off his nose to enjoy a few minutes of leisurely talk. But for all that it is not to me, as I say, a place of very happy memories, because my father's spirits tended to be low there; and I never knew anyone whose moods, however carefully he guarded them, so affected the spirits of the circle by which he was surrounded.

The return to Eton, and his residence in London during portions of the holidays, brought Arthur for a time at least on to the fringes of high society of the late Victorian period, the years when the Edwardian age had effectively begun, some two decades before the death of the Queen. The changed ethos of Cambridge, while Arthur was an undergraduate, was a reflection of the new style of fashionable living, at its height during the London season, characterised by week-end house parties, the rounds of the London houses of the prominent hostesses who brought together the young and wealthy aspirants to public eminence and the eligible daughters of leading families who could match their opposite numbers in elegance, wealth and wit. Arthur's upbringing and temperament were alien, really, to this world. But increasingly circumstances were offering him the opportunity to belong to it. The group – to be christened by Lord Charles Beresford in 1888 'the Souls' – was, after all, composed largely of Arthur's friends and acquaintances. Arthur Balfour was his uncle by marriage; George Curzon and George Wyndham were his seniors at Eton; Evan Charteris was known to him through his literary circle; his return to Eton would soon introduce him to Mrs Grenfell (later Lady Desborough), Lady Ribblesdale and Mrs Horner. He had also made the acquaintance of the Tennant family. Three of the daughters of Sir Charles Tennant, who took 40 Gloucester Square as his London house in 1881, were – with Ettie Grenfell (the sparkling hostess of Taplow Court) – the most radiant and vivacious of the society darlings. Charlotte Tennant had married Lord Ribblesdale in 1877; both Laura and Margot Tennant, in the early 1880's, were besieged by suitors from within and without the circle.

Arthur met Laura Tennant for the first time at Leckhampton House at a luncheon-party given by Frederic Myers and his wife (Eveleen Tennant) in July 1884. She made an immediate impression upon him – not surprisingly, because she was the most brilliant and witty of the Tennant girls. Shortly afterwards he was entertained at 40 Gloucester Square; and their friendship had matured sufficiently for them to converse together and to take 'an evening stroll'. It came, then, as a shock to him, one morning at breakfast (29 January 1885), when Edward Lyttelton calmly announced Laura Tennant's engagement to his brother Alfred. Arthur did not conceal his surprise, but acknowledged that the match was 'a social triumph . . . the cleverest (as I believe) young woman in England to marry the finest specimen of man'. This was hardly an exaggeration, because Alfred Lyttelton was perhaps the outstanding sportsman of his generation – the most distinguished of all the Lyttelton cricketers and amateur tennis champion as well.

Arthur called on Laura a week later. From the talk they had together, recorded in the diary, it appears that their relationship, if not an incipient romance, was at least a genuine friendship.

> She says that she thinks she would have made such a good old maid, that marriage is rather a come-down; that she does not intend this to diminish her friends but only her acquaintances – a rather curious frame of mind for a lady just engaged. ... In the course of conversation she said she couldn't help wondering that she hadn't married before, so many nice people had wanted to. ... I was wonderfully glad. I think I never was in love with her.

This entry explains an enigmatic passage in the *Memoirs of Arthur Hamilton*, which was published in the following year. Arthur Hamilton is represented as meeting at dinner one night a young lady well known in the fashionable world. A strange friendship is struck up between them – strange, because the lady in question has a certain reputation for her promiscuous delight in male company, and Hamilton is known to be very fastidious, hating any suggestion of vulgarity. She is attracted by the other's mixture of gravity and humour, finding him something of a challenge; he loves her impulsiveness, while provoked by her fickleness and disregard for social convention. When he hears of her engagement to another (an heir to a peerage and with excellent prospects), he secretly believes he might have proved a more suitable match. But – alas – 'I never spoke to her a word of love!'

What might have been! Laura's final comment to Arthur, before her marriage, said laughingly as she wished him good-bye, has a real poignancy as things turned out. 'I shan't live a long life', she said. 'I shall wear out quick: I live too fast.' She died within a year of her marriage. Alfred Lyttelton very soon married again – Edith Balfour ('Di-Di' as she was called), Arthur Balfour's daughter and related to Arthur Benson by marriage. Certainly Arthur never forgot Laura. In 1916 he wrote to his friend Geoffrey Madan, after reading Mary Drew's memoir of Laura Tennant, 'She remains in my mind as a very wonderful figure, so small and beautiful and so quick at understanding things. The pace, I think, killed her. I was just inside it all. ...'

Romance of this sort, or even the hint of it, rarely appears as a feature of Arthur's adult life. And, indeed, no mention again is made in his diary of the Tennant family until he met Margot Tennant at Pontresina in the summer of 1891. In the meantime he had made the acquaintance of another member of the same group – Betty Ponsonby, the eldest daughter of Sir Henry and Lady Ponsonby (near Eton neighbours at Windsor Castle), the very close friend and confidante of Ettie Grenfell. She married a soldier (later Major-General William Montgomery), but from isolated references in Arthur's diary, it is evident that she became a close friend. After Margot Tennant's marriage to H. H. Asquith in May 1894, Arthur and Betty Montgomery met together in London for a long talk, chiefly about the doings of 'the Souls', discussing *inter alia* the distressing turn in the fortunes of Harry Cust.

During this period Arthur was establishing himself at Eton and gaining seniority for a boarding-house. When Edward Lyttelton married (in 1888), he moved his lodgings from Baldwin's Shore to rooms over the bookshop called Ingalton Drake's (later to become Spottiswoode's). He associated these rooms ever afterwards with the return of deep depression. He had wanted to move into a house in Weston's Yard with Hugh Macnaghten and Hubert Brinton, but Edward Impey had taken the vacant place on seniority. Shortly after the move he sustained an accident to his knee and he found that the cessation of regular exercise induced insomnia, to offset which he turned to the writing of poetry, often during the wakeful moments of the night. His nerves went to pieces again. 'The curse was on me.'

In this state he received the news of Nelly's sudden death in October 1890. The family were at Addington at the time, and an outbreak of diphtheria had occurred in the village. Nelly fell victim through contact with the local children in the schoolroom, and died after a short period of intense suffering. So, with hardly any warning, passed away 'the best of us', Arthur lamented; 'gay, adventurous, brave'. Because of the risk of infection, Arthur, Fred and Hugh had a brief word with their mother and father at Croydon, and stayed together for a few days at the Bay Hotel in Seaford. Arthur was frantic to get some exercise and took Fred on long walks against his will. 'It was a horrible dreary time. We wrote innumerable letters and tried to be cheerful. I remember one night being seized by faintness, and creeping up to my room convinced I was going to die.'

In the following summer he took a holiday at Pontresina. These weeks, he wrote, 'came like a light in the cloud. I was well and happy there; and a rapid friendship formed with Margot Tennant was a great pleasure and delight – but I do not think it can be kept up.' The depression returned as soon as he made for home, which may account for the pessimistic appraisal of his chances of any enduring link with Margot. He did not see her again until July 1893, when they met by chance at Lord's. Her manner, Arthur recorded, was 'very generous'. Eight months later he heard of her engagement to Asquith. He went to see her at Gloucester Square. She confessed to Arthur that she had been friendly with Asquith while his first wife was alive, and he had been a sort of 'father-confessor' to her. 'Then he had pushed Fred Milner at her and said "Marry him" but had watched the attempt with a gloomy eye. She would as soon have married F.M. as a coal scuttle and had realised that it was unselfish of A. and that *he* was devoted.'

On 12 May 1894 Margot Tennant and Herbert Asquith were married – the most fashionable wedding of the season. Arthur attended the occasion. He had no feelings of jealousy. His account of the ceremony shows more interest in the memorable sight of the 'G.O.M.', 'very toothless and hairless' talking at length to Arthur Balfour on the vestry stairs 'with the pathetic reverence of old age for youth and success'. It is not the last reference, however, to Margot. Years later they met in Cambridge, when Asquith (then Earl of Oxford) was addressing a liberal party meeting in the Guildhall in March 1925. They both dined with Arthur at Magdalene. Margot did not recognise him at first; and she too had changed – 'very witch-like, long face, long nose, with a hat with odd black puffs'. But memories flooded back. They talked of their meeting on holiday. 'She remembered, and we talked about our symptoms – with many nudges and hand-pattings from her. She certainly has a real charm. . . . She had a little olive-wood cigarette box, the counterpart of the one she gave me.' After the meeting, Asquith called her away from a temporary flirtation with one of the Aldermen. The crowd closed in and Arthur could not get through to have a last word. But Margot had not forgotten. She made her way back through the crowd to clasp his hand. "Good night, old *friend*", she said.

*   *   *   *   *

So Arthur parted from the brilliant society figure whom Jowett (who loved her dearly) had called 'the best-educated ill-educated woman that I have ever met'. It is barely conceivable that Arthur could really have fallen in love with her, and certainly Margot was not in love with him. But the linking of the Benson and Tennant families by marriage would not have been a defiance of social convention. Much has been written in recent years about the emergence of an intellectual aristocracy in Victorian England which gradually formed itself into a caucus of power, strengthened and perpetuated by intermarriage. The Benson and Sidgwick families were certainly part of this intellectual aristocracy; and as the century progressed so one begins to see families which had tended to confine their ties to the ecclesiastical and academic world beginning to encroach upon the political world, a reflection of the shift of élitism away from the Church towards politics. Arthur Benson's domestic milieu was the cathedral close and the bishop's palace. As the Archbishop's son he might have been expected to make an alliance similar to the union of the Davidson and Tait families or to the union of the Inges and the Spooners. But not necessarily so. The circle to which he belonged was naturally widening to become, if not noticeably less intellectual, at least rather more aristocratic and political. His own world was now very definitely the milieu of Eton society. Secondly, the marriage between Henry Sidgwick and Nora Balfour had linked the family to the aristocracy, for Nora Balfour's mother was Lady Blanche Gascoyne Cecil, sister of Lord Salisbury, and her brother was an up-and-coming statesman, later to become Prime Minister.

In this way Arthur could make a natural entrée into that family of uniquely brilliant alliances – the Lytteltons. George William, fourth Baron Lyttelton of Hagley in Worcestershire, had fifteen children; twelve by his first marriage (to Mary Glynne, sister of Mrs Gladstone), and three by his second (to Sybilla Mildmay). Not only did all his eight sons display outstanding ability as cricketers. Five of them achieved eminence in other fields – two statesmen (Viscount Cobham and Alfred Lyttelton), one bishop (Arthur Lyttelton, Bishop of Southampton), one general (Neville) and a Head Master of Eton (Edward). By marriage the children linked with the Talbot family (two daughters marrying Talbot brothers), the Stuart-Wortleys, the Cavendishes (Lucy Lyttelton marrying Lord Frederick Cavendish), the Tennants and the Balfours. The youngest daughter of the second marriage (Hester) married Cyril Alington – so that within the same family and a single generation, one son (Edward) became Head Master of Eton, while his step-sister married the man who was to become his successor. The eldest daughter of E. S. Talbot and Lavinia Lyttelton married Lionel Ford, Headmaster of Repton and Harrow. In two generations of Lytteltons, the names of four Prime Ministers appear (through marriage) – Gladstone, Lord Salisbury, Balfour and Asquith – and four cabinet ministers besides.

Yet another link between the Lytteltons and the Bensons was the Strutt family. John William Strutt, fourth Baron Rayleigh – one of the most brilliant physicists of his day (Cavendish Professor of Experimental Physics at Cambridge, President of the Royal Society and Nobel Prizewinner) – married, in 1871, Evelyn Balfour, sister of Arthur Balfour and Nora Sidgwick. Many times Arthur stayed at Terling, in Essex, the great family estate of the Rayleighs, and there he would meet the other members of the circle, especially Jack Talbot and his wife ('a regular Lyttelton', as Arthur commented). Arthur was fascinated by Lord Rayleigh – a delicate recluse with 'his laughing, rather muzzy eyes, his straggling moustache and whiskers, his lounging attitude', who had found Cambridge too taxing for him and had abandoned the management of his large estate to his brother in order to work quietly at his researches; as his keeper told Arthur, 'his lordship spends most of his time in his lavatory'. With Lady Rayleigh he exchanged political gossip and views on education. He became, after all, housemaster to two of their sons – Arthur and Willy Strutt – as he did to three of the Lyttelton boys, Jack, George and Caryl.

This was a thoroughly Eton circle. With the Strutts, Arthur felt conscious of being in the company of aristocracy rather than part of it. He was pleased, however, at dinner at Terling in January 1903, while talking with his neighbour, Lady Alice Archer-Houblon, to note 'two small trifles ..., Lady Alice saying to me, over and over again, "in *our* class" – "we in *our* class" – including me. Now, I should not have thought that I should have been considered by her to belong to her class. When we saw the A.H.'s off, Aunt N. [Nora], Lady R. and I went back to the library and Aunt N. said fervently "Well, now at last we are left alone". I was pleased to be in the inner ring.' The Rayleighs made one 'feel like a relation'; and the two boys never showed the least embarrassment at having their housemaster as a guest. Arthur was particularly entranced by Willy; relishing the sight of him, aged twelve, just before coming to Eton, 'standing in his little riding-breeches and slim legs before the fire, with his wide-apart blue eyes, and asking with the utmost simplicity and unconsciousness the questions of an intelligent man of 30, ... so absolutely guileless and unpriggish – with a natural blush after his questions'. He took the lad off to the dentist's, and tipped him gruffly on their return, saying: 'I must do this when I can. I shan't be able to when you come to Eton.'

Arthur never felt so kindly disposed towards the Lytteltons. His closest friend among the family was Spencer Lyttelton, who had been private secretary to Gladstone. He was a regular visitor to summer reading-parties and shooting expeditions in Scotland. He had an affection for Jack and George, and found Caryl's good looks totally disarming while not trusting him an inch. 'It is strange how much one can *like* a boy for whom one has no respect and in whom one can put no confidence.' As a family, Arthur thought the Lytteltons 'uncivilised', pretentious and self-conscious. Things came far too easily to them. They achieved eminence for no good reason and did nothing once they had aspired to responsible posts.

When Edward's appointment as Warre's successor as Head Master of Eton was announced in April 1905, Arthur recalled with delight the remark of his brother, Bob Lyttelton, to Lord Wemyss: 'What a family we Lytteltons are! There's my brother Alfred a total failure at the Colonial Office, and my brother Neville making a dreadful hash of the army at Aldershot, and now my brother Edward is going to be the worst Head Master of Eton that has been seen for a century. But the public seem to have such a love for the Lyttelton family, that there is no institution they won't entrust to us and beg us to ruin.'

Lady Lyttelton (the second wife of the fourth Baron) was 'an inveterate matchmaker'. Bachelor masters at Eton, destined for important headships, or Cambridge dons who might become Heads of Houses, were definitely on her list. Arthur watched with amusement, in 1907, her attempt quite shamelessly to interest Monty James in one of her unmarried, but very charming, daughters, and confessed to feeling a pang of envy. 'I wish it were going to be my good fortune to deserve her.' He had certainly had his opportunities. Through Edward Lyttelton's good offices he had been brought into the social circle of Sir Henry and Lady Ponsonby at Windsor Castle; and having been scrutinised carefully, as was Lady Ponsonby's wont, he became a very regular guest at her dinner-parties, developing at least a crony-type relationship with both Betty and Maggie, her able and outspoken daughters. Mrs Cornish, at her various gatherings 'full of the scent of Paris, and French literature, and cosmopolitan culture, and the world, and music', did her best to fulfil her avowed intention to find Arthur a suitable bride. It would have to be – she conceded – a perfect match, like her own, she would say, looking 'mistily out of the window' at 'the little wizened V.P. [Vice-Provost] with his red nose in the garden'. Arthur told Mrs Cornish that he preferred charm to beauty, and she caught hold of this at once:

> 'Your love of boys, of young things ought to help you – I can't imagine you with three girls!' She uttered a cooing laugh – 'but I will give you a brace of boys', and suggested ... reading George Sand. 'It would be very good for you. She was not exactly immoral but demanded that if a woman *must* sin, she should sin *disinterestedly* and for love.'

The family with whom Arthur felt most at ease and who provided him with a second home in the Eton holidays were the Donaldsons. Stuart Donaldson was an Eton colleague, some ten years senior to himself. In temperament he was about as different from Arthur as it was possible to be – a paragon of keenness and hearty clean living; painstaking in everything he did, simple and direct in approach; not a raconteur but a good listener; a good-natured, well-intentioned Evangelical, lacking both subtlety and wit. His father had been Premier of New South Wales and had died while his son was a boy at Eton. Arthur was introduced to the remainder of the family when he accepted an invitation to stay with them at Bere Court, near Pangbourne, in the winter of 1886.

He took to Lady Donaldson, Stuart's widowed mother, at once: a gracious, dignified lady whose serenity and shrewdness provided the strength of the household. This included two other victims of bereavement – her sister, Baroness von Brandt, also widowed, and an Irish friend, Miss Adie Browne, a person of fitful moods, veering from irresponsible gaiety to pugnacious dogmatism, and given to absurd over-indulgence to the whims and appetites of the Donaldson horses and dogs. St Clair Donaldson, Arthur's contemporary in College, and an elder married brother, Fred, a successful engineer at Woolwich, were frequent visitors too. Arthur became a regular member of the party when the Donaldsons moved to one or other of their holiday haunts, sometimes to Aylsham in Norfolk, but more often, until 1901, to Dunskey in Wigtownshire, a large, rambling old house formerly belonging to Sir David Hunter-Blair, which was admirably sited for fishing and rough shooting. Dunskey could house large parties, and every year in late summer a mixture of Etonians past and present, schoolmasters and ecclesiastics, together with family friends and the occasional eligible young lady would meet up for a fortnight or so's shooting.

It was a place of romance to Arthur – of poetical romance, at least. The house was situated at the head of a wooded glen going down to the sea – sublime on a summer's evening. Thus, in August 1897, as Arthur slipped out alone just before dark: 'the lights burnt in the low grey house; the sky was all aflame behind the high trees of the grove, melting into the coolest and most translucent green (how solid, oily, un-airy the green of twilight is). The smoke went up from the chimneys, and I beat the air on wings of poetry. Why? What was the sensation of exquisite beauty that I could not explain? I could scarcely contain myself for pleasure.'

That year saw a typical gathering there: all the Donaldsons and the ladies, their cousins, Algy and Mary Lawley, Cosmo Gordon Lang (Vicar

of Portsea), Winnington-Ingram, Lionel Ford, and a few others. Lang
and Ingram quarrelled together one night over the meaning of the phrase
'salvation is of the Jews', and made Arthur hate the priestly caste more
and more, especially the way they chose to speak of the after-life 'as if
they were the possessors of the mind of God. After death I hope for vast
enlightenment – but they know so much already that *anything* must be a
bouleversement to their ideas.' Lang struck him as dogmatic, stuffy and
rather ill-bred. There was certainly an enchantment about Ingram, a
curious personal magnetism ('I am hostile to him when he is not present
and dominated by him when he is'), and he delighted to hear him admit
that when he had spoken consolingly and – as he thought – impressively
to a young lad on his deathbed, the boy had listened gravely to him and
then said: "I don't believe one single word".

The following year the party re-assembled with some notable
additions. J. E. C. Welldon joined them just after his decision to accept
the bishopric of Calcutta and to resign from Harrow. There was much
speculation as to his successor. 'It would take a very strong man ... to
damage Eton or Winchester', Welldon said, 'but a weak man might ruin
Harrow.' He instanced Christopher Wordsworth, telling stories of the
ineptitude of J. W. Colenso when he was Wordsworth's house tutor;
how, for instance, he devised a new method of heating his house, and
when Wordsworth tried it out, he succeeded in reducing the
Headmaster's house to ashes. 'Colenso was a firebrand then as ever',
Welldon added. This was the explanation of why Elizabeth Wordsworth
was born in a stable. 'Wordsworth was fond of preaching sermons on
Unity', Welldon continued, pointing out that as Headmaster he very
nearly achieved it, by reducing the school to 64 in number. 'Fortunately
Sir Robert Peel loved Harrow more than he hated Wordsworth – so he
gave him with a sore heart a Canonry at Westminster, and saved Harrow
from extinction.' As soon as his appointment to Calcutta had been
announced, Welldon told Arthur, the fashionable hostesses had got busy.
Mrs Leiter, whose eldest daughter had married Curzon, expressed her
sorrow that her youngest daughter was due to leave India just as the new
Bishop was setting out from England. 'I think it would be so appropriate
for you to marry her.' Welldon's reply had been: 'I shall be glad to meet
her half-way.'

The event of that holiday was 'Welldon's bathe'. He had announced to
the assembled company on arrival his intention to have a swim on the
morrow 'on the stroke of one'. Great preparations took place. The

bathing-house was broken into; some very inadequate raiment had to be borrowed from Alfred the footman.

> At one the metropolitan entered the ocean. He was with St Clair. . . . It was a fine sight to see him breast the sea. He walked out with dignity but mincingly like an elderly lady. When once in, his little bullet head made him like a seal. St Clair splashed him. W. splashed feebly back and then made a great gesture, folding his arms. Coming up he spoke of the folly of *announcing* you were going to be a celibate. He added that the only people who were certain to marry were those who announced a celibate vocation and he added that if you hear any man deplore the death of his first wife in at all a marked manner you could be sure that he would very soon marry again. He laughed loudly at this and said to me: 'You and I have pursued the study of the defects of human nature together, my dear A.' I replied that I had always followed humbly in his footsteps. 'Yes, my dear A., if there was ever one defect unnoticed by me, you were sure to lay your finger on it.' He sate alone on a bench after a very good lunch at peace with the world, beaming.

There was a certain irony about all this talk of celibacy and marriage. Lord and Lady Glasgow were frequent visitors to Dunskey. On this occasion their party was joined by Lady Helen Boyle (Lord Glasgow's sister), Lady Alice Boyle (a daughter) and Lady Albinia Hobart-Hampden. Arthur had tête-à-têtes with each of them. He was pleased to register one little social point. Sitting next to Lady Helen Boyle at dinner, he turned the conversation to New Zealand, where she had been staying with Lord Glasgow. She said that 'it vexed her "though I don't think I am proud" to have to meet Doctors and Dentists at dinner. I told her that 50 years ago she wd. have been offended by sitting between two schoolmasters.' So had the profession risen in the social scale. He was quite attracted by Lady Alice (perhaps it was intended that he should be), though slightly offended at being mistaken for the author of *Dodo*. With Lady Albinia, however, he felt less at ease. She was curt with him at first until she discovered 'I was painless'. 'She is a good soul – big, rather pathetically plain, affectionate. . . . She lives, an elect lady, at Hackney Wick, working. Complains of the absence of all culture – is devoted to the theatre. Her extraordinary good-humour and friendliness makes amends for all.' A romance, however, began – between Lady Albinia and one of the other schoolmasters of the party; and in two years time her engagement to Stuart Donaldson was officially announced. In the same year, Arthur met Lady Alice Boyle again at Dunskey. This time she treated his literary reputation with greater respect. 'This somewhat accounts for my finding her very congenial – indeed. . . .'

Others who came that particular summer of 1898 were London friends like Moler Cole (a director of the Bank of England) and young Ronnie Norman, embarking upon a successful career in business – a young man of such striking beauty that Arthur studied him closely in repose to see if he could account for the physical properties that create the magnetism of charm. 'Let me record what a beautiful picture he made lying wrapped in a cloak on his side after the shooting lunch. Tumbled hair; bronzed face and blue eyes. He is immensely admired here. I find myself looking at him and wondering why a face which is so beautiful in detail does not attract me more in its general aspect.' Then Luxmoore, his Eton colleague, came for a few days; and one day, soon after the start of the holiday, Lord and Lady Dunbath with their young son, the engaging Mulholland – a boy in Donaldson's house and in Arthur's division:

> I was coming in from shooting wood-pigeons. I had been alone and got five which I had tied together with a cord from a gatepost, carrying them in a string. On seeing the party I thought Miss Browne was with them and so stepped aside into a bush. I was detected and Miss B. was *not* with them – so I had to come out sheepishly and be introduced. The boy was delighted at seeing one whom he only knew as a grim gowned man in Trials, hot, sweating, with a string of dangling pigeons. ... On Tuesday Lady D. photographed us; the boy was merry and sate beside the seat: H.E.L. caught him, imprisoned him and held him fast in a charmingly easy paternal way which I envied, having been rather racking my brains to think of things to talk to him about and only producing grim and idiotic smiles. The boy snatched a fearful joy from being thus held fast by one of the most distant and tremendous of Eton worthies – a delightful picture.

'I love the mossy sea-woods of Dunskey, where I have had so much happiness', Arthur wrote during the summer. There were to be such holidays again; but leaving, after three weeks, with the prospect of another Eton half before him, he wrote of this place, and the people there, one of the most rhapsodic passages he ever committed to his diary:

> I drove away with sinking heart – tears in my eyes – like a schoolboy going to school. All evening I thought of what they would be doing. I cannot be grateful enough for all that beloved place and the beloved people have been to me. Under the weather-stained sycamores, down the leafy roads – with the high stubble fields left and right ... by the mill, taking last looks at everything. It is a strange thing to do this; to feel that the affection and the spirit of all this is so wholesome and true, and yet that we have no continuing city.
>
> > 'But oh, the very reason why
> > I love them is because they die.'

57

Die not, brown woods of Dunskey, and beat on, dear hearts! Make me more ashamed of my ungentle and illiberal spirit, my love of ease and sloth. With and among you we are all generous and sweet. Valete domum! (This is rather a ranting spring, I think. But it is true, though too rhetorically expressed.)

*   *   *   *   *

Most Easters and some portions of each summer were spent at a strictly bachelor retreat: a house called Tan-yr-allt, near Portmadoc in North Wales. The mention of Tan introduces two more of Arthur's close and lifelong friends: A. C. Ainger and Howard Sturgis. Both were several years older than Arthur. Indeed, Ainger (who had been Howard Sturgis' tutor at Eton) was nearly twenty years his senior, and by the time Arthur resigned from Eton he had himself retired although was continuing to live at Eton in the house called Mustians. He was a confirmed bachelor; lean and rangy in appearance, independent and energetic, a stickler for routine and the self-appointed organiser of any party that he joined, but not easily ruffled and rarely out of temper. His friendship with Howard Sturgis began from the moment that this frail and sensitive boy (the very opposite of his athletic and popular elder brother Julian) joined his pupil-room; and although Howard left Eton early, the friendship was maintained through regular meetings in the holidays; and in 1882 they decided to take a joint lease of the beautiful house above Tremadoc – Tan-yr-allt, once the home of the poet Shelley.

Howard Sturgis' life and life-style exude a real period flavour – a touch of *fin-de-siècle* and very much more than a touch of Edwardian opulence. His background was unusual: an American father who married three times and who became massively rich as a partner in Baring's Bank, living his last years as a delicate invalid. By his third wife he had three sons and a daughter. Julian, the second son and the father of three boys in Arthur Benson's house (Gerard, Mark and Roland), was a writer of delicately phrased and somewhat ineffective novels, living in a magnificent modern house on the Hog's Back. Howard, the third son, started life by studying at Cambridge, spending most of his time at the A.D.C. and then at the Slade School of Art. His studies were interrupted by his father's illness. Thereafter Howard effectively retired from active work. He nursed his parents; he set up house in a beautiful residence near Windsor Park – Queen's Acre (or Qu'acre as it came to be called) – and became a sort of patron both of writers and artists (Henry James was a frequent visitor) and of strange American cousins whose common feature was a propensity to over-stay their welcome. One such – William Haynes-Smith (always affectionately known as 'The Babe') – became a permanent guest: a sturdy young man of rough manners and inexhaustible solecisms, whose status in the household was that of companion and resident male housekeeper. At Qu'acre, Howard lived a life of 'epicurean invalidism'. He was too delicate to take exercise; he eschewed any regular occupation, except to write one or two rather sentimental or morbid books, *Belchamber* being his best known. He was a deft and witty conversationalist, slightly disconcerting his auditors (if they did not know him better) by producing a canvas and silks, as he talked, and executing pieces of fine embroidery.

Arthur met Howard Sturgis for the first time while staying at Tan, on a visit in Tatham's company in 1887. He was perplexed by his effeminate ways and a little nervous of his wit, suspecting that behind the elegant and sophisticated façade 'there was a little creature out of sight which might suddenly put its head out and bite'. The suspicion gave way to a deep and lasting friendship. One evening Arthur called on Howard (he was always known by his Christian name) as he was dressing for dinner, admitted his discomposure, and was rewarded by the characteristic gesture of true friendship (Henry Bradshaw had the same habit) – the presentation of a flower for his buttonhole. This 'was not sentimental in the sense that it seemed like a weak effusion of fondness. ... Howard enjoyed sentiment as he enjoyed his embroidery, as a pretty and harmless diversion, not in itself very important, and far removed from friendship, which was a much more serious affair.'

From 1887 to 1899, when the lease ran out, Arthur went to Tan for a short period every year. For the first years, a meeting there with a reading-party was usually the prelude to some summer expedition abroad, generally in the company of Tatham and one or two other Eton friends. In 1885 he went to Sicily; in 1886 to Rome; in 1888 to Spain; and in the following year to Madeira. During the winter break he would make for the Alps, where he became a sufficiently accomplished rock-climber to be elected to membership of the Alpine Club. He abandoned the practice in 1895 after a holiday with Tatham at Bel Alp, when he slipped down a crevasse on the Unter-bach-horn, a seemingly desperate plight (as he described it later) which nearly resulted in the death of both of them and their guide in the hazardous attempt to haul Arthur out by a rope which was slowly strangling him.

From 1895 onwards his visits abroad came practically to an end. But the holidays at Tan and Dunskey continued. Sometimes, or at least in the earlier days, Arthur and Tatham would cycle all the way from Eton to Aberystwyth at the beginning of the Easter holidays. The parties were heartier too:

> When first I came [Arthur recalled], they were large, boisterous, active: Eton boys were often here; Sydney James and other sudorific persons used to play billiards and squash racquets and bathe and eat and smoke. Long expeditions, starting early and cutting sandwiches were organised – long vague walks, with al fresco lunches and teas in inn-parlours. . . . This has all somewhat faded. There is less organised mirth, more peaceful and sedentary life. The mornings are generally undisturbed: the afternoon is expeditionary – not too long walks or bicycle-rides – after tea is given to croquet, paper-reading, writing – and after dinner everyone reads or plays cards – no constraint. Ainger and Howard between then certainly make wonderful hosts.

At Eton responsibility had come to Arthur – by his appointment to a boarding-house in 1892. His first house was Drury's which he occupied for two years before moving (with his boys) to Gulliver's at the end of 1894. His original house was demolished in 1903, and he watched the process with his colleague de Havilland, perhaps a little sadly as he recalled the moment of taking over and his firm resolution that he would never nag his boys and never set small punishments. From Gulliver's he moved to Godolphin in 1899, taking over from Broadbent in September of that year: 'One of the most *amenable* houses in Eton', he commented, when he had finished unpacking. 'The garden, with the huge old Spanish chestnut is very pleasant to look out on – the birds piped loud there the first morning I went and stood out on the balcony, and the screen of lilacs is so contrived that it hides all walls and buildings – and except for W-Thomson's house, looking like an Aladdin palace, I seem to look right away over country, seeing the forms of tall trees further and further down to the horizon – and to be joined to the garden of Eden.'

The depression which had so incapacitated him after Nelly's death had lifted for a while. He was beginning to acquire literary success and important literary friends. He had had, however, an intensely harrowing time in the two years before he began to compile a regular diary in the summer of 1897. Looking back over 1895, for instance, he notes grimly that a busy year has ended in 'acute and deadly depression – and I record it as my deliberate feeling that I would rather at any time die than live. The whole thing is a heavy enigma. Why should I be born, reared, given a contented temperament with certain definite aptitudes and inclinations, and then pushed, miserable and reluctant, along this stony path? ... I have no faith to help me up, no hope. I am simply one of those unhappy invalids who keep diaries, whom I have so often despised – that is the bare truth.' His father and mother had been pressing him to think seriously about marriage, being very anxious to have grandchildren. 'I feel more and more that even if I were so tempted, it would be *criminal* – even to run the risk of handing to another my own miserable disposition – and to admit another into the torture-chamber which I call my life.'

The nightmares returned – one terrible one in February 1896 about a tramp, seen holding over a well 'washing, but with a kind of amused tenderness, an object that I thought was a rabbit, but I presently saw that it was a small deformed hairy child, with a curious lower jaw, very shallow: over the face it had a kind of horny carapace, ... made of some material resembling *pottery*. I was disgusted at this but went on, and it grew dark: I heard behind me an odd sound, and turning round saw this horrible creature only a foot or two high, walking complacently after me, with its limbs involved in ugly and shapeless clothes, made, it seemed to me, of oakum, or some more distressing material. The horror of it exceeded all belief.' Curiously, his work in school seemed to reflect nothing of this anguish of spirit. At Lord's that summer, Warre took his father aside and told him that he hoped that Arthur would eventually become his successor in the Headmastership. 'I should have thought myself the very last person he wd. have selected', Arthur reflected, 'a layman, a dilettante writer of books, no athlete: but I regard such a prospect with no real devotion, tho' position and traditions are alluring.'

A good summer holiday at Tan and Dunskey – and then a week or so staying with Stephen Marshall and his wife at Skelwith Fold in Ambleside (Annie Marshall was a Sidgwick aunt) – restored his good humour. Then – totally unexpected – came the news of his father's death, in Hawarden Church, while staying with the Gladstones, during morning service, following a most exhausting Irish tour. The family had not known that earlier in the year he had been sent by Dr Ross Todd (the Archbishop's doctor) to see Douglas Powell, the heart-specialist. The prognosis had been very gloomy indeed. There were signs of dropsy, and – unless the Archbishop were prepared to take a long rest and to diet – the specialist could give him no longer than two years to live. According to Ross Todd, who told Arthur about it eight years later, 'papa gaily replied: "And how many of these things do *you* do?"' Actually, the true condition of his heart had not been revealed to him, 'I am sure rightly and wisely'.

At first Arthur was numbed by the news. He thought a break-down to be imminent. But the need to cope with the funeral arrangements, the evacuation from Lambeth and Addington, and to agree plans with his mother and the rest of the family, restored him, at least for a while, to energy. 'I have never worked so hard or so freshly as I have done in the last few months', he wrote in the summer of 1897. 'Is it fancy to feel like Elisha? – a double portion of thy spirit.' He saw his mother, Maggie and Lucy Tait off to Egypt for a holiday, although slightly resenting the expense upon the estate and the amount of planning left upon his shoulders. Nevertheless he was elated at the prospect of having to write his father's biography, which he had decided upon within two months of his death. A terrible Easter Half ensued. A boy (Myers) in his house died from pneumonia. Then news came from Egypt that Maggie had had a heart-attack, following pleurisy, and that her death was hourly expected. Fred went out to help with the emergency and contracted typhoid before he reached his destination. Maggie recovered – it seemed miraculously – but when the family joined up with Fred, Lucy Tait fell victim to typhoid as well. When the party arrived back in England, they were offered a temporary home at Farnham Castle with Randall and Edie Davidson. Beth then fell seriously ill. In the meantime Arthur had to face another disaster in his house. A boy, de Gray, at the beginning of the Summer Half was knocked down by a train at Slough station, dying from his injuries the following day.

At the beginning of June 1897 Arthur felt the strain so insupportable that he decided to write to Warre, resigning from Eton. 'The work is altogether overwhelming. ... At present my work roughly divides itself into three parts – the house, the division, the pupil-room – *one* of which I think I could discharge conscientiously, but as it seems that the only one I can retain is the only one that I least wish to retain (the division), I think it better to place my resignation in your hands. ... The work that has fallen upon me owing to my father's death, and the absence of all my family from England, and their subsequent illness is just sufficient to make the pressure impossible.' The letter was never sent. He thought better of things in the morning. Two weeks later he drafted two angry letters to Warre, complaining of his high-handed treatment of the staff on the occasion of the torchlight procession in honour of the Queen's Jubilee, when masters were offensively upbraided in front of boys. The fact that he never sent these either, or referred to any intention to resign, suggests that Arthur was already emerging from the trough. He was just plain angry, not depressed. In the same week he was offered Sydney James' boarding-house by Warre (on James' appointment to the Headmastership of Malvern). 'I took a Sortes Biblicae before refusing it. I found "Is not the Lord your God with you? Hath He not given you rest on every side?"' He took that to mean that he would be subjected to too much noise from traffic in Sydney James' house which fronted on the street, and therefore declined to move.

He then took stock of his position. The date was 9 July 1897. The impetus to examine his efficacy, or lack of it, as a schoolmaster, came from reading William Cory's *Letters and Journals*; and the self-analysis that followed was infinitely more realistic than anything he had committed to his diary in the twelve years he had been at Eton:

> I ... feel ashamed of myself and my work. I have one of the nicest sets of boys in my house at Eton; good, earnest, pure, willing – and I give nearly nothing of myself to them; am fretful and wearied over my work for them, and save for myself every minute that I can. I have a flood of inaccurate knowledge and I suppose a certain sympathy – an intuitive knowledge of what is interesting to an ill-regulated mind like my own – and so in an ordinary lesson I can interest the boys without taking much trouble. I think I inherit a knack of teaching – and the boys get in a way fond of me: but I am quite aware that my house owes more to Mrs Cox [his matron] than to myself and more still to the accident of having brave and pure-minded boys, with good homes. My own mind is as inconsequent and wanting in grip or hardness as ever. I have a great interest in literature and style and epigram – but no knowledge of history, no grasp of philosophy – a lot of half-fledged ideas. ... Well, I seem to myself a cracked and half-baked urn. But I will leave it in God's hands, who made me, and only ask him that as he has given me the power of seeing faults, weaknesses and follies, he may give me strength to correct them.

This entry, though he did not know it at the time, marked the beginning of a new epoch in his life. Although there were many grumblings and heart-searchings during the years ahead, there were no more cries of dereliction or agonising depressions for ten years. In the following month, Arthur embarked upon his continuous journal, determined at least in that respect to emulate William Johnson Cory. For the remainder of his Eton career, from 1897 to 1904, the coverage is so detailed that his diaries stand as perhaps the fullest account of a schoolmaster's life and trials ever written.

In one other respect, too, a new epoch began. With the passing of his father, he had become the senior male member of the Benson family. For a while he had effectively to make the decisions for his mother until she adjusted to a situation where she no longer had to efface herself and her concerns for the sake of her husband and his important work. The immediate problem was to find a family home. The answer appeared to be solved in the offer of a lease of an old Georgian mansion in St Thomas' Street, Winchester. It was ideally sited for the Cathedral, within easy reach of many friends, and seemingly spacious enough to house the bulk of the accumulated treasures, books and lumber of two decades of palace life. The move was effected. The family all came together for the Christmas of 1897, doing all the things that characterised domestic felicity and harmony within a group of very independent and highly intellectual adults, determined to celebrate the event as if nothing had happened. They played word games, composed magazines and argued strenuously. John Reeve, Vicar of Addington, came to join them, much cast down after the death of his mother, hardly contributing to the festive spirit by vouchsafing his constant prayers that Arthur might be ordained and by asking Fred outright, in front of all the others, whether he prayed for the repose of Gladstone's soul. And a tiresome woman, by the name of Miss Bramston, whom Mary Benson had taken under her wing over the holiday, fidgeted everybody, sitting 'four square at tea like a penguin: she slops her tea about, grabs food, gazes at M.B. and takes no notice of anyone else. She walked with us to Cath. on Xmas Day, in ugly black clothes rudely cut with a large grey woollen shawl round her neck. She is shapeless and walks like a swan.'

Winchester suited Fred, who had smart friends near at hand and was enjoying the life of clubland, preoccupied with golf and cards. But Mary Benson fretted and Maggie, after a temporary lifting of spirits, grew more and more depressed. It was too reminiscent of the old life, while lacking the challenge, responsibilities and position which the old life had ensured. Winchester was too damp in winter and too stifling in summer. The ladies yearned for the country. Properties at Basingstoke and Haslemere were inspected. A small London house, 5 Barton Street, lying just within the precincts of Westminster Abbey, was secured as a base, chiefly for Lucy Tait (who had now effectively become a member of the family through her intimacy with Mary Benson). Then came word of a vacant country-house near Horsted Keynes in Sussex, whose owner (Mrs Hardy of Danehurst) was looking for a tenant. After a single inspection, the ladies of the family decided to look no further, and in the spring of 1899 they moved to 'Tremans'.

Arthur did not see it himself until July. Nor at that time had he any knowledge of the Sussex countryside, especially one of the most beautiful corners of Sussex, the uplands lying between Ashdown Forest, all heathery slopes and pine-clumps, and the Sussex weald: a country idyllically fashioned for his tastes: no massive outcrops of crag or rock (he had had his fill of those in Switzerland); no awesome grandeur to take one's breath away; but rather the heart and essence of the English countryside – furrowed fields, small copses, gentle ridges, quiet streams and hidden pools; contrasts of downland, seen at a distance, and valleys studded here and there with farms and hamlets; a land of miniature glories, subtle contrasts and delicate effects. The house itself was one of the finest in the county – Caroline in part, mullioned windows, stone coigns, weathered brick, high chimneys and a lead-topped cupola, with adjacent farm-buildings, bowling green, cherry orchard, barns and fishponds. It was approached by an avenue of Scotch firs and was screened from the road by a huge yew hedge. It had charm, comfort, dignity; and Arthur fell in love with it on that first summer evening, begging a lift from Horsted Keynes station, and standing in speechless delight as he rounded the bend in the drive and caught his first sight of the big iron gate with the manor-house (for such it really was) beyond.

Thus he saw his family settled where they would live until Mary Benson's death in 1918. His mind was more settled too; at least reconciled, albeit grudgingly at times, to what he was wont to call the 'drudgery' of the Eton system. With the enormous additional work imposed upon him by the Archbishop's biography, he found himself, for the first time in his life, coming to terms with his father. The fitting climax to this epoch in his life was the coming-together of all the family, in positions of honour among the greatest in the land, on the occasion of the unveiling of the Benson Memorial in Canterbury Cathedral on 6 July 1899. He travelled down by train with the Bishops of Durham and Winchester (Westcott and Davidson), discussing the personalities of headmasters on the journey. Westcott told him how Prince Lee had once dismissed a master in front of the whole school in Assembly for daring to comment on his actions adversely in a local paper: 'Mr Collins – You may retire. Your services are dispensed with.' It was personality that made the greatness, not scholarship or accuracy or the method and style. Arthur agreed, thinking of Warre. 'His eloquence is nil, his argument unsound; his knowledge limited; his prejudices extreme; but yet he is personally impressive in a high degree.'

The station was lined with red–carpeting and hangings with a guard of volunteers and an escort of lancers to greet the Duchess of Albany who was representing the Queen. The Dean of Westminster (Bradley), looking as if 'he had come from a race-meeting' accompanied Arthur to the cathedral close, where they were greeted by the Farrars. Dean Farrar was so overcome by royalty that he mistook Arthur for Lord Mt. Edgecombe. It was stiflingly hot and thunder-clouds gathered as they entered the cathedral for the service. Thirty bishops were present. 'The Archbishop very hairy and dusty and quite blind.' During the prayers before the monument, the storm broke. 'Hail fell crashing – in stones as big as eggs – so that I thought at first that the one or two I saw thro' open door were fireballs.' In between flashes of lightning, the flare of magnesium 'for photographic purposes gave a great scare. A man said close to me "Good God! The cathedral is struck and is on fire!". . . . The thunder muttered at intervals, like a bourdon pedal.' There were addresses from the Lord Chancellor and Lord Mt. Edgcombe. Mary Benson walked up alone to pray on the steps of the monument. She was presented to the Duchess of Albany as she returned. She met her 'with outstretched hands, bent and kissed her, and M.B. held her hands in both hers while they talked. It was a most touching womanly scene and made me cry.' As a lesson was read by the Archbishop of York, there was a terrific peal of thunder, a great rumbling in the roof and then a cataract of water fell into the aisle. A. J. Mason confirmed to Arthur that the cathedral had been struck.

As the royal party prepared to go, Arthur watched with fascination Archbishop Temple making an obeisance. 'He executed a most extraordinary contortion: all his back, like the back of a bullock lay beneath me while he shook hands – an extraordinary gymnastic feat.' Arthur was asked to travel back with the Duchess of Albany in the royal coach to Victoria. He came back to Eton feeling rather dazed. 'I was profoundly grateful and thankful for the majesty and solemnity of the day. It is, as it were, the closing life-ceremony. Now E.W.B. will be a memory, a figure of history. ... This taste of the world, of a sham importance, has a curious intoxication for me; but I am an earthen pot not fitted for it – and the draught even on the lips was bitter. Still there is an intense pleasure in being *in* it – being a personage – which beams from a man like Creighton; and Mrs Creighton too.'

He was brought down to earth very rapidly.

Came back walking and talking with a kind of foolish dignity, till I fell over a

1 A. C. Benson: the diarist

'*What an odd book this diary is! It amuses me to write it.*'

2 At Tremans, 1904. A.C.B., Hugh, Fred, Maggie with Roddy, Mary
Benson, and 'Beth'

*'We have got a middle-class taint about us. We are none of us aristocrats in
any way.'*

pail in the passage, placed there by providence – broke my bad shin, and became an ordinary human being in five minutes.

*   *   *   *   *

Was it such drudgery to serve at Eton? The trouble was that masters were expected to do too much. 'We are here', Arthur wrote in October 1901, '(1) a maître d'hotel (2) a clergyman (3) a lecturer (4) a coach (5) a policeman – most of us are athletes too – and Warre has made many reforms and *all* have added to the masters' work and responsibilities.' On 1 October 1900, he described a particularly arduous day in his life. He rose at 7 a.m. to take an hour's Greek Testament lesson from 7.30 to 8.30. He had a half-hour break for breakfast, followed by forty-five minutes correcting verses. Then followed two periods with his division, doing Latin prose and construing. He attended Chambers (the morning concourse with the Head Master present) from 11.15 to 11.30. He corrected proses until 12.15, and was then in pupil-room (doing individual coaching) until 2 p.m. From 2.00 until 2.30 he lunched with his boys in the house, followed by an hour of Greek exercises. Between 3.30 and 4.00 he took a short walk with Tatham and returned to correct more verses and have a short sleep. He was with his division again from 5.00 until 6.00, teaching Virgil and then had a quick break for tea, followed by half-an-hour's preparation for his Private Business lecture on Napoleon which he gave from 6.45 to 7.45. He continued with corrections until supper at 9 p.m. He then spent an hour walking round his house, seeing all his boys individually before bed (a nocturnal obligation incumbent upon all Eton housemasters then as now). He took himself off to bed at midnight after another hour's corrections. 'Not a good day for anyone concerned', commented Arthur, 'either teacher or taught.'

It was even tougher during the week he was 'in desk' – taking official school duty, having to 'call absence' and attending every chapel service in a supervisory capacity. The fate of a schoolmaster at a public school, Arthur would complain, was to live 'a hurried, snippy life'; and because so much of what one did was ignoble and unproductive, no wonder it was often regarded as a 'dingy trade'. The time spent on corrections was perhaps the most soul-destroying work (e.g. writing out model classical-verses for one's pupils on work often set by other masters). This would take some six hours every week, with two more on the same exercise in school. By the time he left Eton, he reckoned that he had devoted three thousand hours of his life to this futile pursuit. He felt, in his exasperation, like going round to 'throw a stone through [Warre's] dining-room window'. It was the routine that got one down in the end – not only the tyranny of the clock, but also the maddening predictableness of the day's programme and the behaviour of one's colleagues. On 26 February 1900, Arthur observed Ainger setting off for a walk with Cornish at 3.45 on the dot – 'a thing they have done at 3.45 on Mondays for 35 years. If only people wd. do something different!' Two years later, in mid-February again, Arthur was much in the same mood: 'Today floods me with wild impulses to rush off somewhere, to see something new – not to hop pompously about in cap and gown, with a fine chain round my leg, trying to pretend that I am a very useful person in the world.'

Warre once said to Arthur, who had tactfully suggested that the Eton day was too demanding on the staff, that he was unwilling to relax the timetable because masters would misuse their leisure time. They would spend it not on reading (the essential daily occupation of a schoolmaster) but on play. He was generous enough, however, to exempt Arthur from his condemnation. Certainly Arthur read widely enough in the field of literature, at least at this stage of his life. His complaint was that there was never time to read enough to enliven and stimulate one's teaching. So much of one's teaching, therefore, consisted of transmitting the same corpus of knowledge, the same slender stock of ideas, without the opportunity of leisured re-appraisal of what one was attempting to transmit – 'pumping up the muddy waters of irrigation', as he was to put it in *The Upton Letters*. The teaching of classics, anyway, he found dull and deadening. The subject occupied far too dominant a place within the Eton system. 'The classics are poor pabulum I fear,' he wrote in 1898. 'I live in dread of the public finding out how bad an education is the only one I can communicate. We do nothing to train fancy, memory, taste, imagination. We do not stimulate. We only make the ordinary boy hate and despise books and knowledge generally; but we make them conscientious – good drudges, I think.'

It was by the prosecution of this criticism of the classical curriculum, not only among his colleagues, but also to the world at large in *The Schoolmaster* (1902) and *The Upton Letters* (1905) that Arthur earned the reputation of a liberal. He maintained this particular stand for the rest of his life, attacking compulsory Greek in the 'Littlego' at Cambridge and allowing himself to become such a publicist on behalf of a modern curriculum that he forfeited (as he believed) all chance of gaining further Eton honours, in particular a place on the Eton Governing Body, the ambition of his later life.

He was a classical master and he had to operate the system; but because, within that system, he took every opportunity to enlarge and enrich his pupils' knowledge of English literature, he became an exceptionally successful teacher, and year after year his division secured commendable results in Trials. But what might he have achieved, given a better system? 'I could interest themselves and myself fast enough if I could choose my subject', he wrote in July 1902, 'but as for teaching them Herodotus, Livy, Virgil, Horace, Theocritus and Sophocles – the thing is rot.' What made it particularly difficult was the 'mixed ability' (as it would be described today) of the typical Eton division: '20 great duffers, huge mild boys with voices like mice, and 6 clever collegers'. Did one wonder that the King's Scholars were neglected and frustrated? He did his best to find interesting material for Private Business, giving history lectures on Napoleon, Gustavus Adolphus, Mahomet or St Francis (a difficult subject for Eton boys naturally to identify with); and sometimes smiling to himself at the absurd mannerisms and calculated gestures which a schoolmaster has to adopt to gain the affectionate respect of his boys. One day he heard from his window a man in the street below addressing his horse 'in the gutteral simulated wrath which is supposed to appeal to horses. Rather like my own pupil-room manner, I think.' He certainly had the art of captivating a boy audience – on a chosen subject like Lewis Carroll, for instance, or in telling fanciful historical tales (in slightly stilted language) and ghost stories to his boys on Sunday nights.

One other feature of the Eton system really enraged him: the passion for athletic pursuits and the glorification of athletic success. All the public schools had been moving in that direction while he was a boy, but at least he had found that he could escape from its worst excesses. 'I was not in the least interested in the victories of the School at football or cricket, and I don't think I ever talked about such things.' In the 1890's, however, most of the masters (and especially Warre) fiercely encouraged such fanaticism, and the boys had become 'prostrate in mind before athletics'. The result could only be harmful, in the end, to both the School and the country. This absurd lack of proportion had wrought within the upper classes their 'deplorable barbarism' and that 'absence of the development of intelligence, of which the disastrous results are now apparent in South Africa'. Hence the well-deserved 'scorn felt for our utter stupidity in

Germany and France'. What else could one expect from the Eton philosophy of 'Do your work conscientiously – it is dull, but never mind. Then *play* for all you are worth.' As a housemaster, it gave Arthur mild pleasure when his boys won a match because it gave them 'a sense of dignity and of the dignity of the House', but he confessed, in July 1902, that he was secretly rather pleased that his cricketers had been promptly beaten in the House Ties because this meant that there was no obligation upon him 'to go and watch, which I detest'.

There were better ways of spending one's time in an afternoon – like finding a congenial colleague and going off for a walk or bicycle ride together. On Sundays, in his later years as a housemaster, he would always walk with Walter Parratt, organist at St George's Chapel; on other days, his companions would vary. If it were cycling it would usually be Ainger who, with disconcerting regularity, would confound and confuse him by taking the turn he least expected. If walking, it might sometimes be Rawlins, when they would talk together 'like two grasshoppers, sawing out thin and dry music'; more often, it would be with Tatham, Luxmoore or Macnaghten – 'fragrant walks, made warm by a feeling of mutual liking', talking between themselves 'without gêne or theorising or priggishness', airing 'faint plans of life', talking of boys and colleagues. These were the blessed hours of every day – visits to Staines via the reservoir, and Stanwell Church; up to Dorney Common and round by Boveney, grassy lanes overhung by elms, with 'the river running full and dark, the red osiers and the shadowy hills beyond'; to Langley via 'The Crooked Billet', to look into deep pools and muse, or to watch the great freight trains at Slough. Just occasionally the tête-à-tête would be broken by the tagging-on of unwanted colleagues – Broadbent and Cornish, for instance, stealing up behind Luxmoore and himself '*secundum usum* – and our little talk was spoiled, and we all jawed together like four starlings on a roof-ridge'.

There is a real sense of confraternity here – of male camaraderie – redolent of a vanished age. At least both style and occasion have seemed to change with the different world of the twentieth century. Of an evening, masters dined together in each other's houses. A solitary bachelor meal was a rare occurrence (on Shrove Tuesday 1903, Arthur noted the first occasion that Half for his taking 'a lonely meal'). Arthur preferred a gathering of no more than eight, and disliked the more formal evenings when ladies were present, such as a rather grand party given by the Vice-Provost in the Audit Room in July 1903, when such a high level of conversation was somehow expected that actually no one dared speak; and when anybody tried to break the embarrassing silence, he was left high and dry holding forth nervously, surrounded by 'a circle of chilly faces', all seeming to say 'Well, that's not up to our standard.' Worst of all were the dinner-parties given by Warre, which tended to evoke from the host a series of dull, inconsequential monologues to an unappreciative audience consisting largely of the family, some visiting cleric and mild, faded women-friends of Mrs Warre. After one such, in March 1903, Arthur recalled how, at the close of dinner, Lady Barbara Yeatman 'with eyes like pebbles' sat with Mrs Warre 'like two faded dolls, on the sofa, nodding at each other and uttering sounds. God knows what dim communication of trivial thoughts took place!'

Schoolmasters are notoriously vulnerable to caricature, both in their professional capacities and in moments of relaxation. It was ever so. And Arthur, with his spectatorial gifts and his eye for the absurd, was merciless in his descriptions in his diaries. He mocked them standing on the touchline at football matches – 'a lot of listless beaks, incapable of walking, talking or even smiling, "looking" dreamily on in Aquascuta like opium-eaters'; or exuding bonhomie amongst parents and old boys at a cricket match, Rawlins 'reeking of geniality, which gushes like the light from Moses' head, buttonholing man after man'. He mocked the inveterate defenders of the ancient ways in upholding the inviolability of classics and the tutorial system – A. B. Ramsay, Churchill and Wells – as those 'who sit on thrones judging the tribes of Israel'; and he mocked the tentative interpolations of colleagues when Warre was holding forth in Chambers. Remington White-Thomson 'rose like a ghost of a king, and made a spectral speech about the importance of morality'. On being told that this was irrelevant, he 'resumed his seat and sate staring at the paper with bewildered solemnity'.

Hard work, if it is congenial, is never drudgery; and the recurrence of that emotive word in Arthur's diaries is probably explained by the fact that his term-time entries were usually written up when he was irritated or feeling unwell. The chief cause of professional malaise – in schoolmastering as perhaps in all occupations – is the sense of being unnoticed and unappreciated; that, and the feeling of obstructiveness in one's colleagues, rendered the worse by living so close to them within a largely bachelor community. Everyone likes to feel that he is important. As Arthur himself put it: 'We are sent on our little journey through the world, by God, like a child on an errand ... like a child who, to dignify an errand, has to pretend to be a train or a ship or a tumultuous sea. The nature of the teaching profession ministers to an unconscious self-aggrandisement. Schoolmasters so easily become sensitive to criticism, vulnerable to threats of invasion of their territory and protective about their boys. Arthur enjoyed watching the posturing of his colleagues, while admitting to vulnerability himself. There was de Havilland, furious with the classical tutors because they enjoyed a higher status than the mathematicians; there was Dyer, newly-appointed to a house, becoming pompous with Lloyd, the Precentor, over times at which his boys might go for music-lessons; Lloyd himself, irritating everybody by 'leaping about' under their conversations 'like a thrush in a strawberry net'. 'Lloyd is a bird-like man – he is inquisitive – he hops and pecks. Most of us here have to struggle with the *beast* within us: Lloyd has to struggle with the *bird* – to resist the temptation to hop and peck, the temptation of the *desultor*. .... He is thoroughly conscientious, but I expect he wastes 2/3 of every day in little starts and rushes and sidelong jumps.'

Arthur himself was quite as sensitive to lack of appreciation as any of his colleagues. While on the one hand he refused to accord to schoolmastering the qualities of some charismatic mystery, he hotly resented any depreciation of the profession by outsiders. Politicians were the worst offenders with their habit of dogmatizing airily on a subject they imperfectly understood. 'Education is the one thing in which everyone thinks himself an expert', he wrote sadly in April 1899. The next menace, as far as Eton was concerned, was the 'crapulous O.E.', who imagined that a schoolmaster's duty was to preserve customs and conventions inviolate as if they had been handed down by Moses from the mount. Parents, sometimes, were little less idiotic. The worst kind was the totally insensitive father who would say to a housemaster: ' "Well, I'm afraid books and sap weren't much in *my* line, Benson – but Jack must be different" – and Jack sits there and doesn't see why he should be different. He likes his father as he is.'

As a housemaster, Arthur's relationship with the parents of his boys was exceptionally close. His correspondence, for instance, was prodigious. At the end of the Summer Half of 1901, Arthur commented on the easing of his burden of letter-writing, once he had completed his father's biography. Even so, 'I find I have written 700 letters this half, which will bring the average up to over 3000 this year.' Most of these letters were to parents, a load which in any case was liable to be heavier at Eton than at most other schools because of the practice of housemasters admitting their own boys. He believed in keeping parents regularly informed of their sons' doings – should they be ill, fractious or even mildly in difficulty with their work. He wrote lengthy letters to all of them at the end of each Half. Indeed, it was not unknown for him to visit parents in the holidays. Of course, with exceptionally eminent parents, it was both simpler and more proper for him to visit, for instance, Claremont than for the Duchess of Albany to descend upon Eton to discuss the progress (or lack of it) of the future Duke of Saxe-Coburg. With parents for whom he had a special affection he might stay several days – as with Julian Sturgis, at his curious oriental-style house (Wancote) on the top of the Hog's Back, or – for a memorable few days in January 1902 – with the Earl of Cadogan, Lord-Lieutenant of Ireland, staying at the Viceregal Lodge. Eddy Cadogan had just left and Alec had just been elected to 'Pop'. At a dinner party there one night, the guests included a little Eton boy (Lord Holmpatrick) with his mother and sister, and after dinner 'the rugs were bundled up, the pianola turned on, and there was some lively dancing. It was amusing to see Alec dance with Holmpatrick, H.P. conscious of the honour of dancing with a boy in Pop – but A. deserted him suddenly, and I fancy that he thought I should not like it.'

All his boys were conscious of a strong, paternal interest shown towards them by their housemaster; much more so than Arthur himself had sensed as a Colleger. When he had welcomed his new boys, with their parents, to his house in September 1901, he commented afterwards: 'I do not find these scenes less emotional – and can still vividly recall the timid and dreary way I slid into them myself, a bewildered thoughtless scrap; if anyone had even simulated half as much interest in me as I try to show to these boys, I should have been much happier. I see each new boy alone; try to find out where he stands with regard to moral difficulties – and then with all my might I try to convince him that whatever happens, even if I am officially cross, we are *friends*.' He talked frequently with his boys, individually or in pairs, sometimes finding it difficult to be easy and natural with them while preserving his dignity, and occasionally falling into the temptation of saying indiscreet things about his colleagues and School policy in order to maintain a relaxed atmosphere. Sometimes he asked them frankly what they thought about the house and their tutor, as with Mark Sturgis, one evening in December 1901. He received the answer that the boys felt 'that I was rather "down" on small things and rather grim. But ... I was regarded with real friendliness all through the house, and that the boys were proud of the house, and proud of its good

73

tone. . . . He said "There is not a boy in the house who would not rather be punished by any other master than be spoken to by you." '

He hated addressing boys *en masse*. As a medium of censure, especially on moral problems, it was almost always ineffective. 'To speak to boys together', he wrote, 'is like throwing pails of water over a set of jugs to fill them. They need to be severally dipped.' He took to heart the wise precept of St Vincent de Paul who once replied to a teacher, who confessed his inability to convey effective moral teaching to boys – 'Take my advice – talk a good deal less to them about God – and talk to God a good deal more about them.' So we find him on 31 December 1898, as the old year died, putting the precept into practice:

> I do not think that evil is at work. . . . FAXIT DEUS. Just before the New Year struck, I went away – named over to myself all my boys and commended them to God. There was no sentimentality in this. I cannot help loving 'agnos quos dedisti' – but I try to speak the truth to them, and I am often quite unnecessarily harsh – though it is not agreeable or natural to me.

The attitude in boys which most aroused Arthur's ire was 'loafing', whether it was the arrogant indolence of the 'wet-bob' or the furtive listlessness of the adolescent which could so easily lead into 'talk of a Rabelaisian kind' and thence into moral depravity. This was his perennial anxiety. He had his fair share of weak characters in his house of thirty-seven boys who needed watching and protecting. There was young Lord Eliot who was taken up by two boys in Pop and who walked around with them arm-in-arm, and then started to pester 'a lower boy-friend' in Austen Leigh's; Hugh Northcote who purchased 'a complete set of evils', which he feared might circulate among the boys. When he heard of his successor's (A. M. Goodhart) anxieties for Caryl Lyttelton and Alastair Leveson-Gower – 'little attractive boys' called repeatedly as fags to the rooms of 'big and unscrupulous boys' – he confessed in his diary: 'it is a dark corner of the world. Am I selfish in being glad that I am out of it?' Fortunately he had a succession of fine House Captains in whom he was able freely to confide – Percy Lubbock, Edward and Alec Cadogan, E. H. Ryle, G. W. Lyttelton.

There is little doubt that Arthur Benson proved an excellent housemaster. He felt for his boys; he did not allow them to dominate his life, adhering to a strict routine whereby his own privacy could be guarded and he could indulge his passion for writing. On the whole he trusted them, despising unceasing vigilance, and he rarely resorted to punishment. It is not surprising that when important headmasterships became vacant, he was approached with invitations to apply. In 1897 his name was mentioned in connection with Charterhouse; in 1900 the Bishop of Hereford wrote inviting him to stand for Clifton as Glazebrook's successor; in 1901 he was strongly pressed to apply for Winchester. On two occasions, Warre had talks with him about the advisability of taking Orders, it being his personal wish that Arthur should succeed him at Eton. To none of these invitations could Arthur accede. Something always held him back. He would have liked the honour, the deference, the prestige. He would have hated the actual obligation of command – the restless energy and self-importance and the commitment that such a responsibility entailed.

This dilemma – the need to decide on some positive commitment – recurs time and time again through Arthur Benson's life. At this stage of his career he was not even sure that schoolmastering was his proper trade. He was nervous of responsibility; but he hated being a subordinate even more. This being so, he reserved his fiercest strictures, in his private diary, for his taskmasters, those who created the drudgery he detested so much, and with whom he felt so ill at ease when it became necessary to protest or complain. The evil genius of the Eton system – to Arthur – was the Provost, J. J. Hornby. He, after all, had created the Head Master, Warre, in his own image, and was determined, with all the courteous charm of indolent old age, to ensure that no effective steps were taken to modify or to adapt Etonian ways. He was a remarkable old man, for sure. In his eighties, he took himself to a doctor with a pain in his head; and when told that he was suffering from a headache, nodded gravely: 'Ah, is that it?', he said, 'I suspected it might be that, but I have never had one before.'

His good health was certainly not the result of luxurious living. Arthur described a visit to the Provost's house in March 1903:

> This cold, dirty house, with the peeling pictures and the general air of frowsy neglect is very painful. The Provost's own study is the most cheerless room I have ever seen. The curtains, carpet, chairs are incredibly shabby. There are no arrangements to read or write comfortably – a poky writing-table with a few sheets of paper on it, an extraordinary heap of gloves, stoles, waistcoats, comforters and things on a table – and a similar heap on a chair by the window – two or three priceless pictures, of the collection, hung close to the ceiling – frowsy gowns and cassocks in a corner – a dirty old dog with asthma on the fire-rug – and then this polite, humorous, courtly, vigorous old gentleman in the middle – perfectly complacent, perfectly contented

75

with everything – shirking every duty he can, and living an indolent, secluded, shabby life – yet never getting eccentric, rusty, odd-mannered. It is a *very* curious problem, and I don't see what it means.

Nothing would stir him to action. 'He is like a frozen mammoth: it is just as if he had been knocked on the head and frozen hard in 1884, and was entirely unaware what had happened since.' When Arthur and Tatham contributed £100 to plant some trees in Agar's Plough, Hornby stopped the planting without a word to the donors. Arthur's rage was almost uncontrollable. 'We are sacrificed to a pig-headed selfish man, the most unconscientious and indifferent official in England, who spends nothing on the place, sees no one and treats his big house, great position and large income as a pension for a headmastership when discipline was bad, the tone of the School infamous, and who did less to command the respect of the future than any Headmaster on record.'

Probably Arthur would have vented his spleen on any headmaster set over him. He did not actually dislike Edmond Warre, and indeed wrote a generous, if critical, account of his Head Mastership in *Memories and Friends*. He admired the strength of his personality. When not feeling threatened, he was amused by him. Staying with him for a week-end in the holidays at his Somersetshire home, Baron's Down, in January 1903, he could not fail to note the affinity with Hornby in the indifference to domestic taste and comfort. The study exuded 'that peculiar type of ugliness which Warre communicates to the rooms he lives in. The paper hideous; the fireplace of a sort of "Maple-Smith" type. There are huge chairs – one called by Warre "Great Snorum".' Mrs Warre was as vague as ever, 'nodding a good deal with a vacant eye, addressing me some mild and rather unintelligible remarks'. When it was found to be too snowy to make the journey to Church, Warre read prayers to the assembled company very fast 'glasses off, holding a book to his face, and screening himself from the bright sun with a huge, soft hand'.

He could be, in a grand and magnificent way, effective when deeply moved to address sections of the School for misbehaviour or unworthy conduct. Often enough in Chambers he was embarrassingly long winded and indecisive. 'Wretched Masters' Meeting', Arthur wrote in his diary in September 1902. 'Warre's speech entirely devoid of courage, shrewdness, counsel, or help; he might have lived all his life in a country rectory and been suddenly put in here – he seemed to have no experience, and no programme. Yet he is a great man. We talked, whispered, and made our own arrangements freely and indifferently meanwhile.' Later in the term, he paid Arthur a visit to inspect his division:

> Very courteous – made me sit down – apologised to me for interrupting – talked about everything in the world. . . . At one time the lesson resolved itself into our conversing amiably forgetful of the boys, with our backs to them. Then he told a long story about a Colonel whom he sate next to at dinner, who told him that all his life he had been regretting that he did not know Greek. That when he was younger he felt his loss about once a week, but now he felt it every hour. 'Odd, wasn't it?' he said to me. 'Very' I said grimly.
>
> Then he blazed out into rhetoric and said that the people who talked about Greek having no practical use were as foolish as people who said that the foundations of a house were no use, because unseen. What wretched logic! . . . He then said, 'Now boys listen to me – You ought to have some ideas about grammar which are not only *on the surface*. This is the philosophy of Grammar' – and there came out all the rot he talks to VIth Form, which Cadogan told me. . . . Then he broke off 'There, it is good for you to have gone down a little beneath the surface' and he sailed away in high good humour, his silk sleeves bellying in the wind.
>
> He has been telling us to register as teachers. I am sure no Inspector who had heard him talking today wd. have felt justified in allowing him to register; it is simply senile . . . yet somehow great.

There were times when Warre drove Arthur to near distraction – 'that desperate man, the Head'; 'May God forgive Warre! I cannot'; 'Warre has a municipal mind, and loves a job.' He would not act when it was necessary. When things went wrong, he preferred not to know. On one occasion, Arthur had been approached by Scotland Yard about an undesirable character who was lurking dangerously near the precincts of the School. He went at once to report the matter to Warre.

> Found him with Felix playing patience, apparently, with Trial slips. The idea of Warre wasting his time over such a thing – but he loves slips, marks, foils and counterfoils, ruled compartments – it is his idea of intellectual systems. He listened to me as tho' he grudged the time – made a listless note – and went back with avidity to his slips.

He was at his worst, Arthur thought, over the appalling episode of the great Eton fire. At 4 a.m. on 1 June 1903, a fire broke out in Kindersley's house. The boys were evacuated, but two (Lawson and Horne) found themselves trapped in a room with barred windows and were burnt to death. It was a nightmare situation. All the Fourth of June festivities were cancelled. The School was stunned with horror, and the Press had a field day. Warre did his best to suppress all reference to the bars on the study windows. It was interesting to see how different members of the community reacted. Mrs Cornish was heroic. She attended to the two corpses, washing the bodies, dressing them in nightgowns, making immediate arrangements for flowers and for coffins. Luxmoore wrote at once to the Kindersleys an exquisite letter of sympathy. But Warre never even attended the funeral. He 'lies abed very comfortably, reading Dickens, and occasionally bursting into tears. A thousand things ought to be done.' The Bursar was not much better, indulging in hysterical lamentations about fire extinguishers. 'Occasionally he goes in to see Warre and they sob together, like two Mock Turtles – and they are like the Mock Turtles in this too, that if any practical question turns up in the middle, they leave off their tears, and become intensely irritable and acrimonious.'

There is something, perhaps, a little glibly dismissive in this. Arthur was in no position to know what Warre suffered or what decisions he had to take. He was recounting Eton gossip at a time of fearful strain. Nor was the strain over. A few days later, the fire-raiser was caught: a seventeen-year-old boy called Moore, evacuated from Kindersley's to Rawlins' house, where he attempted to commit the same outrage, only to be apprehended by a little fourth-form boy (Levett) who followed the other out of bed in the small hours of the morning. It was thought right to say nothing to Warre until the boy had been removed by his parents.*

The whole tragic affair was hardly calculated to make for Arthur the prospect of becoming a headmaster any more attractive; nor did it endear him any the more to Edmond Warre. There was, he admitted, an indefinable greatness about the man; but Eton, in his later years, suffered from 'this heavy apathetic rule'. What chance was there of anything constructive being achieved from a man who sat so ponderously on his clutch of 'addled eggs'?

* * * * *

The drama of the Eton fire of 1903 was one of those rare tragedies that occasionally beset a school. Although dozens of little dramas act themselves out year by year in the life of a boarding-school, they become part of the rhythm and tempo of a housemaster's life. Because they recur with passing generations of boys, he learns to anticipate them and to cope with them, as they arise, so that – in one sense – despite the vitality of his charges and all the dynamism created by their mingled anxieties and

* Cf. L. E. Jones, *Victorian Boyhood*, 178–9 where Warre's rôle is described much more sympathetically.

hopes, his life is a curiously static one. Arthur, unusually for a schoolmaster, had a life of increasing consequence outside the world of school, and was beginning to make a name for himself in other fields. But the issues that involved him at Eton, the battles that he fought and the triumphs that he cherished, were – on the whole – the normal concerns (and none the less important for that) of any schoolmaster. The events of the outside world, in any dramatic sense, rarely impinged upon his professional life. He deplored the South African War; he sorrowed over the death of the Queen; he shuddered at the vulgarity of the demonstrations at the news of the relief of Mafeking.

> I don't really enjoy this sort of thing. I don't think I was ever really young – ever tasted the joys of brave, inconsiderate, headstrong, irresponsible youth. ... I suppose we all have different ideas of what hell is like, but mine is a torchlight procession – to plough one's way through hot, lighted excited streets – crowds made not goodhumoured by excitement but offensive – to be tapped on the hat with a whistle or bladder by a female of doubtful character, or a redfaced owlish man – with the taste of hot paraffin smoke in the air.

Apart from the nuisance and anxiety of receiving, in June 1902, a series of offensive and obscene anonymous letters, following the publication of *The Schoolmaster*, which caused him to pay a visit to Scotland Yard, the dramas of his professional life were small, internal and parochial ones. But perhaps only a schoolmaster can know how taxing upon the emotions such dramas can be. The real trials and private agonies of a schoolmaster lie within the emotional sphere. It may be a rewarding occupation – the most rewarding that a sensitive man can enjoy – but it is also unceasingly a trial of his emotions. As Arthur put it in September 1897: 'It's a precarious trade, and depends much on calm nerves.'

Why does a man become a schoolmaster? It may be because he is a compulsive communicator or an educational idealist; it may be simply because he has not grown out of boyish enthusiasms and wants to perpetuate them if he can. Arthur's first reason for returning to Eton was the excellent and perhaps most important one of all – his 'liking for boys', his undoubted susceptibility to boyish charm. At the root of the profession, if a man is really to succeed in it, is a genuine sensitivity to youth; but there can be deeper instincts too, which may sometimes rest dormant or even unsuspected for years until some mysterious chemistry impels them to the surface, so that in the mutually vulnerable relationship between the teacher and the taught, the consciousness of

79

some particular or personal rapport becomes quite literally a sort of heart-hunger – an almost irresistible stretching-out towards an intimacy of union: heart strives to speak with heart. At that point professional detachment is most severely put to the test. What, after all, is true vocation if it is not the yearning to arouse, to enkindle, to elevate, to improve, to open up new horizons, to share excitement with others, above all – to give? These are all functions which lie athwart the tenuous dividing line between the intellect and the affections. This line is the tightrope that many schoolmasters have to walk. But not all who walk it can perceive the abyss at their feet; and even those who do, and who are brave enough to keep on walking, cannot always reach the end.

Such a man was William Johnson Cory – 'Ionicus' – poet of the romantic bond between master and boy. Cory's triumph and disaster haunted Arthur Benson all his life. From his *Letters and Journals*, Arthur wrote in 1897, 'I received such stimulus both general and professional . . . as I have not received since becoming a schoolmaster.' He never actually met him. Cory had left Eton before Arthur arrived; but he felt for him a love perhaps more intense than anything he felt for even his closest friends. 'I wonder', he wrote in October 1902, 'why the thought of Wm Johnson is so often with me and stirs the deepest founts within me – the *lacrimarum fons*. . . . What is the attractive thing about W.J.? It is, I think, that with a perfectly furnished mind, strong, virile, self-possessed and liberal, he yet deliberately put the intellect far behind the affections. Hence comes the coolness and depth of his poetry – the romance, the heart-hunger, the eye for beauty (in character and in the few outward avenues of perception nature allowed him) – the tenderness.'

He did not know the whole of the Cory story. Perhaps nobody does. His teaching was unforgettable, his influence (upon a few) overwhelming. He loved intensely and he loved unwisely. Even Arthur conceded that he had to go. Pressing Cornish for more details, Arthur was warned off. Of the lonely life at Halsden, Cornish could tell, or chose to tell, very little. Any more writing, he said, 'would only stir the wasps who sit upon his tomb'.

If only he had not been 'tainted'. Arthur could hardly bear to think of this. 'The fact that he is so remote', he wrote, 'like a figure at the end of an avenue, averts the necessity.' Then again:

> He had no *morality* technically so-called – but he hated all that was cold, or low, or mean, or petty, or ungenerous, or hard. I think it was a very beautiful soul . . . and pulled off its pedestal by the foul cur which he could not control.

... The letters about his boy-friendships are very touching. It is odd to be surrounded, as we are still, by all this charm, and not to feel it. But those lost and haunting presences of whom he writes – those boys with serene eyes and wind-stirred hair ... with low voices, full of the fall of evening, and feet with the swiftness of the dawn ... they stand in these pages in a magic light which no mortal could ever have for me. ... I almost wish it were not so; if one could passionately idealise, like Newman, how much happiness, ... how much pain, ... and no one sees the dangers more clearly than I do. So to this old and sorrowing soul, so pierced with woes and humiliations – so eager, and loving, and generous; so easily reviving after his strange wounding, I stretch out my hand over time and I say 'be comforted' – I really love W.J. and I cannot help feeling that my love helps him somewhere, *si quis manibus est locus*. This is very transcendental; and yet it is very real.

'Heart-hunger' is a good word to express such a complex of emotions, embracing all the pathos of the loneliness of the sensitive man set by nature or circumstance to guide and live among boys with whom he can never attain anything more than an ephemeral intimacy and from whom he is bound to stand professionally aloof. It is the very essence of 'bitter-sweet': to feel a love that can be agonisingly real – whether it be the paternal yearning for the son that never was or the romantic sublimation of some physical desire – but which can never be fulfilled. Age pays court to youth: but youth is too young to understand or to recognise the need of the other; and youth must move on while the other remains.

It is a hard fate to love the untouchable. Everything in Arthur Benson's temperament seemed to pull him that way. Comparing himself to his friend Bob Norton, in the Foreign Office, he observed how, in their attitude to relationships, they were poles apart. 'Norton is a worshipper of the eternal feminine: the fact that a woman is a woman gives her an *ipso facto* advantage in interest over a man with him. The exact reverse is the case with me.' In a group, Arthur always gravitated, by a sort of invisible, unconscious propulsion, towards *the boy* – if boy there were. At a shooting-party, during a holiday at Aylsham in September 1902, an ordinary day of enjoyable relaxation was rendered blissful for him because the keeper had brought with him his son and a friend – 'two of the handsomest boys ... I have ever seen in different ways. One roguish, English, with a perpetual smile and large white teeth – a common country boy, but of extraordinarily graceful carriage. ... The other, the keeper's son, could have been dressed up to make a really beautiful woman.'

This might, indeed, be Cory writing. But there was a difference. They shared the heart-hunger; but Arthur had inhibitions for the lack of which

81

Cory was to suffer in middle life. Yet Arthur envied the other's ability so freely to express his love. 'I am not affectionate', he wrote. And again: 'Cory reserved his romance for people, while to me it lies in nature.' While he felt intensely the attraction of the young and ingenuous, he could find no means of responding to it except in a spectatorial way. In a boarding-house he was surrounded by boys whose charm was almost irresistible. They were so near, in one way; so far, so distant, in another. One night, going the rounds of his house, he stopped at the doorway to watch (unobserved) young Compton (the eldest son of Lord Northampton) getting ready for bed. The maid was tucking him up and the boy was 'prattling away with intense amusement and interest' about his tutor and something that had been said to him. 'I envied the boy's maid', Arthur wrote.

The cruelty of advancing years was that, while you felt yourself to be just the same person as you were when a boy, with the same sensations and the same longings, you lost – or feared that you lost – all too rapidly the physical capacity to charm. Arthur, with his spectatorial gifts and discerning eye for beauty, was hypersensitive, as many large and bulky men are, to his own physical infirmities. He felt himself to be ponderous and clumsy, and – despite evidence to the contrary – could not be persuaded that he was other than physically repugnant to others. This is a recurring theme in the many passages of self-analysis which appear in his diaries. Giving tea one day to those young Apollos, Julian Grenfell and Edward Horner, Arthur did his best to charm and woo them. 'I tried to be funny', he wrote, 'but ended in prancing heavily, like a cart-horse.'

The boy in his own house whom he felt most tempted to woo was Mark Sturgis, Julian Sturgis' eldest son. From the moment that he arrived in the house, Arthur was fascinated by him. 'I think if I had a son', he wrote in his diary, 'I would like him to be like Mark.' In the holidays he stayed with the Sturgis family, revelling in one particular golden day, telling stories in the heather, Mark hanging on every word. Somehow – wonderfully – the rapport had been achieved. Mark 'pleases me by wanting to be about with me, to walk with me, to sit with me, and by not being afraid to say so. ... This was a cheerful, wholesome day which I shall long remember for its odd glow and brightness.' There were many trials and tribulations to come; many heart-aches. In March 1902, Arthur commented sadly, 'this boy whom I always looked forward to having as my great friend and ally ... is the only one who won't do as I want'. Long talks ensued, and the boy – alone with him – was sheer

3 'Benson's', 1893.
Percy Lubbock, top right:
Mark Sturgis, bottom left
*'The boys get in a way fond of me –
brave and pure-minded boys with
good homes.'*

4 Julian Grenfell, 1906
*'The beloved Julian, with his curly hair
and honest snub-nosed face.'*

5 Edmond Warre, Head Master of Eton, in the year of his retirement, 1905
'That desperate man, the Head.'

6 M. R. James, as Provost of Eton
'He hates being Provost, yet he would hate not *being Provost worse.'*

delight. In the way that boys are, Mark was conscious that he was a favourite and sometimes took advantage by assuming an air of amused superiority when he was with others. It was not he who suffered. As it must be, it was the schoolmaster, who watched his hopes and expectations dashed.

There is a passage in *The Upton Letters* where Arthur expresses with exquisite sensitivity the schoolmaster's emotional predicament. The truly limiting factors within the relationship between a master and a boy come down to these. In the first place, try as you will to distort or to disguise the roles, you can never be other than a schoolmaster to the boy. Thinking of his leavers at the end of a term, he wrote:

> I am here, a lonely man, wondering and doubting and desiring I hardly know what. Some nearness of life, some children of my own. ... But ... these boys who are dear to me have forgotten me already. Disguise it as I will, I am part of the sordid furniture of life that they have so gladly left behind, the crowded corridor, the bare-walled schoolroom, the ink-stained desk. ... They like me well enough – for a schoolmaster.

Then, secondly, in any relationship the schoolmaster has to make all the running, so that with the boys you love, you try too hard and usually fail. With Mark Sturgis very much in mind, he described it thus:

> I have had the feelings of my disabilities brought home to me lately in a special way. There is a boy in my house that I have tried hard to make friends with. He is a big, overgrown creature, with a perfectly simple manner. ... I have done my best ... to make friends with him. I have lent him books; I have tried to make him come and see me; I have talked my best with him, and he has received it all with polite indifference; I can't win his confidence, somehow. I feel that if I were only not in the tutorial relation, it would be easy work. But perhaps I frightened him as a little boy, perhaps I bored him; anyhow the advances are all on my side, and there seems a hedge of shyness through which I cannot break. ... I have made friends a hundred times with a tenth of the trouble, and I suppose it is just because I find this child so difficult to approach, that I fret myself over the failure; and all the more because I know in my heart that he really is a congenial nature, and that we do think the same about many things. Of course, most sensible people would not care a brass farthing about such an episode, and would succeed where I have failed, because I think it is the forcing of attentions upon him that this proud young person resents. I must try and comfort myself by thinking that my very capacity for vexing myself over the business is probably the very thing which makes it easy as a rule for me to succeed.

Arthur was never anything other than scrupulously correct in his dealings with boys. He was certainly the better schoolmaster for his sensitivity and for the realistic way in which he recognised the precarious element in his trade. He knew what was right. 'I don't want the boys to grow up like myself at all', he wrote in May 1902. 'My attitude is much too spectatorial and intellectual. I have an eye for beauty – but not I fear a love for beauty of ideal or character. I don't rest in the wholesome humanities of life, but in the dangerous arts of expression and superficial emotions. I am quite conscious of my weakness in this respect, and wish I were different.'

All schoolmasters are vulnerable. The important thing, in the end, is to know oneself and to know where one's temptations lie. Arthur believed that his diary helped him in this respect. 'It has made my own weaknesses more and more clear to me.' And what is the most that one can ask? – that one helped, and did not harm. Reading the eulogy of Arthur Benson, written by Sir Mark Sturgis some months after his old tutor's death in 1925, we can be sure that the boy who might have suffered most from possessiveness and unwanted emotionalism was actually barely aware of the heart-hunger he had awoken in the older man. Sturgis commented on the extraordinary frankness of Arthur in his private talks, but – above all else – 'he was a gentleman to his fingertips, and treated us as such, and to some extent we reacted, and "Benson's" was the result'.

'A precarious trade' – 'I ... rest ... in the dangerous arts' – 'No one sees the dangers more clearly than I do'. Arthur Benson was a romantic; he was also a realist: a good combination for a successful housemaster. He was rarely free from emotional tensions, but he walked the tightrope to the end.

Chapter Three

HOPE AND GLORY

> No doubt it was the first time that a schoolmaster pure and
> simple – not a headmaster or clergyman – had ever sat at that
> table.　　　　　(Dining with the Queen, December 1899)
>
> I *couldn't* live in the atmosphere of false deference and
> elaborate ceremony. I can't really breathe there. . . . It isn't my
> *monde* at all, and it is too late to begin.　　　(January 1905)

An Eton housemaster might expect to move, at times, in dignified and
eminent circles by virtue of his position *in loco parentis* to many of the
highest-born in the land. Surveying his outgoing post one evening,
Arthur could not fail to remark what a 'curious budget' it was – letters to
the President of the U.S.A. (about a special ode), the Duke of Saxe-
Coburg (to congratulate him on the award of the K.G.), and the
embassies of Japan, Teheran, Rome and Johannesburg (to old pupils).
Two years later when, by the same post, letters arrived to him from the
Archbishop of Canterbury, the Bishop of Winchester and the Primus of
Scotland, Arthur allowed himself to muse on how many people, let alone
his colleagues, might expect to receive three such letters in a single batch.

　　In his last years as a housemaster he was himself beginning to be
regarded within the Eton community as something of a celebrity. After
all, his literary output as a schoolmaster was quite exceptional. In
addition to the two youthful indiscretions (*Arthur Hamilton* and
Archbishop Laud), he had published four volumes of poems and lyrics
(with John Lane), a collection of literary essays (with Heinemann) in
1896, a great compendium of biographies of Eton worthies (*Fasti
Etonenses*, published by Ingalton Drake in 1899), and a classic biography
of the monumental proportions expected of eminent nineteenth-century
figures – his *Life of E. W. Benson*, in two volumes, published by
Macmillan in the same year. In 1902 he produced *The Schoolmaster*, the
first of many publications with John Murray, and was working at the
same time on three other projects, all of which came out in the following
year: a life of Tennyson, a selection from the writings of Whittier, and a
volume of his 'medieval tales' (the stories told on Sunday nights to boys

in his house), published by Isbister under the title *The Hill of Trouble*. *The House of Quiet*, his first experiment in the genre to which he was to become so compulsively attached in later years, was already completed, awaiting publication in 1903. 'Had any hardworking schoolmaster ever *three* books in the press at once before?', he asked himself in March 1903, acknowledging the uniqueness of his position.

To say that he had a facility for writing is to state the obvious. It was his relaxation. Rapidly it became a compulsive outlet. He was always miserable if he had no book on hand or if he was lost for a subject immediately to switch his mind to, as soon as a book had been completed. The medium that came most easily to him was verse. Even he had to admit that he amazed himself at the rapidity with which he could produce an ode, a lyric, a sonnet practically to order. Asked to compose an Ode for the thousandth number of the Eton *Chronicle*, Arthur set to at once. 'It is odd what an extraordinary facility and rapidity I have for this kind of thing', he commented afterwards. 'I wrote it in about ten minutes – and though it is not *good*, it is not bad at all.' Word came from Windsor Castle that special hymns for the confirmation of Prince Leopold of Battenburg would be appreciated. Arthur wrote two immediately. 'I wrote them in the train from London to Horsted Keynes.'

In the middle years of the 1890's he became somewhat disenchanted with his efforts to become a poet. None of his volumes made any appreciable mark. He was perhaps too fluent; and – in any case – no poem, written by the very greatest of poets (he believed), was ever improved by revision. His last volume (at this stage of his life) – *The Professor*, published in 1900 – prompted Arthur to call it a day. 'It is a crime at my age to peddle with verses, I think.' He would respond to special requests or to royal commands, but there would be no more volumes of verse. He soon discovered that he possessed a similar fluency in prose, and that he was as little amenable to the discipline of revision and correction in his prose-writing as he had been with his poems. It was the act of composition that was so satisfying. A portion of each day, even when he was a hard-pressed schoolmaster, had to be set aside for this indulgence, the best time being the two hours between tea and dressing for the evening meal. Then the words would flow across the page without a single erasure. It was the same with the diaries. In the particularly productive years when he was taking his leave of Eton, working on Rossetti and embarking upon the tedious work of editing Queen Victoria's letters, the diaries were being produced at the rate of nearly two volumes a month. The only erasures are the deliberate scoring-through of entries felt subsequently to be too intimate for posterity to read.

Perhaps it is hardly possible to produce a great book – a masterpiece – in such circumstances; and none of Arthur's early publications, with the exception of his father's biography, can make any claim to lasting distinction. They did not bring notable financial rewards, until his fortunes turned with the publication of *The Upton Letters* in 1905. But he was gaining sufficient recognition to encourage him to think of the possibility of leaving Eton and of taking his chance to make his living as a writer. He consulted his accountant in October 1902. From his father's estate primarily, but also from his royalties, he had been able to purchase a house in Windsor worth about £2000, which he was letting to tenants; there was about £16,000 tucked away in investments. Without his Eton salary, and with the possibility of a pension from the Governors of £100 p.a., he might count on about £900 p.a. He reckoned this to be enough.

More important, he had begun to make really influential friends within the London literary world. How he first came to meet Edmund Gosse is not certain. It may well have been through Henry James, who had befriended Arthur from the moment he first met him – at the same luncheon party in Frederick Myers' house in July 1884 when he had been introduced to Laura Tennant. He took both of them afterwards to King's for a chapel service and entertained them to tea in his rooms. Henry James 'never lost touch with me from that hour'. Arthur lunched with him subsequently at De Vere Gardens; Henry James stayed with the family at Addington – a significant occasion because a conversation with the Archbishop implanted in the other's mind the original idea from which *The Turn of the Screw* was to grow. Through the interest that James showed in him, sooner or later he was likely to encounter Gosse. Their paths had not crossed at Cambridge, where Gosse had been Clark Lecturer in English Literature at Trinity from 1884 to 1889. Arthur never visited the little colony of semi-Bohemian American artists and writers who, in the 1880's, settled at Broadway, in the Cotswolds, where Gosse, Henry James and John Sargent came together in 1885. From a diary entry of 22 January 1893 – 'an opening friendship with *Edmund Gosse* very delightful' – it appears most likely that they met in London.

It was a friendship that rapidly matured, and lasted – with occasional bouts of temporary estrangement – to the end of Arthur's life. In July 1893, Gosse stayed with Arthur at Eton, an occasion described by Maurice Baring, who had just left Eton himself and was visiting the

Cornish family at the time. They all met in Arthur's house after dinner. When Baring arrived, Gosse was holding forth from the depths of a leather armchair, smoking a cigarette. As soon as he discovered that Baring was destined for Cambridge, he expatiated at length on the young, but mild, 'decadents' to whom he had been something of a father-figure. Baring was puzzled that he should have described serious intellectuals like Oswald Sickert and Eddie Marsh as in any sense decadent. Gosse expressed an interest in Paul Verlaine, and Arthur Benson confessed his ignorance of French poetry. Baring's description continued:

> Words of a foreign language, he said, to him were symbols, like the figures of a Noah's Ark, whereas in English every word fired a train of association, and sometimes a single word was enough to redeem a whole page. I said I thought Racine's verse was enchanting. Gosse gave me a look of piercing benignity through his spectacles and said, 'enchanting – that's just the word'. ... From Racine we got to Baudelaire. Swinburne's elegy on Baudelaire was mentioned, and Gosse said that the poem had been written in a Turkish bath, and A.C.B. said he was not surprised that a poem should be written in a Turkish bath about a man whose whole work seemed to have been written in a Turkish bath. 'Of course it's howibly good', he added. ... The next day I saw A.C.B., who said to me: 'Wasn't Gosse delightful?' I thought indeed that never had I heard such intoxicating talk, and was amazed at the dexterity and ease of his diction, his fund of amusing illustration and episode, and his deft descriptions and living thumb-nail portraits.

Through Gosse, Arthur entered the London literary world. He secured invitations to write reviews for the *National Review* and the *Pall Mall Gazette*. They went on holiday together to Switzerland, where the young Maurice Baring joined them. He was invited occasionally to join the circle who lunched regularly at the National Club, at a reserved corner table, where Gosse – who delighted in drawing together eminent literary figures and up-and-coming young aspirants to literary glory – held court with Alfred Bateman, Austin Dobson, Chauncy Cartwright and (a little later) Maurice Hewlett, Victor Lytton, Eddie Marsh and Hall Caine. In February 1895, after staying with the Bensons, in the company of Henry James, at Addington, Gosse asked Arthur to become his literary executor, spicing the request with his usual dollop of literary gossip. 'He told me a sad tale of Stevenson, whose last letter, written on the day of his death, he read me. Some years ago Stevenson named H. James his lit: exec: but made a later will nominating no one. The instant the telegram of S's death arrived, H.J. hurries to renounce probate, afterwards proved unnecessary, so he only gave pain. Meanwhile Colvin comes posting to Gosse, to beg *him* not to take the position, because it ought to belong to him by rights. A piece of the grossest ill-taste. I had always thought Colvin refined, if stiff and feeble. But now I know that he is vulgar.'

In Gosse's company – either at his house in Hanover Terrace or in one or other of the London clubs – he met Philip Bailey ('Festus'), Max Beerbohm ('a smiling, bullet-headed man, stout, well-dressed, redolent of cigars, with grey eyes under a heavy brow'), exhibiting his superbly witty caricature of Mr Gladstone in Heaven; and the novelist Rider Haggard. He visited Haggard again at his house at Ditchingham, while on holiday with the Donaldsons, and was surprised to hear him quoting the Odyssey 'with gusto' in the course of a disquisition on mining in Cyprus; but then, as he was assured later, Haggard was not really a well-informed man; he just knew how 'to butter his knowledge very thin and make it go a long way'.

Arthur saw Gosse at his best and at his worst. His best, as a raconteur, was very good indeed. At a luncheon party at Hanover Terrace in January 1900, Gosse was host to Sir Courteney Ilbert, George Armour (an American millionaire), J. M. Barrie ('a little pale, ill-dressed, weary man, very taciturn, and with no look of the gentleman. I should have taken him for an overworked clerk'), Stephen Spring-Rice, Maurice Hewlett and Stephen Phillips. Arthur was present, and described the occasion in his diary. 'Gosse was of course the most brilliant, flitting about like a butterfly and talking beautifully of a Russian Novelist Dostoievsky (?) (Crime and Punishment), in which he said you as it were opened a door and went in to another life – it was your own life that became unreal – you throbbed and thrilled with the tragedy of the book. You felt yourself close to the very bone and fibre of life.'

Gosse concluded the party with an account of the latest absurdity of Montagu Butler, the Master of Trinity:

> The Master ... came up to town for some function and came in canonicals – gown and bands and cap. Instead of taking a cab he got into an omnibus. Everyone regarded him with amazement, as he sate like a dissipated Stewart prince, with a serene and all-embracing smile. Who should get in but the Master of Jesus, rough Morgan, who took a place at the far end, hoping to be unnoticed. At last Butler's eye fell on him. He nodded and smiled and said, across the bus: 'Ah, is that *you*, dear Master of Jesus, and how are you?' There was a sudden sensation in the bus, the spectators suddenly perceiving that B. was a lunatic, and they sate looking at him, ready to dart their eyes away if he looked at them.

The conductor collected fares, but he was so afraid of Butler that he thought he had better leave him undisturbed – but the Master, seeing the conductor leaving the bus, called playfully 'Boy, boy – what are the expenses of this transit?'

The conductor was so horribly taken aback that he said nothing but held up two fingers.

Butler looked vacantly at him and then turned to Morgan. 'And now, dear Master of Jesus', he said, 'I must ask you to interpret this symbol for me.'

Morgan lost all sense of decorum at the scene, and said loudly 'For God's sake, Butler, pay your twopence and have done with it'.

On the other hand, Gosse could be waspish, petulant and prickly. 'He is the imperishable child', Arthur wrote in July 1895, 'I must not forget this.' He did not. Their friendship was punctuated by little quarrels, mutual takings of offence and somewhat unsteady reconciliations. Gosse (like Arthur) could be very scornful of a friend who seemed in any way to snub him; and he could posture pathetically before eminent persons, becoming arch and ingratiating with titled ladies (Lady Londonderry, especially), even pretending a deep interest in golf in order to gain the friendship of Arthur Balfour.

But this was the London literary world. Robert Bridges explained to Arthur in 1897 what he might expect to meet there, if he took up writing as a career. He 'talked very interestingly about the horrible logrolling atmosphere of London literary circles – being asked to meet reviewers; having it hinted that if you will be civil to so and so he will give you a good review and so forth'. Gosse took his education further. There were the bitter rivalries to watch out for – especially the cliques who admired or detested Swinburne. He told him how George Meredith, after a quarrel with Swinburne, kicked him down the front steps of Cheyne Walk. 'It positively made me physically sick to hear the noise – thump, thump – that his horrid little body made falling down the steps! They did not meet again on amicable terms.' How Swinburne took delight in his savaging of Emerson, writing him a letter bidding him to remember 'that he is a debilitated and now toothless ape who, first lifted into notoriety on the shoulders of Carlyle, now spits and splutters from a filthier platform of his own finding and fouling', all this with shrill cries of laughter and the cracking of his little fingers.

Arthur listened to the gossip and recorded it faithfully in his diary – the pathetic efforts of Hall Caine to seduce his reviewers by sending out five hundred presentation copies of a book, all carefully inscribed; the shabby

way in which W. E. Henley treated Stevenson after his death, making out
that his whole life had been a pose when, in fact, Henley had been
privately pensioned by Stevenson 'and drew his pension to the day of
Stevenson's death', – an act of 'foul and perfidious malice'. When he
heard of Henley's death, he wrote in the diary: 'May he rest in peace, and
not have to meet Stevenson in paradise.' This was a back-biting world,
amusing to watch, enlivening occasionally to enter; but it was not one
that Arthur was seriously tempted to join.

Henry James, while not exactly standing aloof, had a greatness and a
lovableness of his own, which put him really into a different league.
Arthur loved the man if he could not understand his work. He thought
his writing convoluted and tortuous. 'This voluble delineation, this
spouting cataract of analysis deafens and bewilders me', he wrote, after
vainly trying to get to grips with *Wings of a Dove*. 'A book is for me a *house*
which I can *enter* – not a castle, half-hidden in woods, round which I
walk, thinking myself lucky if I ever get a glimpse of it at the end of an
avenue.' But as a friend, counsellor and *convive*, Henry James had no
equal. There was the measured, elaborately structured diction – affected,
no doubt, but all part of the image that Arthur came to love. Passing him
in the Athenaeum, Arthur asked him whether he would give him his
blessing. 'My dear Arthur', Henry James replied, 'my mind is so
constantly and continuously bent upon you in wonder and goodwill that
any change in my attitude could be only the withholding of a perpetual
and settled felicitation.' Asked by Gosse if any of a party of actresses who
called with Ellen Terry to meet the great man struck him as being
particularly pretty, 'H.J. turned up his eyes and held up his hands in
speechless horror at the indelicacy of the suggestion. Then after a long
pause, he said "I must not go so far as to deny that one poor wanton had
some species of cadaverous charm".'

In January 1900 Arthur spent a night with Henry James at Lamb
House, Rye. Inevitably they talked literature and literary gossip:

> He refined and defined, was intricate, magniloquent, rhetorical, humorous,
> not like a talker so much but like a writer repeating his technical processes
> aloud – like a savant working out a problem. He told me a long story about
> Heinemann and spoke with hatred of business and the monetary side of art.
> He evidently thinks that *art* is nearly dead among English writers, no
> criticism, no instinct for what is good. He spoke of G[osse] with affectionate
> compassion. He talked of Mrs Oliphant, Carlyle – whatever I began. 'I had
> not read a *line* that the poor woman had written for *years* – not for years.
> When she died, Henley – do you know him, the rude, boisterous, windy,

headstrong Henley – Henley, as I say, said to me "Have you read *Kirsteen?*"
I replied that as a matter of fact, No – h'm, I had not read it. Henley said
"that you should have any pretensions to interest in literature and should
dare to say that you have not read *Kirsteen!*" – I took my bludgeoning
patiently and humbly, my dear Arthur. Went back and read it, and was at
once confirmed, after 20 pages, in my belief – I laboured through the book –
that the poor soul had a simply *feminine* conception of literature – such
slipshod, imperfect, halting, faltering, peeping, down-at-heel work –
buffeting along like a ragged creature in a high wind, and just struggling to
the goal and falling in a quivering mass of faintness and fatuity ... Yes, no
doubt she was a gallant woman though with no species of wisdom – but an
artist, an artist!' He held his hands up and stared woefully at me.

... H.J. works hard. He establishes me in a little high-walled, white
parlour, very comfortable – but is full of fear that I am unhappy. He comes
in, pokes the fire, presses a cigarette on me, puts his hand on my shoulder,
looks enquiringly at me and hurries away.

The nearest that Arthur came to committed membership of the London literary circle was in 1903 when he received from Macmillan the
commission to write the first of his contributions to the *English Men of
Letters* series – a study of D. G. Rossetti. Other volumes were to follow –
Edward Fitzgerald, *Walter Pater* and *William Morris*; and at this stage he
could at any time have abandoned Eton for a London base, casting his lot
with Gosse and his circle in the world of London letters and journalism.
He secured the entrée to the surviving preserves of Pre-Raphaelitism:
improbable treasure-houses tucked away in drab corners of London's
suburbia, where the flame still flickered and elderly devotees of a dying
fashion hoarded the relics and transmitted the mysteries to honest and
appreciative enquirers. On a memorable day in early April 1903, Arthur
cycled from Eton to Putney, stopping unbelievingly before a
commonplace, yellow-bricked semi-detached house, with a tiny
straggling garden in front, where allegedly Algernon Swinburne lived
with his elderly, solicitous and self-important companion, Theodore
Watts-Dunton. 'The house was redolent of cooking, dark, not very clean-
looking, but comfortable enough – the walls crowded everywhere with
pictures, mostly Rossetti's designs in pen and ink or chalk.' Watts-
Dunton conducted him to a study above the dining-room.

There stood before me a little, pale, rather don-like man, quite bald, with a
huge head and domelike forehead, a ragged red beard in odd whisps – small
aquiline red nose; he looked supremely shy, but received me with a
distinguished courtesy, drumming on the ground with his foot and uttering
strange little whistling noises.

... On the fender was a pair of brown socks. W.D. said to me 'he has just come in from one of his long walks', took up the socks and put them behind a coal scuttle. 'Stay!' said Swinburne, and took them out carefully holding them in his hand, 'they are drying'. W.D. murmured something to me about his fearing they would get scorched and we sate down. Swinburne sate down concealing his feet behind a chair and proceeded with strange motions to put the socks on out of sight. 'He seems to be changing them', said W.D. Swinburne said nothing but continued to whistle and drum. Then he rose and bowed me down to lunch.

Swinburne said virtually nothing during lunch, but began to talk quite animatedly at the end, as Watts-Dunton stroked his small pink hand, which elicited from Swinburne a 'schoolboy smile' of pleasure. In the study afterwards Arthur was treated to a long disquisition and some readings, punctuated by a necessary visit to the medicine chest. A long talk with Watts-Dunton afterwards provided Arthur with the material he needed – and a certain amount of scandal besides – a parcel of Rossetti sketches and the passport to other repositories of Rossetti treasures.

One such was a dingy villa near the waterworks on Primrose Hill, where Ford Madox Brown had lived, thereafter the house of William Rossetti. Over tea, Arthur was plied with valuable Rossetti MSS, watched suspiciously and disconcertingly by a 'malevolent lady' – 'an old solid scowling lady in black silk and a kind of mantilla, who rustled in, accepted tea, ate and drank, looked at me fixedly, and said not *one* word of any kind, except to make an obscure sound which Miss R[ossetti] seemed to interpret to be a sign of dissatisfaction with the chair she had been sitting in – so that it became painfully clear to me that *I* was in her chair'. But the most propitious meeting of all came in June 1903, when Arthur again made a tentative and enquiring journey through 'unemphatic suburban streets' to seek out 111, North End Road, the home of Charles Fairfax-Murray, the art-collector, in the house where Rossetti himself had lived and where Burne-Jones had set up his studio. This was a treasure-house indeed – priceless pictures, manuscripts, autographed copies and first editions, mainly amassed by the extraordinary dwarf-like man with bandy legs, who had started life as a shop-boy and developed both a passion for beautiful things and the expertise to find them where their true value was unknown. This was the first of many meetings from which – in the long run – through Arthur's good offices and the generosity of Fairfax-Murray, the Fitzwilliam Museum at Cambridge was to derive one of its most valuable collections.

Circumstances seemed to be pulling Arthur towards London. He was appointed in 1902 to membership of the Nobel Committee to nominate the winner of the literary award. The Committee met under the chairmanship of Lord Avebury, and Arthur and Gosse agreed beforehand to press strongly for Herbert Spencer. Austin Dobson and Thomas Hardy 'sate together like good little boys – Hardy very faded and feeble looking. Dobson very round and sleek. Hardy would have voted for Swinburne.' Spencer won; but the following year Swinburne carried the vast majority, a few votes going to John Morley, George Meredith and Rudyard Kipling.

Although Arthur had, by this time, resolved to leave Eton, he had more than one reservation about moving to London. He was unmarried; and too obviously eligible a catch, within the world of letters, for the intense female prophetesses – like Mary Cholmondeley, for instance, who wrote incomprehensible books like *Moth and Rust*, and tried to entice him into her web, soliciting for confidences in 'hollow whispers'. Arthur had first met her at Qu'acre with Howard Sturgis, and had been for a while mildly enchanted. But by 1903, after she had paid two visits to Tremans, Arthur felt it right to draw away. He liked her sense of humour, but shrank from her propensity to pontificate. She would speak 'as though *she were called to be an Apostle*', while having a mind 'like a house full of crooked passages, useless flights of stairs and blind doors'. As it turned out, Mary Cholmondeley did not admit defeat easily. Sensing his withdrawal, she wrote an earnest letter to him in February 1903, confessing that – from their very first meeting – she had felt 'a kind of large and predestined friendship' coming into being – 'strong, natural, long-standing and indestructible!' Arthur at once shied back. His friendship with Mary Cholmondeley had never been anything more than 'a pleasant feeling of real camaraderie – entire frankness – until it began to be overshadowed by her mysteries and riddles'. Besides that, 'I am entirely a person of *male* friendships. I don't like "exultations, agonies". I like a friendship where I can say exactly what I like, as much or as little: speak angrily or affectionately, and never be misunderstood. *The bond must be unconscious.* I could not bear conscious bonds. They would fret me, not help me. ... I must really tread very cautiously among these eggs.'

At least Arthur knew quite definitely what he did not want. 'I *hate* London', he wrote in April 1904, 'the noise makes me ill.' Success and acceptance depended upon one's readiness to meet and mingle with the society figures of real influence, and to ape the manners and *mores* of rich and shallow-minded people. Fred, his brother, was entirely at home there. He loved the London social round; the parties, the life of clubland, the 'week-ends'. For Arthur, however, a conversation with his friend Bob Norton in the summer of 1904 about the literary 'log-rolling' of the Edwardian age confirmed him in the decision already made that to abandon schoolmastering for a literary career would only be congenial and productive if he remained within a primarily academic setting. Norton assured him that he would loathe the London 'week-ends' and 'the utter *pretentiousness* of the literary talk of the fashionable world; he hears a great deal of it. What interests me most is that he says it is all interlaced with *sexual* relationships, not necessarily immoral at all, but a kind of shifting kaleidoscope of relations, excitements, passions.' The morals of high society were 'worse, more *unashamed* in London than at any other capital'. The women delighted in talking about their intrigues – especially the Taplow Court set, the Grenfells, Balfours, Elchos and the Asquiths. 'The whole picture of the week-end is not attractive. The ladies don't generally appear on Sunday morning. There is golf, bridge, and so forth.' The wonder was that Bob Norton survived it all innocent and unscathed. 'I wonder if *he* has ever been in love? except with the fair witch herself [Mrs Grenfell, the future Lady Desborough]: that is one of the conditions of the circle.'

So Arthur turned his back on the London circle, while keeping up certain important friendships there. But none of these quite took the place of friendships which linked him with the carefree relationships of the Tan and Dunskey days. Mary Cholmondeley once tried out her 'dreadful game' on Arthur – putting him in the imaginary predicament of having to take three real friends to the top of St Paul's Cathedral, duly to find when he got to the top that he could take only one down again with him. One of the others had to be pushed over to fall to his death; the third had to stay on the top for ever. How would he make his choice? Actually Arthur did not hesitate: 'I pushed *Henry James* over, as fittest to die, left *Gosse* on the top, and brought *Howard Sturgis* down.' He would have liked to keep his literary friends; but he did not really need them any more.

*   *   *   *   *

He had acquired for some time important friends at Court. His father's position had helped, of course. Through his father, and in his capacity as his father's biographer, he found himself in 1897 the guest of Gladstone

95

at Hawarden, and of Sir William Harcourt (ex-Chancellor of the Exchequer) at Malwood. Both visits were memorable and both faithfully recorded. When he came to Hawarden, Gladstone was 87 and had less than a year to live. Arthur dined at the old man's table on the evening of 24 August. Only Dean Wickham and his wife, with certain members of the family, were present. As Arthur came in, 'Mr and Mrs Gladstone were sitting on a sofa, side by side, hand in hand, like two lovers.' Mrs Gladstone was full of messages for Arthur's mother. ' "I do so want to send my dearest love to your dearest mother – she must come here when she can". . . . She has a touching way with her kind old face all wrinkled up with attention and sympathy, of saying "Dear" "Dearest" as little ejaculations at the end of a sentence – not addressed to the speaker, but descriptive of the person described.' There was a slight jostling for places at the dinner table, and the G.O.M. insisted on Arthur sitting on his right – 'My left ear is useless', he said, touching it.

They began talking about Eton at once. Gladstone described the solitary occasion on which he had been flogged by Keate, whose rule over the school could be summed up in the phrase 'terror without cruelty'. When Arthur ventured to suggest that Keate's image had been misunderstood by posterity and that he had probably been quite a humane man, Gladstone laughed. 'I don't know about that', he said. 'Where do you get that from? There was not much humanity.' He then turned to the joys of Eton friendship – Arthur Hallam, who always had a curious flush on his face, caused by overwork, 'the most brilliant personality he had ever encountered'; and Milnes Gaskell and his passion for politics. 'We were not liberals or tories in those days', he pointed out. 'We were Canning or non-Canning.' He then said 'The story of M. Gaskell's friendship with Hallam was curious; you know' – with a smile – 'people fell in love very easily in those days'.

> He ate and drank little – a glass of champagne and a curious little cut glass full of port – his own particular glass – with cheese. He ate soup – but spilling much of it and rather vague with his spoon. Fish and some bread pudding only handed to him. He took no coffee but another glass of port (it was rough light new port, not good), asking the butler loudly 'Which is the port? Is it this?' He had on rather a high dress waistcoat, unbuttoned, a watchguard round his neck – a tie tied very badly into a kind of flat knot on one side and high collars. . . . He was most animated and talked the *whole* of dinner. They told me it needed a *visitor* and a *topic*. . . . After dinner he played backgammon with Stephen, saying sternly and loudly to Stephen when his attention wandered, his own last score 'Three and one, three and

one'. He played with great concentration, his face puckered up, rattling the dice vigorously and jamming the dice box down. Once or twice when the conversation grew loud, he said suddenly and severely 'Don't *chatter* there, chatter not'. Everyone laughed, and talked on quietly.

As Arthur got up to leave, he was puzzled to pass a desk with an inkstand, against which was leaning a card with 'LUMBAGO' written on it – nothing else. He enquired delicately what it meant. Mary Drew (Gladstone's daughter) laughed: 'It's one of the words my mother forgets. She is suffering from lumbago for the first time in her life, but can't remember the word.'

The visit to Malwood later in the year, although equally domestic, was a livelier occasion and the conversation more political. Arthur had been invited to lunch with a purely family party (Lewis, the eldest son of Sir William Harcourt – known as 'Lulu' – Bobby, a Miss Harcourt and Lady Harcourt's married sister and her husband – Colonel and Mrs Mildmay). The lunch was a sumptuous affair – 'tables and sideboards groaned with food – cold game, pies, boar's head etc. in profusion', and justice was fully done to it, especially by Sir William. A discussion began on the salutary effects of taking regular exercise, and Sir William pooh-poohed the idea. 'More people are killed by *exercise* than by staying at home! I never leave the house if I can help it except to stroll in the garden – Fawcett died of exercise. Chamberlain, the Duke of Devonshire and I are the strongest men I know and we never take exercise.' A particularly rich confection was brought on at the end of the meal, a wedding cake with sugar and almond paste. Sir William helped himself to a large slice, but when his sister followed suit, he snatched the cake from her plate, saying 'No, no, you don't – You're younger than I am and I can't allow you to tamper with your digestion!' and he flung the cake on the table.

He then took Arthur off to his study, booklined with a sofa with 'a huge permanent depression at one end where the statesman sits' and cigar-boxes easily to hand. He plunged immediately into reminiscences of Disraeli: how solitary he was, how he would hardly ever speak if there were more than three people present, and was totally silent at dinner-parties. Lady Beaconsfield? – 'She had been a pumproom barmaid at Bath and had the manners of her class', a model of indiscretion. Disraeli told Harcourt, after dinner at Hughenden, 'She's such a bright gay creature. She knows nothing of the *past*. She does not prognosticate about the future. She lives entirely in the present. She never can remember whether the Greeks or Romans came first.'

He saw much of Dizzy. . . . Said that D. before he died said 'I have been killed by Afghanistan and the Transvaal' – When Ld. Rowton told him of the sympathetic crowds waiting outside at Curzon St for news of his health, he only said 'Yes, but they turned me out'. . . .

It was Gladstone's 88th birthday. 'Ought we to send a telegram?' said Lady H. 'Certainly not.'

Harcourt pressed Arthur to stay the night with them. ' "Lulu will lend you some things" – and then with a glance at my form – "and I'll lend you my waistcoat" – and added "You shall have the Chancellor of the Exchequer's gold-laced robe to wear if you like." ' The best remark, however, about Disraeli which Arthur learnt from the Harcourts was vouchsafed by Lulu on a later occasion. He recalled his father being asked 'What sort of a person was left when Dizzy was absolutely alone? I can't think what the *real* Dizzy is like – what is it that *goes to bed*?' Sir William said firmly: 'Perhaps you would find a small snake coiled up on the pillow.'

Arthur's entry into Court circles came via the Ponsonbys. Throughout his time at Eton, Sir Henry and Lady Ponsonby lived in the Norman Tower at Windsor Castle. After her husband's death, Lady Ponsonby moved to Gilmuir, a house and estate near Ascot. Arthur was a frequent visitor. Lady Ponsonby loved to keep abreast with what was happening in political and literary circles; she liked the company of cultivated men and women, cutting right across the generations – Ethel Smyth, Vernon Lee, Mrs Cornish, Maurice Baring – and she would discourse on books and personalities, lacing her remarks with French expressions (not always intelligible) which she had acquired in her girlhood from her French governess. She was – as Arthur described her – 'a relic of that almost extinct species, the old *Whig*': radical ideas, backed by a conscious sense of superiority and the value of birth. She liked unconventional people and blunt, unaffected talk, but she never quite allowed her guests to forget her position. She was the 'wicked fairy', who would scoff at idealism about 'love and self-sacrifice being the only things worth having. No – food and drink and occupation and books and talk – all the furniture of life – would all be appraised justly and duly by Lady P. . . . She is somehow the best specimen of the *great lady* I know.'

Arthur had been admitted into her inner circle after passing inspection at a lunch party in the late 1880's. Thereafter Lady Ponsonby was prepared to open for him such doors as he wished. She would speak very frankly to him about the Queen, sometimes warning him against writing an account of what she had told him in his 'too accessible diary'. She explained how her husband had learnt the art of persuading the Queen to change her mind. Confronted with one of her typically indiscreet and obstinate decisions, Sir Henry would say: 'Well, Ma'am, you are right no doubt, as I think you generally are: but there is this and this to be said, and they are considerations of a kind that usually prevail with you.' 'No [the Queen would reply], I am quite decided: my mind is made up.' 'Very well, Ma'am.' A week later: 'Sir Henry: you said that there were some points on that matter which you thought I should be likely to consider. I do not mean to change my mind, but I should like you just to note down what the points were.' The decision was then silently reversed. Arthur asked Lady Ponsonby what the Queen would have been like if born to a humble state. 'A good Scotch cottar's wife – very sententious and always right', she replied. She added, a moment later: 'It was very odd that she should have come of a long line of Kings who believed in the Divine right of monarchs, and that she substituted for that the Divine right of herself.'

What doors did she open for Arthur? Perhaps the introduction to the Duchess of Albany, which resulted in the young Duke being entered for his house. More probably, it was through Lady Ponsonby that Arthur gained his position as 'unofficial' poet laureate to the Court at Windsor.

The young Duke of Albany was entered for Arthur's house in July 1894. Arthur stayed with the Duchess at Claremont for the first time in December 1897. This was the beginning of a new and significant friendship. Helena, Princess of Waldeck-Pyrmont, had married Leopold, Duke of Albany, fourth son of Queen Victoria. Leopold died in 1884. They had two children – Princess Alice (later Countess of Athlone) and Charles Edward, who was born in the year that his father died. Arthur described his first visit to the household:

> To Claremont. . . . Was met at Esher by Sir R. Collins and the little Duke. He is much more robust than when I saw him last and is a sweet-tempered innocent-looking boy with big eyes. I drove in state, they bicycling like outriders. A frosty day. Had tea in the library, but went to see the Duchess first – in her room where she was presiding over some encaustic work – a hot point with a benzoline spray – little Princess Alice a charming child, with a delightful laugh, the most merry and liquid sound. The Duchess' sitting-room was Prince Leopold's, and was the anteroom to the room where Princess Charlotte died, the King wringing his hands. . . . Talked for an hour and a half to the Duchess and told her all about Eton. She most sensible and wise, wants Albany to be treated *exactly* like everyone else. . . .

We dined at 7.30, a long and elaborate dinner, with tall old men in red waiting. I took in the Duchess and sate between her and Prin. Alice. We all pulled crackers and were very merry. Sate afterwards a long time in the Library, the Duchess working something for the Queen as an Xmas present and making Collins show me scrap-books of Prince Leopold with many interesting letters. The Duchess was in white with a white silk cap worked with gold. Very little ceremony. A little bowing and curtseying, and the invariable 'ma'am'. She has great ideas that children should not 'loaf'. Afterwards I smoked with Collins in the same room and he showed me the Queen's room, very shabby, old-fashioned chintzes and bed, tables and chairs all after an exact pattern. Saw also Princess Charlotte's clock which plays an old tune with variations in flutes, blown by wind. Prince L. when he left Claremont for the last time, heard the clock begin just as he was going out – and said 'There's the dear old clock!' and heard it play its tune. Since then the Queen has never allowed it to get out of order and spends a large sum on putting it to rights.

Slept in a large room with a fine alcove. Everything nice but rather old – holes in the sheets etc.

Next morning breakfast at 8.30, the Duchess pouring out tea etc. and very sedulous of my comfort. Then saw the house and Clive's marble bath – all very fine. Had a little more talk to the Duchess, and Collins insisted on giving me lessons in boxing before her, which amused them.... Albany was sent for to shake hands, and told his mother afterwards he thought me very kind. The Duchess is big and solid, with a kind, plump, easy-going face, very genial and friendly smile and absolutely simple. ... I came away refreshed by finding all so simple and good.

Albany stayed at Eton for a little over a year. His mother reluctantly agreed to his becoming Duke of Saxe-Coburg, the Connaughts having declined the succession. It was deemed necessary for the remainder of his education to be completed in Germany. Arthur prepared him for confirmation before he left, and attended the special service in Windsor Chapel conducted by Randall Davidson, Bishop of Winchester. 'Poor Albany was in tears most of the time, and his little treble "I do" sounded pathetically earnest.' The leave-taking was very emotional. The Duchess placed on her son's finger his father's diamond ring with TREU UND FEST in diamonds. Collins then took Arthur aside to give him the Duchess' personal assurance 'that I should not be forgotten, but should count in the inner circle of their English friends'.

The Duchess was as good as her word. An earlier stay at Claremont, in 1899, had established a more relaxed relationship between them. Arthur found he could talk to her without consciousness of her high rank; and she in return opened her heart about her childhood; how she had once, as a child, upbraided an equerry for letting one of her roses die; and how, next day, she had overheard him talking about her to one of the ladies-in-waiting. 'An odious girl – Princess Helen' – 'Yes, indeed', was the reply, 'I don't know what will become of her.' She was mortified – too proud to tell her mother, and suspecting for years afterwards that any kindness shown to her was merely acknowledgement of her rank. 'She talked of the little Battenburg and how the Queen spoilt him and how conscious he was of being her favourite. She said that Arthur of Connaught was bullied and sat upon by his mother and sister – that the Duchess of Connaught had a fretful character, developed by a very ill-tempered father – and other interesting(?) stories.' She was worried then about Albany – the way he talked and the way he walked. She was therefore anxious to confide in Arthur about his problems after he had left England.

There were many subsequent meetings. He had tea at the Castle with her in December 1900, and was entertained by Princess Alice while her mother was still with the Queen – 'almost a young lady ready to go out – but so welcoming and smiling and brisk. She told me that on her first introduction to Lewis Carroll she said to him "Why does your mouth work about so funnily?" and was in great disgrace.' Through the Duchess he was invited to attend the Mausoleum Service at Windsor in the same month. He tried not to stare too hard at the Queen as she came in 'leaning on her Indian', very small and bent, her bonnet hardly reaching up to the rim of the sarcophagus. He took an instant dislike to the Prince of Wales – 'like an old fat fox – such tête fleuré eyes'. Princess Alice was the sweetest of them all.

In July 1902 he was at Claremont again, the place all 'muffled in cloths' as the electric light was being installed. The Duchess spoke very frankly about her concern for Albany. He was expected to proceed to Jena University, in Coburg, 'where she thinks he will be toadied and flattered'.

> She wants him to go to Bonn with the Emperor's second son to whom he is devoted. She says that a great danger is the very corrupt tone of Coburg. 'You know what the Prince Consort's brother was', she said. 'Well, he has set the tone of Coburg. There is hardly a respectable inhabitant of the place who would not consider it an honour for his daughter to be dishonoured by the Duke.' She said that even now the most audacious attempts to tempt him were made. 'He is quite innocent. He brings me the letters and says "I don't understand what the woman wants".' She said she would have liked me to meet the Emperor. 'What a pity you won't come to us at Potsdam!' Collins and the Princess came to say good-bye. 'Don't forget us', said Collins. 'We don't forget you.'

The Duchess got her way over Bonn. Arthur next stayed at Claremont just after Christmas in 1903; and Albany had come over to celebrate the new year. Princess Alice was now engaged to Alexander of Teck (as Collins privately confided to Arthur – the possibility of a haemophiliac strain had put a more ambitious marriage out of the question). Albany impressed Arthur very favourably – 'tall and slender now, with a beautiful complexion, and the same look of innocence he always had', although he disliked his foolish stories of the ragging and fagging of junior cadets at Bonn. They had a very grand dinner, with Albany in his Garter ribbon, Château d'Yquem being served by chasseurs in the Saxe-Coburg livery. Afterwards they relaxed over games round the billiard table. 'The blowing game, however, put everyone at their ease', he wrote. 'It was funny to see people look like old pictures of winds. The Duchess purple, inflated.'

A year later Arthur was entertained by Princess Alice and her husband in the Henry IV tower at Windsor. He liked Prince Alexander whom he thought much changed from the rather stout, black-haired, bright-eyed boy whom he remembered. 'Now tall, thin, brown, but German-looking. ... I reflected what a fine thing this royalty is for giving a man good, easy unembarrassed manners. He is not a clever fellow – and has something of the funny trick that Prince Eddy had of putting a string of words together as if he was not thinking of the meaning.' He had also acquired 'the odd royal laugh ..., rather too loud – and the odd royal habit of getting a book to look out something and getting lost and bemused over it'. The atmosphere was so relaxed, however, that Arthur found that he was quite unable to refer to them as 'Sir' and 'Ma'am'. A few days later they travelled up together to spend Christmas at Claremont. Arthur drove there in the royal car, sitting in the back with the Princess wrapped in rugs and furs. 'We talked and giggled like two relations – uncle and niece. The Princess isn't in the least like a married woman, but like a very simple and merry girl.'

This was Arthur's longest stay at Claremont. He celebrated Christmas with the family; interposed a few days at Tremans, and then returned to see the new year in with Albany who had come over from Coburg again. He accompanied the Duchess on her rounds to all the families on the estate, presenting joints of beef to the men, Princess Alice holding her train as she walked. He took part in innumerable round games ('rather terrible ... it was all hearty, simple, friendly and German'). Presents were distributed after dinner on Christmas Eve; and Arthur was given a little oak clock and a paper weight – a silver skate lying on a block of crystal, like ice – both having belonged to Prince Leopold. One little episode rather jarred with Arthur:

> The odd fondness that Royalty have for 'ragging' other people and laughing at their discomfiture, when they are sure they will never be made to look foolish themselves (Cf. the King of Portugal cramming handfuls of snow down the necks of his staff at Windsor and hurling huge snowballs at them – they in return making up snowballs of the size of marbles and throwing them gingerly back, taking care to miss). Someone had put up some mistletoe under the chandeliers. Teck (who is always ragging Lady Collins) dragged her beneath, and Royle [Prince Leopold's doctor] kissed her! Very vulgar, very harmless: but stupid too and out of date. The Royalties screamed with laughter. But if ... I had dragged the Duchess underneath and embraced her, how wd she have liked it? It wd have been 'a liberty'. Well, why is it not a liberty with Lady C.? Because of the d————d feeling that makes horseplay from a Royalty into a piece of gracious condescension. That is why I couldn't bear to live among them.

But it was a rare privilege none the less. There was the Christmas service at the tiny tin church at West End, occupying the Claremont pew which was the size of a room – turkey-carpets, noble tapestry and deep armchairs. Arthur disgraced himself by going to sleep during the sermon and snoring. There were more intimate talks with the Duchess about life with the Queen: how she had taken Leopold as her favourite after the Prince Consort's death, and worked him so hard that she drove him to his early death; how ill-tempered the Prince Consort was with his children; how John Brown acquired his influence over the Queen, and how 'she was never at ease with a *man*'.

As they said good-bye, the Duchess said to him: 'I wanted you to see our German Xmas and to see Charles and to be one of us.' Arthur noticed, in the Visitors' Book, that this was the fifth occasion he had stayed with her. It had been an extraordinary experience, but he was loath to repeat it. How impossible it would be to '*live* in that atmosphere of false deference and elaborate ceremony. I can't really breathe there.... It isn't my *monde* at all, and it is too late to begin.' He kept in touch thereafter, but he was never to stay there again.

*   *   *   *   *

All through this period Arthur was rendering a service to Royalty in return by producing hymns and odes for special occasions as they were required. The first was a Wedding Hymn, written originally for the

marriage of his Eton friend Willy Boyle to Eleanor Curzon, but which
was actually sung in July 1896 for the wedding of Prince Charles of
Denmark to Princess Maud of Wales. He was then invited by the Queen
to write an additional verse to Bishop How's Jubilee Hymn. From that
moment the requests came thick and fast – hymns for the Mausoleum
Service, one set to music by Queen Victoria herself; a christening hymn
for the Prince of Wales, set to music by Princess Beatrice; a hymn for the
South African War ('O Lord of Hosts'); another hymn to mark the
proclamation of peace; two confirmation hymns for Prince Leopold of
Battenburg. He was invited to write an Ode to commemorate Queen
Victoria's visit to Ireland; and then another to celebrate the Japanese
alliance of February 1902. He received two commissions for the
Coronation of Edward VII – to provide the words for Wagner's
Kaisermarch to be sung at the service; and to write a special Coronation
Ode – 'Crown the King with Life'.

As is well known, in this last commission, he found himself
collaborating with Edward Elgar; and the most famous lines he ever
wrote – 'Land of Hope and Glory' – were inserted at the King's own
request to provide words for the trio melody in Elgar's 'Pomp and
Circumstance March', no. 1. Originally the invitation to write the music
was extended to C. V. Stanford who objected to Novello as the publisher.
'He was blowed if he wd write a line of music for the blackguards', he told
Arthur. 'He thinks they will come a cropper by miserliness soon; they
have alienated Elgar.' Elgar, however, accepted the commission, and –
according to Walter Parratt – Stanford was deeply offended that none of
his music was played at the Coronation – 'simply furious. ... He
considers himself so much the first of all English musicians that this is to
him a deadly rankling insult.'

Arthur met Elgar for the first time at the performance of the
Coronation Ode in the Queen's Hall in November 1902. He had only
once been to the Proms before (with Lionel Ford, when he had watched
with amazement a display of 'animated photographs' in the interval). He
had not anticipated the crowds. He walked straight to the ticket-office,
ignoring the long queue, and persuaded the protesting party to buy his
ticket for him. He sat through a Saint-Saens march, a Tchaikovsky
concerto ('my idea of music'); 'then came the Ode. Elgar stepped to the
box; he is taller and shapelier than I have imagined ..., a long nose – red
hands – large cuffs. He conducted with a smiling aplomb – has a funny
fumbling movement of the hands after *end* of piece. The Ode did both

please and impress me very much; it is wizard-like music – I like the softer portions best.' He went to the 'Premier Artists' room afterwards, and was admitted immediately on production of his name.

> I found Elgar with his artists. I ought of course to have thanked them – but I was too stupid – and just had three pleasurable words with E., who was very genial and pleasant. Once or twice I detected a twang, I thought.

This was not to be their last collaboration nor their last meeting. In the following year Arthur provided the words for a melody of Elgar's – the song 'My Heart' – writing it in only ten minutes. In 1904 he was invited to Boosey's where the proposition was put to him to collaborate with Elgar in providing the libretto for an opera on the theme of Cleopatra. 'I did not refuse though I doubt if I have either time or power: the *dramatic* part would be difficult – but I suppose there is not much drama about an opera, ... that it is mostly isolated lyric. He was highly complimentary, and said I was the only man in England etc. He promised me that it would be highly *lucrative*, and that I can well believe.' Arthur never followed it up – probably wisely.

He had already collaborated with Sir Hubert Parry twice before. The first occasion was in December 1898 when Parry set to music Arthur's verses 'Home of my Heart'. This was performed at a Madrigal Concert at Windsor Castle before Princess Christian.

> Parry conducted his own songs. He blew on the pitch pipe, which was first silent and then emitted a kind of groan. He said, in a silence between laughter, 'I knew I couldn't get the right note out of the beastly thing – Here, Lloyd!' and threw it twenty feet over the singers to Lloyd [Precentor of Eton] in the orchestra, who missed it: it hit the wall and fell on the ground. Lloyd burrowed, roars of laughter, Princess Christian looking shocked. At last the right note was produced. When the thing was over P. Xtian swept out, but turned to bow to Parry, who stood with his back to her talking loudly and mopping his brow. 'Look at that', said Lady Parratt to me (I was sitting next her), 'Sir Hubert Parry is no *courtier*', with bitter emphasis.

The 'Ode to Music', written in 1901 to mark the opening of the new hall in the Royal College of Music, was also set to music by Parry. Arthur attended the first performance in June of that year. Stanford conducted, and royalty was represented in the person of the Duke of Cambridge who entered to the National Anthem 'with his face like a damaged double strawberry, looking very infirm. He was taken to a red armchair in the front, where he dozed; in the soft passage of the violin movement, a few minutes later, all the books and papers they had given him fell out of his old, drowsy hand on the ground, and he did not even pick them up.' The piece was enthusiastically received, and there were cries of 'author, author' at the end.

Of all the musicians he knew or collaborated with, Sir Walter Parratt, Organist at St George's Windsor, was his closest friend. He wrote for Arthur the music of one of the Mausoleum hymns, and Arthur himself testified to the particular pleasure that this little commission gave him. 'It enables me to do something for the Queen, whom I regard with an extraordinary love and veneration. . . . And secondly, it gives me many sights of Walter Parratt, who is a very high-minded, affectionate and able man – more suggestive and less *limited* than any musician I know. They are a *durum genus*, musicians. Their minds seem to be enclosed in a small park. They are without humanity, absorbed, fond of details, fond of bad jokes, desultory, apt to consider small things important.' But Parratt was the exception. He became Arthur's regular companion on Sunday walks. He would take him up to the organ gallery and play for him – or let him play himself. Sometimes he would smuggle Arthur up there, with C. H. Lloyd, if he were playing for a very private royal occasion, and let them peep down to watch. One afternoon, Arthur was up there with Lloyd and Tomlinson (a young musician just down from Oxford) to witness a private performance by a cello and organ duo before Princess Henry of Battenburg. They watched with amusement the arrival of the cellist – 'a hotfaced man in a frockcoat, very nervous'. Then the royals entered. Suddenly to their horror they saw 'a bonnet with an aigrette' bobbing up the stairs to the organ loft and a lady emerged from the dark recess. It was the Queen. Arthur was well concealed by the small choir-organ and was therefore able to watch the whole scene unobserved. 'I giggled insanely in my terror at the sight of Lloyd and Tomlinson, with fear written in every feature, bowing wildly from the waist in all directions.'

Arthur's expression of affection for Queen Victoria was entirely genuine. He was first presented to her on 24 May 1899, on the occasion of the annual Madrigal Concert by Eton boys at Windsor Castle to celebrate the Queen's birthday. He was amused at the demeanour of those waiting for the moment to be announced. 'Poor Grundy was frightfully nervous – his face saffron yellow, his knees trembling.' The Provost made a complete nonsense when his turn arrived, forgetting about the backward walk, stalking firmly off with his back to the royal presence. Just in time an equerry whispered to Arthur to turn his trousers down as he was about to be called. He made his obeisance, the Queen said a few words, and –

'what was an *entire* surprise to me – and will remain with me as long as I live – was her voice. It was so slow and sweet – some extraordinary simplicity about it. Much higher than I had imagined, and with nothing cracked or imperious or (as the imitations misled me into thinking) gobbly.' When it was over, the Queen was wheeled forward to the window, clutching a pair of opera-glasses, to listen to the singing. 'Somehow I could not get out of my head that it was like an afflicted person, at the side of an ocean steamer.'

Next month he received an invitation to a command performance of two operas (*Le Chalet* and *Pagliacci*) at the Castle, and was presented again. He felt rather less at ease. He was the only person present without an Order; and he found himself tongue-tied when the Queen began to ask him questions. 'I felt like Storey, who to everything the Queen said, not hearing a word, said "Yes, mum" – so that the Queen after said: "How funny Mr Storey is! He said 'Yes, mum' to everything I said to him."' The whole thing was like a sequence in a play, the Household 'all just the same with soft, caressing manners and low voices', and the group of those who had been presented watching the proceedings from a further door, giggling and whispering to each other with a sort of frantic relief.

In December 1899, just after the publication of his father's biography, and the Queen's acknowledgement of her presentation copy, he was invited to dine with her at Windsor Castle. He spent the whole day in a state of helpless nerves. Once admitted to the royal apartments, however, his nervousness evaporated. As he was being shown the table-plan, he heard a lady-in-waiting saying urgently to a page 'the Queen wants the address of the Commander-in-Chief in Ireland *at once*' ('I little guessed that next day we should hear of Roberts' appointment and his son's death'). Then the party was formed in a line in the corridor between the private apartments and the dining-room.

> The doors flew open – a page with shawls, fan etc – Then the Queen very much bowed, leaning on the arm of the Indian attendant, a handsome young fellow, almost as if being dragged along. Princess Henry, Princess Christian, Princess Victoria. We bowed and nodded. They went in and took places; then we flew in – the Dean had already said grace in response to the Queen's invitation. . . . The room was ugly – an awful portrait of the Queen over her head. The table ugly – arrangements and everything old-fashioned e.g. sherry glass mouth downwards in finger glass. All silver-plates, soup-plates etc., which set my teeth on edge. A long dinner with a great many things rapidly handed. Everyone ate fast, and plates were whisked away if you laid down your fork for a moment – 2 soups, 2 fish, 3 entrées, a joint, then plum-

pudding (I think) cold beef handed round – *then* quails – a vegetable – cream, savouries – ices. The dinner *not* very well cooked, and rather cold. The dessert knives, spoons, forks of pure gold. Madeira, champagne, claret etc. . . . Everyone talked very low. . . . I descanted on social disabilities of schoolmasters. No doubt it was the first time that a schoolmaster pure and simple – not a headmaster or clergyman – had ever sate at that table.

The Queen was, I was told, much depressed about the war. She talked very little, ate quick, bending over her plate – asked 'What is that?' a good many times of her neighbours. I heard her say 'Terrible, terrible!' in a tone of great feeling about something said to her.

After dinner, Arthur was presented. 'There was no one in hearing – and I had no feeling of tremor whatever. She put me at my ease in a quite remarkable way.'

'I am very much pleased to see you, Mr Benson. How is your mother? Where is she living? She tried Winchester, I think. Why did she leave that? Oh, I had hoped your sister was better – Is Miss Tait still with you? . . . So much pleased with the book – shall read it with great interest. I had a great affection for the Abp. I am to spend Xmas here. The Duke of Albany is coming. Have you heard from him? How does he like it? He enjoyed Eton. It was a pity to take him away, but quite unavoidable –' and so on (I suppress my answers) for nearly quarter-of-an-hour. All this with little reassuring nods, and every now and then the most motherly and delightful smile. She played with her rings a good deal as we talked, and shifted her foot as if in pain. Her hands looked rheumatic. . . . Then came a little silence – and then a smile and bow – 'Very much pleased to have seen you, Mr Benson!' I bowed and backed away. . . . I can't describe how or why one's devotion to her comes. She is so simple, motherly, shrewd, good. . . . Certainly I feel, without any exaggeration or hysteria, that I wd do anything in my power for her.

He felt nothing like the same respect for Edward VII. The Victorian age in the twilight of its senility and passing had lost its ardour and its idealism. Its values had become shallower; its way of life more moneyed and brash. This was the age of the millionaires, Arthur had conceded in an interesting talk with the Duchess of Bedford at Tremans early in 1903, when the world was beginning to recognise its new masters who controlled governments and dictated policies. The despots had passed away, but had given place to the new 'tyranny of wealth'. The king personified the vulgarity of the times. When the news had broken that the coronation had to be postponed, because of the King's illness in June 1902, Arthur and his colleague, H. E. Luxmoore, mused over the irony whereby 'this bourgeois, ungraceful, small-minded, gross, kindly man' had had 'the cup (which he made no pretence of not enjoying) dashed from his lips'. Luxmoore suggested that it was 'like a chapter out of the Old Testament. . . . The King has done evil in the sight of the Lord, and . . . this is a sort of grievous chastening.' Arthur expressed it more realistically: 'The Coronation was to the King, I fear, the Apotheosis of Buttons not the consecration of life to service.'

The King recovered; the great event took place in August. Arthur was there to hear the choir sing his words. It was an occasion packed with opportunities for spectatorial delight. Typically, Arthur noticed the little things – the absurd vignettes, the fumblings in the wings, the tiny dramas enacting themselves within the congregation as the gorgeous ceremony pursued its course: 'a little red-faced peer, with a coronet down over his ears, sitting and kicking a white leg on the arm of the King's Recognit. chair'; 'a delightful little page of about 8 carrying a huge coronet and enjoying himself thoroughly though he had to take a run, after looking carefully round his burden, to get up the choir steps'; the 'lightning flash' as the peeresses – to a woman – all looked at the mirrors in their fans before the moment of the 'putting-on'; the embarrassing incapacity of Archbishop Temple whose legs gave way under him like the legs of a doll, after the King and attendant bishops had had to help him up from a kneeling position during the homage. 'But the worst of all was the communion – he could not see where the King was, and went to quite the wrong place to administer and nearly put the bread on the carpet.'

It was interesting, too, to note how very quickly the atmosphere of the Court itself changed. So Arthur observed at a command performance of Barrie's *Quality Street* at Windsor Castle before the King and his royal guest, the King of Portugal ('a very common-looking young man, like a Scandinavian tenor, or a well-to-do shopman'). The Victorian atmosphere had gone completely. 'It is much more genial, considerate, *equal* – it lacks the grim and ugly stateliness of the old time; but it also lacks the dignity. When it was said that the Queen is coming – that she wd receive, courtiers ran about like frightened hens – and were horribly afraid of her, knowing she would notice everything. Now, no one could be exactly *afraid* of the King!'

Doubtless the recognition that Arthur received from Windsor was a source of gratification to him, perhaps even of pride. But the social occasions themselves were a trial. They did, however, provide an excellent vantage point for the observation of very interesting people at reasonably close quarters. After all, the essence of humour is the incongruous – people trying to act naturally and unconcernedly in unfamiliar surroundings, or – as can often be the case with royalty and royal circles – people whose claim to eminence and deference lay purely in their inheritance, exposing in public their singular lack of any other qualification for the deference shown to them. There was the Duke of Cambridge, for instance, whose conduct during a religious service could usually be relied upon to produce almost uncontrollable mirth. He would either sleep soundly or talk – both activities being exceedingly audible. As the parson was reading the lesson, so the anecdote went, he came to the phrase 'with trumpets also and shawms'. 'God bless my soul', said the Duke, 'What are *shawms*? I have often wondered.' The parson lent forward from the lectern and whispered 'musical instruments, sir'. 'Eh, what?', said the Duke, 'Do they *blow* them, do they blow them?' As the service progressed, the Duke had to listen to a sermon on the iniquity of swearing. 'Damme, a *damned* good sermon', he pronounced loudly as he came out of the church.

Images – vignettes – descriptions – absurdities: these one might glean in abundance; and, in any case, in court circles one could never be anywhere but on the periphery, the ideal point for observation. Arthur would not have wished it otherwise. The great occasions were not for him. Valuable conversations could only really be tête-à-tête, not within the artificial atmosphere of public dinners or prestigious parties. When he heard Maurice Baring boasting of his great 'flat-warming party' to which Asquith, Haldane and a host of lesser luminaries had come, Arthur commented bluntly: 'I would not myself dine out to meet the Twelve Apostles; but I should enjoy having them to myself two or three at a time, and asking them seriously how they did.' The Twelve Apostles, however, would have found the life-style of the Edwardian aristocracy very little to their taste; and one of the most fascinating incongruities of all, to Arthur's discerning and disrespectful eye, was the adaptation of the princes of the Church to the social demands of the Edwardian age.

*   *   *   *   *

He had seen it of course in his own family. How else – but through promotion in the Church – could a middle-class family like the Bensons find themselves living in a palace, with their father in the House of Lords, and mingling with the aristocracy on seemingly equal terms? 'It is an interesting record intellectually – Proctors, Bensons, Sidgwicks, Jacksons, but more intellectual than successful. We have got a middle-class taint about us. We are none of us aristocrats in any way.' It was amusing to observe how it affected different people in the same predicament. With some, like the Creightons for instance, it went to their heads. It was typical of Mrs Creighton, Arthur thought, that when they were leaving Peterborough on Mandell Creighton's appointment as Bishop of London, she should take the wife of his successor (Lady Mary Glyn) aside to beg her 'to *insist* that the clergy should call the Bishop "My Lord" and not "Bishop". "I have always done so and it seems to me due to the position." "I am afraid *we* shan't claim so secure a (social) position", said Lady Mary. Mrs C. seems to have taken it as a testimony to her own and her husband's merits.'

But the Creightons came from the same background as the Bensons. Their rise into aristocratic circles made them self-consciously arrogant towards those with whom circumstances had enabled them to rub shoulders. Mrs Creighton, Arthur noted, was essentially 'cultured lower middle-class', along with the Bensons, Sidgwicks, Herbert Spencer, Gosse, Dean Farrar (and most headmaster-bishops) – 'people whose manners are not quite up to their positions. . . . They think that socially they have nothing to learn – that they are fit for any society and not only anyone's equal but anyone's superior.' As the years passed, Arthur got to know Mrs Creighton (and Gemma, her daughter, who married Cyril Bailey) well. They frequently stayed at Tremans. He even rather liked her for all her self-conscious sense of superiority. But he could not resist analysing what lay behind it:

> She is a stupid, self-confident, self-righteous woman; but she has a strong sense of duty. She does not wish to serve or help others, but to alter them. That is why she is such a failure. She is nothing but an organiser and a member of many useless committees. But I think that if one went to her in trouble she would try to help in a blundering way. She would pour in wine without oil. She would give tuppence to the host, and say that one must oneself be responsible for the extra charges.

Basically both mother and daughter were middle-class through and through – 'not socially so much as mentally – but socially too. A tendency to talk to each other in public as though they were at home, and in rather a dowdy home.' As they left Tremans, all set to descend upon 'some sphere of radiant activity', Arthur took back a little of what he had written. 'I am sure her faults are mainly superficial. Possibly she is even humble on her knees!'

Some princes of the Church cultivated a hearty, back-slapping, man-to-man approach with their clergy and their friends as a means of disguising their inner joy at rising into the ranks of the aristocracy. In some ways this was worse because insincere. It was the tendency of those to whom promotion had come very early in life – men like Michael Furse, Cosmo Gordon Lang and Winnington-Ingram. The humility of a near-saint like Francis Paget was genuine; but Paget had never suffered under the illusion that he was accounted a 'good fellow'. Could one be quite sure, however, of the young Bishop of London, fascinating and engaging though his conversation could be? Arthur described meeting Winnington-Ingram at a dinner party given by the Provost of Eton in July 1903:

> I was amused on being introduced to the Bishop in the drawing-room to be greeted as 'my dear old friend' – and to be reminded of caustic reviews writ-ten for the P.M.G. at Dunskey, and other passages. This is, of course, rather irresistible; and it is part of his power. I watched him carefully – he looks tired and pale; but happy, like a man who thoroughly enjoys his work. He is a little balder, but he has the same odd snake-like look I used to notice in him. He looks very neat in his purple coat (I *think* he wore a purple cassock and his cross by a purple cord) and he has considerable dignity of carriage. He certainly seemed to me very simple, friendly and kindly. Not egotistical, and not in the least degree pompous or *exalté*. In fact, I think he has improved . . . by having ambition gratified and by finding himself (probably) not quite so adequate to his duties as he had expected (There are some illnesses, says Sir J. Stephen, 'that are only cured by promotion'). But I think he is a Christian and a fellow-labourer – and certainly less egotistical and self-seeking than I used to think him. His goodness shines out more and there is less art. But I am not his 'dear old friend' – I am sure he doesn't particularly like me. The only thing that seemed to me to ruffle his dignity a little was when Hargreaves [Conduct of Eton], like a good bumble-bee, came buzzing round and begged him to come and see him in Windsor, calling him 'the little Cox' (I gathered that the Bp had steered the boat at Oxford in wh. Hargreaves had rowed) at which he rather winced. It is all very well for these personages to treat other people like men and brethren – but when an old College friend who is a school chaplain comes and treats his Reverence like an m. and b. his Reverence does not feel it quite so appropriate. One wants to do the condescending oneself, to come down from the pedestal, not be pulled down.

The natural courtier was Randall Davidson; and here indeed was a primate fit for the times. Frederick Temple, like Arthur's father, had belonged to the Victorian age, and he had come to the primacy late. Neither Randall Davidson nor Arthur could find a good word to say for him as Archbishop. He had been a very fine headmaster, and there was a certain greatness in his character which compelled respect; but Randall, who was a natural administrator, deplored his inefficiency, and Arthur – who had seen the extent of an Archbishop's obligations and commitments in the relentless pressure upon his father – was indignant at the casual way in which Temple neglected his duties. 'He became idle, believing still in his industry. . . . He grew to think he could not improve. He stood, as it were, looking at himself in a mirror, and bursting into tears at the thought of how rugged, sincere and faithful he was.' It was amazing what tears could do! 'He said in public that he was nothing but a worker, and burst into tears. Everyone who heard him burst into tears too and thought how splendid he was. They did not know that he never answered letters, played patience half the day, and read schoolboy stories in bed.'

Randall Davidson's appointment to the primacy in 1903 linked the Bensons once again with Lambeth. Lucy Tait was the elder surving sister of Randall's wife, Edith. Since their marriage, the Davidsons and Bensons had met regularly; and after the move to Tremans, it became customary for Randall and 'Edie' to spend a few days holiday with them every year. The Bensons, in return, felt welcome in revisiting their old London home. When Arthur heard the news of the appointment, he saluted it in typical fashion, by writing one of those disturbingly shrewd and frank analyses of a personal friend's character which made his diary less and less a document that his closest friends might read:

> I am very glad: he is the only man I have any confidence in: I have *none* in the H[igh] C[hurch] party. Randall is *not* a great man: but he is a splendid combination of good sense, good feeling and dutifulness. He is avid of affairs, interesting, stimulating – he is not a mystic or a poet – has no idea that a dreamer of dreams is anything but a fool – and that *he* should be the chief exponent of the religion of Jesus of Nazareth is strange. Randall would have listened to Xt politely, but without interest, and then would have gone back to the Sadducees and arranged a little matter of legislation. He *is* a Sadducee, but he is just and fearless and high-minded and there is no *nonsense* about him. He is a good watchdog: and he respects emotion though he does not feel it. I wrote him a very frank and careful letter. He said talking to M.B. the other day that *if* this occurred, and that it wd be affectation to pretend it might not, he would not have the confidence of the clergy. He will not: – nor of the laity. His strength is that people should know him *personally* and then they trust him. I wonder what he feels – whether he is elated, confident, cheerful. I think he probably is. He knows he can – and will – do useful work, and his fingers itch, I expect, to be at things. I shudder to think of the ghastly load of depression under which I should labour were I in his place.

Randall Davidson was no scholar, and would frequently pick Arthur's brains – to find a suitable text for a Spital Sermon before the Lord Mayor; to draft lectures for him to a conference of schoolmasters; to write Latin addresses. In return he would freely discuss ecclesiastical appointments and listen seriously to Arthur's views. Within a month of his elevation he was obtaining Arthur's ideas about his successor at Winchester (dismissing Lang out of hand – 'it would turn his head altogether. ... It is very nearly turned now'); he accepted Arthur's suggestion that Hugh Childers should become actuary to Convocation; and followed up the suitability of F. H. Chase, President of Queens' College, Cambridge, as the successor of the aged Compton, Bishop of Ely.

On the whole their prejudices were the same, as were their ideas about social class. Discussing, as he frequently did, the extent to which he was himself moved by the snobbery which he disliked in others, Arthur conceded 'I fear I have a *little* – rather of R.D.'s type – the liking for *interesting* people: but I think that I *cd* make friends equally with an earl or a solicitor – if only either were interesting.' Actually, he was acutely class-conscious. He loathed being snubbed or being made to feel conscious of the middle-class background he prided himself on. When Mrs Grenfell ignored him at an Eton gathering because she had a cabinet minister in tow (St John Brodrick), Arthur wrote in his diary: 'I don't really care: my life lies outside the life of these swells. ... But I thought Mrs G. was of a finer kind of clay. Her behaviour today was the behaviour of a second housemaid, ingratiating herself with the butler!' But he was himself very quick to discern conduct or manners that denoted whether an associate was 'not quite a gentleman'; and prone to stand on his own dignity if he felt that his rights as a gentleman were being offended. When a group of hop-pickers invaded his first class compartment, while travelling from Victoria to Horsted Keynes, he wrote to the railway authorities to report the guard for not inspecting their tickets. He frequently upbraided his brother Fred for hob-nobbing with the titled and wealthy; and – one has to ask – were they necessarily less interesting or congenial than the titled and wealthy friends of Arthur himself?

There is, then, a touch of hypocrisy in Arthur's castigation of his class-conscious friends. 'I hate *airs*', he wrote in June 1904, after dining at Lady Burghclere's with the Lord Chancellor (Lord Selborne), Sir Arthur Godley, Lady Caernarvon and Lord Peel as guests. 'I hate a world where everyone is arranged according to due degrees of consideration, and where there is little simplicity – and the pretence of a great deal of interest in big things, without any reality. .... I will go to none of these parties.' This may explain why Arthur, at heart very much a Victorian, disliked the values of the Edwardian age. But every man reflects something of the age he lives in, however much he may express his dislike of it. And Arthur knew himself well enough to recognise that the faults one most clearly discerns in others are often enough the faults of oneself writ large.

*   *   *   *   *

It was Randall Davidson who procured for Arthur the means and the opportunity to shed the cares of Eton. The King had expressed his willingness to allow the vast collection of Queen Victoria's letters to be worked through and a discreet selection (for the period 1836 to 1861) to be published. Reginald Brett, Viscount Esher, was to supervise the work, but a suitable scholar was to be appointed to do the bulk of the selecting and editing. J. E. C. Bodley, who had edited the Coronation Book, regarded himself as the obvious choice, but he had alienated the King by allegedly sulking at the inadequate honour he had received for his earlier royal service, and other names were therefore considered. Randall Davidson was consulted and strongly recommended Arthur Benson on the strength of his reputation as a biographer and his known literary services to the Crown. In July 1903 Arthur received a telegram from Lord Esher asking him to visit him at his house. The summons was entirely unexpected. In a sort of daze, he strolled with Esher through the shady walks and elegant terraces of Orchard Lea in the afternoon sun, as the proposition was unfolded. Not for a moment did Arthur hesitate about accepting.

> Here am I crushed with work at Eton, hardly strong enough to wriggle out, and yet with no motive to go at any particular minute. Suddenly in the middle of all my discontent and irritability a door is silently and swiftly opened to me. In the middle of this quiet sunny garden, full of sweet scents and roses, I am suddenly offered the task of writing or editing one of the most interesting books of the day, of the Century. I have waited long for some indication – and was there ever a clearer leading?

He wrote his letter of acceptance that night; also a letter of resignation to Warre. It gave him profound satisfaction. Earlier that evening he had witnessed Warre at his very worst, presiding over a special committee to consider fire precautions following the disaster at Kindersley's:

115

Warre began by reading the report aloud; a cat which had been sleeping in a chair sate up when he began, looked at him with horror, and then slunk to the ground and after trying to get out in vain, wailed deplorably. When order was restored Warre made one of the most confused speeches I have ever heard: he said he would renumber the points for consideration – and he then referred to them either by their original number, or by the new numbers or by both. We then considered point by point, Allcock talking desperately all through. At each point Warre said that it must be carried out, and we gave conclusive reasons why it *could not* be carried out in the interests of discipline. . . . So that each time that Warre made a command, we carried the opposite. When we had done a little of this, Warre as a counterstroke told the Bursar to add to each of our resolutions that he, the Head, approved of the original suggestion, and that any master who failed to carry it out did so at his own risk.

We hardly got through any of the report; and then broke up. Warre's demeanour and speeches throughout were simply childish – those of an old, nervous, rather silly and timid man by an alehouse fire. It was a really dreadful exhibition. . . . Whatever happens, either way, he wants to be in a position of saying 'I told you so'. . . . In fact for a lack of commonsense, good feeling, statesmanship and leadership I never heard it equalled.

To escape from all this! 'No Bishop ever believed himself more truly called', he felt as he read the announcement of his appointment in *The Times*, noting with satisfaction that in one newspaper he was described as 'a great personal favourite of Queen Victoria'. He was invited to the Castle to meet Lord Knollys and to discuss arrangements – a memorable visit, if only because it provided Arthur with his first sight of a telephone being used ('it is *very* funny to hear this done'). He also had to discuss the implications of his resignation with Warre who had written him 'a gloomy note of acquiescence'. During this talk 'all my scruples vanished. He was *very* kind – but once sure that I wd not reconsider my position, he washed me off the block with the utmost readiness. I was no longer Eton, and being no longer useful to Eton or to him, I was no longer in the least degree interesting, except as an old friend to whom it would not be decent not to show a certain tenderness and kindliness.' Warre then spoke at length of why it was imperative for Eton that he should remain as Head Master for some time yet, there being no possible successor that he could envisage. 'With which watery harangue he washed the last shreds of compunction out of my mind.'

He had looked forward to the day of his going for some time; and he had already decided where his base should be. In October 1902, on a visit to Cambridge, he had looked over the Old Granary in Silver Street, owned by George Darwin and adjoining the Old Mill House where Darwin and his family lived; a most remarkable residence 'with the garden on a kind of archipelago of islands, connected by bridges'. The nearness to the river attracted Arthur; and although the rooms were small, its charm lay in its quiet and detachment from other buildings either in front or behind. Cambridge seemed to offer him all that he craved for at that moment. He had many friends there – Aunt Nora at Newnham, Monty James, Walter Durnford and Marcus Dimsdale at King's; and there would be young men who held out the promise of friendship, with whom one might be able to relax without the inhibition of being *in loco parentis*. 'I should like to make some younger friends', he wrote in January 1903, 'in a way which is impossible with boys when one is in authority over them. But one schemes and schemes.'

Shortly after accepting the royal invitation, and with only one Half to go at Eton before his release, he spent a few days at Cambridge in August with Walter Durnford as his host. Memory can be very kind. The sadnesses of his undergraduate days nagged him no more; he recalled the golden moments, sublime walks, old friendships. He revisited Linton, taking tea at a farmhouse 'with the Granta flowing in loops and deep pools full of water plants. . . . Linton, how well I remember it, in the half-sad, half-ardent Cambridge days.' Surviving figures of the past had aged somewhat, he thought, as he noted Sir Richard Jebb passing him in Silver Street, looking like 'a dissipated hairdresser . . . very much bowed, with tremulous leg on a tricycle'; but the undergraduates seemed – on the whole – a pleasanter lot than he recalled of his contemporaries. He attended a smoking-concert after dinner at King's – the men coming out into New Court carrying chairs and smoking pipes 'under the great elms, with the moon rising'. They 'seemed to me to be quieter, wiser, more sensible than we were'. And there was one undergraduate whom he had met after dinner on the previous night who had stirred old feelings. This was Oliffe Richmond, a bright and talkative classicist, who had made Arthur conscious of the sweet melancholy of middle-age. 'I felt some of the old glow at making friends with a congenial and ingenuous creature, with all the charm of clever, self-conscious youth.' Travelling back through London, he blessed his good fortune – to be free from Eton, to return to Cambridge, to have a stake in the literary world and yet to avoid the metropolis, its bustling, self-seeking and scalp-hunting centre.

Earlier that month he had had a very satisfactory meeting with John Murray. He had been treated as a celebrity; swept into the inner sanctum while Mr Justice Kekewich was kept waiting outside. The ledgers were brought down so that he could inspect Theodore Martin's profits from his life of the Prince Consort. He was assured that the Queen's letters should produce royalties well in excess of £5000. He had already received the distinction of being selected by 'Spy' (Leslie Ward) for one of his *Vanity Fair* caricatures. 'He mostly used vermilion and prussian blue. I must be depicted like a turkey-cock', Arthur mused. In the same mood of excitement and anticipation, he returned to Cambridge in September to join a shooting party with the Donaldsons at Linton. Although the Old Granary was as yet sparsely furnished, he entertained the Donaldsons and the Dimsdales there for dinner, exulting in the view over Coe Fen. He spent a hilarious evening with Monty James, laughing over old memories and discovering a romantic element in Monty which he had never before realised. 'I was touched by his getting out an envelope containing a large bundle of my old letters to him.' He made expeditions to two places which became peculiarly dear to him in later years: by train to Hitchin, and then a cycle ride through Baldock to locate the springs of the Cam – cold streams gushing out of the chalk; and then, on another day, to St Mildred's Well near Exning on the site of the palace of the old Saxon kings. 'I never saw or dreamed of a sweeter place; there among the elder thickets, by day and night, the springs wink and bubble, and the water races away in the stream, ever since the days of Etheldreda.' All these were soon to be near at hand. 'How much life has developed in the way I had hoped', he wrote, adding rather ominously 'Of that which a man desires in his youth, he shall have enough in his age – says Goethe.'

Still, there was one more Half to face at Eton. As he returned he thought of his feelings as he arrived there as a new master. He was still using the same mark-book, so that his whole career there seemed spread out 'as in a map'. Of course he had mixed feelings as the days passed. Eton had sunk deeper into his affections than he sometimes cared to acknowledge. Earlier that year he had expressed the dilemma exquisitely as he described his feelings on returning one evening to his boarding-house after teaching in school: 'When I came back . . . my house stood up so square and big against the sunset, the glazed bricks in the front lit up mysteriously – lights in windows and cheerful voices. How one ought to love it all! . . . How well I know all the fields round here – every little field-path, every tiny streamlet, pool, tree, house, ditch! How I shall think of them someday and believe I was so happy. . . . But now my whole mind is bent on flight, and I sit like a caged bird.' This was a recurrent reflection.

'It is a wonderful place to have spent so much of one's life in. But I desire to be gone, not ungratefully; and I shall not fail to pray for the peace of Jerusalem; and I shall not forget her, though I be myself forgotten.'

Congratulations and regrets at his departure poured in from all sides. He reckoned that he was answering letters at the rate of fourteen a day. Speculation mounted as to his successor. De Havilland dearly wanted the house, and was enraged when the choice fell on A. M. Goodhart, Master in College. Arthur was profoundly relieved because it meant that his boys could stay where they were. There were inevitable sadnesses to face – the distress of parting from his House Captain, E. H. Ryle, and of passing to another the decisions as to the fortunes of his boys; the realisation of the affection felt for him by Mrs Cox; and the difficulty in discriminating between his servants – those whom he should discharge and those who would accompany him to Cambridge. He needed a husband-and-wife team to look after the Old Granary, and he engaged a Mr and Mrs Hunting, who had been in service with a Wellington housemaster. He kept on his housemaid, Sharp. The other servants were liberally rewarded by gifts of £1 apiece for every year they had been in his service – an outlay of £45 in all.

This was a fair sum at a time when Arthur was conscious of his need to retrench. He actually travelled second class for the space of a few weeks while he worried over his financial position once he had lost his Eton salary. He was therefore deeply offended by the niggardliness of the Eton Governing Body in granting him a minimum pension of £100 p.a., when he had allowed himself to expect up to double that sum. 'My *exact* due, no more', he fulminated in his diary; it demonstrated 'the *sickening insincerity* with which compliments about one's work and the value of one's work are framed. ... So here goes another master from Eton snubbed and humiliated, after having done his best for the school, by a G.B. whose policy is to raise rents, sweat the masters, spend thousands on unnecessary buildings.' At first he showed his chagrin by refusing the invitation to his last Founder's Day Dinner. He relented in the end, much as he disliked gatherings of this sort: being herded into Hall 'like driven pigs'; the fatuous speeches; the racket of the assembled company in Election Hall afterwards, tongues loosened by drink, making 'a row like ten thousand poultry yards', so that one had to pause to wonder at the absurdity of the amusements which the human race created for itself.

His last Founder's Day made him no more enamoured of Eton in festive mood. The guests provided some amusement – Montagu Butler,

Master of Trinity, looking 'like the Almighty in Blake's design for Job'; an 'absurd, rather shy, youth, of about 18, with red hair, who turned out to be the great Professor [J.B.] Bury', and Oscar Browning, 'very heavy, rather blear-eyed, and fearfully tubby'. In Election Hall, 'O.B. drifted slowly up, like a porpoise and talked dreamily about himself and how bored he was in the evenings – and (a wicked lie) how he played piano duets with a great pianist now at Cambridge. O.B. is an execrable performer, who bangs a few notes of a piece and those wrong. Yet the man has genius somehow about him; and a warm heart, though overlaid with egoism.' Actually Arthur missed the whole point of his attendance. At the close of dinner he slipped out to do his normal nocturnal round of the house, and discovered on his return that, in his absence, the Provost had delivered his leaving panegyric.

The leave-taking itself was painful. He had tried to avoid Warre, but got caught by him while talking with Cornish. Arthur cut the conversation short deliberately and was then suffused with guilt. 'He turned away looking old and kind, and somehow pathetic, so that my heart rather went out to him; but I persisted stupidly and went on; and I think I shall be sorry all my life.' Two of his servants broke down in saying good-bye, Bradley telling him to remember 'that I am your servant as long as you live, and ready to come to you and do anything at any time'. He gave presents to each of his boys and tried to be cheerful, because boys have such 'a great dislike of all emotional scenes'. He had a walk with Ainger to have a last look at the trains passing and to see 'the Dutchman thunder under a bridge'. He received a tremendous ovation at the Concert when his own leaving song was sung, and the audience called for 'author!' The sight of his house on the last night, luggage packed, and his own effects stacked in the hall, made him catch his breath. 'The old life all breaking up and going. Well, it has been a happy time – happier and happier in many ways. And most of all I thank God for giving a very timid, feeble and weak-minded person the chance of doing a little useful work. But I won't repent or look back: I made a deliberate choice; and I think God meant me to make it. But, alas!, for the good hours that have come to an end, and can never be again.'

The boys departed. The furniture vans arrived the following morning, while Arthur breakfasted in the bathroom. He had lunch with Goodhart. When he returned, he realised that the house was actually no longer his. Life would go on there; the boys would tumble back – but he not there to see them. He decided to leave at once. 'I did find myself in darkness and sorrow then. The light was very low: a dark foggy day, but driving over Fifteen Arch bridge I looked back and saw College and Chapel: and the elms and the pool, and College field; as I remember glancing back at them in 1881, when I left Eton, as I supposed, for ever.'

It was left to Hugh Macnaghten to publish Arthur's Eton epitaph; and he did so exquisitely in a sonnet published in the *Spectator* (5 December 1903). He recalled the housemaster who held his younger boys spellbound on Sunday evenings by the tales of medieval mystery and romance; who preferred to run his house on trust rather than severity of punishment; who took a stand among his colleagues for a liberalising of the Eton system, notably in challenging the traditional domination of the classics; and who – for all his quickness to take offence and his propensity to grumble or to fume at the soul-destroying drudgery of a boarding-school routine – valued most highly the qualities of kindliness, good-humour and friendship: the friendship that cuts across the generations and achieves the union of youth and age.

ARTHUR CHRISTOPHER BENSON
ETONA DISCEDENTI

FRIEND, 'he shall reign who wonders', is it so?
Then you have made us kings, who thrilled to hear
Your golden legends, as you brought so near
The shadowy past, and left our hearts aglow.
And all, to whom you gave the wish to know
Realms undivined, because you held them dear,
Quickened to love and trust and persevere,
Would thank you once today before you go.
And yet because your every thought was kind,
And you, alike to youth and age allied,
Believed the good, to which our eyes were blind,
Inspired the peace our petty lives belied,
Friend, of the liberal and loving mind,
Tis only we that pass, but you abide.

Chapter Four

'AND I NOT THERE'

> When one thinks of death one *resents* so the idea of life and the world going on, *and I not there*. Why is it that one doesn't resent the sense of the past enacting itself before one came into being? (June 1904)

> Watching two poor lady-birds, who are perambulating the window, one inside one outside, stopping to make signals, and bewildered that they can't touch the little body that is so close, just beneath their feet. That is a parable. (August 1904)

The very day that he left Eton Arthur felt uplifted by the sense of release. He was now a free-lance; nobody's servant; no obligations; no ties. He could not begin work on the Queen's letters until February at least. He could savour his freedom without counting the days until the start of a new Half. He celebrated that night (spent at Lucy Tait's pied-à-terre in Barton St) by dining with Gosse at the National Club. Although he eschewed the exercise of tuft-hunting, he had to admit that he rather enjoyed being accepted so readily by the eminent group whom Gosse had drawn together. H. G. Wells was there – 'full of nerves without and within', and obsessed by class-consciousness in harping on his humble background (his father was a cricket pro) and in revealing his ignorance of public schools; but the most conspicuous guests were H. H. Asquith and Lord Haldane. Arthur watched them with interest. 'Looking at and listening to these two men I felt I partly saw what success in England was. It is *health* mainly. Asquith is simply a very healthy machine, with a firm intelligent brain. He ate, drank and smoked deep – five or six cigars – much champagne, port and a liqueur. His clean, pink, smooth face, with no hollows to the eyes and no touch of sweat, was that of a man in *prime* condition. Haldane, a big white pig-like face; not quite so *healthy*, but massively strong – but Haldane had great humour and something more – a sort of tenderness, I felt. Asquith had neither.'

After dinner, Arthur had a long talk with Asquith in the billiard room. They discoursed on music, and then passed to a discussion of the Church and the lack of really strong men on the bench of bishops. They both admired Randall Davidson, but – as Asquith put it – 'in any other profession he would not be a *first-rate* man – but a very good one'. He compared him to Arthur's father. 'People might discuss your father as they liked ... but no one ever doubted he was a *great man*.' Winnington Ingram? – 'a dear little fellow – but in a great place!', Asquith commented, recalling that the best that Creighton could find to say about his successor in the see was 'He is a very good *dancer*'. He had made a fearful fiasco of his sermon before the Judges at St Paul's, sobbing out stories about the East End, when he might have taken the opportunity to discourse on the *Republic* of Plato. The star of the evening, Arthur conceded, was Gosse, who was perfectly at ease in such company, with a fund of anecdote. He recalled Herbert Spencer's remark to a young man whom he had challenged to billiards and who had opened with a break of eighty: 'Young man, the game of billiards, played with moderate and temperate skill, is an adornment to life; played as you play it, it is evidence of a mis-spent youth.'

On the following day, he made his number at the Athenaeum, to which he had just been elected, reflecting on the conversation of the night before. 'I did not feel awkward or distrait with these people, or uncomfortably conscious of inequality – tho' I felt a little rusty.' More satisfactory still, these leading men 'made me, so to speak, one with themselves'. He decided that he would use the Athenaeum for his London base – 'but where my money is to come from I don't know – I am £2000 overdrawn!!!'

So to Cambridge to superintend the move into the Old Granary. Percy Lubbock was already there to help him, and Mrs Cox had preceded him to ensure that everything was to his liking. Arthur, in gratitude for their long association at Eton, gave her a leaving present of £100. These, too, were golden days. There was a large Eton gathering at King's (as always at that time of year). They played charades in Monty James' set (with Monty stealing the show by a ludicrous imaginary dialogue through the window on the theme 'Where did you get that hat?'), followed by games of grab. The next evening he and Monty James both read ghost stories which they had composed, before going off to dinner with the Provost of King's. This proved a bore. 'The great cold ugly rooms were full of Austen Leighs young and old, all cautious, prosperous, prudent, trivial.' Edward Austen Leigh tried to persuade Arthur not to lodge with Ainger at Mustians, while he was working at Windsor Castle, but to come to stay with him. Not a good idea, Arthur thought; the Lower Master was too like his brother, Augustus, the Provost of King's, who certainly failed to impress him favourably that night. 'The Provost, with his swollen finger feeling his head, shrieking with laughter, the slave of a fat poodle, was really rather a depressing figure: not fit for a great place. He is a worthy, friendly man – but I do crave for a little profundity, distinction or bigness somewhere.'

There followed a particularly happy Christmas at Tremans. Lionel Ford, now Headmaster of Repton, joined the family party; a bit too absorbed in his responsibilities, Arthur thought, but excellent company. He was busy initiating liberal reforms and having trouble with his staff ('It must be terrible work conciliating those grumpy, ill-paid, rather feeble and discontented men'). Within a fortnight of his stay, the news broke of his engagement to May Talbot – yet another link with the Lyttelton circle – and Arthur was put out to receive the background story from Prothero at the Athenaeum. Hugh was away, studying for the priesthood in Rome; Fred was there, fretting to be back with his moneyed friends in London and irritating the household by loud, coarse strumming on the piano; but otherwise the atmosphere was relaxed and congenial. Arthur had several walks on sublime December days, noting delicious vignettes – 'the sheep in a frosty meadow, cropping the cold grass, with a dark copse behind them. ... How I love the kindly, quiet, tranquil earth – and the pomp of sunset and the green skies of evening'; the view from Wych Cross, the 'rosy light of evening everywhere as I went up its bare heathery shoulders – and the valley spread peacefully below me: it is one of the most beautiful views in England'. As he descended, the sunset took his breath away – 'the sun going stilly down into a great misty, frosty silence; all flushed with gold. Lights peeping from the plain; and the shadowy ridges lying one behind another out to the shadowy downs. Again the unutterable peace and beauty baffled me.'

So he reverenced the Sussex countryside on the last day of 1903 – a wholly memorable year for him. 'I have at last cut adrift from a slavery which was becoming intolerable: but I have also given up a fine work, work which I could do in my own way, a band of old comrades, boys whom I love, a large income and a place in the world. I don't know how I shall do in my new work: but it was given me to do, if ever work was given to anyone in this world – and with it comes a curious courage which is not characteristic of me. Well, God be praised for such happiness and activity.'

His new freedom was to give him more opportunity to stay at Tremans and to draw nearer to the family. Mary Benson, Maggie and Lucy Tait (and Beth, of course) had thoroughly settled there. Fred came but rarely. Hugh, who had spent a while in the Community of the Resurrection at Mirfield, had decided to put himself under instruction for the Roman Catholic Church in July of that year. It did not come as a surprise. Mary Benson took it calmly. Arthur was less indulgent. 'Philosophically I don't dislike the step', he wrote in his diary. 'Practically I dislike it very much indeed. I hate, too, the thought of my father's son doing this. . . . The idea of the old cords snapping, all the old tender associations cut adrift . . . are nothing to him by the side of satisfying his childish whim. He was always like that. Nothing would serve but to obey the impulse of the moment – and yet in his own mind I have little doubt that he thinks that his idleness at Eton and at coaching and his consequent abandonment of the Civil Service – and then his taking Orders and following since every whim of his own mind – that all these are the tender leading of the Hand of God. . . . Well, perhaps they are!'

When Hugh returned from San Silvestro in June 1904, he seemed little changed – 'as natural and cheerful as ever'; indeed, less contentious (for a while), and absence had made all hearts grow fonder. Arthur was amused to note that Hugh had not learnt industrious ways at any rate. He knew not a word of the language after eight months in Italy. He was full of stories about Rome – the ignorance of the clergy, the endless audiences one had to have with Cardinals, the experience of meeting the Pope and exchanging skull caps. On the second evening after Hugh's return, the two brothers went out together before retiring to bed in order to search for Roddy, the collie dog they had recently acquired. Arthur went ahead and looked back to see what Hugh was about. It struck him – perhaps for the first time – what eight months away had wrought. There he was 'in cassock and tippet, with skull cap, bending forwards by the old doorway, with the creepers, candle high upraised'. What would his father have thought?

They saw a lot of each other at Tremans that summer. Arthur's searching and critical eye observed some characteristic quirks, especially Hugh's delight in his distinctive dress – 'a sort of gown and tippet all in one', and the biretta which he wore throughout the day ('I rather like it; but I think I should like it more if I did not feel that *he* rather liked it too'); the curious independent life he seemed to lead, with no apparent cure of souls. He was for ever searching out his little server (the son of a humble neighbour) and going off for walks with him, armed with sandwiches. He would glow over the most trivial things – 'a monsignor's dress with purple buttons, a Papal procession – things which seem to me pretty toys'. The old argumentative side was still very much in evidence too. On a walk to Scaynes Hill, they discussed superstition and credulity, and discovered the vast difference between them. Hugh was easily satisfied on the scantiest evidence because he wanted to be; Arthur demanded an abundance of proof because he preferred not to believe. Hugh was a disciple of authority, approving 'in a general way' of the Inquisition; Arthur was the upholder of liberty, saluting the French Revolution. They agreed on one point. As Hugh put it: 'What one knew compared to what was hidden was only like the faintest crescent to the whole new moon.' But then, as Arthur added, 'Of course, *I* believe that too; only I think the Romanists describe and define a good deal more of the crescent than they can see.'

Tremans had turned out to be the anchorage which Arthur had so much needed. In the summer of 1904 he took stock of the customary and comfortable routine. His room was too small for his liking, and sometimes his mother and Lucy, who shared a large double bed in the room adjoining, would disturb him by their talk and devotions. When Hugh was there he would celebrate Mass in the little oratory (again, an adjoining room), which he had appropriated – much to Arthur's indignation – for his own private use. The first sound, in the morning, would be the tinkling of the sacring bell and then the mumbling of Hugh with incoherent interjections from his little server. Tea was brought to the bedroom at 8 a.m. Arthur would then read for an hour in bed, invariably avoiding family morning-prayers, but noting the distant strains of the organ. He came down to breakfast at 9.45. The papers came at 11, and the post about noon. In the summer, Maggie would go to her 'shelter' in the garden; Mary Benson would go to her room to deal with the day's business. Beth would be conducting a vague superintendence, sorting out the linen, but spending – in later years – most of the time in her room. Lunch was at 1.30.

The afternoon was for walking or cycling, as far as Arthur was concerned, whatever the weather. The Sussex countryside was a joy to him – 'the quiet exploring of green, embowered lanes, old farm-houses, open heaths, shady woodlands'. The walk through the woods to the Paxhill Road, returning across the water-meadows was – he adjudged – 'one of the most beautiful rustic walks in England'. On other days he would make for Heron's Ghyll (where Coventry Patmore lived), or Wych

Cross, or Scaynes Hill. He would cycle to Ashdown or the countryside around Ardingly, with superb views in all directions. Occasionally he would take a train to Lewes or to Hassocks to walk the downs over Mount Harry and Ditchling Beacon. All his expeditions were timed to bring him back to Tremans for tea at 5 p.m. Sometimes visitors would have arrived, who would hold Arthur up, encroaching upon his sacrosanct two and a half hours between tea and dinner when he did his writing. The worst offenders were the McDowalls. His cousin Kitty McDowall was a compulsive talker, 'so intensely interested in the right kind of things, so anxious to please, so officious, so affectionate and grateful – and spoiling it all by thinking not of the thing, but of the effect she produces'. Her father – 'Uncle Andrew' McDowall – was even worse: 'a terrible old man, and a bore of penetrating horror'. Both were at their worst if Arundell Esdaile (Kitty's fiancé – they married in 1907) was also present. Uncle Andrew made no secret of his disapproval of his future son-in-law, and Kitty did her best to magnify him in everybody's eyes, while the poor Arundell who, since publishing a volume of poems, had taken to growing 'his hair in long and tangled elf-locks', looked on 'like a very battered edition of Oscar Wilde'.

This was ungenerous, but then – as for the rest of his life – Arthur found it difficult to forgive anyone who disturbed his routine, especially the time set aside for writing. At 7.30 the warning gong for dinner in half-an-hour's time would sound. Arthur left his changing until 7.55 and would join the company on the stroke of eight. He would smoke after dinner; read or join in whatever the others were minded to do until evening prayers or compline. This ritual was a great trial for Arthur. He hated kneeling upright on the floor; he felt foolish singing hymns in a domestic setting (hymns 'bearing the same relation to poetry and music that onions and toasted cheese do to claret and peaches'); and he regarded compline as 'the one perfect symbol of *all* that is unreal and fantastic in religion'. When this was over, he retired to smoke again and thence to bed.

The talk, of an evening, was 'remarkably good – very brisk, humorous, fanciful; and even serious. Arguments are sustained with force and ingenuity. ... It might appear forced and smart, like the crackling of thorns. But perhaps it is saved from that by a vein of poetry. Lucy talks less than we do: but argues with greater tenacity; and her laugh is delightful.' Maggie could be – by contrast – somewhat sedate, picturesque in her use of words, poetical by temperament, and perhaps the least prejudiced in her sentiments. Mary Benson, however, was the finest talker of them all – 'really brilliant: so fanciful, humorous, suggestive, incisive; and her power of transition so great'. Fred was always vivacious and full of stories when he arrived, but rapidly became bored, letting the others argue vigorously over his head, wearing 'a dark, crucified kind of expression' on his face. Hugh veered between perverse and unreasoning argumentativeness and bubbling good humour. He and Arthur had always laughed at the same sort of things: an absurd proposal in the House of Commons to ban the use of the word 'Mass', so that Christmas would have to be called 'Christ-tide', a notion rendered the more ludicrous by the fact that its proposer's name was Thomas Massey, who would therefore have to change his name to 'Totide Tidy'. They both dissolved into tears at a story which Hugh brought back from London in April 1905: how Maurice Baring, Margot Asquith and some other society darling had taken a box, for a joke, at the Albert Hall to watch the great Torrey-Alexander Mission. They soon, in fact, began to get bored and started to chatter amongst themselves, which was – admittedly – bad manners. Torrey, on the platform, detected them and stopped a hymn in mid course. 'There are two ladies and a gentleman who are talking together in a box', he thundered, 'Now they must come to the front and sing the next verse alone.' 'Maurice Baring fell to the ground and lay there – but Margot Asquith and the other came cheerfully forward and, in the silence, accompanied by a vast organ sang the next verse in tones like the squeaks of mice or rats to the Great Hall.'

After dinner, if they had talked long enough, they might play games. One of Hugh's favourites was a sort of 'Consequences' called 'Heads, Bodies and Legs', making grotesque figures out of cards; or an acting game, when the others had to guess pairs of improbable characters – Mary Cholmondeley and Randall Davidson, Queen Victoria and Cleopatra – but, as with many families, their minds worked so much in sympathy that they would always guess the solution too quickly. Since they were all of them compulsive writers, they would sometimes compose extracts of autobiography and then read them aloud. One particular occasion, some years later, has been immortalised by Fred: when each of the three brothers amused themselves by writing a parody of one of the other's stories. 'Like three Cains each preparing to murder an Abel', they set to. Arthur began. 'He had been studying *The Light Invisible* by Hugh, and he had laughed so much himself as he read the impression it had made on him, that his eyes streamed and he had to wipe his spectacles. . . .

My mother, by this time was laughing helplessly and hopelessly, with her face all screwed up, but Hugh sat, leaning forward, so as not to miss a word, puzzled and inquiring, and politely smiling.'

Fred's turn came next.

> I had skimmed through several of Arthur's books and presented the musings of a wise, patient wistful middle-aged gentleman called Geoffrey, who sate by his mullioned window and looked out on the gracious flowing meadow below, where a stream ran between banks of feathery grass and willow-herb and loosestrife. ... Once again my mother was helplessly giggling, but, as I read, I became aware of a draught or a frost or something inclement in the room, and looking up, I saw a pained expression on Arthur's face. ... 'Now for Fred', said Hugh, and then it was my turn to know what a brother thought of me. Hugh's composition seemed to me to miss its mark. Those babbling puppets with their inane inconsequent talk had no individuality; there was nothing in them. Really this composition made no impression on me; I could not see the point of it. ... But here was my mother for the third time wiping tears of joy from her eyes, and Arthur and, of course, the author were much amused. 'Oh, you clever people!', said my mother. 'Why don't you all for the future write each other's books instead of your own? You do them much better. Give me all those stories. I shall read them when I feel depressed!'

There were often visitors to Tremans. Most of Arthur's friends spent holidays with him there from time to time. Of their near neighbours, James Bryce, who lived at Hindleap, came over frequently to talk politics and education, especially when Arthur was there: 'a small man, with lined healthy face, ragged white hair; roughly dressed ... a very downright free-trader. It is odd that he is not popular in the House, as he is a very simple and courteous man, with no idea of his importance.' On one occasion he brought the great A. V. Dicey with him, and again Arthur was struck by the humility of the scholar in a totally assured position, noting too his complete disregard for sartorial impressions, his clothes grotesquely ill-fitting and 'his waistcoat riding up behind higher than his coat'. The night before, in a half-waking state, an absurd limerick about the day's guests had come into his mind, 'which then seemed to me an *extraordinarily* funny and satirical rhyme. Now it only seems rude:

> There was a Professor called Dicey
> Whose manner was trenchant and icy:
> He came with James Bryce
> Who was almost too nice:
> O that Dicey were nice, and Bryce icy.

The neighbour who fascinated Arthur most was the celebrated, and enormously prosperous, ecclesiastical artist and designer, C. E. Kempe, who lived at Old Place, Lindfield. They shared, of course, a passionate interest in cathedrals, churches and liturgical science. But their views were poles apart. Arthur liked his company but disapproved of everything that Kempe did – his flaunting of his wealth and style of living; his dogmatism on matters artistic; above all, his own tasteless stained-glass windows which were so much the vogue at the turn of the century that one could scarcely find a church on which he had not left his trademark. His windows were like the man – not only quite literally, because his own face appeared in all his characters, but they fascinated by their very vulgarity.

> We do *not* want unadulterated Kempe everywhere [Arthur wrote in August 1903]. We don't want Mr Kempe as St Peter, only bleached like celery, without the wholesome oranges and purples of Mr K's face – talking to Mr Kempe as St Andrew – with two Mr Kempes walking in the distance; and Mary Magdalene (as Mr Kempe shaved and feminised) falling to the ground under a weight of Turkey carpets. We want strong ugly faces in glass, like the Fairford windows – even like Peckett's grim, smoke-stained saints, scowling and pink.

Seeking out Kempe glass became almost a recreation for Arthur on his travels. There he was at Evesham ('rabbit-faced people in carpets, and angels with ragged wings'); and again at York, and at Bridport, and at Winchester ('with everyone in the window like him in feature, as usual – even Queen Victoria!'). But for all this, Kempe was a man of consequence; to be seen to be believed; and a visit to Old Place to meet him became as much a part of the itinerary for a guest at Tremans as the view from Wych Cross. 'I *do* like Mr Kempe', Arthur wrote in September 1904. 'I have a *warm* regard for him, almost an affection. I don't agree with him on any point. But I like that he should be there, going about so solemnly in his rich house, and making such a minuet out of life. Let him dance on!'

Three or four times within the year, sometimes for several weeks on end, Arthur returned to Tremans. Its predictable routine was a real relaxation. There were the servants who welcomed you back – Rymans, the gardener; Marshall, the coachman; the excitable Roddy, surely the most timid dog that ever ventured out of his own domain. The most innocuous object – a milk-churn, a tiny kitten – was a potential lion to Roddy, and in his terror he would put 'his tail so much between his legs that it came out under his chin', and he would then go 'trundling along, like a hare, with a round back'. Arthur recalled his adventures in a delightful essay, published in *Along the Road*:

> There was a cottage gate close by, where he once, when walking with me, put his head in, and was greeted with a bark let off straight in his face, like a peal of thunder, from a chained retriever, just round the palings. He came up to me, pale under his coat and shuddering, with a look of horror at a world where such terrors could be. There was even a farmyard from which he had fled in hot haste, pursued by an elderly hen.

On every visit one could count on two little ceremonies performed by Beth. She would choose her moment to come to your room to have a quiet tête-à-tête, talking of old times. The little tap on the door was the sign that the moment had come. Then she would insist on doing the packing when the time came to leave; and when the baggage had been taken down, and you walked out to Marshall, waiting at the gate, she would be at her window, waving a handkerchief until you were out of sight. 'What a *wonderful* thing it is this absolute devotion to a family without any tie of blood', Arthur wrote after leaving Tremans in late September 1903. 'Beth is nearer to me than almost anyone in the world, I think. Her whole life from morning to night is spent in doing some kind of work and looking after someone. . . . I think her life one of the most beautiful things I know.'

Arthur sometimes grumbled at the expense of the upkeep of Tremans. He contributed his share each year; but the cost of the whole household, with the rent, amounted in 1907, he reckoned, to £2000 a year. But how much should one pay for peace of mind? For a person of Arthur's tastes it fulfilled all he could ever have asked – above all 'its perpetual feast of little simple, ancient, homely beauties: always waiting at every turn; never flaunted. The quiet, the twitter of birds, the rustle of trees, the green hills and woods in all directions: make it the very sweetest home imaginable.'

*   *   *   *   *

On 16 January 1904, Arthur returned to the Old Granary with the prospect of a whole month at Cambridge before starting work at Windsor. How would he find Cambridge as a resident, as opposed to being somebody else's guest? What would Cambridge make of him? The Provost of King's arranged a special dinner-party for him so that he could meet various Cambridge worthies – Montagu Butler (whom he knew already), Adolphus Ward (Master of Peterhouse), E. S. Shuckburgh

(Librarian of Emmanuel) and A. E. Shipley, Fellow of Christ's, who allegedly 'runs the University'. Arthur Mason, now Master of Pembroke, invited him to dine with just his wife and himself so that they could reminisce freely about Truro days. Arthur recognised at once 'the old laugh, the old smile', but felt a little disappointed in observing that 'the old radiance and grace seem to have hardened on to a little knobby core, and not to be the outflow, as I used to think, of a beautiful soul'. A dinner-party, given by Sir Richard and Lady Jebb, was hardly calculated to raise Arthur's spirits, for he found himself in the midst of the militant defenders of compulsory Greek. Even Monty James showed himself to be a 'horrible Tory' on the issue, and he sensed war clouds on the horizon. Nor was he impressed by his first encounter with Professor Bevan, who was one of the company – 'a man like a polite, rather timid, hen, or some other kind of seed-eating bird. Excessively polite, with a gentle cackle. A distinctly absurd man.'

Arthur welcomed these attentions. They were, however, opening courtesies. It was up to him to gain acceptance; and these alone could not fill the void. Eton had given him young companionship, and where was he to find this? There was a promising pair of Etonian classicists at King's, still undergraduates – Stephen Gaselee ('fond of ancient things and things ecclesiastical and ... rather a viveur') and Oliffe Richmond, who had aroused his interest on an earlier visit. They seemed to sense his need and invited him to their rooms. On the first occasion, Arthur felt strangely nervous, so anxious was he to be accepted. On the whole the evening passed well. 'I really did not feel older than they: they heard my stories with respect and some show of amusement.' He took to calling on Richmond after dining at King's (he had been granted dining-rights), just as he would pay nocturnal calls on boys in his house, not knowing whether his interest was really appreciated. Could they genuinely welcome such intrusions from 'an elderly and tiresome man'? 'It *is* so hard to realise that one is not the same age as these young sparks. ... One never thought in the old days that Dons wanted to *please* one: and yet God knows how tremulously I try to interest these young Apollos.'

There was much to savour and to enjoy: the tranquillity of the Old Granary, for instance; the joy of the weir close by – 'the rush of the green water in the sluice, the dancing of white waves in the pool, and the spray flying like smoke in the dark gate'; watching two thrushes hopping morning by morning on the two great mill stones set in the ground across the stream. But then a touch of melancholy would take possession. 'The good hours pass on – "it passes, it passes" as Fitz said.' There were the walks, sometimes to places he had never visited before or to Colleges he had never before had time to explore. Magdalene was one such, known shortly to be appointing a new Master. A courteous porter took him round. Arthur was at once captivated by its miniature delights – the treasures hidden from the public eye: the back court with the Pepys Library, 'the stiff formal grassplot, the limes planted too close to the walls and grown up to them – mysterious doorways leading nowhere'. But it was in a sad state of neglect. The Hall looked dirty, slipshod and slovenly. The Chapel was characterless, 'a feeble modern Gothic building, no organ – all the same. The Master's stall and candlestick feebly and cheaply decked in black.' It needed someone to love it, someone with imagination. Above all, he would need 'money, patience and courage'. He speculated on the chances of Walter Durnford, and then played with a pleasing fancy – 'I should like to try and raise it out of the dust.'

He had been barely a week at Cambridge when the sad truth struck him. He was lonely. 'I feel a shadow, at the loss of old ways and old companions.' A few days later he counted up his many blessings, and then added: 'the *only* shadow over this place is the want of company. I left Eton as rather a swell, rather a distinguished person, whose company conferred a favour. Now I knock humbly at the doors of undergraduates and implore elegant young men to come and see me, which they won't do. I am not wanted!

> "Tomorrow" and "Today" they cried.
> "I was of yesterday"

But this will do me good. I was too much focused on myself, and I don't altogether mind it. Indeed like Christian and Hopeful I find the plain of Humility an easy place to walk in.'

But he also had an uneasy feeling that he might not quite belong within a world of academics. Their minds were so fastidious, their talk over dinner (perhaps, even worse, their silences as they listened to you trying vainly to keep up) could be excessively daunting. 'I am afraid of these acute and learned persons, I think', Arthur confessed, after trying to keep an intelligent conversation going with an economist at the King's High Table, and having spent the afternoon in the company of Walter Headlam, who personified everything that Arthur found disconcerting in the donnish make-up. He knew more Greek than anyone in Europe, but was too fastidious ever to commit himself to paper. Even a congenial companion like Monty James lived largely in a mystifying world of his own. 'The more I see of him the more I feel what a funny comfortable little paddock Monty's mind is', Arthur wrote. 'Every year the hedge grows a little higher. I suppose it is the same with all of us – but I am dimly conscious of the streets and the fields of stones and the great bare hills outside. . . . I don't like them, but the wind blows from them. All the time Monty smells his flowers and eats his peaches, for all the world like Omar Khayyam himself.'

York Powell once said of Benjamin Jowett: 'How he hates learning!' – its narrowness and parochialism, the arrogance of mere erudition, the false sense of perspective that comes from over-sedulous attention to minutiae. Arthur recognised a kindred spirit. 'It is true of me', he wrote in 1907, deploring the extent to which many of his Cambridge associates and companions expended their energies on 'poky work'. How, then, could one survive in such an atmosphere? Some could – and did – make the chief object of their interest and attentions the undergraduates, the mass of whom, at any one time, would share this repugnance to learning for learning's sake. Others became resentful, through insecurity and consciousness of exclusion, and tried to make a virtue out of their inability to comprehend the scholarly mind. Such a one was Oscar Browning, a terrible object-lesson for anyone who sought to survive in Cambridge too self-consciously as an undergraduates' don. Arthur spent an appalling evening with him during this first month of his sojourn at the Old Granary, ostensibly to receive from O.B. his ideas about the role of political science in the teaching of history.

The setting was O.B.'s luxurious rooms in King's, where dinner was served off gas-rings in a gyp-room, by his young resident servant, a 'sleepy-looking handsome sort of boy', who actually slept behind a screen in an adjoining room so that he could be at hand to minister to O.B.'s needs in the night, should he be taken ill. There was no conversation; only a monologue and a harangue; a personal tirade against the Dixie Professor (E. M. Gwatkin) and Stanley Leathes who had adjudged there to be no *prima facie* case for the award of the Litt.D. degree to O.B., whose published works had been returned to him with the pages uncut. This was explained as the jealousy of timid and inarticulate dons at the facile writer who could command the broad sweep. There followed hours of pathetic self-justification, with O.B. 'wallowing in this dreadful slough of self'. After a while, Arthur took refuge in a game which he had learnt from Gosse in coping with the 'jawing' or 'prosing' of an egotist: you sat back and counted the number of times that he used the word 'I'. By the end of the evening Arthur had reached the total of 1,260!

From the outset, then, it looked as if Arthur's life at Cambridge would follow the pattern which his temperament and talents had devised for him throughout his experience so far. He would try to be uninvolved and detached, except in seeking agreeable companionship. He would gravitate naturally towards the outskirts, to a position where he could observe both the charms and the absurdities of Cambridge life, without himself becoming anything more than a peripheral figure. He could watch Cambridge, as it were, from his window, and record it in his diary. Perhaps one day a definite, if not too demanding, post would come his way, and he would find himself a secure, if modest, role within a College community. Until then, the view from the Old Granary window must suffice.

So we may picture him in April 1904, back in Cambridge after a spell of work on the Queen's letters at Windsor, ruminating on the Cambridge scene. Stuart Donaldson had just been chosen by Lord Braybrooke as Master of Magdalene. Arthur confessed to feeling envious. 'I have thought very tenderly of the poor little college – so beautiful and stately and venerable: and yet so out at elbows and out of heart. I made a prayer that I might be perhaps allowed to raise her up. There are very few posts in England that I desire; but this is one. I should like a small, definite, thorough job to do. I don't suppose I *should* like it really. ... Well, Donald has taken it; and he is an *ideal* person. ... He is industrious: the undergrads will adore him; he will coach the boat, he will do everything I could not do, and lift the place on his shoulders. All that is wanted is that he should go and laugh in the courts, once in each, and the place will recover heart at once.'

The view from the Old Granary window certainly had its compensations. It provided him with some delightful vignettes. 'It amuses me to watch the movements of the household of the miller who lives opposite. There is a small active child in a green frock ... who is very comical.' Arthur studied her games carefully, once observing how she wandered too far off until cut off from return to safety by some grazing cows. She took up a stance like Saint Perpetua 'as they came, cow after cow' until she could stand it no longer and 'ran like an india rubber ball home'.

> Then she played with a blue balloon; and in the bright day her mother, who generally goes patiently about her work, became young again and played

135

too. They romped together – and the only disapproving spectator was a large white cat, who sate in sullen anger upon the doorstep because the door was not opened instantly for it. Think how a dog wd have rejoiced in their joy. But the cat sate furious till the door was at last opened, when it flew in and disappeared, like a merchant to his office.

And the university was a wonderfully rich scene for the *voyeur* with the ability to translate his pictures into words: Professor Gwatkin dining at King's, for instance, exhibiting what always excited Arthur's mirth – the predicament of a highly unusual person performing a perfectly natural act. 'Gwatkin was the terrible sight, eating like a wild beast, looking like a Cyclops, with his whited eyes turning all ways and fringed with grisly hair. He managed to make each piece of food that he put into his mouth look like a worm or grub. He flung things at his mouth, often missed it. But it would catch in the hair on his face, and he would pull it in and swallow it somehow.' Contrasts and incongruities caught Arthur's eye – the contrast between the tremulousness of old age and the easy precision of the young; the incongruousness of trivial pursuits being taken with a deadly seriousness. The tow-path in May could always provide such scenes; the old and the middle-aged looking on with wistful envy, the 'strong, fresh-coloured, slim, neat-limbed young men, in the striped jerseys: so intent on the nonsense of rowing. A coach in a red coat ... riding in deep thought like Napoleon before Waterloo.'

This took one back to Eton and the summer Half. Arthur was, in fact, living much of his time at Eton still. Ainger had offered him lodgings at Mustians while he worked on the archives at Windsor, and he had therefore the strange experience of mingling with old friends who were no longer colleagues, of meeting daily with boys over whom he no longer had any responsibility, and of living the life of the *revenant* without any prescribed routine. It proved highly unsettling. In the first place, Arthur very soon found that the work on the Queen's letters was dull, laborious sorting and editing which was totally uncongenial to his tastes. Such scholarly zeal as he could muster very quickly evaporated. He enlisted the support of Hugh Childers to do the bulk of the selecting; he engaged the services of a translator (Dr Eugene Oswald) to cope with the German correspondence, and he hired a secretary (Miss Williams) to do the transcriptions. For a while he put in about six hours a day at the Castle (from 10.30 till 1.30, and from 5.00 till 8.00). All the difficult problems were referred to Esher who consulted the King's wishes.

In the second place, Arthur had to adjust to the difficult and unfamiliar situation of living for long stretches as a guest in somebody else's house; and it is a tribute to Ainger's patience and imperturbability that the arrangement lasted so long and that their friendship survived it relatively unscathed. All this Arthur readily conceded. But he missed his own servants; he fretted at not being master of his own routine; he grumbled at Ainger's new passion for playing billiards after dinner; he felt himself under an obligation to accept his companionship in walks and cycle-rides (with all the subordination to his maddening habit of choosing eccentric and devious routes that walking and cycling with Ainger entailed); and, on the occasions when Arthur was in the mood to wax intellectual, Ainger would unerringly find a way of puncturing his airy flights and of reducing the conversation to the little parochial concerns that dominated his own comfortable and unruffled life. One evening, Arthur lent back in his chair to expatiate to the other dinner guests on Maeterlinck and Emerson. ' "As philosophers, they were like men finding a difficult path over the mountains with a box of matches – every now and then comes a spurt, a pretty circle of light; and you see something of broken rock and heather; but it is no lantern. ..." Then Ainger in his dryest voice said: "What is the present position of the report of the committee on the teaching of Latin prose?" Our little card-house fell to pieces.'

Thirdly, Arthur was sorely tempted to intervene in the troubles that Goodhart was facing in the house. Rather shamefully he did not always resist the temptation. Mrs Cox wanted to pour out her troubles to him, and he lent her too sympathetic an ear. Once, when Goodhart had shingles, Arthur went back to the house to perform the nocturnal rounds in his stead (a painful experience, as it turned out: 'I did not know I had so much heart'). He listened to Willy Strutt complaining of Goodhart's unpopularity and his 'everlasting corrections and alterations'. Arthur unwisely commented in his diary: 'I must try to speak to G. about this.' Of course it was a difficult position. Sometimes Goodhart wanted to consult him about individual boys, and it was so tempting to undertake a private talk with the boy concerned, especially as Arthur was rather naturally disposed to feel that the reason for the deterioration in character or behaviour was largely due to the removal of his own personal influence. He viewed it all with mixed feelings. He was relieved at the freedom from responsibility; but the needs of the boys themselves, and their pleasure at talking with him again, awoke old feelings.

One hot summer night in July, feeling lonely and depressed (hot weather was always a trial to him and caused 'the wrong things ... to bud and flower within me'), he went over to Goodhart's and offered to do the rounds. There was Eliot in bed in his room, without a rag of clothes on, partially covered by a single sheet, pleased to see him, ready to sit up and talk. Arthur returned to Mustians almost overcome with the old feeling of heart-hunger. 'I reflect sadly that I see so little of these boys. I implore them to come and see me, but they never will – I know I should have done the same.' Probably, he mused, his rather daunting manner put them off. 'But I do rather hanker for some nearer tie – someone to whom it would be natural to come and linger about. And yet I fear that it would fret me too. I think I am more like Papa in many ways than I thought!'

Two boys, however, began to cultivate Arthur's friendship during these months, and became regular visitors. The first was Julian Grenfell, the eldest son of William and Ettie Grenfell of Taplow Court (whom Arthur met at Walter Parratt's within a week of his return to Eton). The second was Edward Horner, who although a King's Scholar while Julian Grenfell was in Somerville's, had been a close friend of Julian's at their previous school (Summerfields). They were to go up to Balliol together in 1906. Arthur had first noted Horner when lunching in College Hall and had commented on his 'very curious and special charm. ... I have not often seen a boy who without or nearly without physical comeliness is yet so attractive in manner and gesture. I should like to see more of this boy.'

Circumstances determined that he should. Quite by chance, a few days later, he was at a dinner-party given by Gosse and found, as his neighbour, a 'statuesque nymph' by the name of Cicely Horner, who turned out to be Edward's sister. 'I have seldom had so pleasant a partner', Arthur recalled. Later in the same month, on Confirmation Day, while Arthur was fuming to himself over the unreality of the occasion (like 'a huge garden-party, slightly overshadowed by a sense of religion'), he received two unexpected visitors. 'It was my Diana of the Gosse-ways – Cicely Horner and . . . the delightful Edward. Really it was very odd – the two human beings who have interested me most of all that I have met lately are this boy and girl.' He had thought to himself how restrained he had been in not going out of the way to attract Edward Horner's attention, feeling that he had been perhaps already rather spoilt by the attention of clever people. Arthur was a little nervous at first, sensing a dawning friendship. 'At such times I become painfully conscious of my own heaviness, bigness, slowness, ugliness. I feel like Quibus Flestrin, the Man-*mountain*; like a dancing bear.' It was foolish really; he could make friends easily enough. 'Yet I am so profoundly conscious of *unattractiveness* both physical and mental.'

A week later he invited both Julian Grenfell and Edward Horner to tea. At the beginning of the next Half, returning to Mustians after a walk, he found they had both come over of their own accord. Julian Grenfell 'with his imperturbable smile and his curly cherubic hair, is the *beau ideal* of an honest, intelligent, good, happy, wholesome boy. Ed. Horner has a curious attraction for me; he was silent, unembarrassed, clever, natural, sweet-tempered all in one. When people are like that, I feel a great wish to please them; and I suppose that an attraction like that is unconsciously felt; for the boy stayed behind to speak to me, and asked simply if he might come to see me! This is a very unusual sort of experience, for boys are very shy about such things. I think he will come ... so that this has been a happy, a very happy day.'

*   *   *   *   *

The friendship with Edward Horner brought the Spring back into Arthur's life. He had not felt a love like this since those isolated happy days (and they had been few enough) of blissful rapport in the company of Mark Sturgis – and then his love had been incommunicable. So perhaps this might have to be, too. When he returned to Cambridge the day after having Julian Grenfell and Edward Horner to tea on the eve of the Easter holidays, he found himself in high spirits. In such a mood he left for the Cotswolds with Hugh Childers to meet Tatham for a holiday based on the Lygon Arms at Broadway. It was one of the happiest holidays of his life. His sense of beauty had never been so sharp: his desire to express it in writing never so compelling.

From the moment he drew aside the curtains, at 5 a.m. on the first morning of the holiday, and saw a 'divine morning coming in over the stable yard – cocks crew faintly and horses rattled and munched in the stables', he sensed the joys that were to come. They visited Tewkesbury, Arthur exulting in the graves and monuments in the Abbey, experiencing 'a great going out of the heart to all these people, who lived and loved the earth and the glory of it, who have died and gone into the darkness. I remembered them all in a little prayer before the altar.' He and Tatham cycled thirty miles in the day to visit Honeybourne; and the following day they went – on Luxmoore's recommendation – to Chipping Campden.

> The half of it was not told me! I don't honestly suppose there is any town so beautiful in England. ... Beauty, beauty! What is it? Is it only a trick of old stone and lichens and sunlight? ... One can't explain it, but it is there. I

shall remember this sweet place as long as I live. It is not only the place; but it lies, like a lark's nest, among soft green hills and woods, living its own quiet and grave life.

There followed a pilgrimage to Stratford-on-Avon to see Shakespeare's monument and tomb. 'And there he sleeps! I stood and prayed with all my might over his head, to do worthily; he is the Father and Head of all our English writing, poetry and prose; and a writer may well pray there for a double portion of that Spirit.' A certain lack of charity crept into his reveries when he was told that Theodore Martin had purposed to erect a bust of his wife just opposite Shakespeare's ('that pestilent old man', whose plans had been frustrated by 'the still more pestilent Marie Corelli'). They then visited the Theatre and the Shakespeare Museum, Arthur being particularly delighted by the absurdity of the Macbeth pictures. 'In one two men with blue hats are talking to three Highland girls. The landscape something like the Cliveden reach on the Thames, wooded heights with castles. One of which is in flames, with the lightning that kindled it still visible across the sky. A high wind blowing; and more blue-hatted men exhibiting the most absurd and unreasonable terror of the girls.'

Visits to Evesham, Malvern, Gloucester and Cheltenham followed, and the mood of contentment prevailed, as did the urge to record every incident and whim: a hilarious statue of Jenner in Gloucester Cathedral 'which though of white marble tends to convey the impression that he had a heavy cold and a red nose. There are two angels apparently squabbling over a medallion, on which is depicted a very bluff and fierce old man in high collars.' In Cheltenham his roving eye picked out two contrasting vignettes, each giving play to the imagination:

> Two little things I noticed in Cheltenham which I must record: one a complacent, red-faced, flourishing looking old gentleman, apparently in bed, at an upper window open to the street, suffering I suppose from gout, and looking most benevolently about him. The other a very different kind of invalid, pale, worn, sunken over the temples, with lank hair, driving with his mother – he was quite a young man – she, looking so tenderly at him, said something as we passed – he frowned and shook his head. He looked *afraid*.

This was what life was about – ordinary people, with their individual dramas, their joys and sorrows, the places where they lived, the beauty of small things that were so often passed unnoticed. Was this worth writing about? Arthur felt that somehow he ought to compile a book about it all. 'Like Cobden's daughter I haven't very much to say. I only want to put into words some of my love for the dear earth, its hills, its flowers, its dingles – and for the houses that have here, as it were, grown up out of it.' It was Maurice Baring who gave him the idea of the appropriate medium – a book of letters between imaginary correspondents, enunciating the philosophy of things observed, and what might lie behind. It was typical of Arthur that once he had settled on the idea, he proceeded immediately to work. The first of the *Upton Letters* was written the following day.

Arthur was always at his happiest when he was writing a book that he wanted to write. *The Upton Letters* promised well: *The House of Quiet* had gone into a third edition and was nearly sold out; and an invitation was awaiting him from Macmillan to add Edward Fitzgerald to his assignments for the *Men of Letters* series. He had therefore plenty of congenial work on hand. He spent the summer between Eton and Cambridge, apart from a spell in London in June acting as one of the examiners for the Admiralty Board selecting candidates for Osborne. Off and on he saw Edward Horner and Julian Grenfell, but not as often as he wished, feeling a pang of jealousy when Henry Bowlby vouchsafed with satisfaction how the two boys would freely seek his company for weekly and intimate talks. 'I wonder why I can't get boys to do this', Arthur lamented. 'I have no doubt it is that I don't really want to see them so much as I want to write my absurd books.'

The smallest act of unsolicited friendship from boys like these could, however, transform Arthur's moods. At the end of the Half, Edward Horner came to ask Arthur shyly if he could visit him to talk, confessing that though he had many acquaintances, he had very few friends. Arthur's heart glowed with delight. Although the Half was ending, and the boys were departing for the summer holidays, some earnest of enduring friendship had been given – and given freely without pressure from the older man. Arthur surveyed the familiar scene of a bustling community swiftly sinking into emptiness and quiet, as the boys dispersed – 'the deserted playing-fields very wistful and pathetic; the summer half, all the games and the friendships and the irrevocable joys over:

> Alas that Spring should vanish as the rose
> That youth's sweet-scented manuscript should close!

Little groups of friends and colleagues dined together in the evening, as they always did on the first night of the holidays, discoursing relaxedly, with no nocturnal rounds to make, and talking inevitably – for such is the way of their world – about individual boys. Arthur dined that night with

Hugh Macnaghten and Cyril Alington, and they talked about Julian Grenfell, whom Macnaghten described as 'one of the strongest and purest boys he had ever seen'. Arthur agreed, feeling a little sad that the 'beloved Julian' had not looked in to say good-bye. He need not have worried. Julian returned the next day from Taplow Court, riding on horseback in the rain, to supply the omission, telling Arthur how he and Billy Grenfell had the great house to themselves and had fixed up a small Eton gathering there of Julian's friends together with a group of younger Eton boys who belonged to Billy's circle. Arthur thought how little he would have approved of such a mingling, as a housemaster. 'It is just the sort of time and place for the worst kind of mischief.' But somehow, with Julian, it would turn out all right. Arthur was charmed by the boy's frankness and courtesy, watching him ride off back to Taplow Court 'all drenched and grown out of his things, with his curly hair and honest snub-nosed face'.

Never had the sense of bitter-sweet seemed so strong as during this long hot summer. There was so much to be happy about – so much beauty to absorb and to describe; and yet some inner indefinable sadness too, a sense of the transitoriness of the blissful moment, a malaise arising from the consciousness that the future was uncertain and that whatever the setting of this or that particular joy, one's own role within it was much more that of the spectator than the participant. There were many fretful days. Arthur was never at his best in hot weather; he was sleeping badly (the worst series of sleepless nights since 1892, he mused in mid-July); he was a mass of small, irritating ailments. He was unsettled, too, by a prospect which had come up quite by chance in a talk with Stuart Donaldson in early May. Stuart had been expatiating on his plans for Magdalene and the difficulties facing him for want of money. In particular, the College needed more Fellows, but there were insufficient funds to provide the necessary emolument. Arthur had suggested – half-humorously – that he would be himself quite happy to accept a Fellowship without any stipend at all. 'I should like to be connected with the dear little place. To my surprise he caught at it; and I really think it may possibly come off. I *should* like a definite tie at Cambridge – and I think I could help a little.'

The thought, having once been expressed, began to build up into definite prospects and plans. A month later, however, the secret got out. A message from Stuart Donaldson, delivered to Arthur while he was at a dinner-party at Goodhart's, was hastily seized upon by de Havilland, who said to the assembled company 'Hullo! Reduced already to apply for a lectureship at the feeblest College in Cambridge!' To make matters worse, the message seemed to dash Arthur's hopes. The Fellows of Magdalene had plans of their own, and serious consideration was being given to the appointment as Pepys Librarian of E. K. Purnell, an old member of the College and an assistant-master at Wellington. Donaldson reported gloomily that he thought it right to drop the matter for the time being. Arthur felt duly chastened: 'It is a lesson to me not to try and help myself to the pleasant things on the table, but to leave it to God to help me.'

Typically he now began to prepare himself for the worst. At the end of August, he waved aside Donaldson's vague assurances. The Purnell party would surely win the day. It was his own fate 'to be one of those people ... who just don't get things. I never got any prizes; I just don't manage to bring things off. Consider all the posts I might have had, and have not!' Hearing that Professor Newton (the sole Magdalene Professorial Fellow) had written privately to Gosse about him, and that it might be necessary to compile a *curriculum vitae* to satisfy the Fellows of his ability to undertake some teaching, Arthur objected strongly to the appearance of his going 'cap-in-hand' for a post that he was prepared to accept without any payment at all. 'I don't really care if I am elected or not. ... I really shall be almost relieved, I think, if I *don't* get it.'

This, of course, was sour grapes. What had his liberty secured him? – an editing chore which he found more and more laborious; an 'unreal existence' at Eton, lodging as a guest with a long-suffering friend, and getting on everybody's nerves. 'It is very undignified.' He was 'in Eton and not of it ... I long to be gone.' It was scarcely better at Cambridge. No one had really any time for a man who was outside all the recognised circles; and what he had seen of the life of the average don did not greatly attract him. With the exception of the very few, like Monty James and Walter Headlam, the Fellows of King's 'are engaged in working hard, teaching stupid men, going to meetings, trying to make money, marrying and begetting children. There ought to be more peaceable unoccupied men, neither idle nor peevish, living quietly among books and dreams – a very innocent life, and not *less* valuable than a Bank Clerk! – Why do we connect Practical Activity with Virtue so closely in England?'

Even the little friendships – pathetic romantic questings across the barrier of age – were enchanting illusions to satisfy the moment and no more. He did not really belong to the circle of the Horners and the

Grenfells. His own need of them was far stronger than their need of him. In the end, he was merely a spectator of their elegance, ingenuousness and charm. 'I stand on the outskirts and applaud', he wrote sadly in June, noting the admiring group of which Edward Horner was so naturally a part. It was the classic agony of middle age – the fact that one yearns for a relationship more poignantly than one did when young, while the capacity to achieve it rapidly fades. 'I am unstrung and weary.... Yet my brain and emotions are all alive – the latter (it seems to me) more alert and youthful than they have been for years. Things move me easily, and I seem to see beauty and pathos everywhere. I suppose it is a last flicker before I settle down into middle age.' The more beautiful the setting, the happier the hour, the more enchanting the companion, the greater the sense of imminent loss. So he mused, during a 'very sweet, but sad, hour' at Cuckoo Weir in early August, escaping the trippers at the Castle on a Bank Holiday Monday. 'I trailed my wrist in the clear water. Everything unutterably dreamful, peaceful, contented – all but myself. I wondered why the sweet minutes must pass so quick; and my joy in the present was overshadowed by the thought how we are all racing on to the darkness. Why must one spoil peace thus, by vain desires and dreams?'

What did he really want from life? There were moments when he conceded that he had created his own solitariness by eschewing marriage. 'One *ought* to be married, no doubt: but it is too late now ... and I think I love my liberty better.' If liberty were all important – liberty to achieve what? That he could not easily answer. All he knew was that he was restless, more restless than he had ever been in his life before. 'Like the little man in Blake, who has set his ladder up to the moon, I WANT, I WANT.' He found himself looking for signs and omens. Walking from the Castle back to Mustians, one day in late July, he noticed for the first time the row of carved heads on the parapet of the Wolsey Chapel, and observed with amusement that one, wearing a mitre, had a strong resemblance to his father. 'So I said to myself that the next head, left, should be myself. And this was rather a foolish person, in a laurel-wreath.'

*   *   *   *   *

Perhaps, indeed, this was what fate decreed. Foolish persons in laurel-wreaths were doomed to be spectators. They might earn their laurels for their glib facility with words; the essence of their folly was their preference for describing life rather than living it. In December 1902,

Arthur had perceived this truth about himself. 'I can see life as a series of beautiful pictures', he had written. 'I cannot live it.'

He could live it, of course, in his imagination – and this was one of his qualities as a diarist. He was so absorbed in what he observed that he allowed his imagination to colour everything that he saw. Tiny images, momentary vignettes that would impinge for a second on the average person's mind, would – with Arthur – become little human dramas worthy of record and suggestive of sympathetic elaboration. A family group, having tea in a Cotswold garden, leads him to picture 'the boy going to school, the marriage party and the funeral crossing the court with the beating bell'; three Welsh women returning from market with their unsold cow become a miniature tragedy – their dressing up in their best in the hopeful morning, the sad, unsuccessful return journey in the evening – 'the three strong unhappy women, in the flat marsh road with the watery wild sunset behind'; a man and a child singing softly together on Coe Fen in the dark of the night, moving Arthur almost to tears, communicate to him their 'sense of hidden companionship'. He sees at once the romance implicit in the spectacle of two earnest amateur painters, copying a portrait in the Tate, one a quiet handsome boy, the other (near him) a girl 'with parted lips, not looking at the picture but at him'. A whole story suggests itself by the sight of a little boy with an amputated leg on Longstanton station being hugged affectionately by an older boy. He anthropomorphizes the predicament of the animals in a van on the Windermere train, seemingly going to slaughter: 'poor calves tied up in bags, fat, sighing ducks, agitated out-peeping fowls, all equally sad'.

Even inanimate things could inspire a sort of sympathy or awaken old, irrational childish fears. Staying at Dorchester in 1905, Arthur subjected to scrutiny a pleasant stone mansion called Colliton House, perceiving an 'odd stone head, at the arch top, that generations of boys have flung stones at, until one has filled the poor mouth with a huge pebble. The poor chipped and leprous face hangs there so solemnly, choked by the stone, apparently trying to reject it.' There was a very beautiful garden at Cliveden which Arthur visited in May 1904. He was fascinated by a particular statue – 'an old man in a flat cap, with an unpleasant smile'. So far, so good. But then comes the characteristic Arthur Benson touch. The figure had 'some unaccountable object in his hand, which rather frightened me'.

Not surprisingly, Arthur had a very acute historical imagination. He could feel for the past; pick up, as it were, the vibrations of historical sites and buildings that he visited. Staying with Tatham at Wooler in April 1899, he walked over the site of the battle of Flodden Field and looked in at the nearby church. 'I dare say it saw horrid scenes the day after the battle, as many wounded must have gone in there', he wrote. 'Groans and smells and horrors – fancy what the so-called Doctors did! All the day I was haunted by "They pass and smile the children of the sword, No more the sword they wield". . . . Many Yorkshiremen must have died there.' Probably some Benson ancestor 'poking with a billhook at anyone within reach, in a shabby leather coat and leggings. But the whole place gave me a deep-seated thrill, I don't know why.' In Dorset, at Chalgrove Field, his imagination strove to reconstruct the scene of Hampden's death. 'There was a sort of horror over the place – the stream ran heavily by choked in grasses. I thought of how pale faces must have looked from the upper windows as the tired troopers drew off from Chalgrove Field and carried Hampden past.' A monastery, a Roman Camp, prehistoric caves, a gibbet-tree with initials scratched out in the bark – these were enough to call his fertile and graphic imagination into play. Further than that he would not go. Historical research – and the scholarship of Stubbs and Freeman, even of his close friend G. T. Lapsley – bored him. To picture life as it was lived; to recover the tears and laughter of ordinary people long ago, and the absurd trifles that aroused them – these were what excited the *voyeur* part of Arthur's mind, in the past as well as in the present.

Deep down, however, was a genuine consciousness of historical roots, and a desire to cling to permanent things. So much of life was transitory. So much of the beauty that one cherished passed away. 'And oh, the very reason why I love them is because they die' was one of his favourite refrains, capturing so simply the mood of 'bitter-sweet'. Either the beauty of the natural order decays and perishes, or the spectator himself passes on. Whichever it is, the moment of enchantment is too often a fleeting one. 'When one thinks of death', he once wrote, 'one *resents* so the idea of life and the world going on, *and I not there.*' So deep was this feeling that Arthur, time and time again, would play, as it were, little tricks to defeat nature, would plant small relics of himself in beautiful or memorable places that would survive long after he had passed away. These he would call 'fetishes'. On a walk to Langley, via 'The Crooked Billet', with Tatham in 1888, they hid in a hollow tree at Britwell a little tin box 'containing a silver pig and other mysteries'. They visited it again in 1902 and transplanted it 'beyond Lynch Hill, like two children'. In an apple-tree in the Mustians garden lies concealed the knob off the cover of a vegetable dish; an old rusty key reposes in the sixteenth tree (a willow) from the right, as one turns from Barton Road to Coton (it was still there when Arthur went to investigate nine years later).

There are fetishes concealed carefully in various chosen spots in the Lake District, mementos of happy visits or holidays at Skelwith Fold or Loweswater: at Holker Moss, on the summit of Grasmoor, under a boulder on the top of High Stile. In Harston Church (in a secret place) Arthur has concealed an actual relic of himself – a tooth which had been extracted a few days before and which his hand touched in his pocket as he was walking round. 'I did not see why it should not lie in consecrated ground.' Unknown to Arthur at the time, his brother Hugh shared the same whim. On a walk together in December 1904 they came to Coton Church. 'There followed', Arthur recalled, 'a funny little event. I had, as I still love to do, hidden a fossil shell in a secret cleft of the porch. I found that Hugh had done just the same; but his was a penny and a pencil, buried in the churchyard. So we looked at our treasures!'

Arthur Benson loved life passionately, even if – in a sense – he could not live it. He loved people too – people and places; things of beauty; and not necessarily the things which other people (especially the experts) deemed to be beautiful. A great manufactory at Carnforth, a complex of grinding wheels, pulleys, chimneys and iron balustrades, was somehow beautiful because it denoted life, function, drama, reality. But, on the whole, it was the simple and commonplace beauties of nature that Arthur delighted in – the things that the mass of men took for granted and passed by unobserved – the expressions on people's faces, the sound of a laugh; above all, old, permanent things that evoked the continuity of simple lives, divorced from affectation or contrived and pompous grandeur: a blacksmith's forge, silent woods, farm-yards. Exploring the countryside round Coniston with his cousin, Cordelia Marshall, he looked covetously at a farm-house at Oxen Park which was up 'To Let': 'I do like these old, stone-built, roughcast farms, so solid and sturdy, with a garden full of flowers, big barns and granaries and a yard full of farm-lumber and litter. I am sure my old dalesman ancestry makes me feel unconsciously at home here.' When he saw life as 'a series of beautiful pictures', he indulged a compulsive curiosity not so much in the affairs of the great, or the grand artefacts of acknowledged masters of their craft, but in the miniatures fashioned by nature and the vignettes of ordinary people simply living what might seem to others unremarkable or humdrum lives. 'I gather the harvest of a quiet eye', he wrote in 1901, 'and I have constant thrills of homely beauty everywhere.'

In some ways this was unashamed self-indulgence; sometimes, too, sentimentality. It is certainly an *aesthetic* approach to life. He tended to regard the world, the people within it, the scenes that passed before him, as objects of aesthetic enjoyment to himself. They excited his sense of humour, his perception of beauty, sometimes his contempt for ugliness, meanness or cruelty. His role was that of spectator; the others presented the drama for him to observe. This was true throughout his life. Even when he achieved fame and responsibility and could not avoid attending meetings and committees, his main preoccupation was never the subject under discussion, or the contribution he might himself venture to make, but the attitudes, expressions, posturings and inanities of his fellow men. Wherever he found himself – at a conference-table, at a public dinner, travelling on a train, worshipping in church – his first attention was to his companions, noting their movements, their voices, their mannerisms, with the eye of a cartoonist; only a cartoonist in words.

He was, essentially, a *voyeur*, blessed with the gift of describing accurately what he saw and with the imaginative power to extract humour and drama out of the scenes that he witnessed. The *window* image recurs again and again. Not for nothing did he achieve his greatest fame by his collection of *Cornhill* articles under the title *From a College Window*. He had been looking out of windows all his life: watching the antics of the miller's daughter from his window in the Old Granary; surveying people in the street from his window at the Lygon Arms at Broadway, speculating about 'an old lady in a cap' who 'sits all afternoon looking quietly out'; philosophising from his seat by the window at Mustians. 'From my window I can see by the cemetery chapel spire a little blue hill, over soft woodland ridges, waiting, under the evening sky: unutterably peaceful and sweet. Nearer, it would all fall into fields and elms: but seen like this, it is just like a retrospect of one's own life.' When he was having his portrait painted, years later, he was content to sit passively by the window, being 'much interested in a room across the street, at the window of which kept appearing a lovely girl in pyjamas with her hair down, smoking a cigarette. I asked Nicholson about her but he would not take any interest.' If he could have his wishes truly granted, he wrote in 1907, he would ask for complete seclusion by a window where he could look out over the whole world.

But windows were equally enticing objects from outside. When he had time to kill, waiting for a train, he would walk the streets by the station, looking in at windows, imagining the lives of the people whom he might espy: the curious domestic lives of the inhabitants of Clerkenwell; listening in at a window of a board-school at Sandown on the Isle of Wight, hearing 'a male voice, a baritone, sweet and full of feeling, sing a song, self-accompanied on an old cracked piano – followed by applause and then laughter. It was a singing lesson, I think.' Sometimes the image came completely unlooked for, and caught the eye unawares. In May 1904 Arthur was walking back to Mustians one night, having dined with Stuart Donaldson:

> Such a little picture coming back: the lane was still as death, fragrant and cool. Impey's house loomed up, mostly dark. There was a window lighted up, full of flowers: the room inside still: but just as I came past there came a boy in a nightgown to the window with a candle, put it down; and began to move the flowers, smiling. It seemed so strange to see this, hung like a picture, high in the air: like a window opened in heaven; and yet he was so unconscious that anyone saw him, down in the dark. And then came a further surprise, of which I will not here speak, but which I shall not easily forget.

The tragedy of the *voyeur* is the very obvious one, which Arthur himself conceded, that one cannot actually experience, except in the imagination, much of what one so eagerly regards. You can see life, but not live it. This was the essence of Arthur Benson's personal predicament. It affected his attitude to every community he belonged to, limiting the degree of involvement he was prepared to give. It affected, too, his attitude to personal relationships, holding him back, always, from total commitment and the willingness to make himself vulnerable and open to suffering and hurt.

It was not that he failed to understand the demands of love. He had himself – he believed – been through the fire and had been badly scarred by the experience. The memory of the bitterness of his 'great misfortune' at Cambridge had sunk deep, and left him with the firm resolution never to expose himself again. Basically, however, his love of his own independence, and his refusal to disturb his own chosen path, inhibited close relationship. So, of course, did his very strong spectatorial instinct. 'I take an interest in other people', he wrote, 'but I draw fancy pictures of them – and then when people behave in a way that I don't wish or expect, I am vexed.' The closer he came to a person, as a friendship advanced, the more keenly he found himself perceiving his or her faults, not forgiving or ignoring them.

> My experience is that I have *never* cared much about a person without making *him* care much for me; and that this has always been very easy to do, though accompanied with a sense that I have always to work very hard indeed to make myself acceptable or tolerable; and moreover with a perfectly hard, accurate, ungenerous perception of the friend's minutest faults, with nothing blurred over or extenuated.

This is tantamount to saying that he never really allowed himself to fall in love. It is not entirely true. He was to find, in the years to come, that he was more vulnerable than he cared to admit, and as he grew older he became more tolerant and rather more understanding of the sexual basis of romantic love. Not that that made his own predicament any easier. He was always more powerfully attracted to male beauty than to female, and this in itself created natural inhibitions in him against the physical expression of his inmost feelings. At one level (and for him, a deep one) the very thought of the physical expression of the sort of love he felt was a spectatorial absurdity – almost a monstrosity, as he mused to himself during a walk with a young, attractive undergraduate from Repton, by the name of Nash, in the summer of 1910. Arthur had just returned from a painful and gory operation at the dentist's.

> Nash chattered away very ingenuously – and I felt that I could almost be sentimental with the boy, who would respond to sentiment very swiftly – but just could not. It might amuse me, but it would be like an intellectual flirtation, or emotional sensualism. I should not want to give anything, only take a little ripple of emotion – how hideous to talk so! I suppose that one ought to do uncalculatingly what one desires for the minute; or else tread it all down; not dally with it. However, being fat and hot, and with my face in a large black bandage, I could realise how even the dimmest approach to sentimentalism was grotesque, and refrained from all but paternal growlings.

At another level, Arthur had to come to terms with a psychological and emotional deprivation. Nature debarred him, or so it seemed, from the inner life of true involvement. That was sometimes hard to bear. In the summer of 1904, at a time when he was feeling exceptionally heart-hungry and yearning for a relationship – 'the very thing I have turned my back on all these years' – he walked back from Cuckoo Weir to Mustians, picked up a volume of Cory's letters, and then tried to do a little writing. But his mind was not on his work. He looked over at the window.

There he saw:

> two lady-birds, who are perambulating the window, one inside one outside, stopping to make signals; and bewildered that they can't touch the little body that is so close, just beneath their feet. That is a parable.

How much less complicated life would be – for some – if one were sexless. The thought had crossed his mind when at Stratford-on-Avon during the Easter holidays. He had re-read a number of Shakespeare plays and come to the conclusion that *The Tempest* was his masterpiece. The character of Ariel entranced him:

> I think Ariel is the hero of the piece, that pretty, sexless creature, the dreaming spirit of wood and flower. It takes hold of me to think of Ariel serving so zealously and only waiting for his escape to the blossom that hangs on the bough. Then Prospero giving up his enchantments and the isle full of noises to go back to the world and business. I am sure that was a parable of Shakespeare's own life. Macbeth frightens me and Hamlet bewilders me; but the Tempest leaves me happier at heart.

Later that year he went to see *The Tempest* at Her Majesty's. He found Viola Tree's Ariel 'enchanting', but – alas – wanting in its portrayal of that perfect sexlessness. Once the idea had seized his mind, he could not leave it alone. Time and time again, the image of Ariel flits through his books. Shakespeare's own art was the art of Ariel, 'that dainty, delicate spirit, out of the reach of love and desire' that yet could 'delude and bemuse the human spirit'. Ariel is the bright spirit that flits through the air and sunshine while the rest of the world is enshrouded in mist and fog. Ariel can be a 'tricksy spirit' having fun at the expense of mankind; but he can also be represented as the spirit of beauty – 'some ethereal, soulless creature . . . floating at one's side, directing one's attention, like a petulant child, to the things that touched its light-hearted fancy, and constraining one into an unsought enjoyment'.

So, perhaps, here was his solution: he must be Ariel, as he conceived Ariel to be; a somewhat ponderous Ariel, no doubt; but at least Ariel's spirit at work in his generation. He had thrown off his own bondage; he would give himself to the woods and the flowers; he would put himself out of reach of love and desire; he would sometimes poke fun at mankind; he would show his generation where beauty – homely, simple beauty – could be found, so nearly within their grasp.

It was a pleasing, and not entirely absurd, conceit. Whether he succeeded or not would be for others to say. What he wanted from his life might be gathered from what he wanted of immortality, and here Arthur was perfectly explicit. He described it to Percy Lubbock some six years later:

> I detailed for him my own idea of pleasurable immortality, flying all over the world, like Ariel, just simply *looking* at things. My interest in looking at things and people is just what it was, unabated. . . . As a bee flies and buzzes for hours over a rock-face, looking hard at the crannies, so would I buzz and hang over the world, looking into streets and houses, bedrooms and drawing-rooms – and then off to some wild mountain and do just the same.

He had now found some ethereal patron to whom he could dedicate his work; he had found a way, perhaps, of making a virtue out of his own impediments, as well as out of his spectatorial gifts. At least he knew more clearly what he wanted to do. As for what he wanted to be, it seemed that nature had already decided that for him. He would be a *voyeur* to the last.

Chapter Five

FROM A COLLEGE WINDOW

> I felt somehow very near the secret of it all; the spirit stood,
> finger on lip, and smiled at me.   (June 1903)

> So I am stranded at 44 with a corner in a tiny college, writing
> books that go straight to the heart of a few hundred of the
> unctuous and sentimental middle-class.   (July 1906)

The period in limbo was drawing to an end. In the late summer of 1904 Arthur spent three weeks in Scotland as the guest, first, of the Donaldsons at Humbie (a house rented from Lord Polwarth, near Tynehead, in fine shooting country not far from the Lammermuir hills), and – secondly – of Reginald Smith, the publisher, at his house at Burnside. The break itself provided the tonic that Arthur needed; unfamiliar terrain and different companions supplied him with a wealth of fresh ideas and new incentives to write; and with Reginald Smith he struck up a close friendship which was rapidly to develop into a significant partnership.

Within a day or so of his arrival at Humbie, however, two small clouds appeared on the horizon. The first was the news that representations had been made to Edmond Warre by members of the Eton Governing Body that the time had come for him to retire. There was immediate speculation as to his successor: F. H. Rawlins, perhaps, the obvious candidate on the spot; Edward Lyttelton, Headmaster of Haileybury; Lionel Ford, Headmaster of Repton ('I don't think he would be very good with masters', Arthur thought); Sydney James at Malvern ('an excellent kind of purser – but rather a bully and unintellectual'); even Arthur himself. As soon as the possibility was mooted, Arthur felt stirrings of interest. He reckoned that he might be the choice of Eton parents, but never of the staff. He had made too many enemies by his attack upon the classical regime. He surprised Stuart Donaldson, however, by confessing to him 'how poisonously ambitious I am'. He tried to put it out of his mind, but could not succeed entirely. 'Both for books or for active work I am alike in God's hands.'

153

The second unsettling sign was a grim warning about the state of his host's health. Stuart Donaldson collapsed during their first shooting expedition after suffering a violent convulsion. Arthur, who was with him at the time, believed him to be dying. It was actually a severe epileptic fit, and Stuart admitted to Arthur, when he regained consciousness, that he had been witness to his 'thorn in the flesh'. He tried to make light of the whole episode, realising the other's concern. Indeed Arthur had never seen anything like it before. 'It was like a resurrection from the dead.'

They were a strangely assorted party. A. S. Ramsey, Bursar of Magdalene, had arrived on the previous day and this was Arthur's first meeting with a man whom he would shortly come to know as a close colleague for over twenty years. 'A quiet, sad, pleasant, donnish man', Arthur thought, 'who finds the world rather hard'; but then he was exhausted after examining in the Mathematical Tripos, and – like most tired men – could not be prevented from talking shop. The other male member of the party was a young seventeen-year-old Wellingtonian, called Arthur Mills, who had apparently just been expelled for indolence and insubordination.

Arthur fell for him at once, especially after witnessing Stuart Donaldson taking him sternly to task for his lack of drive. 'I like this boy', he wrote. 'I expect his great personal beauty was the chief mischief, as it has been to so many poor boys before him.' He set out to enchant him in the hope of establishing a little romantic friendship. They had quiet talks together about Wellington and the sneaking habits of Wellington masters (schoolmasterng could be a very 'dingy trade'). On one of their expeditions Arthur engineered himself the seat next to the boy and talked light-heartedly with him for the whole of a long journey, only to be put out, on their arrival at Humbie, by the boy saying 'Well, I *am* glad that ride is over!' A second attempt to dazzle young Arthur Mills met with a similar rebuff. They had been joined by Geoffrey Young, an Eton master, and he and Arthur talked together airily after dinner, when the men had been left to smoke, and touched the heights of brilliant conversation. Arthur looked round to see the effect. Stuart Donaldson had fallen asleep and Arthur Mills was reading a novel.

Arthur enjoyed the company but decided that he was not very taken with Scotland. 'I can't make out why the country is not more *pleasing*. It is somehow featureless and lacks charm. Very Scotch, in the latter respect!' On a visit to Haddington, he conceded that the place had 'all the elements of romantic beauty' while somehow failing to be beautiful.

Then he discovered the reason:

> John Knox was born there. This unamiable, fiery, uninteresting man broke down one tyranny and substituted another nearly as dangerous, quite as stern, and far uglier. He broke down the Abbey and set up the Kirk. He belongs to the class of people who *know they are right*, and all who disagree are damnable. I would not go to see his birthplace, the wild old boar!

He intermitted his holiday at Humbie by his week's stay at Burnside with Reginald Smith. There were more visits; more shooting expeditions, rendered delightful for Arthur by the presence of 'a little groom, James, aet 15, a pretty London boy, of whom R.J.S. and Mrs S. make a considerable pet ... a nice boy, a regular cockney'. On his return to Humbie, more guests had arrived: Hugh Macnaghten and his sister ('very wild and blowsy, with her eyes all twisted up') and an old Eton and Cambridge contemporary, J. E. K. Studd, a renowned cricketer and an inflexible Evangelical. Arthur avoided his company studiously. He 'devotes his whole life to Polytechnic work. . . . He has no sympathy with weakness or failure; doesn't want to help lame dogs over stiles, but wants everyone to be strong, ardent, good, and to be converted and sing hymns in a brazen voice.' He had two 'frank, jolly keen boys', one at Winchester, the other on the *Britannia* – 'breezy, clean-limbed, clean-minded'. Arthur sighed for Arthur Mills.

Two interesting visits took place during this final stay at Humbie. The first was to Abbotsford, the shrine of Sir Walter Scott. Arthur was not much impressed. 'Scott appeared to me here what he was: a great big jolly *child*. Making a toy-house at Abbotsford, collecting old bric-à-brac, pretending to be everything but what he was, and enjoying *that* like a child.' He did not approve of his careless approach to his writing. He was 'not a wise, tender craftsman ... but a rollicking teller of tales. An artist ought to be more of a *priest*, I think.' Arthur prided himself (rightly) on his own fluency, but it was nothing compared to what Scott reckoned to achieve. He aimed regularly to write 9000 words a day. 'That is an enormous amount. I find that it is *very* difficult to do more than 2000 at a sitting. And this would mean four sittings in a day. . . . It wd be hideous drudgery.'

The second visit was a social call: a lunch party with A. J. Balfour, the Prime Minister, at Whittinghame. A huge family-party was there assembled, because it was Balfour's practice to keep open house for any member of the family while he was in Scotland. Arthur was amazed at the homeliness of it all – the Premier doing all the carving of the saddle of mutton for the whole company; the time he was prepared to spend in showing them all round the house and gardens. 'Who could believe that this childlike naive smiling man, with just a touch of the spoilt child in his voice, moving about, a little bowed, a little shambling, with apparently nothing to do but loaf about and talk to his visitors, could be the Premier?' Arthur snatched a few words with Aunt Nora who was also present. She put down Balfour's ease and equanimity to his 'complete absence of mental restlessness', which was true of all the Balfours. They were all good sleepers, and 'never troubled by anything'. As they were leaving Whittinghame on their bikes, Arthur skidded and nearly fell off as he was crossing a bridge with a low parapet in the drive. A whimsical thought occurred to him. He would undoubtedly have been killed had he fallen. His father had died while a guest of the Prime Minister.

The Scottish holiday had been a success on all counts. Arthur had enjoyed the company of his *convives*; he had been totally accepted by the Donaldsons as one of the family. In the course of his visit he had been enlivened by an abundance of images that had appealed to his particular sense of humour – Lady Hobart shrieking into the ear of a deaf lady with an ear-trumpet, not appreciating that the instrument was excessively sensitive to sound, so that the deaf lady winced in agony at every word; a passage in a chronicle of Dryburgh Abbey which recounted how the Abbot, during an audience with the Pope, had presumed to tell the Holy Father a silly story, 'at which (says the Chronicle) the Pope laughed *very earnestly*'. He had discovered some superb examples of tasteless religious art, which he always sought out when visiting churches he had never seen. One picture stuck in his mind – 'The Madonna of the Sparrows':

> St John, presenting it, is a merry curly-haired Italian child. How easy to write nonsense about the child Jesus; to say he has a far-off look in which is written tenderness for all his creatures etc. The real fact is that he is, in the picture, a child whom the artist has tried to make also resemble a Dean.

A month later, while he was at Eton working again at the Queen's letters, he received the news he had been waiting for. On 8 October, a telegram arrived from Cambridge. 'I had been unanimously elected at Magdalene.' It had not been plain sailing. Reservations had been expressed about the quality of his degree – a First Class, certainly; but he had never proceeded beyond Part One of the Tripos. When the Master's assurances of his standing at Eton had been accepted, the Fellows seemed still divided. There were only four of them. The Bursar (Ramsey) followed the Master's line; so did Vernon Jones (Pepys Librarian and an Old Etonian). Peskett, the Tutor, wavered between Benson and Purnell, but eventually agreed to support the Master. The last to be won over was the eccentric and fiercely perverse Professor Newton, who was never happier than when in a minority of one.

Despite the fact that his Eton colleagues were somewhat unenthusiastic about the honour – the Lower Master congratulated Stuart Donaldson on his piece of 'jobbery', recalling Tom Carter's description of Magdalene as a 'hole and corner place', and even Walter Parratt remarked on the College's 'miserable reputation' – Arthur himself was delighted. It was real recognition of his position. While he would maintain his connection with King's, through being a member of the High Table, he now had an honoured status within the University and a small teaching responsibility. On 11 October he wrote in his diary: 'Today eight years ago Papa died. I can't help wishing that he could know about my Fellowship – Perhaps he does? I am sure that it would have given him great happiness.' He celebrated the event by purchasing a fine piece of Capo di Monte ware depicting 'the woman taken in adultery' (perhaps the Magdalene herself), and arranged for it to be set in oak that it might dwell in his Magdalene rooms for ever.

On 15 October he went up to Cambridge for his installation, arriving at the College in state in a victoria, feeling rather as if he were about to be consecrated bishop (a collision in Magdalene Street slightly detracted from the dignity of his reception). He robed for the ceremony in Chapel; took the oath at the altar steps; viewed with satisfaction his stall (he was to be a Founder's Fellow, he noted), and inscribed the great book of the College. He relaxed with his new colleagues over dinner in the Lodge, taking an instant dislike to Mrs Peskett ('a pushing, consequential redhaired woman'). There was still some talk about Purnell ('If they proceed to elect *him* a Fellow it will be awful', Arthur privately observed, feeling that it would remove his sense of triumph). Vernon Jones immediately offered to surrender the Librarianship to him, but Arthur – suspecting some fresh drudgery through having to play cicerone to visitors – demurred. He found himself at once embroiled in College intrigue and sized up the situation at once. 'I see that poverty and covetousness are the curses of this place.'

He liked Professor Newton on his first meeting. He was clearly a character: very lame, full of personal idiosyncrasies, but 'a real old gentleman' with a most charming voice. Attending morning service the next day, he had his first spectacle of Newton at worship. What emerged from his house as the chapel bell was ringing was 'a figure of fun: a surplice down to his knees; legs bent; crinkled feet; leaning heavily on his two sticks; a hood thrown over one shoulder, the white lining a kind of coffee colour with age – torn into strips and hanging out – and an old greasy battered tall hat at the top'. His responses in chapel were belligerently audible, in tones such as a man at a meeting might adopt when declaring 'Well, considering everything, I will withdraw my opposition for once.'

It was tiresome to have to return to Eton for a further spell on the Queen's letters, especially as the news of Warre's resignation had just been announced and well-wishers were already approaching him. 'My own position is clear', he wrote. 'I don't desire it; I mistrust my own stamina and strength. I don't think I have enough patience and good humour and tact. Enough for a little place – not enough for a big one. But if it were *offered*, I should of course have to consider it. I might even find it a duty to accept it, but I know I should be very unhappy. . . . Stand I will not. That is my position.' But this was easier said than done, especially when Warre himself told him that he regarded Arthur as his natural successor, when friends wrote to press him to let his name go forward, and when it became clearer who the possible rivals were. He would have been happy for Rawlins, although sorry for his colleagues and guests who would have to endure respectfully his absurd conversation. Lionel Ford made overtures to Arthur to find out how the land lay, telling him that although Repton had intimated to him that he should feel free to apply, he had no real desire to do so. 'Sydney James *does* want to stand – God help us!' But the real menace would be Edward Lyttelton.

Being a Lyttelton, he would expect to receive it, almost as of right. What he heard of him at Haileybury gave Arthur no confidence that he could cope with Eton. He was assured and dogmatic, and would be prepared to do the sort of things which Arthur could never have contemplated. He had publicly flogged boys at Haileybury, following a great row and a march of rebels into Hertford; he had pushed himself forward into the arena of pompous educational debate.

> He goes to conferences, he makes speeches. I have no great confidence in Edward's judgment myself; it is a shallow stream. Lionel Ford told me that he had met him at Cambridge and that E's talk was lively and continuous, but mostly consisted of things he had seen in the papers, which he thought the most interesting and valuable suggestions. It is this distractability that I

dread; he does not seem to me to have solid aims or a big policy, but to be like a little skiff that dances merrily before any breeze. But his incisive speech, his crisp talk, his strength and self-reliance are all superficially impressive.

To add to this he had become cranky, especially since his marriage. He had become a mass of stupid fads – living in the open air, for instance. He and Mrs Lyttelton slept on Jaeger beds out on a balcony ('Fancy if he comes here, his sleeping out on the roof!'). When that was not possible, so the gossip went, Mrs Lyttelton would insist on sleeping with her head out of the window and the rest of her inside the room! He was 'a very brisk and brave personality', Arthur conceded, 'but a man of no literary sense, and with a really fundamentally unbalanced mind. These silly crazes about health are all part of it. He is so easily converted to any point of view that is strikingly put; and his own convictions are both fluid in essence and definite in form. That is always a dangerous thing.' Typically, Edward Lyttelton wrote at once to Arthur, as soon as he heard that Warre was going, to ask him 'his intentions'. He even asked him outright – 'Am *I* wanted?' This was not an easy letter to answer. 'I could not frankly say "No" as I ought to have done', Arthur mused. Still, the thought that Lyttelton might secure the post was the strongest temptation to Arthur to enter the lists himself. It was clear that his colleagues expected him to. He could not help noticing the subtle change in attitude towards him in both masters and boys – 'a certain increase of anxious civility – how truly absurd!'

Deep down, however, the prospect troubled him – either way. If he refused the post, were it offered him, could he ever forgive himself? If he accepted, could he possibly undertake the responsibilities, however much he might enjoy the position and honour? The problem began to nag him in his dreams. One night, before Warre's retirement had been announced, he dreamt that the Vice-Provost had summoned the staff together and announced the election of the new Head Master – an unknown by the improbable name of Finske! Objections brought about a re-election and the chosen candidate was his dearest Eton friend, Herbert Tatham. 'I struggled with violent emotion ... thought T. was unfit ... tried to make believe I was not jealous of my old friend.' A few months later he dreamed that Sydney James had locked Warre up in Chambers, and had then handed the key to Arthur with the words 'You are the right person'.

All in all, Arthur wanted to be away from Eton. The atmosphere had become gossipy and intriguing. Somehow he had contrived, too, by his over-fondness for Edward Horner to bring about a temporary rift between him and Julian Grenfell. To make matters worse, another possible Eton honour was coming up for appointment: the position of masters' representative on the Eton Governing Body. This Arthur wanted unreservedly. It would give him a real position at Eton and a chance of prosecuting the reforms he dearly wanted to see, while not interfering with the hopes and plans which his new situation at Cambridge held out for him. Unfortunately, this prospect turned sour almost from the beginning. As soon as it became plain that the anti-classics faction on the staff had approached Arthur (led by Allcock and Somerville), the opposition turned to Monty James. The whole thing rapidly degenerated into a party squabble. A. B. Ramsay wrote to Arthur begging him not to stand. Arthur and Monty James decided that it would be better for them both to withdraw to allow the election of a *tertius gaudens*.

Arthur was profoundly upset. 'I have missed the one thing I desired, a seat on the G.B. – though assured to me by a majority.' The experience was 'humiliating and mortifying. Moreover it makes it clear to me that I could not accept the Headmastership. A man *must* have the confidence of his staff; and I have not got it. . . . I must try to be grateful for the fact that a mirror has been today held up to my spirit, and I have seen an ugly sight. . . . I must acquiesce in being a failure – a man who might have done big things, if. . . .' Although in actual fact, Arthur's own (reluctant) interest in the Head Mastership was not stifled by this rebuff, a wound had been inflicted which would take many years to heal. He had no doubt, either, that the man who had worked against him, and who was therefore enduringly his enemy, was A. B. Ramsay. 'I must not pretend not to recognise that this is the end of my connection with Eton', he wrote. 'I must throw in my lot with what is I suppose the smallest educational establishment in England, instead of the largest.'

Not quite yet, however. Off and on he was at Eton until Christmas 1904. And it seemed ironical that at the moment he was preparing to end his year-long sojourn at Mustians with Ainger and emotionally transferring his allegiance from Eton to Magdalene, his little friendship with Edward Horner reached the stage of a genuine attachment; or, at least, there appeared from the boy himself the wish to make their relationship closer. He had admitted to Ainger that he was 'heart-broken' at Arthur's going – 'with an unutterable look'. Both Edward Horner and

Julian Grenfell were seeking Arthur's company to speak about the other alone. Horner wanted to warn Arthur of Julian's reputation for priggishness; Julian to tell him that Edward had become highly unpopular in the school because he was thought effeminate. He also wanted to enlist Arthur's help to rescue his younger brother, Billy, from some corrupt elements in Goodhart's house. The help was forthcoming over Billy. Arthur talked to Mrs Cox, and found that Julian had every cause to be alarmed. There were several heart-to-heart talks with Edward Horner, who felt he had cleared himself from the suspicion of effeminacy and dilettantism by recently obtaining his House colours. 'He is now very nearly at ease with me', Arthur wrote; 'and, except Percy Lubbock, he is the most interesting boy to talk to I have known; he is so mature and quick; and yet not priggish or superior. I hope to keep this friendship.' And then again: 'I like the *unsentimental* character of a friendship like this. What I hope I have established is an easy and equal kind of relation – so hard to establish with a boy. I only twice before succeeded.'

But Magdalene was calling him now; and a new compulsion to write. He had completed both the book on Fitzgerald and *The Upton Letters*. In January, Reginald Smith accepted the latter for publication. More than that, he came forward with a proposal that exactly suited Arthur's needs. He had enjoyed writing *The Upton Letters*. He yearned for some other medium to express and develop his philosophy of life.

> I am getting very desirous to write one good small perfect book. Since I left Eton, I find my theories of life, art, education etc all strengthening and becoming more lucid. . . . The form is the difficulty. I am not a philosopher: but I can write with some *charm*, some trenchancy, even some humour. Which to take? It must be a mingling, I think. I have no power of planning and carefully working out a book. It must be a series of rapid impressions.

What Reginald Smith proposed was a series of articles for the *Cornhill* – 'a monthly *causerie*' – twelve numbers in all, each about twelve pages in length. Arthur jumped at this. It was 'a delicious task'. He immediately thought of the appropriate role. He would write 'as a don', reflecting on life and people's doings as seen from the tranquillity of a Cambridge College. So came into being his most famous and popular book. Reginald Smith provided the outlet. But already Arthur had realised that, in writing *The Upton Letters*, he had discovered the genre that came most easily and naturally to him. Summing up the remarkable events of 1904 in his diary, he wrote as follows:

> I have made a real stride in art. . . . I seem to have become a citizen and a

denizen of the City of Art – the city whose luminous and radiant towers I used only to see across the rivers and the plains.

The citizens of that city know one another when they meet, like two freemasons, even if they are trafficking far from home; and they know too who is of the company and who is not; and smile to hear the pretentious clamours of those who would claim citizenship and do not possess it.

In one sense, it was like a conversion experience: the consciousness of being one of the Elect. In another, it was a real mark of having *arrived*, of being accepted within the inner circle of the world of letters. 'It is like being a Fellow of a College.' The title of his most famous book, then – *From a College Window* – has a double meaning. It states quite literally what it purports to be – his reflections on life and the world, written as a Fellow of Magdalene. But what he reflects is also a sort of gnosis: an inner secret vouchsafed in accommodatory form, whereby one who has attained initiation delicately tutors those with eyes to see.

*   *   *   *   *

Arthur Benson's output as a writer was prolific. By common acknowledgement he wrote too much and too quickly. His writings divide into nine categories, only four of which – at this stage – warrant some detailed evaluation. The odes and lyrics have already received at least passing mention. The editorial work on Queen Victoria's letters was untypical both of his genuine interests and his particular talents. The books on Eton (*Fasti Etonenses*; *The Schoolmaster*; *The Myrtle Bough*) were either historical collections or *livres de circonstance*, the ideas of which are better and more fully illustrated from the diary coverage of his Eton career. His excursion into novel-writing was a later phase of his literary career (*Watersprings*; *The Orchard Pavilion*; *Chris Gascoyne*; *The House of Menerdue* and several others even less well-known) and wholly unsuccessful, although the lack of success did not deter him from frequent experiments. A series of literary studies, mostly compiled for the 'Men of Letters' series – a *Life of Tennyson*, studies on *Rossetti*, *Edward Fitzgerald*, *William Morris*, *Walter Pater* and (a later work) *Ruskin: A Study in Personality* – helped to establish his position as a writer of charm and a critic of perception, but none of these works has stood the test of time. Four categories remain – his 'medieval tales'; his biographical studies of people whom he personally knew; his quasi-autobiographical pieces, many of which make the transition from autobiography to fantasy and were vehicles for the expression of his own

7 The Master of Peterhouse meets the Master of Trinity outside the
Senate House
Sir Adolphus W. Ward: *'a fine old corrupt figure.'*
The Revd. Dr Henry Montagu Butler: *'like the Almighty in Blake's
designs for Job.'*

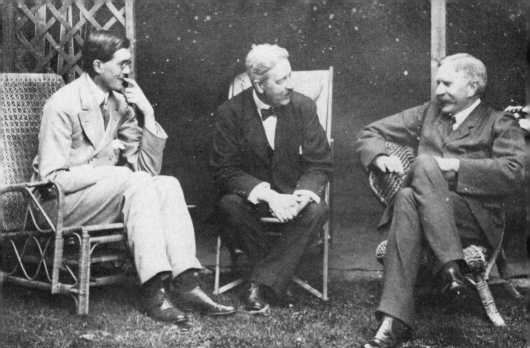

8 Percy Lubbock, Howard Sturgis and A.C.B. at Hinton Hall, 1906
   'I cannot conceive *how Howard can talk as he does all day.'*

9 Thomas Hardy and Edmund Gosse, at Max Gate
   Thomas Hardy: *'like a retired half-pay officer from a not very smart
   regiment.'*
   Edmund Gosse: *'He feels, I think, that he has climbed the social ladder
   and is among the Upper Ten. But it is all a sham.'*

philosophy of life. Finally, there were the most self-conscious *belles-lettres* – collections of reflective essays, elaborating this same philosophy.

The 'medieval tales', published in two collections as *The Hill of Trouble* and *The Isles of Sunset*, and in a revised single edition as *Paul the Minstrel*, were all expanded versions of tales told to boys at Eton while Arthur was a housemaster. As tales of the supernatural, written at the same period as M. R. James' *Ghost Stories of an Antiquary*, they lack the graphic horror, the touch of humour, and the sense of conviction arising from the erudition of its scholarly author that all Monty James' stories could command. Their language is stilted and self-consciously archaic. When told by an expert narrator, with an attractive and expressive voice, they were doubtless compelling in their way. Written down, in their elaborated form, they are curiously flat. There is a sameness about the plots, situations and characters – an excursion, despite warnings, into some forbidden place; the meeting with some evil influence, perhaps as the innocent victim of some fearful curse; virtue, normally through some spiritual force, intervenes to ensure that good triumphs over evil. Basically they are moral tales, couched in a studied romantic terminology to demonstrate, as Arthur put it in his preface to *Paul the Minstrel*, 'the poetical and beautiful side of virtue, to show life as a pilgrimage to a far-off but glorious goal, with seductive by-paths turning off the narrow way, and evil shapes, both terrifying and alluring, which loitered in shady corners, or even sometimes straddled horribly across the very road'.

They are naive, both in expression and content. Walter Durnford, who never hesitated to be brutally frank, complimented Arthur on the 'somnolent' quality of *The Isles of Sunset*, praising the *Guardian* reviewer for his 'remarkable penetration' in dismissing the book as 'a sugar-and-water, schoolgirl, pious feeble book'. Even Arthur conceded that there was some truth in this. 'The book is to the Greeks foolishness. The outer meaning is slight and even silly. I should be surprised, and not much pleased if W.D. *did* like it. This is quite honest, and not put down with clenched teeth for the benefit of readers.' He would have succeeded better if he had not tried so hard to cultivate 'the purest English I could write'. This is what gives the impression of flatness and exhibits so nakedly the actual thinness of the plots. The message of the tales is genuine enough. Indeed they were allegories of Arthur's own predicament: his consciousness, even in his happiest moments, of 'the wild beast, moving silently through the forest beside me'. There is a wild beast lying in wait for all of us if we do not cling to the road. He explained this most fully when it came to his notice that the Duchess of Albany had complained that *The Hill of Trouble* frankly gave her 'the creeps'. 'But the creeps is only on the threshold; and I want it to be *beautiful* rather than frightening – mysterious rather than terrifying – a sweet mystery', Arthur wrote. The motif could best be understood by conceiving life as a river 'crowded with holiday folk, running between high banks – within a stone's throw, but shrouded with wood, is a hamlet and a church. The bright thin definite stream of life runs thus. Sometimes we see tree-tops, blue hills; or even a strange face looks over; but we are mostly bounded by the banks – and *that* is the mistake – not to believe in the great and beautiful tracts on either side.'

Arthur really showed his quality as a writer when circumstances determined that he should devote himself seriously to a biography of someone whom he knew closely and whom he had ample opportunity to observe. *The Life of Edward White Benson* is by modern standards an unwieldy, unselective study, in part church history, in part a personal document. It must be judged, however, by the accepted canons of official nineteenth-century biographies of leading public figures, often enough useful but wearisomely uncritical works of filial devotion. Amongst the lives of Victorian churchmen, Arthur's life of his father stands very high indeed, if not alone. In the first place, it was written by an accomplished writer of natural fluency; in the second, although undertaken as an act of duty, it became – almost reluctantly – an act of love. In the course of its composition, Arthur became reconciled to a figure whom he had but dimly understood and whom he feared rather than loved. Despite its massive size and abundant quotation, it is full of atmosphere and presents a credible and moving portrait of a real man. In many ways it was unfortunate that Arthur did not himself perceive the magnitude of his own achievement. It was not until much later in life that he returned to the same theme. In the judgement of posterity, the finest books that Arthur wrote were his works of family reminiscence and studies of men and women whom he had personally known: *The Leaves of the Tree* (1911), *The Trefoil* (1923), *Memories and Friends* (1924), and – to a rather lesser extent – his *Hugh. Memoir of a Brother* (1915) and *The Life and Letters of Maggie Benson* (1917).

These were subjects perfectly suited to his style and talents: his gift of acute and discerning observation, his natural sense of structure in devising short pieces, his humour, his vivid imagination and graphic memory. They possess – above all – charm. Because he is writing of real people in actual situations he abandons, in these studies, the affected style of detached urbanity which gives to so much of his reflective writing a dated flavour and a tone of lofty condescension. He was writing of 'men of large hearts and passionate impulses, who, in spite of faults and sorrows, have made a gallant and heroic business out of life'. Their images could only be enhanced by being lovingly disrespectful in representing their weaknesses and foibles as well as frank and ungrudging in eulogising their virtues. Of all his writings, these essays approach most nearly the tone of Arthur's private diaries. He was thinking less of his audience than of the subject he was trying dispassionately to portray. They are miniature classics, both as examples of the dying art of *belles-lettres* and as object-lessons in the true meaning of 'sympathy' in the biographical art.

If Arthur had written these works alone, he must be accounted a figure of some consequence in the history of English literature. Ironically, however, his fame was secured (and his fortune made) within a genre of far less enduring quality – his volumes of reflective essays and quasi-autobiographical studies – exercises in homely philosophy which became almost like a drug both to his none-too-intellectual reading public and to himself. Critical and contemptuous as he could sometimes be of his own most popular writing, he found it almost impossible not to repeat the dose every time he settled down to write. This was not a case of cynical insincerity or of self-conscious prostitution of a great natural gift. What Arthur wrote he believed. What he could not rid himself of was the tone of patient and patronising didacticism which his public seemed to like and expect, but which he knew was alien to his true personality and a source of embarrassment to his friends.

The books fall into two categories, differentiated not by their content but by their mode of presentation. The first category – the majority of his books – tries to veil the autobiographical element by purporting to be the publication of letters or diaries of some 'friend', who has lived a placid, reflective life in the course of which he has had to face deprivation, either by way of sickness or tragic bereavement. Obviously elements of fantasy creep in when the life of the 'subject' overtakes the actual point in time when the author is writing. So, with *Arthur Hamilton*, much of the book is fantasy because the autobiographical element ceases when Arthur Hamilton (Arthur Benson) goes down from Cambridge. In *The House of Quiet*, written in 1899, the friend goes through most of Arthur's early experiences until he discovers that he has a serious heart condition (fantasy) and must be content to occupy 'a backwater of life', which means that he has the time to reflect and to communicate his reflections. The imaginary writer of *The Upton Letters* is a schoolmaster ('T.B.') who expounds his thoughts on life to an invalid friend ('Herbert' – Herbert Tatham?) who has been ordered to live abroad. *The Altar Fire* (1907) is – in fact – the same situation in reverse. The diary published is one kept by an invalid friend who dies while abroad. The hero of *Beside Still Waters* (1907) is 'Hugh Neville' (A.C.B.) reflecting on his life from the vantage-point of the Old Granary, Cambridge. *The Silent Isle* (1910) is Arthur again, musing on the doings of the world from his self-imposed exile at Haddenham in the Fens. *Thy Rod and thy Staff* (1912), *Where no Fear was* (1914) and *The Child of the Dawn* (1912) are more personal documents, the first two recounting experiences of mental breakdown, the third giving his personal view of life after death. *The Letters of One* (1907), *The Gate of Death* (1909) and *Meanwhile* (1916) are all imaginary letters from unknown subjects 'discovered' by Arthur Benson, describing – in one situation or another – how one copes with unrequited love, bereavement and war. *Father Payne* (1915) is a fantasy-picture of a wealthy, eccentric patron of young writers who forms a sort of community where the deeper lessons of life and art can be learnt, chiefly from the prolix homilies of Father Payne (an A.C.B. figure) himself.

The second category of reflective books extols the same philosophy in a collection of articles and essays, supplied to the *Cornhill* (*From a College Window*, 1906, and *At Large*, 1908), or the *Church Family Newspaper* (*Along the Road*, 1913), or the *Century Magazine* (*Escape, and other Essays*, 1915). *The Thread of Gold* (1905) and *Joyous Gard* (1913) consist of connected essays which did not previously appear as magazine articles. In all, this amounts to nineteen books which were attempting to say the same thing in not very different ways. Undoubtedly the most successful – in terms of its presentation – was *The Upton Letters*. The volumes of essays read well as essays, especially *Along the Road*, which contains some very fine pieces. The fullest expression of the philosophy appears in *The Thread of Gold*, *From a College Window* and *Beside Still Waters*.

What was this secret of life that Arthur had discovered? At root, it was a determinist philosophy, exhorting people to stop worrying needlessly about matters over which they had no control, partly because most of the things we agonise over never happen, or when they do, they are never so appalling as our apprehensions allow us to suppose. Life is a mixture of beauty and ugliness, good and evil, light and dark, it is true. But running through our lives is a 'thread of gold' – 'a golden thread of hope and love interwoven with all our lives, running consistently through the coarsest and darkest fabric'. What one must seek are the various manifestations, always so close at hand, of this thread of gold – the simple beauties of patient, uncomplaining lives; the natural miracles of enchantment that take place round us every day; 'soberness and sedateness of mood, a smiling tranquillity'. Often enough this last quality is found amongst people who are the least obviously endowed with material blessings: elderly people, the afflicted, the simple and industrious who work with their hands; not pompous, active, strident people who strut fiercely about full of their own self-importance and believe themselves to be reforming the world. The virtue to cultivate – in a word – is serenity. This did not mean idleness or cultivating a life of reflection. It meant serenity of spirit – seeing the beautiful within the ugly, the harmony within the disordered, peace within the tumult of life.

We suffer from some ingrained habit of mind which Gray called 'leucocholy' – the tendency to vitiate our blessed moments by too keen an awareness of the pathos of the evanescent; instead of living for the moment and basking in it, we are tinged by the awareness that it must pass even as darkness must follow light and death succeed to life. And yet this consciousness of the 'bitter-sweet' in nature takes us to the very heart of nature's secret. It is the essence of beauty itself, which requires sensitivity to *lacrimae rerum*, the sadness of things, the mingled joy and sorrow of creation itself.

It is a sort of quietism; the deepest sense of religion and, indeed, the deepest truths, are imparted through meditation of nature and the allegories of the natural order. 'If I could make a religion', Arthur wrote in 1915, 'I should make water its symbol – so pure and cool, so capable of being fouled and spoilt, and yet capable again of laying all its filth aside. I think that human life is perhaps like that – beautiful and sweet and silent, much dirtied by use, and yet always capable of beauty again.' If one looks at clouds forming, when a swift change in the weather takes place, 'like all great movements in the world, the impulse does not come slowly in – it starts at the same time in many corners'. The manifestation of the divine in the world is beauty: natural beauty rather than man-made beauty. It is seen in beautiful lives. '*The only thing I will admit to be higher than the pursuit of beauty, is the gentle diligent care for the happiness of others*', he wrote in 1904: 'and that, I believe, to those who practice it faithfully, is in reality an instinct for beauty too.' In a remarkable passage of his diary in February 1907, when describing a walk with A. E. Shipley in

Longstanton, viewing the great flat fen from a quiet belt of woodland, he ascribes to nature the highest and fullest therapy for the troubled spirit:

> Something of the Peace of God settled in my unquiet heart – humanity never affects me like that! Men and women are all on the same bitter and grievous pilgrimage. They know and guess and conjecture too much – but here is a living thing, this sweet copse, which has its seasons of sun and bleak rain; and sympathises without *understanding* – this is what I want – the sympathy of perfect knowledge or perfect ignorance.

Much of the language is romantic – the search for the enchanted place; the experience of the blessed mood, which gives to the recipient the consciousness that he is indeed of the Elect. 'Only those who have visited the Holiest place know those others who have set foot there, and they cannot err.' Such places, and such moments, one does not publish abroad; nor even describe too exactly in one's private diary:

> I went the secret way behind Hedgerly Park by Bulstrode garden wall [Arthur wrote in June 1903]. I stood a long time looking out into the quiet valley near the hill-top, birds chuckling and whisking thro' the deep grass – the green valley rich and dim with trees below me – the sun streaming down; all simply *made* for peace and rest and happiness. While I stood came a sound of a gun from a copse-edge: so some poor life fell, I suppose. I felt somehow very near the secret of it all; the spirit stood, finger on lip, and smiled at me. Strange to think of the little fringe of life, living just on the surface of the great flying ball of earth – so self-conscious and vexed and important: if one could only draw some strength from one's insignificance, instead of merely sipping despair.

Now all of this is of a piece with the man whose diaries reveal more and more of himself. It is certainly not insincere. It is the faith of a man thrown temperamentally on his own resources through his inability to achieve real intimacy with another human being; who found, as a boy, his love for places so much stronger than his love of people; who valued so highly his own independence that he acquired a real detestation of dogmatic, assured, emphatic people, who *knew* what was right and tried to make others accept their dogmas – experts in the field of art, Roman Catholics, ardent Evangelicals, people who lost their tempers in talking about politics, those who thought that classical learning gave them a greater insight than others into the nature of wisdom, all the *cognoscenti* who sought to impose their views by authority or on grounds of higher scholarship.

It is also a classic example of a man creating a philosophy (if such it can be called) out of his own limitations – and no less admirable because of that. Arthur was naturally gifted with the power of exposition. He had been much struck, as a young man, by sound advice given by J. R. Green: 'The only way to have a style was to write and write and get entire facility.' That was sense. 'I think I have got it', Arthur acknowledged in 1902, 'but it is sauce without meat.' The phrase itself was used by John Morley in criticising a short story which Arthur submitted for publication just after he went down from Cambridge, and it stuck in his mind. It was his major problem. As he put it in *The Upton Letters*, 'My deficiency is now in ideas and not in the power of expressing them.' If, however, you come to believe that the most significant things in life are the small, everyday, trivial things, then to write interminably about the commonplace acquires its justification.

Probably this was unconscious. He had a genuine power – almost a mission – to put into words sensations and fleeting thoughts which are shared by most people, who either lack the ability to describe them or who think them too trivial to comment upon. After he had returned from lunching with Balfour at Whittinghame in September 1904, he noted in his diary: 'three absurd things – but they are the kind of things that everyone experiences, and that no one puts down or says: (1) the cool wind which seems to blow in one's mouth when one eats a peppermint, (2) the shrill bursts of cheering which one hears from children at crossings as one goes past in a train, coming so suddenly, dying away so quickly, (3) the way in which music seems to fill the silly conventional painting of a theatre drop-scene with a strange and brilliant excitement.' It was from notes such as these that material was collected for essays and articles; sometimes whimsical, sometimes sentimental, but – in their way – compelling, because they evoked some memory of a shared experience and established an affinity with the writer.

One of the commonest criticisms that he had to face was that what he published was so intimate and personal as to appear indecorous, if not indecent. Both Shuckburgh and Lady Jebb took him to task over this aspect of *The Upton Letters*. 'I worried my own thoughts about too much, took the world too much into my confidence etc. I dare say that this is to a certain extent true. ... I look upon publication as a way of putting my feelings in the hands of the right people – the others don't matter.' He had to harden himself to a series of brutal reviews. *The Thread of Gold* was savaged in *The Times*: 'complacent fluency ... highly scented', the author pictured as 'writing day and night, with both hands, with an ineffable air of detachment and repose'. Arthur excused himself by pointing out that his reflective books were 'only *sketch-books* of a certain amateur type – handed round for the pleasure of an intimate circle', but secretly admitted that he had been too facile and too impatient to make a better job of it. 'It comes straight out of my mind; and as to the expression of it, well, I don't think I ever better my writing by patching it. The book aims at two or three distinct points – quietness, gentleness, perception of beauty, that the best things of the world are given, not gained; and so on. But I don't expect much now from any of my books. It may be said, why then not try to fall in more with the taste of the time, write a novel or something similar? I cannot! And for some obscure reason which I cannot fathom, I believe I am intended to put out my little careful fantastic books, which no one very much reads or cares for.'

People read them all right – although not the reading public that Arthur would have chosen. His books went 'straight to the heart of a few hundred of the unctuous and sentimental middle-class'. 'How strange it is', he wrote in 1915, 'that I should have captured, quite unintentionally, a second-rate and uncultivated public – that people like P. Lubbock should think my books silly, fatuous, unworthy of me. That I should yet seem to myself incapable of producing anything else – and that though my actual reputation as a writer is far more humiliating than gratifying, the practice of it is still an exquisite and constant joy to me. P.L. etc say that my writing isn't even *like* me; just as I can't recognise Hugh in his priestly letters. Could I write a book in any other style? I don't think I could. My letters and talk are different – more trenchant, I think. Well, I don't give up my hope of writing something good yet. It's very *odd*, because *I don't ever write with either money or fame or audience in my mind.* I can say that quite honestly.'

What Percy Lubbock was objecting to, in Arthur's reflective books, was not so much the philosophy he expressed – he would have no sympathy, for instance, with those who accused him of lack of robustness – and certainly not the style. He had the deepest admiration for Arthur's style. 'I could read a book on the fiscal policy of France, if you wrote it', he told Arthur in November 1904. 'I believe you were born with the gift and didn't acquire it by writing a great deal.' He took him to task on two counts, both of them valid. After *The Upton Letters*, which he regarded as a fine book, he felt that Arthur's *tone* changed, while his ideas remained the same. The tone of *From a College Window* is elderly and sedate, self-satisfied and avuncular:

Here is going to be a sedate confession [so the book begins]. I am going to take the whole world into my confidence, and say, if I can, what I think and feel about the little bit of experience which I call my life....

... So I sit, while the clock on the mantelpiece ticks out the pleasant minutes, and the fire winks and crumbles on the hearth, till the old gyp comes tapping at the door to learn my intentions for the evening; and then, again, I pass out into the court, the lighted windows of the Hall gleam with the ancient armorial glass, from staircase after staircase come troops of alert, gowned figures, while overhead, above all the pleasant stir and murmur of life, hang in the dark sky the unchanging stars....

... One may meditate more upon one's stores, stroll about more, just looking at life, seeing the quiet things that are happening, and beaming through one's spectacles.

There is more to life than this; or at least there should be. If these are feelings of self-contentment, natural to all men at certain moments, should they be expressed with quite such complacency? Worse than that, it comes ill to receive oracular utterances on Cambridge, college life, and the follies of less fortunate people from somebody whose experience as a don was both untypical and very short. It was certainly one of Arthur's most feebly resisted temptations to write as one of the *cognoscenti* almost on the instant that he enjoyed a new experience.

Secondly, however sound and sensible the philosophy, it could not bear interminable repetition. Indeed, by over-writing he weakened the homiletic effect. His views on life came to look threadbare. He repeats the same themes; he supplies the same examples; he frequently uses the same quotations. Little idiosyncrasies of language become tiresome through avoidable repetition ('sate' for 'sat'; the use of the word 'sedulous'; overuse of adjectives like 'grave', 'sad', 'sweet'). If one adopts – to use his own description of the confessional manner of 'Father Payne' – the 'demeanour ... of an indulgent uncle', then the prose itself becomes urbane and prim, deteriorating, as the books multiply, into cliché. The kettle 'sings its comfortable song'; gardens are 'peaceful ... with smiling lawns'; trees 'rustle'; pigeons 'roo-hoo'; one hears the 'fluting' of the birds. In *The Thread of Gold*, fowls are represented behaving 'with a desperate intentness' twice in three pages.

This was unworthy of Arthur Benson's gifts. The distinctive quality of his prose, at its best, is indeed his fluent command of descriptive vocabulary. It is not easy to describe laughter, a sneeze, a nuance of expression in the course of conversation. Arthur loved to do so. Entertaining his Eton colleague, Vaughan, to tea, Arthur made him laugh. And the laugh is described in the diary – 'a strange writhing or convulsion accompanied by a series of harsh dry sounds, like wooden machinery'. Sitting next to a Miss Gardner from Newnham College, at a dinner-party given by G. T. Lapsley, he notes that he managed, once, with an amusing story 'to raise . . . a curious mechanical sound, like an old dog barking'. Who, but Arthur, would have noticed (and noted) that when Monty James took his glasses off 'he became an old wrinkled, furious, red-faced man with a glassy stare'? When Henry Jackson yawned, 'his face became purple and he made a loud roaring sound while his mouth opened wider than I have ever seen a human mouth open'. One of his peculiar joys was to observe old and eminent men relaxing in the Athenaeum:

> One incident remains in my mind of the afternoon [he recorded on 23 June 1906]. I wonder if it was as funny as I thought. A dignified, melancholy old man in the Ath. with a parchment complexion and a white moustache, fell asleep over a book and was awakened by a sneeze so sudden and so violent that his pince-nez flew from his nose into the middle of the room. He looked round ruefully and then went to pick it up. I shook for half-an-hour with secret laughter.

The same felicity of wording is displayed in his description of animals and birds, where he finds exactly the right anthropomorphic quality or simile to make the vignette graphic. Walking from Hawes to Long Preston in the Yorkshire dales, he 'found a comfortable hen, with puffed feathers and a furious eye, lying in a bed in the road'. On the Slopes at Eton, 'rooks, like grave old hooded women, sate croaking among the branches'. In Hyde Park, with Hugh Childers, he watched with interest pelicans looking 'like swans muffled up for sore throat'. On a summer evening at Mustians, he was 'much beset by clouds of black flies, whirling in a giddy dance, as tho' determined to get the most out of life. They dispersed at the waving of a hand; but instantly returned to their chosen place and their Dervish whirlings.'

His similes were sometimes inspired. A major on a shooting party had 'a look of having been cured in smoke'. A group of tired guests in an over-hot sitting-room after dinner sat together 'like sacks in a granary'. A Miss Jenkinson of Newnham had 'a face like a porcelain witch'. Stuart Donaldson, after baptising Vernon Jones' son, solemnly kissed the baby 'after it had been made a child of God etc. as if he were biting at an apricot'. Leslie Stephen's *Reminiscences* left a taste in the mouth 'like stale oatcake'.

Much of the effect is gained by the subtle choice of adverb. At the

United Services Club, he bumped into C. V. Stanford looking shockingly ill. 'He shook hands, looked at me wildly, staggered to a cab, sank back.' While sitting in the train at Liverpool Street, he saw A. H. Mann, Organist of King's, in the tea-room. Arthur waved to him, 'my signal intercepted by a strange parson, who waved feverishly'. But the most interesting and distinctive stylistic trick is the conveying of delicate nuances of expression by the use of oxymorons. Examples abound. Stuart Donaldson, after dinner, is represented at the pianola 'playing ... grimly'; he dreams of the Vice-Provost of Eton having committed a horrible crime and discussing it with a 'vile gaiety'. Looking out of his bedroom window to see the dawn, he 'shuddered luxuriously'. Talking to Charles Gore, he notices that he has acquired the habit of public men of listening to you with 'courteous inattention'. A. E. Shipley, in his old age and unpleasing corpulence, sat at a meeting of the Council of the Senate 'like a quivering statue'.

The oxymoron is the grammatical expression of the incongruous in its neatest and most epigrammatic form. It also epitomises the deepest truth of life – its 'bitter-sweet' quality, which was the way in which Arthur tended to regard both the drama of life itself and the characters, major or minor, who make up the play. The dignified become undignified in standing on their dignity; old men become like children; babies look 'fat and solemn' like old men; pompousness is actually vulgar; the most rugged people are usually the most wistful; the thing closest to hand is often furthest away; the height of bliss is the awareness of the sadness of things.

Style is the man. Did any writer skirt so perilously near the sentimental without actually being a sentimentalist? Arthur, after Hugh's death, took to task his former Magdalene pupil, Richard Keable, for writing of Hugh as if he were a sentimentalist. 'Hugh was *not* sentimental. Anyone who thought him that had not got inside his mind. He was not even very emotional. He attracted far more affection than he gave; and at the bottom lay the *artist*, that impulse to create beauty, which is essentially a lonely thing.' In truth, he might have been writing of himself. 'The sentimentalist is more pained by the tears of a child than by the sight of a drunken man. I don't think Hugh's emotions ran away with him. He was *tough* in dealing with people, and it did not pain him to be severe.'

Arthur, too, was of a far tougher fibre than his reflective books might suggest. *From a College Window*, and all the other books of the same genre in which – perhaps sadly – he allowed himself to become trapped, were the wistful expressions of a very rugged personality indeed. Only the tone was out of character; certainly not the style. And if the ideals and the philosophy were some distance removed from the restless temperament of their author, then it must be remembered that men will more freely write and expatiate upon what they would like to be rather than on what they are. Arthur Benson was, a little shamelessly perhaps, aware of his own faults. He conceded very readily most of the blemishes in his books. 'I think I can spread the butter as thin as any living author', he wrote in October 1912. But this did not mean that he was content with the infirmities that nature, or inheritance, had given him. At least he knew what he *wanted* to be.

*   *   *   *   *

In the early months of 1905, the pressing question, however, was 'Did he want to be Head Master of Eton?' Had the possibility come up a year earlier he might have felt more enthusiastic. As it was his affections were rapidly transferring to Cambridge, and to Magdalene in particular. 'I realised what a perfectly enchanting place it is. . . . It is really a garden of delight; and to have been picked up by Providence and put down in a place like this, such as my whole soul desires, ought to give one faith.' He had selected his rooms, which had meant ousting an undergraduate called Leslie Pym, who fortunately bore him no resentment. He approved of the view 'from his College window', from which he could watch a colony of thrushes and turtle-doves and admire 'the deep emerald grass, the radiant trees, the shadow-flecked sun, the glint of sapphire water thro' the tree-trunks'. He had set about furnishing them in typical fashion. He put up some huge oil-paintings, having 'no merit of design, but much of colour'; one called 'Morland', which cost him 30/–, depicted 'a kind of gypsy encampment, under a brown tree; in the background a furious sea, in a storm, with a fierce thunderflash. No sign of rain or wind in the encampment.'

He had begun to involve himself in College life. At Stuart Donaldson's request, he attended a conference of College chaplains and deans at Magdalene on the eve of the Lent Term on the subject of 'Agnosticism', which caused him some quiet amusement – an assemblage of 'bird-like men from unknown colleges, pale and anaemic parsons'. He advertised a series of lectures on the romantic poets, and although horribly nervous when the day of the first lecture came, he was gratified by the size and vociferous appreciation of his audience. Forty-two ladies had been turned away at the door of the Magdalene Hall. 'I am glad for the sake of Magdalene that it was a success', he commented. 'I don't suppose that there has been such a gathering in the little Hall for years and years.'

He had several literary projects on hand – the *Cornhill* articles for Reginald Smith, and a new invitation for the 'Men of Letters' series (a study of Walter Pater). Assessing his financial situation at the end of the previous year, he found that although he had lost his Eton salary, and was to take no emoluments from Magdalene, he was still reasonably in credit. His receipts had been:

£701 from investment.
£120 Rent of Gatehouse (his house at Windsor).
£100 Eton pension.
£391 by my books.
£ 42 Admiralty.
        Total: £1354.

Expenditure: £1050, but living with A.C.A. has proved expensive – £200. Made 3 small investments.

If he were to become Head Master of Eton and received Warre's salary (which he calculated at £6000), he would become a very rich man. But, as it was, he had no real need to retrench. He had already turned down the offer of the Professorship of English Literature at the Yorkshire University at Leeds with a salary of £600 p.a. (a tenth of the salary of the Eton headship!). His royalties were likely to swell greatly during 1905.

Now that he had an acknowledged position, he could feel more relaxed in moving in Cambridge society, and he was beginning to make one or two promising friendships. In November 1904 he had met at Trinity a young American history coach from Harvard, recently elected to a Trinity Fellowship – Gaillard T. Lapsley, some ten years Arthur's junior. 'I liked this bright, intelligent man, glittering like a diamond, polished, hard as nails ... in spite of his detestable accent.' He was 'eager, epigrammatic, smart, sociable', and although by temperament a dry, unyielding scholar (and therefore inclined to take the opposite point of view to Arthur on almost every intellectual question), they sparred together on their frequent walks perfectly amicably. It was clear, too, to Arthur that Lapsley 'had formed an extravagantly high opinion of me'. By the summer they had become close friends, and Arthur was touched by Lapsley's evident reluctance to leave Cambridge to spend the summer with his family in the U.S.A. 'He is a fine creature; and I seem to have established a friendship of great candour and frankness with him. He thanked me, with great emotion, for being so good to him. But it is all the other way.'

He also discovered, within a fortnight of settling at Cambridge as a Magdalene don, that undergraduates were prepared to seek him out and pour out their private troubles to him; and that just as he had become a sort of father-confessor to Edward Horner and Julian and Billy Grenfell at Eton, there were others, too, at Cambridge who needed his help on intimate matters and were prepared to cast him, uninvited, in the same role. On 24 January 1905 he received a visit from an Emmanuel undergraduate, Hugh Walpole, who had written to ask him for an appointment. Arthur little realised how full of consequence this first meeting would be:

> Then I came away [from King's] to see Hugh, the son of my old friend Walpole – an undergraduate at Emmanuel Coll. This boy had written to me about taking up *writing* as a profession. I had dissuaded him as plainly as I could. ...
>
> He appeared at 9.30. Rather a handsome, sturdy, neatly made fellow, short-sighted, with a pleasant smile and manner. He began to talk about History, difficulty of concentrating, the passion he had for literature, possible profession. Then he went on to religious matters – he is evidently finding all his faith breaks up. This is a hard trial, I think, for people brought up in ecclesiastical households. I said what I could; but I am not sure that he wanted advice. I don't think people in that state do. They *must* follow the labyrinth, unless one is prepared to come forward, as an R.C. priest would do, with a handful of little paper books, touch the hat, and say 'I am an authorised Guide'. I don't want to do that sort of thing – one must tread the wine-presses *alone*.
>
> Then he said 'And then there's another thing' and then came out one of the most *intime* confessions I have ever heard, which I must not speak of here. The boy is evidently in very deep waters. But I could not help admiring the spirit he reveals. I don't think he is giving way. He said with a shudder 'I could manage it all, if it weren't for my dreams.' I asked him many plain questions, and I think he is living a sensible and manly life. His heart and his desire are on the right side.
>
> But the thing is really very ghastly. Why does a boy of this kind have this sort of burden to bear? Are there many who have it to bear? My impression is that of the many who I am sure have to bear it, the majority give way. The horror of it is that the voice of God, of conscience, of association is on one side; and on the other the strong, silent, force of nature, pulling blindly, heavily, constantly. How *is* one to believe in a God who sets these two forces at work against each other, to tear a soul in pieces?
>
> I tried to say what I could – but one seems stupefied in the presence of this dilemma. The horror is that a thing which is in itself absolutely natural

should assume this aspect; and seem to the boy himself to taint and blacken him in a stainless world. He seemed pretty desperate. But I think he is a fine fellow. He evidently has the artistic temperament very strong – and a great fund of wholesome affectionateness and healthy instinct. But it is a dark place to have looked into, and I leave it with an immense compassion for him for many reasons, and a strong desire to help. But why this should all be told to a stranger is hard to see. I don't gather that anyone else knows. I don't think he meant to tell me when he came. I hope he won't be ashamed of having done so.

It was not long before Hugh Walpole came again; and in their second talk Arthur discovered why he had been chosen for these intimate confidences about his sexual problems. 'He confessed he had for years made a kind of hero of me! from a photograph, and as E.W.B.'s son: then from books. I never felt less heroic than when he said this. Sleepy, stout, flushed. He said that he must confess that *this* was his reason for getting to know me, not wanting advice etc., etc. .... He is a very highly-strung, neurotic creature, that is plain. .... I never heard a boy talk an odder sort of schoolboy-story type of style, affecting to seem unaffected.'

A very significant friendship was forming here; and in the midst of it all, Arthur's mind was being tormented by pressures from outside. The appointment of Warre's successor would be made at the beginning of April. He made no move. But while that was in the offing, another event of consequence took place. At the end of January Walter Durnford arrived in Arthur's rooms in tears to tell him of the death of Augustus Austen Leigh, Provost of King's. He had had a heart attack the night before (while playing chess with his wife!). That this might open up another possibility did not strike Arthur at the time. He went to the funeral, partly out of respect, partly because he enjoyed such occasions for the spectatorial delights they invariably provided. He was not disappointed. 'There was the horrible mixture of geniality and gloom which is produced by funerals – elderly men, flushed with sherry, and with a subdued twinkle of the eye.' There was the usual self-conscious jostling for position in the processions, and a service of some power, enlivened for Arthur by Herbert Ryle's (Bishop of Winchester) reading of the lesson 'in a voice like the quacking of a gigantic duck – that horrible guttural twang he has lately caught'. Arthur's roving eye moved to the organ loft. 'Mann in surplice and Dr's hood looked well in the loft, but spoilt the Western view by letting Mrs Mann in black spectacles and a hideous bonnet look over the gallery, like a witch uttering charms.'

It was his brother Hugh who dropped the bombshell. He had been talking with A. W. Verrall who had told him that Arthur was being discussed as a possible candidate for the Provostship. 'Good God, how I wish *that* were to come true!', Arthur exclaimed when he heard the news. A fortnight later Monty James talked the matter over with him, pressing him to allow his name to go forward. Walter Durnford was not considered sufficiently eminent; Prothero would not be acceptable. Monty did not wish the post for himself. 'I had an excellent chance. . . . Well, it needed no consideration. It is difficult to imagine anything I should like better. . . . It wd suit me ten times better than Eton.' How oddly one's circumstances could change at a place like Cambridge, Arthur mused a day or so later, on the occasion of a Magdalene Feast. Admittedly his guests were distinguished enough for a possible Head of a great House – Austin Dobson and Edmund Gosse. But at Magdalene he was the junior fellow and had to sit in a lowly place.

Then an official letter from the Provost of Eton arrived. Arthur had been warned by Cornish that he would receive an invitation to stand. Within hours of his replying to decline the invitation ('I did not think I could form a *ministry* – and that I certainly would not compete'), Monty James told him that his hopes of the Provostship of King's were fast receding. Arthur felt, in a way, relieved. 'I feel like Xtian in *Pilgrim's Progress* when the burden fell off his back and rolled into a pit that lay on the bottom, *and he saw it no more*.' It was not, however, to be the end of the Eton affair. Private representations came from two of the Fellows of Eton, and eventually Arthur agreed, while not being a candidate, to accept the suggestion of Sir William Anson that he should submit a memorandum on the needs of Eton as he saw them and to discuss the matter with the Governing Body, should they wish to follow it up.

The pressure built up immediately. A *Daily Mail* reporter sought him out for an interview, and Arthur turned him away by stating categorically that he was *not* a candidate. This was published the next day, and Edward Lyttelton took immediate umbrage. He wrote Arthur 'a snappish note' to say that 'he doesn't understand my line. He says that Cobham had told him I am sending in a memorandum like the rest of them.' A further letter, in reply to Arthur's explanation, upset him deeply.

> Surely no one but a Lyttelton *could* take the line of dissuading one (that is what he practically does) from attempting a post for which he is himself a candidate. He says that I ought to decide now whether I will accept; he says that to be offered it and to refuse would be very serious for the G.B. and for myself – why, I don't see.

10 Hinton Hall, Haddenham

'It was there that my illness crept on me.'

11 Tremans, Horsted Keynes

'The very sweetest house imaginable.'

12 Hugh Walpole, from a drawing by Jane Emmet von Glehn

'The word affection seems to him to mean something which he takes, not gives.'

13 George Mallory

'I suppose many people would not call him handsome but it is to me a beautiful face.'

Although he had already agreed to meet the selection committee on 29 March, Arthur felt that it would be better for him to withdraw. He drafted a letter and sent it to Randall Davidson for his comments. He received no sympathy from that quarter. 'He knocks my *faute de mieux* argument to bits by saying that he himself, and many others, were *faute de mieux*. . . . If I chose my profession deliberately, I ought to be ready to bear its highest responsibilities.'

In the same week, Monty James gave him further news of the election at King's. He told Arthur privately that the Provostship had been offered to himself, and that he was in great perplexity about accepting it. Arthur had little doubt that he would, while musing over the curious chance that both he and Monty, friends together of such long-standing, 'should thus lie under the shadow of great posts. Who would have guessed it four-and-twenty years ago? And if we *had* been told of it then, which of us would have dreamed of the possibility of refusing?' What does one do in such a circumstance? 'If one is bound anyhow to relapse into stupidity and bufferdom, had one not better compromise by taking a situation of dignity like this? To be called Rabbi seems so attractive at a little distance; but near at hand such a poor gaud for which to barter away one's liberty.'

Privately, he felt very angry about King's. Monty accepted the Provostship, and Arthur was under no illusions over the reasons why his candidature had not been taken further. He had had insufficient connection with the College over the years and had not acquired notable academic distinction. 'They did not give me a Fellowship – that was quite right and natural – but when I came up here they made *no* attempt to give me any connections with the College, except to say politely, when I was elected at Magdalene, that they were very sorry they hadn't secured me. And yet I can say frankly that I am certainly one of the very few, perhaps a dozen, fairly prominent Kingsmen. And now they won't hear of me as Provost.' As he walked back with Monty from attending morning service at King's that Sunday, three days before he was due to meet the Eton Governors, he felt strongly that Monty was 'already enjoying the consciousness of new dignity. I wish he wouldn't fall back *quite* so much on its being done from a sense of duty.'

At last the fateful day arrived. Arthur lunched at the National Club with Gosse before going over to the House of Commons where the selection committee was meeting. When he was asked to come in, Lord Haldane rose to vacate his seat next to the Provost to allow Arthur to sit there. Anson, Cobham, Roscoe and Cornish all put questions to him about his memorandum. The others said nothing. Even at such a moment as this, Arthur could not restrain himself from observing his neighbours closely, savouring one particular vignette – the Lord Chancellor doodling as the interview progressed. Arthur took a peep at what he was scribbling: the words 'Headmaster, Housemaster, Headmaster, Housemaster' in a column down the page. During the interview he felt quite composed. The Provost put the direct question to him: would he accept the post if it were offered? 'The Governing Body would not wish to be put in a position of having its offer refused.' Arthur replied: 'In that case I feel the offer should *not* be made.' Sir William Anson intervened rapidly that Mr Benson had expressly said all along that he did not wish to be considered a candidate. And so it went on, leaving Arthur in little doubt that at least *one* person present – the Provost – was decidedly against him.

Two days later he received through the post a printed notice giving particular of the appointment – the salary was to be £4750 p.a., plus house and many other perquisites. A day later, Anson himself wrote asking Arthur privately to make his decision. Arthur interpreted this to mean that he had the majority vote of the committee, but no unanimous decision could be secured. This was not a clear enough mandate. It would mean that his task would be a hopeless one, bearing in mind that the staff would be split right down the middle. He then took the decisive step and wrote to Anson to say that he would definitely refuse the post if it were offered to him.

Why, in the end, did he back away? Frankly, he did not want the responsibility. He knew himself too well: how easily hurt he could be, how fatally ineffective when in the grips of depression. 'But I don't want to make myself out both as happy in my refusal *and* pathetic. I *am* happy, unreasonably and absurdly happy. I feel ... like a mouse who hears the trap snap just behind him. The pathos lies further away, the pathos of being somehow, in spite of certain gifts and powers, a *failure*: just not effective. It is the secret core of weakness, selfishness, softness in one coming out. I feel as if I should like never to see Eton again, except in dreams. . .'

He was inundated with letters, approving and disapproving. Luxmoore pulled his heart-strings rather by saying that 'in presence, in impressiveness, in winning hearts, in keeping our place in the great world of English historical life, in serious love of culture, above all in

determination to uphold discipline and keep our society lofty and pure, I believe you would and could do more than anyone'. But he still would have voted against Arthur because of his depreciation of the role of classics! No words, however, spoke more truly to his heart than a passage which he discovered for himself in W. B. Yeats' *Ideas of Good and Evil*:

> Shakespeare saw indeed, as I think, in Richard II, the defeat that awaits all, whether they be Artist or Saint, *who find themselves where men ask of them a rough energy, and have nothing to give but some contemplative virtue, whether lyrical phantasy, or sweetness of temper, or dreary dignity, or love of God, or love of His creatures.*

This would have been his predicament – to Eton's loss, and certainly to his own.

So Edward Lyttelton was appointed on 6 April 1905. Arthur had regrets only for Rawlins, and perhaps for Eton too, although he felt angry when he heard that Lyttelton had written to Rawlins to declare that 'they had had a good neck-to-neck fight, and that *now there would be no heart-burning*', feeling that such an expression would have come more appropriately from Rawlins. It amused him, also, to learn that Mrs Lyttelton had let it be known that her husband received a decisive majority, and that it was absolutely untrue that Arthur Benson was offered the post. 'Edward was the only person ever really thought of for a moment.'

On his forty-third birthday, he took stock of his position, as was his wont:

> I am now exactly as old as papa was in July 1872, when he gave up his headmastering. He had 24 years of life before him; and he became by swift degrees a much greater man, after he left Wellington. He had lived till then in the poor dream about the Classics being the end of life, in which my unhappy colleagues are now sunk! Lincoln made papa humble, I think, and more tender. He had to rule by tact and not by position. Then Truro gave him daring, boldness; and there he really put out his genius. And then came Canterbury, in which he was never at home, though he was just, I think, learning to be when he died. But his early training, the starvation of dignity and social ease made it very difficult for him to be *tranquil* in so high a place.

And what of himself?

> I want to make a beautiful thing of some kind: a book, no doubt. I want to try and put into a few people's heads the ideas of simplicity and quietness. It is not a gospel suited for all.

He was not, by nature, a great doer, enamoured of good works, fussing around at Boys' Clubs and the Y.M.C.A., laying down programmes and grasping at opportunities. He wanted to proceed 'step by step; as a man crosses stepping-stones; the next stone the inevitable one. And I want to be humble in mind; not self-deluded, self-deceived. The temptation is to feel *interesting* – but one is cured by realising again and again how dull and poky one's whole view appears to many brisk and radiant people – the majority of people, indeed.'

In May, G. H. Wilkinson, now Bishop of St Andrews, came to see him. They went together into Magdalene Chapel and prayed. He laid his hands on Arthur's head.

> A kind of consecration of my life to Magdalene – who knows? . . . It was just the peaceful, patriarchal blessing I wanted and needed. . . . I think it was the solemnest act I have ever taken part in.

Now Magdalene would come first. He was not sure that he would ever visit Eton again.

Chapter Six

PASSION WITHOUT TAINT

Sometimes when the *real* thing has come suddenly near, dropping from the sky ... it is so unlike the imagined emotions that one cannot write of it. ... The oddest thing is that all my life I have been the *wooed*, not the wooer.

(June 1906)

I think I have a very Greek fibre somewhere within me

(July 1910)

The Eton affair preyed on Arthur's mind for many months. Attending a chapel-service at King's three months later, he exulted in the beautiful reading of the Old Testament lesson by an Old Harrovian, Milner-White. The lesson seemed addressed to him: 'Because thou hast rejected the word of the Lord, he hath also rejected thee from being King.' Was it as simple as that? He had shrunk back at the last, but 'who made me what I am?' Eton had become to him 'a place, *ubi sicut Stephanus lapidatus sum*'. 'I feel as if I should not mind if owls were to roost there and satyrs dance among its ruins. This is ungenerous but true.' He felt little more forgiving to King's, deciding that he was not really wanted there, and it would be better for all parties for him to resign his membership of the High Table, ostensibly on the grounds of its expense.

While the tumult was subsiding, he had taken a holiday with Tatham at the King's Arms, Dorchester. This had convinced him that his true mission in life was to write. He had experienced once more the sensation of romantic vision, one of those 'spots of time' when he had felt overpoweringly that nature was revealing to him its inmost secrets. It was at Winterbourne St Mark, by the Black Down monument, walking over the barrows on the downs, with a view of the sea and Weymouth and Portland in the distance. 'I ... had a glimpse of the central mystery.' Stamping his foot on one of the barrows, surrounded by a great ditch, and covered in bramble and gorse, the words came to him: 'Sleepest thou, son of Atreus?' 'Audisne haec, Amphiaroë, sub terram condite?'

> I tried to hold out a hand of fellowship to the old chief that lay there. *Then* the feeling came to [me] for an instant, that all the world was one. The secret

183

came close . . . out of the air, over the sea . . . and was gone again in an instant. The thought of the death that overhangs the world, that waits for me, clouded my peace for a time. . . . The long procession of those who have lived and who sleep . . . calling the world their own for a space, and then disappearing so utterly. What is there behind it all? Why should one love and hope, be full of eagerness, desire, beauty? Only to die and be silent in the dust? The poor snails which we crushed in the turf, what of them? And all the time the breeze blowing cool off the sea, the shadows of clouds racing over the turf, as they did a thousand years ago. What can one add to the world, what can one leave it?

To go back from this into the bustling world! Actually what he returned to was a bustling, fashionable, ecclesiastical wedding – to act as 'best man' to Ralph Inge at his marriage to Kitty Spooner in Canterbury Cathedral. They arrived only three minutes before the bride, thanks to Randall Davidson telling them (but subsequently forgetting) that they could wait in the Palace until he came back from the Cathedral to admit them by his private entrance. The signatures in the register revealed an extraordinary linking of episcopal families – Lucy Tait, Arthur Benson, William Temple, Edie Davidson. It was the first time that Arthur had talked at any length with Frederick Temple's son. 'I rather liked William . . . a bluff, clever, stout, Oxfordian, like a great bumble-bee, with a loud laugh.' The ceremony ended with an appalling reception in the gymnasium of the King's School.

The desire to escape haunted Arthur throughout 1905. *Aut Caesar, aut nullus.* If he could not achieve great recognition, he would like to bury himself as a recluse somewhere in the country. Perhaps the Fens, for which he had developed a mounting passion. The first thought that he might acquire a Fenland retreat in exchange for the Old Granary began to take shape in his mind during the early summer. It was superb cycling country. One of the most sublime cycle-rides he had ever taken was along the tow-path to Milton, thence to Waterbeach and into the open fens:

> The space between the towpath full of masses of cow-parsley: the river sapphire blue between the green banks – the huge fields running for miles to the right, with the long lines of dyke and lode; far away the blue tower of Ely, the brown roofs of Reach, and the low wolds of Newmarket. It was simply *enchanting!* . . . I declare that the *absolutely* flat country, golden with the buttercups, and the blue tree-clumps far away backed by hills, and over all the vast sky-perspective is *the* most beautiful thing of all.

Longstowe would be a possible place, with easy access to a station; possibly Haddenham, totally out-of-the-way, in the heart of Fenland, but near enough to Ely for purposes of travel, and with a breath-taking view of the Cathedral on the horizon. He talked the matter over with the Huntings, his servants at the Old Granary, and they seemed happy. There was a fair chance of his securing the lease of Hinton Hall there, the house and garden with 700 acres shooting for only £70 p.a. The prospect seemed inviting.

But he had pledged himself to Magdalene, where he must content himself with being junior fellow. He could not entirely evade reminders of what might have been. He agreed to meet Edward Lyttelton at the National Club in May to talk about his criticisms of the Eton system. For a moment he allowed himself to be impressed. 'I liked Edward's candid gaze, the smile which broke out all over his face, his splendid laugh. He is a mere brown skeleton; but hands still red and stumpy as of old. I felt a mixture of confidence in his strength, and entire mistrust in his judgment.' Later that month he met him again as a guest of the Conybeares, with Monty James also present. Afterwards the three of them walked down King's Parade, accompanying Monty to King's. 'So many people gazed with deep interest and excitement at my two companions and had no eyes for me', he wrote. It had not helped to discover, from Lyttelton, that Arthur's reputation at Eton was that of a 'radical'. This made him 'rage and sicken with fury'.

With Monty, however, his relations remained as cordial and relaxed as ever. Although he derided him for attending the University Sermon regularly, simply for the pleasure of being seen processing with the other Heads, wearing his Litt.D. robes, he was quite wrong in his supposition that respectability and office would quench his 'joyous spirits'. He was touched by his refusal to let University or College concerns interfere with his habit of seeking Arthur's company for afternoon walks. His anecdotes were as ready and as disrespectful as ever. They rejoiced together in the absurdities of H. N. Mozley, the 'Old Black', a wildly eccentric Fellow of King's, who would invite undergraduates to breakfast (off cold leg of mutton) weeks ahead of the actual engagement. There was one undergraduate who, on being invited to go sculling with him in October 1897, had consulted his diary and suggested a date in the following March, in the hope that this would prove too long in advance. On 10 March 1898, however, Mozley appeared, as arranged, dressed in a tall hat. They repaired to the river, and the only remark that Mozley vouchsafed throughout the expedition was to say to his companion after an hour or so's sculling, 'the scenery at this point is very fine on *my* left and *your* right'. If Mozley was seen coming out into the court at King's for a walk, and you '*whistled* from a window, he would always return to his rooms for about ten minutes and then try again. M.R.J. said that he had seen this done many times, Mozley sent back to his rooms over and over again by V. Yorke whistling. It was thought that he was either affected by terror, as horses are said to be; or that he thought it was a noise in his head.'

At Magdalene, Arthur set himself the task of getting to know something of all the undergraduates by inviting them in pairs to lunch through the year, a practice he continued, with only occasional breaks because of illness, for the rest of his life. He did some teaching for the History Tripos; he continued his course of lectures; he even began to preach – about once a term – in College chapel. 'It is odd to find', he wrote in May 1905, 'that the idea of public speaking seemed to me a hopeless barrier against my taking any big post. But I find that I can preach and lecture to large audiences with no sense of nervousness at all.' He found himself settled sufficiently in the College to begin to grumble and fume at his colleagues, watching old Professor Newton, for instance, taking his dividend cheque of £200 at the College audit 'with pious complacency. ... He takes this and £500 from the University as Professor', while paying a deputy £100 to do his lecturing for him, and doing nothing himself except to find fault with every arrangement in the College.

Nevertheless recognition was coming to him – of a sort. He was invited to become a member of a Consultative Committee of the Board of Education, chaired by Sir William Hart Dyke. ('Just the fussy, ugly, earnest, enthusiastic people you would expect', he commented. 'Clergymen with large whiskers, or with beards and closed-up eyes, with mellifluous tones – ladies ill-dressed with bright eyes and bags of papers. I augured the worst.') He was appointed examiner for the Chancellor's Medal for English Verse. For some totally unaccountable reason (for his knowledge of foreign languages was minimal), he was nominated President of the Modern Languages Association in succession to Herbert Warren, President of Magdalen College, Oxford. As a literary celebrity, he was invited to deliver papers to College societies. He was sought after for membership of prestigious dining-clubs.

The first of these was a newly-founded dining-club which met over dinner at least once a term to discuss religious questions. Foakes-Jackson of Jesus College was its leading spirit, with R. V. Laurence and E. W. Barnes of Trinity, G. T. Lapsley, E. S. Shuckburgh and Arthur himself.

Three guests were always invited to each dinner. At their inaugural dinner, Shipley and F. M. Cornford were among the guests. Arthur was especially interested in the latter – 'the great agnostic, with a fine, sturdy, pale face and crimped black hair – like a king or prophet of some forgotten tribe'. How serious the discussion was is not recorded. It was rendered memorable for Arthur by a story told by Foakes-Jackson about Montagu Butler when he was dining as the guest of the Master of St John's. Butler was sitting next to his host, and turned to him conversationally, saying:

> in his sweetest tones: 'Dear Master of John's, *you* can enlighten me: with your marvellous memory you will have retained the name of that chivalrous and gentle guide who conducted us up the Schulthorn at Mürren – that model of courtesy and consideration – whose name I have often endeavoured to recall, but without sccess.' To which the M. of J. said very gruffly, 'I suppose you mean Arnold Küpfer.'
>
> 'That was the name!' cried the Master of Trinity in an ecstasy. 'That was the name; and I must endeavour to retain it in my memory. Thank you a thousand times, dear Master of John's, for recalling to me a name which brings back to me some of the best and sweetest days of my life – happy hours when guided by that chivalrous Arnold Küpfer we took the wings of the morning on the Alpine ridges.' He presently withdrew. Someone shortly after said to the Master of John's, 'Was Küpfer really so delightful a guide? I never even heard of him.'
>
> 'Neither have I', said the M. of J. gruffly, choked with food. 'I invented the name. I could not have Butler going on like that.'

Arthur had already dined as a guest of 'The Family', the most prestigious of all Cambridge dining-clubs. Within the next year he became himself a member, meeting three or four times a term for purely social discourse over excessively sumptuous fare the real inner circle of Cambridge worthies, several Heads of Houses and University Professors and men well along the road to high office. It is true that many of them were deaf; and Arthur himself rather doubted their self-conscious claim to constitute an élite ('It is very curious', he reflected, 'that some of these men should have got into this club, when we have simply the pick of the whole place'), but he was pleased at the honour and enjoyed meeting regularly characters like J. W. Clark, J. J. Thomson, Joey Prior and A. E. Shipley. Certainly his widening circle of friends and *convives* enabled him to entertain at college feasts guests of a greater distinction than would normally be expected from the junior fellow. In November 1905 he invited five guests to the Magdalene Feast – the Master of Peterhouse (A. W. Ward), the Master of Pembroke (A. J. Mason), the Provost of

King's (M. R. James), together with A. E. Shipley and Foakes-Jackson.

He was beginning to get the measure of dons: their tendency to pose, their terror of criticism. 'They are timid, with the timidity of clever men', he said to A. W. Ward, as they discussed the breed together at this particular Feast. The young don who took unsolicited refuge in his subject in order to excuse himself from the give-and-take of conversation was the greatest menace. He and Monty met one such a few days later, while dining at Magdalene, when one of Newton's guests was dining – an anthropologist by the name of Guillemand. They were invited to Newton's rooms afterwards – always a trial for Arthur because the room was too hot, there was a superfluity of electric light, and no concessions to comfort, the guests sitting round in upright chairs.

> Guillemand, a man of desperate cultivation, talked with a hard pebble-like eye on matters of absorbing interest, such as why the Dutch sailors who discovered the great Auk called it *appo-rath*. 'I suspect it of being Portuguese', said G. many times, and the nature of certain Balearic dances, which he had seen, and which he imitated on the hearth-rug, and which I thought very ugly. There were more things of this kind; he had got them all *in his notes* – Good God, what a book! and I began at last to feel that I should die if he had anything else in his notes.

One or two guests rapidly tore themselves away, and Arthur followed as soon as he decently could. 'My last glance into the room was of Guillemand pulling out some fresh gem of cultivation, and giving it to the party as bread.'

His favourite companions among the senior members, apart from his old established friends, were E. S. Shuckburgh, of Emmanuel, a man some twenty years his senior who died suddenly in July 1906 to Arthur's great grief ('one of my best friends at Cambridge'); A. E. Shipley, more nearly Arthur's contemporary, who had befriended him from his arrival at the Old Granary and who was a frequent companion for walks. Although he was, to Arthur's taste, overmuch addicted to extravagant good living and good drink, he had a genuine interest in undergraduates and a truly wide-ranging mind. 'I love and admire Shipley', he wrote in November 1904, 'he is so kind, so humorous, so sincere.' He came to know Goldsworthy Lowes Dickinson better, and recognised in him something of a kindred spirit. Despite his reputation for agnosticism, his was really a profoundly religious mind, and his 'soul was bound on a pilgrimage like my own'. They differed in their political ideas, and from time to time exchanged their thoughts on democracy in the course of afternoon walks. Dickinson felt that he *ought* to attack inequality, although he felt nervous lest the democracy might not be able to accept the culture that he offered them. It would be taking the risk of breaking the 'existing lamps, dim and scattered as they are, in the hope of diffusing light'. Arthur had far less confidence. 'To me the democracy seems likely to submerge all I think most beautiful.'

Another kindred spirit, whom his new dining-club enabled him to meet regularly, was R. V. Laurence, the historian, Fellow of Trinity, who although sixteen years younger than Arthur, contrived by his manner to pass for a man of fifty. He stooped, walked lame, sported a pointed beard and prided himself on his greying hair. He, even more than Shipley, delighted in the joys of the table; and Arthur, who rarely noted gastronomic details, invariably made an exception after dining with Laurence, his digestion finding it difficult to cope with a meal that started with oysters with audit ale, and continued with mulligatawny soles, beefsteak pudding, partridge, a savoury, all washed down with 'floods of champagne and port'. As Lapsley said to Arthur, 'nothing that he eats nourishes him and nothing that he drinks hurts him'. D. A. Winstanley recalled being with Laurence when he decided to order a 'scratch' lunch from the buttery by phone – '2 dozen oysters, salmon cutlets, ... etc. etc.' Then he left his desk eagerly to select appropriate wines.

Arthur's friendship with G. T. Lapsley prospered too. 'I could not have thought I could have got to know Lapsley at my time of life', he wrote in December 1905. 'We are very different too. He is polished, brilliant, capable, dry. I am lymphatic, slovenly, muddled, sentimental. Yet we mix well.' After Lapsley had stayed with him at Tremans, Arthur rejoiced to find how naturally he had fallen into the Benson ways. 'He loves the same sort of talk that we love – a sort of casuistical, speculative, delicate, spectatorial criticism of life.'

The new friendships were tending to take the place of the old. Tatham, Ainger, Cornish and Luxmoore still kept in touch from Eton. Howard Sturgis wrote fretfully from time to time, feeling that he had become neglected. But Arthur was fidgeted by the atmosphere at Qu'acre, and found the company – especially the Babe's – unappealing. He was also put out by Howard's mocking displeasure at his new *intime* style of writing, taking great exception to a parody which Howard had sent him, ostensibly for his amusement. 'I appear as a pompous, selfish, hypocritical, elaborate poseur. Surely no one could be *amused* by being represented so? ... The worst of it is that a caricaturist knows where truth ends and exaggeration begins – a victim not. ... I could no more think of doing it to one of my friends than I could put pins in their sofas and purging salts in their tea – and require them to be amused, because I love them so.' Percy Lubbock wrote regularly, mainly about Arthur's books, and keeping him posted on doings in the literary world in London. He was working in the Education Office and yearned for more time to write. In 1906 Arthur approached Stuart Donaldson over obtaining for Percy the post of Pepys Librarian, and secured his election in June. Thereafter their close liaison was renewed, even though Arthur felt that temperamentally they had moved a long way apart. 'The odd thing is that the more I know of Percy the more unlike I find myself to be. He constantly says things which are instinctive to him, which have no echo, no faintest echo in me. He has a fine nature, a nobler sort of feeling, a loftier judgment; while I am perhaps rather more effective.'

He was also seeing a great deal more of his brother Hugh. In 1905, Hugh moved to Cambridge, taking up residence at Llandaff House with Mgr Barnes, working – with almost disturbing success – for the Roman Catholic chaplaincy. In November Stuart Donaldson complained to Arthur about Hugh's proselytising methods, alleging that some thirty undergraduates had resolved that term to become Roman Catholics. He begged Arthur to use his influence with Hugh to check his activities. Hugh assured him that the report had been wildly exaggerated. He was, however, preparing a paper for the Jesuit Society on 'The Conversion of England', which he conceded might not actually take place in their own lifetime. It was 'an ultimate certainty, of course'. Arthur replied that he would rather go to the stake than join Hugh's Church.

Nevertheless their relations were less strained than they had been. 'He is much nicer and easier to get on with in every way, more Christian', Arthur wrote in May 1905, 'but he seems to have a horrible sense of certainty.' He did not, however, approve of Hugh's friends. Staying at Tremans with him in late August that year was none other than the notorious Baron Corvo, Frederick Rolfe, whom Hugh referred to as 'the exorcist'. Arthur liked him not at all.

A very trim, grey-haired priest [he was not actually in Orders]: neat, long-nosed, short upper lip, badly dressed, large silver spectacles, enormous rings. Very silent and deaf at dinner; but not in the least shy or humble or conciliatory. I discovered, by his talk in the chain-room, while we smoked, that he was a great egotist and fancied himself a great writer.

While he was staying with them, he burnt his hand badly when a box of safety-matches exploded in his hand. It was the sort of thing that happened to Rolfe. He had fantastic ideas about the signs of the Zodiac; somehow contrived to make everybody feel ill-tempered; he brooded 'over the house, like the spirit over chaos'. That only trouble would come from Hugh's association with him, Arthur had no doubt whatever. There was something sinister about the whole *ethos* of the man. 'He is *a me alienus*', he wrote, with some relief after Rolfe had left.

Arthur's relations with Hugh were always freer and more relaxed than with Fred, who stayed with him at Cambridge for a short while in July 1906. Fred was contemptuous of donnish life, and full of the scandals and gossip of the fashionable world: how Marie Corelli, for instance, practised daily devotions at Stratford to Shakespeare, whom she regarded as her muse. She could only write underneath his portrait, she maintained. It turned out, however, that the portrait above her desk was actually of Hall Caine. Fred, flushed with the success of *The Challoners* and *Dodo*, was patronising about the literary efforts of his brothers, giving the impression, when visiting them, of 'a great man visiting an almshouse'. He was serenely conscious of 'being in the swim, because he goes to stay with absurd countesses like Lady Radnor whose vagaries I cannot think that he would tolerate if she was Mrs Tompkinson'.

Arthur could not yet emulate Fred's sales, and noted rather covetously that 8000 copies of *Angel of Pain* were sold on the day of publication. But the tide was turning. His own fan-mail, which was to cause him despair in later years, had begun, the first letter a curious missive 'from a virgin of 30, written to me as the unknown author of the *College Window* – in a beautiful, simple style, a most interesting personal document'. By the summer of 1906 the royalty cheques had risen to undreamt-of proportions – £700 from the sale of *Upton Letters*, and £600 from *College Window*. In six months he had made £1400. 'It is only a vogue of course', Arthur commented, 'and I must husband the money – but I cannot deny that it is pleasant.' Five months later he received another cheque from Reginald Smith for £1109, and the total royalties for the financial year 1906/7 came to £3300. He had become a popular writer. By this time, other books were in the course of rapid preparation – *The Gate of Death*, *The Letters of One*, *Beside Still Waters*. On 1 June 1905 he had begun writing his study of Walter Pater and had completed it by 25 August. To his chagrin the advertisement appeared with a grotesque misprint. It was described as 'Walter Water'!

If the writing of *Walter Pater* took under three months, at least the research behind it had proved ticklish and delicate, as Gosse had warned him it would. There were 'dark areas' in Pater's life. Benjamin Jowett had gained possession of certain compromising letters which he had threatened Pater he would publish should he ever think of standing for university office. Arthur's reaction was instinctively to defend Pater's male friendships as never being anything but 'frigidly Platonic'. After he had visited Oxford and talked with Herbert Warren at Magdalen about the Aesthetic Movement generally, he was less happy. 'It will want great care', he wrote. This was 'rather a dark place, I'm afraid. But if we give boys Greek books to read and hold up the Greek spirit and the Greek life as a model, it is very difficult to slice out one portion, which was a perfectly normal part of Greek life, and to say that it is abominable etc. etc. A strongly sensuous nature – such as Pater and Symonds – with a strong instinct for beauty, and brought up at an English public school, will almost certainly go wrong, in thought if not in act. But Warren revealed to me a depth of corruption in Symonds of which I had not dreamed.'

Talks with Oscar Browning had presented Arthur with the problem rather more starkly – both in what he said and in what he exhibited of his own mind. It had all started with a visit, unannounced, which he and Cornish had paid on O.B. one evening in January 1905:

> We found him entertaining tête-à-tête a young handsome undergraduate, with curly auburn hair and delicate complexion – who had lately migrated from Cats. . . . O.B. was awful. He tried to be glad to see us. He read all his letters aloud. He talked incessantly about all his great friends. 'Dear Curzon and I were taken together in Milan in a group, in an affectionate attitude, don't you know' (uneasy laugh), 'and just as the man took the cap off, Curzon said "Surely that is not your stomach pressing against my elbow, O.B.?" Of course, everyone laughed.' So he rambled on – how he had written to Brodrick, what compliments everyone paid him, how immoral French military schools were, how he admired Napoleon . . ., how he hated the Dutch, how immoral *they* were 'and without even any grace to carry it off' . . . and so on – not a word did we say. Then he drove us out, but kept his young friend. In the outer room the valet was snoring behind a screen.
>
> The whole exhibition was horrible, depressing, painful. So much genius and personality all through, but obscured by a torrent of egotism, of a sort of ugly sensuality of view, of grievance; he seemed to take out his very heart and liver, and hand it round for inspection. Then all the handsome furniture and appointments of the room – and yet there is a kind of flesh-creeping feeling about the man, I don't know what, as though there was, or might be, something horrible in his mind. He said good-bye very cordially.

He dined with O.B. a week or so later, and talked about Pater with him ('O.B. was really horrible. . . . "I was very intimate with him – he was very much attached to me" '). The next day, Arthur and Hugh met him on his tricycle going up the Barton Road to 'inspect the Hare and Hounds . . . "because it was so Greek". "Look, look", he said to me eagerly, at the sight of a young man who had tumbled into a brook and whose clothes clung close to him "How Coan that is!" . . . I had been telling Hugh about O.B. and the aesthetic movement – how, last night, as he warmed to his work, he got more and more horrible, leering, satyr-like, and splashed mud on many honoured names. He laughed rudely and triumphantly when I ventured to doubt his aspersions; and ended off by a tirade against Hubert Parry. . . . The mind is really a very poisonous place, but what I dislike is that he is not frank about it. He said: "I never agreed with these fellows – I was very intimate with them, but never shared their views".'

O.B. treated Arthur and Hugh to further revelations about the Aesthetic Movement, talking 'darkly' about the public whipping of a boy, who was bribed for the purpose, by the Oxford aesthetes, the scourge being dipped in red ink. 'This disgusting little anecdote strikes me as a kind of horrid, bestial possession, like the were-wolf stories etc. – a curious searching for any impression that may excite or stimulate. I can conceive of a man having such a perverted sense – but to confess and carry it out in public is simply inconceivable. Well, O.B. maundered on in a horrible way, making everyone and everything vile. I don't think I am an entirely conventional person; but he gave me a disgust for the sliminess of his thought, the ill-masked delight in a sort of evil and ravenous beauty.'

One more vignette of O.B. completes the Pater story. It was in February 1906, just after Arthur's book had been published. Walking through King's one afternoon, he saw O.B. waddling slowly across the court towards him:

> He rolled up to me; he rolled round me; he struck and butted me with his stomach; he discoursed with a fixed eye, thus: 'Hurro, my dear Arthur, so glad to see you. I liked what you said about Pater so much – so true – I was very intimate with Pater, very intimate indeed (an ugly and unctuous laugh) and with all the lot – some day I shall write my recollections of the aesthetes. There was Symeon Solomon – such a dear fellow, who went into the shade. Swinburne I think taught him to drink; he didn't drink when I knew him. I remember a few years ago getting out of a cab in town and finding him on the pavement. It was "Oscar! You here!" and "Symeon! Is it really you?" It was like the meeting of Dante and Beatrice in Heaven. He

193

painted me – such a faint, smiling, ethereal sort of thing – it's down at
Bexhill – Well, I keep all my letters; and some day people will see what a
large part I played in the political and intellectual movements of the time.'
He rolled away, but presently shouted out and came up *running*, to tell me to
read an article of his in the *Saturday*: a bowler-hat, grey suit, overcoat, low
collar – immensely fat and swollen, with a grey pallor.

All this – and Hugh Walpole, clamouring for help over his sexual
temptations, too. Arthur, whose own passions had been inspired by his
love for boys and young men, felt outraged by the coarsening and
degradation of noble and romantic emotions. As a schoolmaster he knew
how easily passion could become tainted. It was the tragedy he grieved
over in the life of William Cory who – despite his faults – was eminently
lovable; far more lovable than any of those who brought him down and
condemned him. It was the same with Oscar Wilde. He read *De Profundis*
in February 1905 with mixed feelings, disliking Wilde's sense of pose and
his refusal 'to feel the ugliness of his vice'; but he was powerfully moved
by the pathos of the scene of Wilde being laughed at by the hypocritical
onlookers as they saw him in convict dress at Clapham Junction. He then
read Wilde's *Life*. What sickened him about it was not so much the
behaviour of Wilde but 'the conventionalism that smashed him. Many
men have been more vicious in orthodox ways, done more harm and
inflicted more misery, who are absolutely respectable and comfortable. I
did not know that he was epileptic and drank. This accounts for
everything. . . . I ended pitying him with the pity one has for the hopeless
and bewildering calamities of the world, a kind of helpless shudder – very
fruitless.' Many years later, he read with interest the report of the Alfred
Douglas trial before Mr Justice Darling (18 April 1913), when one of the
chief points at issue was the publication of a very frank document
intended to form part of *De Profundis*. 'It is a dangerous document',
Arthur wrote, 'because it makes that sort of passion into a noble affair.
Darling was anxious that the sordid side should be suppressed. But that is
more dangerous still, for if one eliminiates the vile and base side of it, one
leaves nothing but what was after all fine enough in Plato.'

And then there comes the question which he had posed before: 'Isn't it
really rather dangerous to let boys read Plato, if one is desirous that they
should accept conventional moralities?'

*   *   *   *   *

'I don't think I am an entirely conventional person', Arthur had written
in January 1905. If anything, as the years passed, he became less

conventional, and certainly very much more sympathetic to people who gave way to sexual temptations, even though he himself remained steadfastly chaste throughout his life. Although male friendships, and all their ramifications, fascinated him, he only once – and then late in life – allowed himself to use the twentieth-century term 'homosexual' (it was first coined in 1897) in his diaries, and then in such a way as to suggest that he had never seen the word in print. This was in 1924, when he discussed its possible meaning in a conversation with Fred:

> We discussed the homo sexual question. It does seem to me out of joint that marriage should be a sort of virtuous duty, honourable, beautiful and praiseworthy – but that all irregular sexual expression should be bestial and unmentionable. The 'concurrence of the soul' is the test surely?

This last sentence expressed Arthur's views exactly. Love is a noble passion; and no less noble for being the bond which may unite two persons of the same sex or of different ages. Such love might, at certain stages of history and civilisation, he considered unconventional, but in itself it is neither unnatural nor immoral. Indeed the propensity to feel such a love, in a schoolmaster or a don, can often be the particular gift which he brings to his calling; and if such emotions were branded as ignoble or base, then it would remove from these professions the inner commitment or vocation which so often inspires them. Who, in the last analysis, is the finer schoolmaster – William Cory, with his ardent love of boys, or Edward Lyttelton, with his equally ardent love of cricket and his taste for power?

While Cory was 'prudent and self-contained', there is no doubt at all about the answer. Cory was a romantic; he exulted in fine ideals, love of country and adulation of heroes. 'I don't suppose that E.L. has ever in all his life felt one touch of the passion which animated W.J. for his land and for her heroes.' But, in the end, Cory allowed himself to become too obviously (as Julian Sturgis once put it to Arthur) 'simply an old Greek – like a philosopher in a dialogue of Plato – born out of due time'. So sad was his falling that Arthur had regretfully to concede that – given the times and given the conventions – 'no one with a strong appreciation of beauty and charm ought to be a schoolmaster. ... Favouritism was so bad, not for the masters nor for the favourites, but for the kind of effect it had on spectators of altogether a lower morale.' This was not a considered judgement; but rather the expression of that occasional self-doubt which any idealistic or romantically-inspired teacher might be expected to feel.

The passion itself was noble. It could, however, so easily give way to taint. The relationship between the emotion itself and the way in which it was exhibited bothered Arthur all his life. When his House Captain, Percy Lubbock, began to form a romantic attachment to Howard Sturgis, several years his senior, Arthur welcomed the liaison.

> P.L. is making a romantic friendship with H.O.S. I think it will do him good – he wants sympathising with. H.O.S. struck me very much last night by saying he didn't want to be one of those men who go on always having romantic friendships with young men – so undignified – but that if he carefully eliminated the mawkish, it would be better – did not give way to sentiment – and pleased me still more by saying that he used not to care whether he did a friend harm or not by spoiling – but now cared very much and would rather break off a rising friendship than do so.

He frequently discussed the problem with Lapsley, who – on the whole – shared Arthur's views. In May 1905, for instance, 'we [A.C.B. and G.T.L.] discussed the ethics of romantic schoolboy friendships, and how far romance should enter into them. My own feeling is that they are very sacred things; that the best kind are simply passions of the purest kind. But that they are better not spoken about, either by people writing *about* them, or by friends to each other. One does not want any sentimentality about it, any glancing or hand-patting. I have myself experienced several of these devotions, early and late – but my best and closest friendships have not been made that way, but have grown up silently and even coldly, with no admixture of sentiment at all.' But perhaps this was being timid and prudish? Lapsley and Arthur agreed, two years later, that the Anglo-Saxon temperament was excessively prudish on such matters, making 'love into a secret and almost filthy business – but with the counterbalancing advantage of an ideal of male chastity'.

It is interesting to note two things about Arthur's own concept of friendship here. In the first place, he needed (as perhaps most people do) two different kinds of friendship. He yearned for romantic passion – in his case, with a young ingenuous male; he cherished steady, unemotional, relaxed friendship with those of his own age. His perfect friendship was his relationship with Herbert Tatham. At the end of a walking holiday, based on Cirencester in 1907, Arthur recalled his 'immense delight to see Tatham again, and to find him so entirely simple and unchanged. He is a strange fellow – so childlike in many ways, so robust, so good-humoured; and yet not really using his great gifts at all adequately, from diffidence and lack of ambition – but he is a very happy person.' They had spent their evenings quietly reading novels with hardly a syllable exchanged – 'the ideal atmosphere of masculine friendship'. These were the friendships that endured because they were totally undemanding.

> To me relations with others are *in no sense* unique. They are only one of many relations, with waves and winds, trees and sunsets. Then I am cursed, or blessed, with an ease of speech, and give my intimacy early, because, I suppose, it is not *sacred* for me. Relations are not holy or solemn or awe-inspiring for me – only pleasant or unpleasant. . . . But to Percy Lubbock and his school, this is a kind of emotional harlotry, I think. . . . Friendships [are] for P.L. a series of deep thrills – exultations and agonies – while for me they are only like flying sunlight on a bright morning.

The second point of interest is this. In so far as Arthur maintained any enduring friendships with women, they were all of the unromantic type; they were *brotherly* relationships and, in no sense, uxorious. He could relax with very few women – the female entourage of Tremans (and Beth in particular), Cordelia Marshall, his cousin who lived at Skelwith Fold near Ambleside and with whom he was to pass many holidays in years to come. He could relax because he felt no claim or call for commitment. He was in no sense vulnerable. When he felt attracted to a woman, this was giving way to an aesthetic appeal; and the beauty that aroused him was essentially a boyish beauty. He was captivated by the daughter of his host at a dinner-party at Exeter, when he was staying with Herbert Ryle in 1903 – an enchantress, aged 27, called Lady Rosaline – 'with her odd attractive smile and boyish look', Princess Beatrice of Saxe-Coburg (to whom he lost his heart) and Celia Newbolt (with whom both Percy Lubbock and Oliffe Richmond fell in love, with Arthur looking enviously on) are both described as if they were boys; the one 'upright, attractive, with sparkling eyes'; the other, as having a Greek beauty, especially when dressed as a boy, 'loosely-dressed in a knitted sort of blouse and cloth shirt'. On a journey to London in 1916, Arthur was entranced throughout the journey by the company 'of a most engagingly boyish girl in the train'. The hero of *Watersprings*, a shy bachelor don, is physically attracted to Maud Sandys because she so closely resembled his favourite, delightfully ingenuous, undergraduate pupil, Jack; and the moment of realisation that he has fallen in love with her comes when he sees her dressed as a boy.

'I am entirely a person of *male* friendships.' 'I am not *puellis idoneus*.' Arthur was entirely honest with himself in this respect. He was, moreover, deeply stirred by physical beauty, especially the combination of grace, personality and charm, which – to him – was the essence of the attractiveness of the young male. This was, to a large extent, a spectatorial pleasure, an aesthetic rather than a sexual thrill, although he came to recognise that, deep down, the pleasure that he took in the company of boys and young men was at root an expression of his sexual need. He would stop to watch 'young smart guardsmen' playing polo at Datchet, feeling 'a soft and filmy-eyed moth beside these bright butterflies'. He would catch his breath at the spectacle of a party of lads in the Boys' Brigade having a 'sham fight' on the downs near Lewes. 'The leader was, what is so rare with English boys, a boy of really extraordinary beauty, so fine that it gave me quite a thrill, because he seemed so unconscious of it. He stood bareheaded on a wall, directing his troops.' This very *unconsciousness* of the beauty and charm that a boy or a young man so naturally and simply possessed – all part of the ingenuousness of youth – was what attracted Arthur so much. A woman *would* be conscious of it and become coquettish. So, again, in Ennerdale, he meets 'a schoolmaster with some smart flannelled boys going to bathe. One of them extraordinarily beautiful, and with a lovely voice, upraised in mirth. It gave me a Platonic thrill. I think I have a very Greek fibre somewhere within me.'

It was not just physical comeliness and grace that caused the thrill. As this last passage shows, the voice played a large part in the attraction. One could fall in love with a voice, Arthur reflected, listening in ecstasy to an undergraduate reading the lesson at King's. At a curiosity-shop in East Grinstead in 1910, when Arthur was spending an afternoon with Fred, 'a big plain loose-limbed reddish-haired boy took us round, with a sleepy smile and one of the most beautiful voices I have heard for a long time. It is quite curious what an inexplicable attraction a *voice* has for me. It gives me quite an odd thrill even to recall the tone of it.' Little things, like hands and teeth, could make the whole difference in determining physical attractiveness. Entertaining a Magdalene undergraduate called Thorpe to lunch on 14 October 1906, Arthur noticed his teeth and experienced an 'ecstasy' of delight. On the other hand, he could not fall victim to the charms of Rupert Brooke, despite his acknowledged beauty, because 'his motions are clumsy, his hands and feet stiff, and his voice is monotonous and strangled'.

There was within Arthur very strongly what lies within most of us – not only the desire for congenial and compatible companionship, but also some yearning to adore, or receive the adoration of, the young hero so

totally unlike oneself, or endowed with the virtues and talents one has
irretrievably lost or maybe never had. It is the sad refrain of William Cory
in *Academus*:

> I cheer the games I cannot play;
> As stands a crippled squire
> To watch his master through the fray,
> Uplifted by desire.

Why else should Arthur seek the company of the young loose-limbed
Welch, the friend of Edward Ryle and a great runner, President of
C.U.A.C.? What had they in common? But Arthur tried to charm him,
and delighted in his success as 'we explored, talked, laughed, became
confidential'. So, with Gaillard Lapsley, time and time again, he would
go off to the river bank to watch the young men rowing. They were
sometimes disappointed, agreeing one afternoon in February 1907 on the
absence, so it seemed, 'of personal beauty among the undergrads',
searching the boats in vain 'like two old pagans, for shapely and graceful
creatures, but found none, none of the sweet Athenian beauty which set
Plato's heart beating and drew charming ironies from Socrates'. Arthur
felt rather ashamed afterwards. 'This was rather disreputable. Perhaps it
is there all the time, and we cannot see it. But our young men are speckled
and ring-straked, like Laban's cattle, moralists rather than hedonists, and
that lines and darkens the face.'

It was, indeed, the form in which the hedonist strain found release in
Arthur. He admitted it frankly. He regarded beautiful young men or boys
as – primarily – aesthetically satisfying to himself. Thus, at a lunch with
A. W. R. Don in 1912, when he met a charming Etonian called Elliott, he
recorded in his diary: 'I *must* try to see more of him, not for his sake but
for my pleasure.' And again, at a shoot at Moor Barns a week later, he
noted that within their company was a youngster by the name of Pease:
'such a handsome boy with curly hair, a charming smile and fine eyes; but
I fear he is quite a barbarian. I enjoyed having him to look at, however.'
So much did he rejoice in the society of attractive, ingenuous, loose-
limbed young men, and so much did his own teaching take fire when his
heart warmed to his pupil, that he was not above making personability a
factor in his choice of undergraduates for Magdalene. While interviewing
for the History Scholarship examination in March 1907, he was greatly
charmed by a candidate from Repton by the name of Cotton. When he
discussed the awards with the College History Lecturer (Hutchinson), he
found that 'the best man at present is *Ward*, a man like an ill-designed

frog, who wrote a hand composed of trailing water-weeds. I don't want to elect him!' In the end, neither was elected; the scholarship went to a man called Ibbetson. But Arthur was not going to lose Cotton. He financed a special exhibition for him out of his own pocket.

This is all very human; perhaps, as Arthur mused to himself, just a little disreputable. But it was very definitely not what he regarded as 'taint'. For these emotions to become base or tainted, certain other factors would have to be present – indeed any one of the following elements: the first was lechery; the allowing of one's aesthetic or spectatorial pleasure to be clouded by lustful imaginings and designs. He loathed, for instance, sexual books, anything suggestive of pornography. He felt sickened by ugly or leering talk, or unashamed flaunting of one's sexual tastes. O.B. could not be exonerated from this charge, Arthur thought; nor the Rector of Coveney, whom he met in June 1907, who 'shook hands with a soft clinging hand that made me creep'. He felt a little uneasy in the company of the Vicar of Richmond (Canon Leigh), while on holiday in August 1908, when he saw the pictures and photographs in his study. There was something distinctly unmanly about him which 'rather bothered me, I don't quite know why. . . . He gave me the impression of being the sort of man that O.B. is – his curious absent-mindedness and self-absorption.' He had the same feelings about a Cambridge 'aesthete' called Case, who would for ever harp 'on his favourite subject of youth and boy friendships. He is an abnormal creature, unwholesomely minded.'

Corruption, or the attempt to corrupt, was certainly 'taint'; so was vice – the unashamed indulgence in sexual pleasures promiscuously and to satisfy lust. To give way to sexual temptation, however, in the course of a love-relationship was far less reprehensible. As he grew older he became less and less inclined to regard such an action as necessarily tainted. Although he was never himself to abandon the ideal of male chastity, he became increasingly conscious of the priggishness of conventional morality and more inclined to wonder whether his own moral ideas had really been a cloak for timidity. He had no sympathy for priggishness at all. He fumed, after listening to a sermon from Henry Bowlby at Eton on boy friendships: 'Why does a man who knows boys say that there can't be a strong friendship between two boys unless they can look each other in the face, conscious of entire innocence. What *Nonsense!*' On the other hand, he was shrewd enough a schoolmaster to know how easily one can be deluded into supposing that one's motives are entirely innocent. Why does one so often want to be the friend and help-meet of *attractive* boys?

He took Oliffe Richmond to task on this, when he heard him stoutly defending his vocation to help and advise the choirboys of King's:

> He told me a long story about his old adventure with the King's choir-boy, and his recent attempts as a Don to frequent the choir-school – but his plans were thwarted by a little boy in the school, a brother of the former boy, complaining to the Master of the Choristers asking that R. might be discouraged from visiting them. If this had happened to me, it wd drive me from Cambridge, but R. takes it with a sort of mild vexation, unintelligible to me. The odd thing is that he tries to disguise his motive in the matter. He makes out that he would like to help and befriend the choristers – whereas he really has a sentimental interest in boys.

How should one advise undergraduates over such matters? Arthur talked the question over with Lapsley. 'The tendency now is for people to have great emotional affection for each other, and to be ashamed of speaking about it or admitting it; though they think it both right and holy and even advisable. That seems to me nonsense. Either the whole thing is wrong, sentimental and effeminate – or else people should not be ashamed to speak of it – among the right people of course. It is the wrong kind of reticence. I gather that Lapsley himself is a Platonic sort of lover. His real passions are given to his friends, of the same sex – he has no love for the feminine; and I think the same is really the case with me.'

This was all very well for Arthur, because temperamentally he was never tempted to move beyond the aesthetic stage of a friendship into something deeper. His romantic friendships, enjoyable and important to him as they undoubtedly were, never threatened, as far as he was concerned, to become physical or unwholesome. Although his sexual urge very obviously determined his passions, his own infirmities protected him from sexual pleasures beyond sight and sound. Sometimes he regretted this. In Tewkesbury, on holiday in 1904, he looked with envy at Laffan, King's Scholar of Eton, walking happily with two small boys 'arm-in-arm'. He could respond to a mild caress, being greatly moved by Edward Ryle who – after receiving a birthday present from Arthur – 'softly encircled me with his arm'. He enjoyed certain gentle physical sensations – having his hair cut, for instance, which produced 'a curious physical effect upon me', the more so when the barber happened to be a very attractive youth with a quiet, gentle voice. But he was horrified when he heard Tatham speaking of his holidays in Skye, where he had had to share a bed with his young nephew. Such close and intimate proximity Arthur could never – as he put it – 'deliberately undertake'. 'I

201

have', he wrote on another occasion, 'a peculiar and fastidious horror of my own kind. I have often to leave the pavement of a crowded street and to walk in the road from a horror of breathing twice-breathed air.' Not surprisingly, love-making rather appalled him. He hated to see lovers locked in an embrace in public. Young Jack Sandys, in *Watersprings*, delights Howard Kennedy's (A.C.B.) heart by telling him: 'I do hate love-making! ... It spoils everything.'

One can look at this predicament in two ways. Arthur was preserved from falling by his commendable sense of restraint. On the other hand, this strength was his very weakness. No deep, enduring relationship can be achieved without both parties allowing themselves to become vulnerable. Arthur valued his independence too highly; or – at a deeper level – his psychological infirmity obliged him to rank his liberty and privacy above any personal commitment. Either way, he was not prepared to take risks in his relationships. Perhaps, then, he should have been less ready to criticise others whose behaviour, in such a relationship, was less decorous than his own. He had himself been greatly taken with an attractive King's undergraduate called Donald Corrie. The 'friendship never flourished'. He was, however, scathing in his remarks about A. C. Pigou who seemed to have more success. Lapsley had told him of a dinner-party given by the Marshalls, with Pigou and Corrie among the guests; 'with Pigou dancing attendance in the road afterwards to take [Corrie] back and let him in the back way. It is really rather *infra dig*: for a Fellow and lecturer to go out to escort an undergraduate back like a nursemaid. Pigou is a fool; these romantic attachments may do great good both to the inspirer and the inspired, but they should be conducted with some seemliness and decorum.'

It may be dangerous, too, to play with emotions; to enchant people for your own pleasure, and then to take offence if they take you at your word. Arthur reflected, from time to time, on the strange fact that in a romantic friendship he often found himself not the wooer but the wooed. He seemed able, very easily, to attract a type of young male to him, but then he would have to consider how delicately he could deliver the rebuff. In May 1905, he wrote in his diary:

A letter from a boy, whom I know slightly, a graceful, ardent, impulsive creature, who came to my lectures; and who writes today a letter such as I have never recd in my life: if it had been from a woman it wd have been simply a very ardent love letter. I was not, in the days of my youth, inexperienced in the sensation of being made love to, so to speak, by older people. But to be made love to in this simple way, with this deep and grateful devotion for nothing in particular except for being what I am, moves and touches me a good deal. I wrote a simple, elderly letter back to say that these things were better not confessed – partly because they must be transitory, and partly because people were not always to be trusted. .... It is a very curious experience.

The interest taken in him by Hugh Walpole was of the same type. After receiving from him a very affectionate letter, Arthur wrote: 'I wish he did not believe so profoundly in my wisdom and kindness: after all, it is the occasion when one is *not* prudent, when one confesses emotion – so long as one does nothing of which one need be ashamed, or give pledges which one can't fulfil – which bring the best blessings.' Having stated the thought, he allowed to himself to consider whether all along he might not have missed something very precious by his refusal to let a friendship of this type be anything more than a pleasing diversion: 'I often wish', he wrote, 'I had not been so cautious and so timid in my relations with others.'

This was in September 1905. Although he did not know it, during the next two years his emotions were to be put to their severest test.

*   *   *   *   *

In the winter of 1905 Arthur made the decision to vacate the Old Granary and to take the lease of Hinton Hall at Haddenham. There were a great many problems to overcome, not least trouble over the water supply, but after lengthy negotiations all was set for him to move in during March 1906. He had no pangs over leaving the Old Granary. It had proved too noisy and too little of a retreat. 'The hot noisy summer gave me a kind of horror of it. But it has been a dear little tent to me for a time.'

He had seen a lot of Hugh Walpole during the summer: advising him about literature; arranging for him to meet Reginald Smith; assuring his father that Hugh's taking a post as private tutor to the son of Sir Archibald Edmonstone at his castle in Scotland, where Mrs George Keppel would be present, should not prove too serious an exposure to immorality; walking and talking, considering whether he had a vocation for the priesthood, speaking frankly about the nature of male friendships. On 4 December 1905, Arthur took a long walk with him in the early afternoon, while he rambled on about the romantic friendships at Emmanuel. 'I preached against sentimentality and in favour of emotion. He said that you could not help expressing to people what you felt, to which I replied that they generally understood it well enough. . . . I felt like an undergraduate again.' When he returned to Magdalene, Donald Corrie had come over from King's to show him some of his poetry. 'So I have spent six hours of today in company with two boys, each of them delightful in his own way; and I not only ought to be but am grateful for this pleasure.'

Indeed he had made a number of promising undergraduate friendships during the Michaelmas Term. There was a pleasant Wykehamist called Edgcumbe, with an attractive husky voice; Leslie Pym, a Magdalene pupil who won Arthur's heart by writing to the *Cambridge Review* to take exception to a vulgar parody of *From a College Window*; and – most propitious of all – a young freshman whom Arthur had espied on the first day of term at morning service in King's, not then realising that he was a Magdalene man: 'a fine-looking boy, evidently a freshman, just in front of me – lo and behold the same came to call on me; and turns out to be MALLORY from Winchester, one of our new Exhibitioners at Magd. He sate some time; and a simpler, more ingenuous, more unaffected, more genuinely interested boy, I never saw. He is to be under me, and I rejoice in the thought.'

He was also seeing something of his former Eton pupils. Edward Ryle and George Lyttelton were both up at Cambridge, Ryle incurring Arthur's wrath for spending too much of his time on athletics, and Lyttelton, who had been recently offered an Eton mastership, staying up to acquire 'a technical knowledge of English literature'. Arthur felt a particularly warm rapport with George Lyttelton. He had about him 'a tranquil kind of wisdom which makes me feel as though he were my own age'. Their sense of humour was similar, too. With savage delight, Arthur recorded in his diary George Lyttelton's latest anecdote about Mrs Sydney James – 'a real Mrs Malaprop, who said that Malvern was about eight miles from Worcester, *as the cock crows*'.

So 1905 ended in an atmosphere of agreeable companionship, young and old; the anticipation of the move to the Fenland retreat; literary success (1500 copies of *The Thread of Gold* were sold on the day of publication), and a sense of great satisfaction with all that Magdalene had to offer. 'This is a very dear and gracious home to me; and I am more happy here than ever at Eton.' The mood did not last long. Once he had moved to Hinton Hall, he wanted time to enjoy his new surroundings, and he became vexed at the claims that Cambridge and Magdalene were making on his time. On 19 April 1906 he wrote angrily in his diary, as he prepared to return for the summer term, full of resentment at having 'to live in a place which I tolerate rather than like, much hustled by many small duties, and – marvellous to reflect – I do this with no motive except a general one of obliging Donaldson and helping the College; and not only does this not *add* to my not very big income, but *actually costs me some hundreds a year.* I pay, that is, about the salary of three curates, in order to be allowèd to do work which I don't particularly like, and which prevents me from earning money.' As soon as he had returned to his rooms, however, and Mallory and Edgcumbe had paid him a visit, he was restored to good humour.

But the move to Hinton Hall had seemed to fulfil everything he had ever yearned for. He was now the resident squire of Haddenham! On the day of the move, he had taken a train to St Ives, and walked to his new property. He was greeted everywhere with deferential respect. The Huntings had seen to all his effects; Sharp (the maid) was delighted at living in the country, and there was a holiday atmosphere throughout the household. He had spent the first evening dining alone, sitting in the drawing-room writing letters and making plans, breaking off to play on his organ for a while. The next day he explored the surroundings – 'the wide, solitary fields. ... No jostling with humanity – the only living person I saw, a shepherd leading his flock in a huge field, with a crook.' He bought himself a piano and a pianola. He invited Fred to stay for a few days, followed by Tatham. He made the acquaintance of the Rector (Mr Morgan), 'a man with a poor face and a big jaw', somewhat ritualistically inclined, but a gentleman and without ecclesiastical pose. Arthur was immediately invited to become a lesson-reader and to preach. He duly read the lessons on Easter Sunday, processing in surplice and hood, and enjoyed the services, not least vespers because he was attracted by 'a jolly little choirboy who sits under me, who sings in a reedy voice like a bird, wholly intent on his music'. The preaching invitation came to nothing because he was furious at being sent, by the Bishop of Ely, a list of questions for him to answer before a licence could be issued. 'I seem to scent out some mild and meek ecclesiastical tyrannising here.' Arthur refused to take the matter further.

His guests at Hinton Hall during the summer of 1906, invited to explore Fenland with him and to ensure an unbroken sequence of companions, read like a catalogue of his friendships old and new: Hugh Walpole, Edmund Gosse, George Lyttelton, A. C. Ainger, Howard Sturgis, Percy Lubbock, Donald Corrie, Edgcumbe, George Mallory,

Leslie Pym, Gaillard Lapsley, the Donaldsons, Maurice Baring, Marcus Dimsdale, H. E. Luxmoore. For a short while during August, Edward Horner came to stay with him at Tremans (to Arthur's joy, suggesting the invitation himself). It was to be a holiday of unashamed self-indulgence, enjoying his new property, getting to know his neighbours, organising outings with his friends. He would accept no commitments. Walter Durnford observed bluntly, when Arthur told him that he had refused an invitation to the Bishop of Ely's garden-party: 'No one in the world has so little idea of doing his duty as you.' Lady Albinia rallied to his defence by pointing out that Magdalene claimed a fair amount of his time. Durnford laughed: 'He only does that because he likes it.'

There was truth enough in that. But if Arthur liked to organise his pleasures along his self-indulgent lines, he could not have anticipated the drama in store for him when Hugh Walpole came to stay. He had been sensing that Hugh's romantic attachment to him had been slightly cooling off, as his enthusiasm turned towards his intended work at the Liverpool Seamen's Mission ('Right and brave', commented Arthur, 'noble work, but how dingy! Should I not hate it?'). Hugh Walpole duly arrived on 14 June, more relaxed than Arthur had expected, and they spent the first evening trying out the pianola and talking 'like old friends', with Hugh sitting at Arthur's feet on the hearthrug. They had an outing to Witcham on the next day, Arthur noting the frankness of Hugh's conversation about his experiences at school and Emmanuel. There were further visits to Aldreth and Ely, and Hugh received the news of his Third Class in the History Tripos with equanimity and good humour. On 17 June, they rode back on their bicycles from Ely 'on a fine golden evening'.

> I like H.W.'s company very much [Arthur wrote], and he has pretty, affectionate, tender ways with him, which a person like myself, who has a shy terror of demonstrativeness, finds rather touching. For instance, tonight, I was reading some scraps aloud out of Cory's Journals, and he was sitting on the hearthrug. He turned half-round as he sate, and just leant his head against my knee as I read, without either sentiment or embarrassment, as if it was just the most natural thing in the world. Not only do I not encourage this; but indeed I think I rather repel it – but he behaves just as a son might, without protestations or gush, simply talking about what he feels and thinks.... Of course I don't suppose that this feeling will last. He will go off to Liverpool and have new interests. I am a bad hand at keeping up relationships. But it will be a tender sort of memory.

Passion without Taint

Hugh Walpole left the next day to attend the degree ceremony at the Senate House. 'It is odd and characteristic of my chilly temperament', Arthur wrote, 'that I don't miss H.W. particularly. I like him to be here. I like to be alone.' He was put out, however, on Hugh's return to learn that he had decided to join his friends for a party at the Ascot Gold Cup and would be curtailing his stay. They sat out in the garden during the evening, 'while the walnuts rustled and the stars came out, and the horses wandered snuffling over the pasture: till I shivered and grew cold. There followed an odd and inexplicable incident which I won't record: unintentional, I think. It gave me a bad night – and I lay awake till 3.' He could hear movement about the house, with doors opening and shutting. Going to investigate, he discovered that the noise was coming from Hugh's bedroom, so he ventured in. He was standing by the window, clutching a chair. His manner was odd, and Arthur concluded that he had been sleep-walking.

They went to Over the next day, the atmosphere slightly strained. In the graveyard of Over Church they started to talk about Hugh's future.

> Something I said, half-humorously, vexed Hugh and he broke out rather eagerly into protestations – He cared for me more than for anyone in the world. I could not believe it. I did not think it would last, but it would, etc. etc. Touching, of course. It is extraordinarily touching, and it is half a surprise, half a relief to me to find that there is anyone who is not put off by the general *ugliness* of body, mind, and spirit, of which I am myself so conscious. It is quite right that he should believe all this passionately; it is quite right that I should *know* that it will not last. Before the cock crows he will have another friend; and it is right that it should be so – our restless souls were not meant to lie at anchor all this time under the lee of some big vessel. I tried to say this as tenderly as I could – said I did not feel anything but *entire* confidence and gratitude – but that I *would* say that if it altered I could never have a word of reproach or thought of reproach. 'It is here if you want it; and if you do not want it, you need not feel that I shall expect you to ask for it.'

That evening Hugh Walpole left. Arthur sat in his drawing-room, stunned: not quite believing that the episode had actually happened. He sat there 'desiring I know not what. . . . Something behind it all, I think, "above the howling senses' ebb and flow". I could not write much. I began and stopped, began and stopped. Somehow when the *real* thing has come suddenly near, dropping from the sky suddenly and unexpectedly, with a whirl of wings, it is so unlike the imagined emotions that one cannot write of it. Is it not odd that a man of my age and make should have such [an] experience? The oddest thing is that all my life I have been the *wooed*, not the *wooer*! And that such sentiment should be showered over one who feels mentally and physically like Mr Back, is a strange experience. . . . It is like a monkey dancing on the passive shoulders of a bear!'

When he woke up the next day (21 June), he still could not believe that the episode had taken place. 'I am not very well', he wrote, sweating in the summer heat. 'What wonder?'

*   *   *   *   *

As his other guests came, the episode receded a little from his mind. There was an exchange of letters, Arthur writing rather frigidly. The visit from Howard Sturgis, Ainger and Percy Lubbock turned out something of a disappointment. There was too much talk for Arthur, and he tired of it. Nor was he entirely happy about the successive visits of his undergraduate friends. Edgcumbe turned out to be rather too much a man of the world; Mallory seemed somehow a little unsympathetic and self-absorbed. Arthur felt rather more drawn to Corrie and Pym, although they stayed only a very short time. He also felt that Lapsley, at close quarters, could be a little wearing. 'I regret to write it; but though I think I admire him more, and respect him enormously, yet I do not think he is as congenial to me as I supposed. We are on quite different pilgrimages.' Somehow the holiday was not turning out as he had planned. He had a few days alone before going off to Tremans to meet Edward Horner in early August, and the alarm bells began to tinkle, albeit from a long way off. 'I like being alone; but I fear it is not very wholesome. All the poisonous weeds of the mind begin to show their heads.'

But it was a joy to see Edward Horner again, after an absence of nearly two years: very tall, very delicate looking, but the charm as powerful as ever. There was much Eton talk, and Arthur discovered that Edward Lyttelton had gone down well with the boys. He discovered, too, that his love for Edward Horner was far more intense, and more real, than any feelings he had for Hugh Walpole; and that the boy's reaction and manner to him were altogether healthier and more wholesome. They walked the downs together one summer afternoon and sat talking on the top of Ditchling Beacon.

> The walk will remain in my mind as a very beautiful and memorable thing. It passed swiftly like a dream. . . . I don't know why I enjoyed it all so much –

yes I do. Because here was an absolutely ingenuous and modest boy, entirely frank, giving me not a peep, as often happens, but a steady look, without any self-consciousness or pose, into a very charming, natural, good, honest, sweet-tempered mind. . . . He loves life and people and things of interest – and then too he has the charm of manner, voice, glance, gesture, that one can't analyse, but which is there, and is so fugitive a thing. My interest takes two forms – one to retain his affection, because he evidently is really fond of me – and the other to give him good advice, which I faithfully did! The pleasure is . . . he has kept up relations all along, and at the most changeable, oblivious and fickle time of a boy's life – and now proposes of his own accord to come here. I find it very difficult to say quite what I feel; and yet I don't think I shall forget the soft green sides of the beacon, as we sate in the grass, falling steep to the plain, and the woods and the tiny hamlets – and how the sun filled all the hollows with a golden dusty light. The plain was merged in haze.

This was exactly what Arthur needed to enable him to see the strange hot-house Hugh Walpole affair in perspective. That had been affected and somehow contrived. His relations with Edward Horner were altogether more natural. 'I hated that the moments should fly. . . . The wonder is that one can talk to a boy as one can to him. I dare say I was indiscreet in some of the things I told him. But one can't help that. . . . All the more I am amazed and delighted that E.H. seems really to *care*. My only attractiveness is a certain trick of sympathetic and sometimes slightly amusing talk; not much of an outfit, in a heavily-built, anxious, timid person to attract the young.' When he left, Arthur found himself 'sad and *distrait*, having lost my dear companion, like the man in the Odyssey. It is very odd, the way in which people are pushed in and out of one's life: how much one cares, how soon one ceases to care! That is the strangest and worst part of it.' The very next day he received a remarkable demonstration of this unhappy truth. The post brought him 'a tiresome letter from Hugh Walpole to which I replied sharply and stiffly. I *hate* sentiment. I suppose I am undramatic.'

After Edward Horner had departed, Arthur found himself sinking once again into a state of malaise. Fred and Hugh got on his nerves at Tremans. 'I have not enjoyed Tremans as much as usual', he wrote. 'Neither, for some reason, has quite as much geniality prevailed.' He felt lonely when he returned to Hinton Hall, and was already questioning his wisdom is settling upon a Fenland retreat. 'If I can't be happy here, where can I be? The real fact is that I ought to be married, at my age: I like solitude and it does not suit me. I must anticipate a very low-spirited age, I think.' He found his moods switching alarmingly. One day his sense of humour would return – as when he visited Dean Stubbs of Ely to congratulate him on his appointment to the see of Truro, finding him looking like 'a faded Dionysus', with Mrs Stubbs 'a thin, sinister, acid woman, who looked as if chipped out of stone, and two speechless louts of sons, who sate and spoke not – so that the Dean and I acted a sort of little play before them. . . . It is these heavy *sons* that are the bane of Episcopal households. . . . I think I wd allow Bishops to marry on condition that they had only *daughters*.' Another day he would be cross and fretful, objecting to the 'young, noisy, ill-dressed town scum, who now that the undergrads are away swarm all over the Backs', taking pleasure in behaviour that they know to be offensive to other people. 'These young toads are so self-conscious – they *like* to be heard and seen. . . . I would far sooner kill a brace of these beastly boys than a brace of pretty partridges.' He was irritated by the torrent of fan-mail he was receiving, usually from foolish spinsters, about whom his diary entries were somewhat less complimentary than his scrupulous and courteous replies.

The untimely reappearance of Mary Cholmondeley on the scene did nothing to sweeten his temper. She had never really forgiven him for resisting her advances. Her revenge was to caricature Arthur in her new novel, *Prisoners*, in the character of Wentworth Maine, portrayed as a 'dilettante egotist'. Arthur was deeply offended. 'This has been a very curious summer', he wrote, in retrospect; 'I think I shall probably look back on it as a very golden time. I have had some great happiness, some consolations of friendship. I have been successful as a writer. On the other hand I have not been very well, not in good spirits.' His writing would suffer, he was convinced. He wrote best in a spirit of contentment. The worst always came out in a mood of melancholy, 'like a moulting fowl, conscious of shabbiness and uncomeliness. It winks its eye; it utters melancholy chuckles.'

One day in late September he decided – characteristically – to seek guidance by taking a *sors*. 'I am fond of little omens, of opening books, and saying that the words I see shall guide me – of putting my finger down on an open map, and saying that the name I touch shall speak to me. I did this just now over the Cholmondeley business, on an open map of Northants. The word I touched was HASSE.' This was certainly not a good omen for marriage! Miss Cholmondeley was assuredly not a candidate, if once she had fondly supposed so. When Percy Lubbock told Arthur that rumours were abroad linking her name with a much younger man, he declared her to be emphatically 'non nubilis'. 'Personally I

would as soon think of marrying Miss C. as of marrying a beech-tree.'
But Arthur knew that his malaise, at root, was a yearning for some
permanent relationship. 'I know what I desire – a new, engrossing,
unselfish relation – but that is what I am not likely to get. Probably the
best thing of all would be to fall hopelessly in love and to be rejected with
scorn.'

He had certainly found that a short holiday in the Lake District, with
the Marshalls at Skelwith Fold, in early October, had lifted his spirits for
a while; and he had enjoyed very much the company of his cousin
Cordelia Marshall with whom he had taken several fell walks – Crinkle
Crags, Pike o'Blisco, the Fairfield Horseshoe, Scafell Pike by Rossett
Ghyll. She proved good company for a man; perhaps because there was
something inherently mannish about her. In a few years' time, he could
picture her as 'a pleasant, sunburnt, thick-booted, frieze-coated maiden
lady, who tramps about her place, like a man, with her dogs'. In the years
to come Arthur spent many happy days with Cordelia, often lamenting
for her that she had never found a husband. They might have suited each
other well.

The new academic year (1906/7) augured well. The College accepted
Arthur's offer to purchase an organ for the chapel and a chapel screen
(even Newton acquiesced); and he enjoyed discussing the plans for these.
There were some interesting new undergraduates to meet – a young
Indian called Nehru; Arthur Grimble (of future *A Pattern of Islands*
fame); a pleasant advanced student from Emmanuel by the name of
Raverat, who proved to be an admirer of Arthur's books. Percy Lubbock
was now close at hand, as Pepys Librarian ('I saw the light in P.L.'s room
and was glad that he should be here'), and Oliffe Richmond was back in
residence at King's. Arthur was invited to a number of spectatorially
promising occasions. At the beginning of term there was a great dinner at
the Trinity Lodge to meet Lord Avebury, with the chief figures of
Cambridge science all present. 'Thomson's harsh voice, strident laugh,
genial smile, snaky locks were notable. M. Foster is rather a silly man, I
think; and sits on a back seat wondering why he was ever on a front one.'
Montagu Butler was host, saying grace, his voice rising 'like a stream of
rich distilled perfume. A nervous don opposite me gave a start and looked
wildly round when he began.' Arthur had the strong impression of faded
glory. The Trinity Lodge, which used to be the centre of Cambridge life,
was now 'merely a colossal almshouse for a distinguished man'.

In December he was invited to lunch with Princess Henry of

Battenburg at Kensington Palace through the good offices of Stephen Gaselee who had become tutor to the Battenberg boys. This was the prelude to Prince Leopold, then at Eton, being entered for Magdalene. Arthur enjoyed the occasion, at least in retrospect. He decided that Princess Beatrice was very definitely *nubilis*. 'I believe she has refused many offers. I don't wonder. That is the sort of person with whom I could fall in love. There were some dim ladies-in-waiting.' At lunch he sat next to Princess Henry. Arthur felt in 'his most walrus mood', but managed to keep his end up. They talked about Ena, the Queen of Spain, compelled to watch bull-fights and nearly fainting at the horrors. Princess Henry talked warmly of the Benson books, being fascinated by the title *By Whose Authority* – 'a book by Mr Benson's clever brother'. During the audience after lunch, 'she soon seemed to be bored, so I said, "I must not keep you, Ma'am", whereupon she shook hands with disconcerting alacrity and real cordiality, and went away with a sort of farouche dignity, as tho' she was not certain how she looked from behind.' Arthur then joined Gaselee who was with Prince Leopold and Princess Beatrice both shrieking with laughter at a telegram. 'One of them used so strongly scented a soap that the mere handshake lent a fragrance to my own hand which I perceived two hours later!'

Just before Christmas Arthur went to stay with the Fords at Repton, where he had promised to give a lecture. He was impressed by Lionel's obvious achievement. He was introduced to the chief housemaster, a muscular Christian by the name of Vassall, of whom he had already been told the story that at House Prayers, on an occasion when the boys seemed particularly lethargic in their responses, he had snapped out at them 'Here, pray up, you boys!' But, most of all, he was moved by the atmosphere of conjugal bliss in which Lionel and his wife so obviously lived. 'Good God, what would not one give to care for anyone like that!' he reflected, noting the adoring glances of Mrs Ford when Lionel returned to the house after giving Arthur a conducted tour.

So yet again he allowed his thoughts to dwell on marriage. Of the eligible ladies he had met during the term, who had showed an interest in him? One, undoubtedly, was Jane Harrison, who had talked very confidingly to him at a dinner-party on the subject of physical beauty. 'Poor soul', Arthur had commented privately. 'She must hate mirrors.' Vernon Jones had done his best to interest him in a young lady called Miss Dobbins, who had been at a convent at East Grinstead with his own wife. She was reputed to be an heiress to a fortune of £80,000 and apparently worshipped Arthur Benson from afar. He arranged for Arthur to meet her at dinner in their house. 'She was a pleasant, pretty, well-dressed creature, clever and agreeable', Arthur wrote. 'We had a nice evening.' But the matter ended there. It was no good. He was not made for marriage. Given the choice, he said to Percy Lubbock at the end of the year, 'I would prefer an eternal solitude. I want to observe people, to know their thoughts, but I don't want to form *ties* with them.' As for such women friends as he had ever had, he had always squabbled with them. 'I *don't* like the sex.'

*   *   *   *   *

So what remained? Edward Horner was passing out of his life as he became an undergraduate at Balliol. Arthur suspected, rightly, that he did not really belong to his world, a fact brought home to him by a visit from Eddy Marsh, an old Eton acquaintance, friend of George Wyndham and the Custs, who bore down upon Arthur in October 1906, full of talk about the Taplow Court set. The reason for the visit soon became obvious to Arthur. 'He had been touring with Edward and Cath. Horner; and it seemed to me that he was épris with sentiment and admiration for both. I could not augur which he loved best. In fact I think I owed his visit to the desire to talk over Ed Horner, and because he had conceived a higher idea of the man whom E.H. liked.'

Diplomatic relations had been restored with Hugh Walpole, after their exchange of letters, and Hugh came to stay with Arthur at Tremans after Christmas. He had decided to leave the Liverpool Mission and, for lack of family funds, needed to start earning right away. At the end of February he secured, as E. M. Forster had done before him, the post of tutor to the children of the Countess Von Arnim, the author of *Elizabeth and her German Garden*; and – since for various reasons the tutors came and went with some rapidity – his services at Nassenheide would be speedily required. This would give him an opportunity to study languages and work at his first novel. Arthur approved. 'I feel myself strangely responsible for this boy. His mother is such an invalid and his father so busy that he has but little home life.'

There was, however, one undergraduate pupil who fascinated Arthur; and who somehow, while being perfectly friendly and courteous, remained distant and seemingly immune to all efforts to charm him. This was George Mallory. Arthur made a supreme effort to make him lower his barriers by inviting him to stay at Hinton Hall during the Christmas vacation of 1906. They cycled off together in a drizzle on 11 December at the end of term.

> Mallory is a delightful creature [Arthur wrote] – very refined, clear-headed, affectionate. We have many common interests. His father is a Cheshire squire, but Vicar of Birkenhead – he deliberately exchanged his own rich and comfortable living for this ghastly work at the age of 45, feeling he was growing too comfortable. The boy a Wykehamist – one of the most ingenuous and purest-minded creatures I know. He is one of my History boys; he is also a great Alpine climber, tho' only 20. He is very beautiful, too, to look at, and finely proportioned, so that it is a pleasure to me to see him move, or do anything – quite unsentimental, tho' romantic. ... He comes with the least little touch of shyness and reserve.

On the second evening Arthur achieved the break-through:

> My companion lost his last shadow of reserve; we had a long talk about religious difficulties, miracles etc. I found him an advanced liberal, but meaning to be ordained. Then more personally still, he told me his early romantic attachments etc. Most interesting – and I had thought him rather a kind of *Ion* in this respect.

Arthur lent him *Dr Jekyll and Mr Hyde* to read. 'As I write this, he sits behind me ensconced in a chair – in absolute silence, except for his breathing and now and then a turned page. I have always liked the boy since I first saw him in King's chapel – and now a little barrier seems to have melted away between us.'

He left on 14 December, Arthur returning to see him off after a meeting with the Rector of Haddenham.

> I came back, through melting snow, and saw my dear companion off. This boy has grown much into my heart. He is so simple, ingenuous, affectionate and grateful. He is romantic, but not at all sentimental, like H.W., and I feel that his liking for me is a kind of filial confidence. Never mind what it is, it is sweet and encouraging. We were photographed at the door, but the results were somewhat grotesque. He appears impish, I like an old bear. ... I ... then took a lonely walk.

Arthur did not rush this friendship. He saw Mallory from time to time during the next term, usually with Edgcumbe. In the early summer of 1907, his new friend began to confide freely in him about his love affairs, especially his passion for a young girl of sixteen. 'I don't wonder at a girl falling in love with him', Arthur wrote, deeply touched. The boy was then taken ill with jaundice, and Arthur visited him, arriving one day together with a florist's boy bearing a bunch of lilies of the valley. 'A gentleman brought them and gave no name', the lad said, handing over the enigmatic note 'From a fair unknown'.

While Mallory was recovering from jaundice, and unable to row in the College boat, Arthur had many chances to walk or cycle with him. On 25 May 1907 – after a day in his company – he frankly admitted to himself what had happened.

> Why should I pretend that I do not love this young friend, and take deep pleasure in his company. . . . I did not sentimentalize for an instant – except just at the end to say that I had enjoyed the day. . . . I don't want to be sentimental myself. It is a different sort of feeling from that. It is a pleasure in the sight of him, the sound of his voice and his company. . . . Pleasure in a very virginal kind of innocence. . . . But he would dislike anything emotional, and so should I; and yet one seems to want *something*. There is some haunting wish to establish a *permanent* feeling, a tie which is impossible. And I suppose that, in reality, far off, disguised, refined, transmuted, it is really the instinct of passion: but how unrecognisable! . . . Well, so we rode together, and walked together, and had tea together, and said many absurd things that came into our heads and smiled at each other like two good comrades. The church at Guilden Morden had the gate tied with a wreath of shepherd's purse – a good omen!

The summer term of 1907 was full of events for Arthur. He was busy working on the final proofs of the Queen Victoria letters, after many mishaps and difficulties, chiefly caused by 'His Gracious Goodness' at Windsor Castle. Arthur decided to take a deep financial plunge and bought himself a car. A magnificent green motor was delivered to Hinton Hall in June 1907, and he engaged Chapman, a Haddenham man, to be his chauffeur. The College was aware, too, that it was about to lose one of its most eminent men, old Professor Newton, who became seriously ill with dropsy during May. He died on 8 June. 'He was a regular old John Bull', Arthur wrote, 'loving his own opinions, hating sentiment, enjoying life in a fine, full-blooded way.' His last words to Stuart Donaldson, who went to pray with him when he was taken with syncope on the night before he died, were 'God bless my friends, and God bless the College – and may Zoology flourish as a study here.' Then: 'Let me die in my chair, like Bradshaw.' They took him to his chair, and 'he died like an old Viking'.

At the beginning of the vacation, Mallory came to stay with Arthur at Hinton Hall. They tried out the new car; and Arthur was not sure that he liked the experience. 'It makes me headachy, giddy and bilious, which is a sad disappointment.' But his guest made up for all vexations. Mallory read some of his poems – 'rather conventional in expression, but full of the joyful melancholy of youth'. They hired a boat at Ely, Mallory rowing 'by deserted wharves, grass-green and melancholy, by cottage gardens and willowy islets to a place where the Cathedral stood up over the orchards like a crag – and here we lunched at our ease and discussed absolute beauty'. They soon got on to the subject of sentiment in friendship:

> I had the feeling ... an uncomfortable, semi-physical feeling – that in my companion's spirit there was a great and deep perturbation of emotion. I felt scorched, as by a fire. Now my own emotions do not scorch – they merely shine and ripple like the waters of a lake; and when I come near this sort of *fire*, it makes me, I think, uncomfortable. His point was that we should *never* express such things. Mine, that if one can *trust* a person absolutely, not to give one away, there is no objection to an easy and natural frankness. I do think we English people are absurdly reticent.

They talked about Magdalene. 'There was much romantic friendship in the air – and then dipped into a darker moral region, the shadow that lies behind such friendships. That is one of the few things about which I do not speak my real mind.'

To Arthur, it was 'a day in a thousand'. Hearing Mallory talk made him feel 'young and rash'. This promised to be the relationship he had pined for. But – could it last?

> I wonder what these affections mean, whether there *is* something real and permanent behind them – or if we merely meet as fellow-pilgrims, love each other, are sorry for each other, and then fall back into the stream.

That day, at any rate, Mallory had 'walked with me as the angel walked with Tobit', whatever the future might hold in store.

Chapter Seven

THE WILD BEAST BESIDE ME

> I should be so happy today; but this shadowy terror, and the feverish reckoning up of contingencies affects me very much. It is all so mysterious at present. It lies in wait for me, whatever I do, like a wild beast, moving silently through the forest beside me. (September 1904;)
>
> The black dog was on my back. (April 1913)

'I reflect sadly', wrote Arthur in September 1904, 'that the very things one schemes and labours most carefully to get . . . in spite of the kind and persistent refusal of Heaven, are the *very* things that may turn to dust and ashes in the mouth, when at last Heaven gives them, worn out by importunity.' There was, indeed, a bitter irony in Arthur's nervous collapse during the autumn of 1907, at a time when so much of what he had striven to attain seemed to have been achieved. He had pined for solitude, declaring confidently two years before 'I shall never be afraid of solitude again', and he had acquired the seemingly ideal retreat at Hinton Hall. He had yearned for companionship to relieve the sense of loneliness that he had then discovered, and at last he had secured the romantic friendship he had worked so carefully to bring about, with his triumphant captivation of the heart of George Mallory. He had hoped for literary success and independence of means – to prove to others, as well as to himself, that his rejection of other courses and other opportunities was, at least materially, justified. By 1907 he had become a famous author, elected to the Literary Society in February of that year, with royalty cheques and a fan-mail to ensure that whatever he wrote in the future would find a market.

It seemed almost as if he had only to articulate a wish for it to be gratified. He coveted the finest residence in Magdalene. On Newton's death, he was offered the tenancy of the Old Lodge, and eagerly accepted it. He wanted to be recognised by those whose professional status was unquestioned; and in a dozen little ways the gratifications flowed in. He was appointed an examiner for the Seatonian Prize, and confessed to feeling pleased and self-important striding through the busy streets of

217

Cambridge in cap and gown to attend the selection committee at the Vice-Chancellor's. At a performance of Elgar's *The Kingdom* at King's ('the music of Heaven, with a strange and unearthly quality about it'), Elgar greeted him as his old friend and collaborator afterwards and went back with him to Magdalene. 'Elgar was interesting. He told me his eyes were overstrained and he could do no work – then he said simply that it was no sort of pleasure to him to hear the Kingdom, because it was so far behind what he had dreamt of. It only caused him shame and sorrow. . . . He seemed all strung on wires, and confessed that he had petitioned for a seat close to the door, that he might rush out if overcome – by shame and sorrow, I suppose.' Edmund Gosse, who had offended him by a stuffy and censorious critique of *Beside Still Waters*, seemed to have become a good friend again, staying with him at Hinton, and accepting – albeit grudgingly – his advice and criticisms of his draft speech for the unveiling of the Whistler Memorial. 'Well, he is a real friend: the odd thing is that I see his faults clearly, but am very deeply attached to him, by a kind of insoluble tie, like relationship.' If only he had a better instinct for dress. 'He walked about Ely yesterday in a flowered lavender waistcoat and a black tail-coat – the whole crowned with a very old cloth cap.' Then, amongst Arthur's fan-mail – admittedly shoddy, sentimental stuff for the most part – came a letter from Princess Beatrice asking him to send her his autograph.

Yet happiness and peace of mind eluded him. Worse than that: throughout the year the storm clouds of deep depression were gathering, reminding him of the mental anguish of his last undergraduate years at Cambridge and the sense of dereliction that had tormented him off and on during his first twelve years as an Eton master. He became more and more self-critical in a futile way – criticising the faults he could do nothing about, or (if he could remedy them) doing nothing to do so. He brooded over his lost opportunities and failure of nerve. He felt taunted and mocked by his very success as a writer, because the audience he appealed to was so little worthy of his real gifts. He became obsessed by anxieties over his health, feeling himself to be in the predicament of the rich fool, awaiting imminent retribution. Where was peace to be found? He tried prayer, or – at least – his equivalent of prayer, slipping down to the court at Magdalene at midnight, 'the moon wading through clouds, with a golden aureole, over the cupola of the Hall. The place absolutely silent and beautiful. I did not exactly pray – but I spoke with God – saying that he knew all I was and all I desired to be, and all I could and could not be, and that I left it all to him.' But the fretful self-questioning returned. If one sought out an enchanted place, the mood that lent it enchantment had gone; the sweet had become bitter. One of his favourite cycle-rides – through Harston, Shepreth, Meldreth and Melbourne – taken to lighten his spirits, only weighed them down still further. 'I don't think I can ever go that road again. I have traversed it three times in a week and all three times in vile gloom.' Self-analysis was certainly no comfort. What did one learn? 'The fact is that out of the six parts of my being I am about one a man and five an artistic female, with all the faults of the sex. . . . My real mistake was giving up the uncongenial life of Eton, in a sort of impatient luxuriousness, with the result that after a year or two of ease I have found suffering.' He schemed for leisure, and was granted his wish. 'God turns the flame of his burning-glass on the writhing spirit.'

G. H. Wilkinson had helped him in the past. Perhaps he could do so again. He met him, by chance or providence, at a dinner-party at the Pembroke Master's Lodge in February 1907. Arthur was at the time rebelling against any notion that God could be Love – so much of what He seemed to do to a man was the very opposite of what might reasonably provoke love. 'He strikes, and does not make one understand, so that one co-operates in darkness and blindness.' Wilkinson took Arthur to another room and they prayed together, the butler coming in while Arthur was on his knees. 'I had the blessed consciousness that I should not have cared if the whole of Cambridge had been looking at us.' For a while he felt relief. But 'I slip from frying-pan into fire and back again with vast celerity.' The trouble was that every cure seemed to be a cause of his malaise. He needed solitude, but that made him lonely; he needed society, but that made him crave to be alone. He had written himself to a standstill and needed a break; but writing was his relaxation and he was always at his most content when he had a load of writing on hand. Perhaps he asked too much of life? He brooded long over the words of a dour Calvinist, advising his daughter who was suffering from great affliction: "Remember that all short of Hell is Mercy."

But perhaps he was deeply mentally ill? His father had suffered the same way. Was there, perhaps, a strain of insanity in the Benson stock? Deep, deep down this unspoken thought gnawed at his mind. There seems little doubt that his malaise turned into a depressive condition following the news of Maggie's terrible breakdown at Tremans at the beginning of May 1907. Arthur received a telegram from Dr Ross Todd, the Benson family doctor, on 4 May and hurried home. His mother and

Lucy, all set to leave for a holiday in Venice, had been living a nightmare existence for the last two days. Maggie had taken to her room, convinced that her soul was totally lost. She had taken Roddy's whip-thong with her and 'I won't describe what Lucy described – but M. said she had been seeing what pain could do.' She had then tried to tie her own hands together. She had begged to be put under restraint. Consultants were brought in, and there were hints of cerebro-meningitis or delirious mania. A third opinion was called for (Dr Savage) and the doctors agreed that she must be confined under restraint at once. Arthur signed the committal order – 'a case of blood-poisoning from influenza'; everybody in the house was told to stay in their rooms while Maggie was brought downstairs and driven off to St George's Convent at Wivelsfield, near Burgess Hill.

Arthur was shattered. 'Why could not she be allowed to have a better time? She did not ask very much of life, and has been disappointed in everything. ... What a beautiful, desirable, sad, treacherous, unjust world it is, little things punished so heavily, big things left alone.' Looking back, he realised how the climax had been building up. Maggie had become curiously dominating, almost as if she had assumed the role and *persona* of her father; very critical of her mother, deeply suspicious of everyone's motives. This was 'all part of the gathering malady'.

Arthur, Fred and Hugh visited Maggie a day or so later. She wanted only to see Hugh. 'I felt today', Arthur wrote, 'that my own dim religious philosophy was a poor thing to ask anyone to hold on to in a state like M's. She wanted the kind of religion that Hugh could give her, the idea of other people's prayers, the personal touch of Xt. Alas, I can't say that even that makes it *true* for me – but I felt that Hugh could help and comfort her and that I could not.' Before returning to Cambridge, he visited Maggie again and found her much more relaxed. She was sitting out on the terrace doing some crochet work. Perhaps she was going to recover.

At any rate, Arthur's spirits rose for a while. Honesty compelled him to admit that he had had a contented and relaxed holiday with Tatham over Easter at the King's Head, Cirencester. He had some work on hand (a collection of 'prose and poems' published under the title *At Large*); there were the sublime few days with Mallory at Hinton Hall, and – for a while in July – while Maurice Baring and Percy Lubbock were with him, he felt that he had fully recovered his sense of beauty. They motored into Suffolk and stopped at a village called Icklingham.

> We had a delicious stroll in wild meadows by a clear stream with gardens
> and paddocks running down to it. Beyond lay wild heaths and warrens with
> belts of firs – very characteristic Suffolk scenery. The sun lay hot on the
> fields and the horses whisked their tails in the shadow, across long stretches
> of meadows deep with sedge. . . . We did not talk much but just murmured
> of what was in our minds. P. an ideal companion, entering so readily and
> easily into a mood.

It was pleasant to discover Percy again, after odd, tempestuous,
emotional entanglements with more transient figures. They instinctively
laughed at the same kind of things. It had been characteristic of both of
them, on a previous walk, to attempt to put into letters the curious sound
of J. W. Clark's voice. How would one render the words 'The Library'?
It would come out 'Ver yibewrwawy'.

The summer continued quite evenly. Arthur had been appointed to
the Council of Gresham's School, Holt, and attended his first Speech
Day there in early July. He enjoyed the occasion, but was highly critical
of everything he saw (a fair sign of restored health). The Headmaster,
Howson, did not impress him at first meeting, his manner being 'self-
assertive, bold and uneasy all in one'. And the speech from Field Marshal
Sir Evelyn Wood (in full dress uniform) was 'the usual rot about ability
being the gift of God, but character being in our power to acquire. Why is
this lie told year after year? . . . I was amused to think how much better a
speech I could have made and how *infinitely* less effective it would have
been.'

A spell at Tremans in the late summer produced further upsets,
however. Maggie was no better and was apparently convinced that the
sisters at the Convent were trying to poison her; the Cornishes came to
stay, trying their best to conceal their recent sorrow at the suicide of their
son-in-law, Reginald Balfour; there were quarrels with Fred and Hugh
over the expense of Maggie's illness, Arthur feeling that the others had
ducked their obligations and were leaving the chief financial burden on
his shoulders. A host of minor irritations accentuated his malaise: there
was a new station-master at Horsted Keynes, replacing the genial and
respectful Mr Chalker; reviewers were griping at the repetitious element
in his books ('Ruskin and Carlyle said the same things over and over . . .
often in the same words.'); Walter Frere and his sister arrived to stay
without Arthur being warned, and it was assumed that he would have the
time to entertain them. This was the sort of liberty that exasperated
Arthur. He took strongly against Miss Frere who had eyes only for Mary

Benson. 'My recollection of her at meals is an ear and the rim of a cheek, her face being set towards Jerusalem – i.e. M. B. She is rather a dull lady. I hear she is semi-learned in Biblical things.' Frere's laugh got on his nerves. 'I fear someone must have told him it was hearty and infectious. It is a great contrast to his worn and rather seedy aspect.'

In this uncharitable state, on 28 August, he went over to see Maggie at Wivelsfield. It was an experience he was never to forget. It was not only that he saw her at her worst – so convinced of the evil designs of the sisters that she made Arthur promise that he would never come again; but – as he was leaving – he heard distinctly the sounds of some poor female inmate screaming in the lower part of the building. The pathetic, tormented cry seemed to pierce his soul. 'This is a place of torture and living death', he thought. He could not rid his mind of it. On the way back, 'I touched as dark and dreadful a depth of despairing bewilderment as I have ever felt, and it seemed better that we should all die and fade away.' What could God's purpose be? 'How is one to believe in love?' He woke up on the following morning in the grip of terrible depression, his mind full of the sickening delusions of Maggie and the sound of those horrid screams. 'Something seemed to crumble in my brain and clutch my heart. I thought I was going to die. . . . I don't recollect having been so depressed since those dreadful days at Cambridge. It gnawed my mind all day long.'

A short respite came. There were two idyllic days by the sea in early September – the first at Seaford with Fred; on the following day at Newhaven with Hugh. All his love of natural beauty seemed to flood back: the sight of a great heron; a sunset of extraordinary splendour; the children on the beach. 'I like the long-limbed, brown-skinned girls and boys, playing eagerly on the rim of the sea. I wished in vain that I had a home and family of jolly children – but these things are given and cannot be taken. The strangest thing of all is one's powers, by imagination and contemplation, of taking into account all these other lives; one is in it all and yet above it; as though one had a particle of God's heart inside one.' With Hugh at Newhaven, they moved on in the afternoon to Rottingdean and sat on the cliffs watching some boys bathing. The appeal to the *voyeur* element in Arthur was almost too strong for him to bear. 'What a beautiful thing the human form is after all, and how vilely we conceal it – a little brown boy, taking headers off the pier was a delicious sight.'

He left Tremans, calling on Ross Todd on his way back to Cambridge. He was pronounced physically sound, but in need, maybe, of a holiday abroad to give him some new experiences. Arthur also looked in on Fairfax Murray; an important encounter, as it turned out, as it led directly to the offer by Fairfax Murray of thirty of his best pictures to the Fitzwilliam Museum. For a while Arthur's mind was diverted from his melancholic broodings by the move of his effects into the Old Lodge (and saying a rather wistful good-bye to his old rooms, with the "College Window" which apparently hordes of visitors had come up to view during the summer – 'This is a kind of fame, I suppose'). He accompanied Hugh to inspect a property at Hare Street, which Hugh was minded to buy as a little Catholic retreat in the country. All in all, he came to the conclusion that 'my good days are beginning to outnumber the evil'. But he was becoming less and less sure of the wisdom of maintaining his exile at Haddenham. 'I have been here nearly two years and yet I know hardly anyone. I feel that I *ought* somehow to know the people, but I don't see how. They are shy and self-respecting folk too, and expect me to make advances.' Just before leaving Hinton Hall for his annual short holiday at Skelwith Fold, at the beginning of October, a strange thing happened. When Sharp brought in his coffee at 9 p.m., she hovered at the door and then blurted out that she was sorry that he was going because she had a 'presentiment I should never come back to live at Hinton'. It was 'the beginning of the end'. Arthur laughed away her fears, but she was not to be persuaded.

All was well at Skelwith Fold: some happy walks with Cordelia Marshall; an amusing encounter with his ninety-year-old great-aunt (Mary Jane Sidgwick), who delighted in maintaining that she was both older and infinitely more hale and hearty than Beth at Tremans. As soon as Arthur met her, she was eager for news of "Elizabeth", manifesting 'a grim satisfaction at any hint that Beth's powers are failing. "She does not really know her age", says my aunt, nodding mysteriously with compressed lips. "She could not produce an entry in a register", and goes padding off, leaving in the mind the impression that Beth would turn out about 16.'

The new academic year started well too. He met Mallory by chance on Bletchley station, on the journey back from Windermere, and they travelled together to Cambridge (Mallory and his companion hastily obtaining first-class tickets). 'Conversations in trains are a doubtful pleasure – and we had a scrappy, bawled sort of talk, being all of us too shy to hold our tongues.' Arthur was enraptured by the view from his new College window: 'simply exquisite – a box-hedge – the N. wall of chapel hung with flowering creepers, a great lime, yellowing with autumn – a perspective of trees and lawns and old walks beyond, and the sombre Lodge looking over to the left'. Indeed he was in a better mood than he had felt for months. He had a row with John and Hallam Murray over misaddressing the draft advertisement for the *Queen Victoria Letters* to "Arthur Berry, King's College" ('the worst of a conference with J.M. is that the doors are open and he is so deaf that one has to shout'). On publication day, another major row broke out over the news that a German publisher had broken the embargo and published in advance of the agreement. But Arthur took this all with equanimity. He was enjoying making the acquaintance of his freshmen: the delightful Cotton from Repton, a tongue-tied boy called Miles ('a rather pretty creature who has had his share of petting'), and a healthy, shy Christ's Hospital boy called Knappett. He enjoyed his first experience of being host to 'The Family'.

On 21 October the depression returned, just after Ross Todd had told him that Maggie was to be moved from Wivelsfield to the Priory at Roehampton. 'There followed a perfectly horrible day, fighting hour by hour against acute and perfectly mechanical depression.' On the night of 27 October, he wrote to Ross Todd asking for an immediate appointment. He tried to be as normal as possible on the following day, giving lunch to his old matron (Mrs Cox) and walking with Monty James ('a perpetual pumping of talk out of the vale of misery'). Todd came to see him and was reassuring, especially about 'what is a natural dread', the possibility that he was about to be afflicted with the same malady as Maggie. On 30 October he was in a state of virtual collapse. He wrote again to Todd asking to put himself in his hands. 'On Friday I shall leave this place, perhaps never to return. I don't write this in any mood of self-pity. I simply write as one who has come into stern contact with an awful reality.' The decision relaxed him. He dined normally that night with Monty James, Walter Durnford and William Cunningham, Archdeacon of Ely. After a sleepless night, he walked round the College mentally saying good-bye. A telegram from Todd assured him that arrangements had been made; and on Thursday, 31 October, his diary ends with a pencilled scrawl: 'Well, enough of this. I must enter into the battle.' On 1 November 1907, Todd placed him under the care of a specialist, Dr Blaikie, at a nursing-home at 9, St John Street, Mayfair.

*　　*　　*　　*　　*

The depressive illness lasted for two years, during which time (apart from the first fortnight at the nursing-home in Mayfair) Arthur maintained a day-by-day chronicle of his miseries, his various treatments, his attempts to return to normality, his holidays with patient friends, as gradually the illness ran its course. The most harrowing time was – as one might expect – during the first six months, as the doctors debated his condition and Arthur resigned himself as a man without hope to a future of chronic neurotic invalidism. The spell at Mayfair lasted a little over three weeks. After a fortnight he felt sufficiently recovered at least to describe in his diary what had occurred.

He found himself in the same room where, two months before, Robert Collins, equerry to the Duchess of Albany, had been operated on for cancer. Once he capitulated to his depression, he collapsed utterly. 'I felt myself brought face to face with the ultimate and inexorable darkness. I saw my wretched, self-absorbed, indulgent life, chance after chance to be noble and good, thrown away; and yet I did not know what the darkness held. ... My past appeared in the light of a golden time of happiness, in which I had thrown away all my chances; my future as, at the best, a broken and invalided shadow; and the present absolutely horrible. ... This surpassed anything of which I had ever dreamed.' He remembered isolated incidents: a few hours of serenity reading *The Shropshire Lad*; a day when two operations were taking place, and seeing from the stairs the great glass container of Biniodide and Boracic, odd wheeled tables with nurses dressed in white, the sickly smell of ether, 'the careworn surgeon and smart assistant carrying the bag of tools'; games of cards with the Irish sister, by the name of Ada; occasional taxi-rides, and memories of East Sheen and Temple Grove, as he crossed Barnes Common; being told that he had been awarded the C.V.O. for his work on the Queen's letters and receiving the news as 'a matter of utter indifference'.

On 23 November he was thought sufficiently recovered to take a holiday at Aldeburgh (the Wentworth Hotel) with Percy Lubbock, and then with Edmund Gosse. It brought no relief, only the realisation that 'the sights and sounds of life fill me with horror, envy, dismay'. On 11 December he departed with Percy Lubbock to Rome, to fulfil his promise to Ross Todd to see if a complete change of scene could help to recover his zest for living. Most of it was a nightmare. He was looked after by an English doctor in Rome (Dr Smallpiece) who could only counsel patience. He tried to be normal, going to St Peter's on Christmas Day ('I thought and even hoped that I might be going to die'), and having dinner that night at a hotel with Cyril Alington and Charles Gore, who were taking a holiday. The Elgars were in Rome too (another case of depression), and Arthur and Percy visited them. 'Lady E. *very* kind, but without charm and wholly conventional, though pathetically anxious to be *au courant* with a situation. Elgar's daughter, about 16, a quiet, obediently silent, contented sort of girl, interested in Rome.' Arthur asked Elgar his opinion of the church music in Rome and received a dismissive reply. "Oh, I don't care about music in church." The great man took a lamp to light Arthur down the stairs. 'The worst thing about him is the limp shake of the thin hand, which gives a feeling of a great want of stamina.'

Twelve days in Florence followed – and still no relief. The beauty did not speak to him. 'I don't think I can ever come to Italy again, whatever may happen', Arthur commented. He returned to England for a short spell at Tremans to prepare himself for the private investiture of the C.V.O. at Buckingham Palace on 20 January. He picked up a volume of Shakespeare's plays the night before and tried the *sors*:

> I opened on the passage in Richard III, when Richard is in his tent on the eve of the battle. Stanley comes in and says: 'Fortune and Victory sit on thy helm' and R. replies: 'All comfort that the dark night may afford, Be to thy person etc.' Very superstitious, no doubt, but it cheered me a little.

Ross Todd gave him a 'nerve-potion' before he went to Buckingham Palace. Hunting came to the Athenaeum to help him dress up in his frock-coat. When Arthur was summoned,

> the King was standing near the door. He looked well and rubicund, his face very much lined and wrinkled, not so stout as I remember him. He shook hands with me with an easy and natural kindness, said he was glad to see me and then gave me the box of insignia, saying he was most pleased to confer it, and held out his hand, which I kissed, a firm wrinkled rather hairy hand.

They had about ten minutes' conversation, the King observing that to continue the series of Victoria's letters would be to tread on 'very dangerous and delicate ground'. 'He saw I think that I was nervous and ill-at-ease ... The King gave me the impression of a jolly, active, bourgeois man, full of kindness and tact, who thoroughly enjoyed being King and doing his job well.'

Todd wanted Arthur to attempt to return to his duties at Magdalene. When he arrived at Cambridge station, there was Lapsley standing in cap and gown to greet him. Arthur lasted two days before wiring for Todd to come at once. Another specialist was called in, and the decision was taken to put him under the care of a Dr Caldicott who boarded a few mental patients at his house in Hampstead. The period at Hampstead (from 22 January to 24 February 1908) was probably the most wretched time of all. Here he was under supervision. He heard the doctors discuss whether he should be allowed to go out alone. He noted, with a sort of horror, 'an ominous scrawl on the window and a sinister little padlock'. He took walks over Hampstead Heath; pointless, drifting strolls down the streets of South Hampstead looking aimlessly at shop windows. He searched pathetically for little omens. 'I was quite upset by a bit of paper blown to my feet, with DOWN printed on it. Yet the next two things my eye lighted on were REPAIRS in one shop window, and REFRESHMENTS in the next. Again as I walked, I wondered to myself where Greencroft Gardens were, from which De Cordova has been writing to me: and I said to myself, "it shall be an omen of good if I pass the street". The *very next* turning was Greencroft Gardens!' He was allowed to visit friends, even to look in at the Athenaeum; but the contrast of happy, normal lives with his own pitiful existence – returning to 'my lonely hermitage', playing schoolboy games with the other 'lodgers' in the evening – sickened him.

When suffering affliction, it comes as a sort of lugubrious comfort to realise that one is not, by any means, alone. Wherever he turned, whatever he read, he came across others whom he knew personally, or knew of, who had to carry this cross: Vernon Jones at Magdalene; Herbert Paul; Margot Asquith; Marcus Dimsdale; Hubert Parry; Edward Elgar; G. H. Wilkinson (whose death he heard of while in Rome) – had all suffered in similar ways. While at Hampstead he read of the suicide of Wilfrid Thomson, son of the Archbishop; he heard, too, that Lapsley had had a collapse through nervous depression. George Prothero – he was told – 'is treading, I fear, the same sad path as myself'. Apparently Von Hügel endured a similar misery for two years on end. Perhaps it was a rare privilege to be spared?

The doctors hoped that he would be relieved by veronal, and on 24 February he was allowed to leave Hampstead with Fred for a spell at Tremans. Fred and Hugh took it in turns to keep him company. 'My brothers have stuck by me of late in a very loving manner', Arthur acknowledged, 'and I am not ungrateful.' On 16 March, Todd tried the experiment of sending him back to Cambridge. It lasted ten days this time, giving Arthur opportunity at least to set his papers in order in expectation of imminent death, and to take a sort of dim satisfaction in noting that Mallory was not being neglected. 'Gaselee is rather épris with M. just now, I gather. Very good for both. G. is a fine old crusted Tory, with a strong dash of the world about him. M. a rather sentimental radical, and they may learn to see if not to respect other points of view.' There followed a month of almost unrelieved gloom at Tremans. Odd items of news from the outside world caused a flicker of reaction. He heard of Cyril Alington's appointment to the Headmastership of Shrewsbury in April, and reflected in his diary:

> He will have a big and difficult job and will do it well; and then he will succeed Ed. at Eton. I wrote to congratulate him; and I had twinges of remorse at the thought of the zest with which he will take up the job, and at the thought of how I have missed my chances, by feebleness and fastidiousness, and general flabbiness, of doing a big work in a fine way.

In May he had a fortnight's holiday at Dunster in Somerset with Ainger. He was a little better, although the memories of previous holidays roused in him 'a poisonous kind of regret for lost happiness'. He heard the news that Percy Lubbock had decided to leave Magdalene and that Stephen Gaselee had been appointed his successor as Pepys Librarian. Gosse, who had recently come into a fortune of £46,000, succeeded Ainger as his companion when they moved from Dunster to Broadway. It was the same problem. These places held too many memories of happier days. Arthur tried to express his predicament through the words of a pathetic little poem entitled 'The Thrush', beginning with the line: 'I have no heart for music now'.

> It was not thus in other days
> When mine own heart did music make:
> But now I have no song to raise
> And so be silent for my sake.

During the summer the illness seemed to pass into another phase. He had occasional days of relief: six days out of twenty-four between the middle of May and 15 June, spent largely at Skelwith Fold; a happy day at Seaford with Hugh on 7 July, playing like children on the beach, throwing stones at a cock-shy and making sand-castles; but he paid for it by a day of abject misery on the morrow. He made a brief visit to Cambridge to attend a College meeting on 9 July, making the acquaintance of Newton's successor as Professorial Fellow (Professor Nuttall) and watching a performance of *Comus* in the evening, memorable for the ridiculous acting of Cornford and his first sight of Rupert Brooke ('beautiful arms and a radiant figure'). On his way back to Tremans, on the train to Horsted Keynes, he seriously contemplated suicide:

> I prayed to have courage to end my life. . . . It seemed to me so easy to lean out and let myself be struck senseless by some bridge or signal post. After passing Three Bridges I was at my worst and we ran quickly into Balcombe Tunnel – and then I could have done it, as the edge of the arch comes so close to the train, but I knew I had not the physical courage.

The company of Mallory, however, at Tremans revived him. He could even laugh at Aunt Emmeline Woodhouse's inconsequential talk. Somebody mentioned the name 'Horatio', and this set in motion a train of thought communicated in a low voice with many 'smiles and winks': "Yes, Mr Lockhart was called Horatio, I am sure; he was brother to Mrs Robertson who had that fine house on the cliff – They lived in good style. I heard all about it from Emma Page, who was my kitchenmaid. She went into service there, but she could not stand the cooking! But now I think of it, it was *not* Horatio, but Terence." Ross Todd had him to stay for a few days at his house at Goring; but at the end of July the suicidal mood came over him again, and he felt certain that he could not last out the month. 'I am sure that some crisis draws near. I was to all intents and purposes mad this morning', he wrote on 28 July. A long holiday with Gosse at Richmond, and then at Sedbergh, where he was joined by Ainger, revived him.

So the moods oscillated over the next few months. In October, Todd decided to try hypnotism and sent Arthur to see a great specialist, Dr Oulterson Wood, in Margaret Street. 'The great man turned out a pompous ass', Arthur wrote. 'Even in my misery I could not help noticing his absurdities. He rolled elaborate phrases on his tongue. "Mental depression – involving as it does the tension of some of the most delicate physical organisms – involves a considerable degree of discomfort." ' He could not treat Arthur himself but suggested one or two other specialists in hypnotism – a Dr F. Woods and a Dr Bramwell. He had five sessions with Dr Woods during October, paying two guineas a time to have his midriff stroked and a soothing hand caress his brow. It was like trying to put out 'a conflagration with a drop or two of scent'. Nevertheless Arthur was back at Cambridge and endeavouring to appear normal and to do some teaching. A whole year had passed since his collapse.

Gradually the depression was abating. He became involved in College business again, taking a strong line over the impending appointment of a College Lecturer in History. He met the young Frank Salter in R. V. Laurence's rooms at Trinity in February 1909 and resolved at once to secure him for Magdalene: 'an *excellent* man – bluff, strong, sensible, amiable – just what we *want*'. Later that month two new Fellows were elected – Stephen Gaselee (without emolument) and Talbot Peel, with Salter as College Lecturer, and Arthur felt well satisfied. He began to take an interest in undergraduates again. Hugh Dalton at King's, the son of Arthur's old friend Canon Dalton, came to call on him to sing the praises of Rupert Brooke. Arthur persuaded Mallory to bring him to tea. He turned out to be 'shy and silent, and would not part with his opinions'. He made the acquaintance of the new Director of the Fitzwilliam Museum, S. C. Cockerell, having tea with him in 'rather a mean house' by the station and noting the artistic young men whom he had collected there, with Rupert Brooke in their midst: 'the sort of young men I could have been excited about how short a time ago. But today I just knew they were delightful.' He started to dine with the 'Family' again, and to become more involved with Gresham's and the business of the Fishmongers' Company.

There were very black days, but they were noticeably fewer; and occasionally the whole nightmare seemed to dissolve, and he was back as he had been before, indulging in spectatorial delights and disrespectful gossip with his friends. At the Pepys Dinner in February, with Shipley and Cockerell as his guests, he was able to relax completely, criticising the speeches, revelling in the singing of a choir-boy from the gallery, and then playing a little game with Shipley by attempting to define the word 'gentleman' in relation to the other members of the company. 'We could not define it, but we took about a dozen of our guests and sorted them, and agreed *absolutely* about them.' As he retired to bed he allowed himself to ask the question – 'Am I really better than I think?' The next day he had a happy cycle ride with Percy Lubbock out to Horningsea.

> We sate under a haystack out of the wind and in the sun. Haddenham tower on the Isle across the wide meadows. I told P. L. exactly how things were with me – and it seemed to clear my mind of some poisonous stuff, for I had an hour of real tranquil joy and hope, content to sit and talk of other things and watch the sun on the old pasture and the far-off clumps and the shadowy hills of the Isle. I do thank God for today. . . . a little space of quiet happiness given to me, with a real sense of returning to life out of my hideous cage of suffering.

He had a grievous relapse in March, but he managed to hold on and remained at Cambridge. At the end of the Lent Term he decided to take the risk of going off on holiday with two much younger companions. Hugh Walpole had returned from Germany, and had secured an assistant-mastership at Epsom. They had met once or twice over the last few months and there had been no repetition of the frantic emotionalism of two years ago. Arthur invited him for a holiday at Ashbourne, where they would be joined for a few days by George Mallory. Certainly Hugh Walpole did not succeed in charming Arthur out of his moods.

> H. W. is full of go [Arthur reflected]. He is publishing a novel, writing another, he reviews all the fiction for the *Standard* etc. He is full to the brim of life and books, but I think he is treading the wine press of books almost too strenuously. ... He makes friends with everyone – his latest captive is Henry James, who writes to him often. All this is very delightful, and I do in my feeble way rejoice in it. Though it makes me feel horribly old and cold and broken too.

He did not greatly approve of the histrionically emotional set in London with whom Hugh seemed to be almost dangerously involved. There was a 'strange jealous' creature called Jennett who accused Hugh of trying to steal one of his closest friends (Spooner), and ludicrously effeminate and emotional scenes followed. 'He seems to have an extraordinary knack of getting taken to people's hearts. But I can't help wishing he could make more women-friends and contemplate marriage. If I were not in so hopeless a mood, I should know how more than happy I am to have secured the affection of so eager and ingenuous a creature. As it is I can only drearily endeavour to behave decently and try my best to make him happy here.'

Mallory's arrival made for difficulties that Arthur had not anticipated. Both young men were highly suspicious of each other to begin with, and Arthur had the strong impression that each would have preferred to be with him alone. But on the first evening, after dinner, they began to talk eagerly together over clothes – a subject 'which rather interests me, but interested them so much that they did not allow me to say a word'. Arthur was thoroughly put out. And the next day was worse:

> I did not enjoy this day at all. H. W. and M. developed strong and youthful mutual interest, and I suddenly became aware that I was the amiable middle-aged man who was only just a figure in their dreams.

Hugh Walpole began to talk about himself – and would not stop.

231

Having told his life-story at length, he then began to expatiate on schoolmastering. 'Even here, where I had some little experience', Arthur grumbled, 'I was still excluded. "Ah, well, I dare say it may have been so in your time – but it is very different *now* – *I* make it a rule, and found it an excellent one, never to take back a punishment etc." Well, one must some time or other be relegated to the shelf and it has come to me now – but in my case, not by age, but by illness. . . . M. curled himself up and listened, while H. W. discoursed . . . with an attempt at self-depreciation which did not succeed.' Arthur felt himself to be 'a faded leaf'. Indeed, he liked not at all 'the rather common fibre' which Hugh Walpole was revealing in himself – 'a sort of rather ugly and chuckling self-confidence'. In desperation, Arthur suggested that they might have a game of cards. Hugh promptly replied that he was too sleepy – and talked for another hour. 'I admit it has been a little trying to find myself, the host, fall between my two guests, and their interest in each other swamp their relation to me.'

Mallory left, after a disgraceful exhibition by both young men during church on the following morning, laughing so much at the Vicar's foolish voice that Hugh had to go out. He tried to make amends with Arthur when they were alone again, by telling him more about his intense emotional friendships, especially with Jennett and Spooner. They travelled back together to London, and at St Pancras station, 'W. fell into the arms of his Spooner. It was painful to me to see with what joy he leapt into his real life. He tried hard to part with me emotionally, but I fear he was thankful it was all over.'

The holiday had turned out something of a fiasco. After a short break at Tremans, which added to Arthur's vexation through Beth being taken ill and his mother's persistent efforts to persuade him to visit a faith-healer, Arthur returned to Ashbourne for a short holiday with Gosse who did his best to revive his spirits. Arthur recorded all his anecdotes faithfully and humourlessly. He was plunged yet again into deep depression, reaching 'the nadir of wretchedness' at the end of the month. He struggled through the next term as best he could, consulting three doctors who gave contrary advice. Todd was convinced that the only thing that would shake Arthur out of his morbid introspection was some sharp shock, emotional or physical. He planned to take him to Harrogate in the summer to receive the full treatment that the Spa could offer. In the meantime Arthur's condition was to some extent worsened owing to his suspicion that his friends were losing their patience with him.

Shipley, for instance, ignored him completely at a presentation ceremony to J. W. Clark at Trinity. 'Since illness and eclipse, I have ceased to be a person of consequence to him, because I can no longer be of use – so he drops me, courteously and good-naturedly – I don't suppose he is aware of this.' He seemed to be drifting apart from Lapsley, too, while both of them were sunk in depression. After an evening together in June, talking about their fears and sorrows, Arthur felt 'we were asking ourselves mutely if this is the end of a friendship and if we should ever meet again'. On all sides, friends and contemporaries were gaining honours and leaving him behind. Alington's happiness and success at Shrewsbury (very evident to Arthur on a visit he paid on him with Ainger in early June) were somehow galling, in a totally unreasonable way. Then came the news of Henry Bowlby's elevation to Lancing.

> Bowlby the new Head of Lancing and Gosse offered the Principal Librarianship of the B.Mus, which he has, wisely I am sure, declined. These opportunities, so well deserved by my friends and so richly earned, pierce my heart. I don't envy them but I feel how sadly and ineffectively I have thrown my own chances away. Yet it is not that – it is a deeper thing – it is the radical thinness and timidity of my nature expressing itself. I had nothing to *give*. I wanted my life to be a pretty portrait, and constructed decoration. Well, I am punished and it serves me right.

It did not even cheer him to receive from John Murray, in July, a huge cheque for £4600, the profits from the cheap edition of the Queen Victoria Letters. 'The sum gives me the income I require for life', he noted unemotionally. A trace of bitterness crept in to his comment on the news that Henry James had formed a close romantic friendship with Hugh Walpole: 'very good and happy for both, I expect. But I feel envious, alas. If I could but experience a real emotion, or find some work, this cloud would disperse a little.'

So to Harrogate with Todd, in late July. Arthur hated it. He hated the place; he was nauseated by the treatment – a 'disgusting process, the details of which are unrepeatable. It is the Plombières treatment. I was left alone in the operating room, smelling of disinfectants, sitting on a towelled couch – and my reflections were of the saddest. One has suddenly slipped into the world of the invalid state.' The waters were horrible too, like drinking the fluid from bad eggs. The whole place 'seemed to me like *Hell* – the crowd of fashionable invalids, the wearisome pleasures, the air of *haut ton* coupled with the sense of illness.'

The shock came, however, at Harrogate, not in the way that Todd had planned. Arthur first read the news, misreported, in the papers; a letter the next day confirmed the worst interpretation he had been able to make of the garbled newspaper report: Herbert Tatham had been killed in the Alps, 'a slip and a fall on an ordinary path above the hotel. He died on the spot.' Arthur was stunned. 'Why was not I allowed to go, who am sick and useless and miserable. I have known him intimately for 35 years and he has been my closest and most congenial friend.' For a while he was plunged into abject misery.

Towards the end of August 1909, Hugh joined him at Harrogate, replacing Todd, determined to make Arthur go out and about. They went to Ripon to be entertained by the Bickersteths, having tea on the lawn with Cyril Bickersteth and two nice girls. A flicker of humour returned:

> They were all engrossed in Hugh whom they knew and loved, till I felt inclined to say 'I also am a man'. So I sat sweltering like a toad swollen with its own venom, trying unsuccessfully to engage jauntily in the talk.

During September the suspicion occurred to him that he was getting better. He had mooched around with Gosse, Ainger and Percy for a fortnight or so at Settle. He then went to Skelwith Fold, discovering that both the urge and the capacity to write had returned. He began composing some articles for the *Church Family Newspaper*. That his touch had returned is evident from his description of meeting old Aunt Mary Jane:

> She said that she hadn't seen me for 20 years and that I was now getting an old man. She especially asked me about my children, and said that she supposed I was the only one of my generation now left. . . . She asked about Beth, and was pleased to hear that she had been ill and seldom left the house, rather disappointed to learn that she was not deprived of most of her faculties. It is very strange this twilight of soul and body and mind – she wanders vaguely about, and sounds the gong whenever she passes it – but does not seem unhappy.

At Skelwith Fold, Arthur came to a decision. He would throw away all his medicines. It did not bring him the immediate relief he hoped; and all Todd could recommend, on their next meeting, was a further course of hypnotism. He had sessions with Dr Bramwell and a Dr Wright ('This is the tenth man I have been to', Arthur commented ruefully). They seemed cheerfully confident, pooh-poohing any suggestion of suicidal impulses or incipient insanity, and after several sessions, Arthur conceded that 'the gloom is a little lightening. . . . Can this absurd treatment be doing me good? It is rather humiliating.' In actual fact he was to all intents and purposes cured. No further reference to his health or state of mind is made in his diary for the rest of the year, except to salute the return of his powers and his zest for life. The two years nightmare was over.

*   *   *   *   *

Arthur Benson described his depressions in *The Upton Letters* as a sort of 'neuralgia of the soul'. He offered varying explanations for the condition: he had overtaxed his brain; he was suffused with guilt feelings over his renunciation of important posts and his self-indulgence, both in his writings and style of living; he was being chastised for his timidity; he was suffering from a Benson malady. But whatever it was that practically incapacitated him between 1907 and 1909, it was something that had lurked within him all his conscious life. It was latently there in his mind; and if dispelled or conquered for a time, it still lay in wait to reassert itself when conditions, circumstances, or crises determined that it should. However it may be described – 'the wild beast', 'the black dog', 'the satyr lurking in the bushes' – it was, as it were, the side of his mind that complemented the gifts of vivid imagination and intense appreciation of beauty, without which he could never have tasted so keenly the pathos of the human condition and the bitter-sweet quality of beauty itself. Because his mind was in tension, he saw with peculiar clarity the incongruities of the natural order, in its simplest manifestations, and how life itself was a complex of tensions – now ugly, now beautiful; now tragic, now comic; now cruel, now kind.

He might be remembered by posterity as a cosy writer, enunciating a cloistered and comfortable creed. Perhaps he had only himself to blame if this is the impression he gave. But this was utterly at variance with his view of life, and of the pilgrimage that all are bound to make. Beyond the river bank, with its high hedges, are not only enchanted places and sacred shrines, but also evil spirits and lurking demons. 'Well I know all the corners of the road, the shadowy cavernous places where the demons lie in wait for me, as they do for the wayfarer . . . in Bewick, who, desiring to rest by the roadside, finds the dingle all alive with ambushed fiends, horned and heavy-limbed, swollen with the oppressive clumsiness of nightmare.' We may talk of life as a pilgrimage, but is not our progress so often – as Arthur saw his own – 'like the abject figure in *The Winter's Tale* of the gentleman pursued by the bear; it was a dolorous and undignified flight, full of miserable indecision and helpless prostration'. As far as he was concerned, Arthur admitted that 'I simply shuffled despairingly away from the monster which pursued me, murmuring apologies, and pleading for mercy.' In his brilliant description of the complex mind of F. W. A. Myers, he expressed how pursued and pursuer can co-exist, perhaps to some extent must co-exist, in one and the same consciousness. Looking at that mind, 'it is as tho' one saw an altar, surrounded by thickets: the pure smoke stealing up; but an ugly shadow behind, a Satyr lurking in the bushes'.

Arthur's eye searched for beauty; but he was fascinated by ugliness and corruption too. After all, if one has spectatorial gifts, the eye will feed on anything graphic, sometimes – as one well knows – in spite of oneself; in spite of one's better feelings and nobler instincts. Arthur could describe the ordinary, and the beautiful within the ordinary, superbly. So also could he describe the corrupting elements and the ugly: a dead rat writhing with worms; another horrible, though pitiable, rodent caught by two dogs who ripped it apart while alive; a dog eating the putrefying skin of a rabbit; a shrike eating the brains of a dead fieldmouse hung from a point of barbed wire; the huge dead worms dug up in Magdalene garden, when drains were being laid, and large vermilion spiders; strips of horsemeat hanging up in a shanty near Barrington; a putrescent cow, skinned after falling from a rock in a field near Ashbourne.

In dreams, of course, one cannot be selective; although something of the state of one's mind can be gauged by what one's subconscious chooses to dwell upon and to invent; and, indeed, to act out. Arthur, like his father, dreamt very vividly and possessed an astonishing ability to recall his dreams. He himself saw his dreams as a curious dichotomy of two parts of his consciousness – the part that invented the situation and predicament; the other part being himself as essentially the observer, sometimes the incredulous, outraged or amused observer of what his consciousness had invented. The spectatorial side was, therefore, very active in his dreams. Just as in his normal life he could detach himself from his surroundings so that he could the better observe them, so in his dream-life that sense of detachment was even stronger. He watched himself doing improbable things, as a spectacle, totally divorced from any moral considerations. He might feel the sensations that he saw enacted – anger, pride, self-importance, fear, lust, envy – but it was more like empathy for a character that he observed than a sense of real personal involvement. As he put it himself, 'the observant part of the mind' is 'utterly unaware that I [am] myself originating it all. And the only natural inference would seem to be that there is a real duality of mind at work.'

236

Because one is the originator, one must reveal in one's creation some interesting insights into oneself. On the other hand, it was rather like watching a play which one had never seen before, with oneself as the chief character; a play, moreover, conceived on a vast scale by an artist who was totally amoral and whose characterisation could be singularly naive and inept.

> My adventures seem interminable [Arthur wrote] – one small inconsequent adventure leading to another – in wonderful landscapes. If dreams reveal a subliminal self, I have an extraordinary power of conceiving landscape, on a gigantic and elaborate scale – and a vast appreciation of picturesque beauty, but no moral ideas, and a very feeble grasp of character. People who come into my dreams are clearly seen, but don't do characteristic things.

'The wild beast' beside him would manifest itself often enough in nightmare form during his dreams. He would occasionally have the classic experience of hearing soft footfalls coming to a door, the handle moving, and then ... nothing but the prints of some unidentifiable beast. Sometimes there would be fantastic horrors in the course of a dream: loathsome offal being stuffed into the head of a Pomeranian dog; removing a coverlet from a bed to discover 'strange, large flies – grey and tufted, others very bronzed and bright'; a sawn-off face dangling from a tree, with a horrid, yellow, viscous substance dripping out of it. The very essence of nightmare is the unexpected change or transmutation, either visually or through other senses – a child who turns out actually to be a wizened old man; a parrot on his shoulder who suddenly bites his ear viciously; when he tries to dislodge it, 'it cracked'.

Nightmare situations abounded, but often became confused with farce. He frequently dreamt that he had been arrested and put on trial with varying degrees of unpleasant penalty to follow. Thus, in September 1904:

> A trial, in which the defendants, or rather prisoners, were myself, a man whom I knew to be Lord Morton, and a third, unknown to me. I could not discover what we were being tried for. It was before a mixed assembly, which I supposed to be the House of Lords; a judge in wig presiding. It was just like Alice in Wonderland. By attentive listening I discovered it to be a case of conspiracy; and the only definite charge that was made was that in the presence of Arthur Heygate, who was a witness, someone had said that the only way to punish the Colonial Secretary for his political mistakes was by not asking him to dinner. To this I was supposed to have assented, though I had no sort of recollection of the incident.
> At the conclusion of the first morning Lord Morton was condemned to be

executed. I saw it carried out. We went together to a place outside, where there was a flight of steps. He laid his head down, and a man with an axe cut pretty deep into his neck. I saw into the cut, it was like a currant tart. He then rose, and walked a few paces with me; but saying that he felt ill (no wonder) sat down, soon sank down and died.

After this the trial, which had before been an amusement, became an anxiety to me. It continued, with all sorts of irrelevant speeches. 'I never will desert the Navy', said one man at the conclusion of an impassioned speech. I beckoned a man in a wig to speak to me, and said to him 'Can't someone make it clear that I know nothing about the case?' He said, 'Oh, it will be all right.'

The Bishop of Winchester [Herbert Ryle] rose among others to speak, very affectedly, dressed in full robes, with many odd ornaments, leaning his hand upon Ed Ryle's shoulder. He said in the course of his speech, which I thought weak, that he had had his pocket picked on the previous day, and had lost a gold pencil-case, which had belonged to his father, and which he greatly valued. 'But far more', he went on, 'did I feel the loss of a MS which the pocket contained – one of dear Arthur Benson's letters.' This I thought to be in poor taste, but saw that it had produced a favourable impression. I was overshadowed all the time by an urgent fear of death, but speculating as to whether the sort of execution I had witnessed would *hurt*. I said to a lawyer who came up, 'I should not so much mind if I were dying in a good cause; but to be executed on a charge which I cannot comprehend, supported by incidents which I cannot recollect, seems almost grotesque.' He smiled, and said, 'Others have felt the same before you', which I felt to be unfeeling. I was then called...

Most of the nightmares were inadequacy dreams: taking a class, not knowing the names of the boys, and when he had procured a list, finding that the class had changed; having to lecture on medieval literature at a convalescent home, and when searching in a despatch box for his notes, finding only a large doll; giving a lecture on 'Immortality', while being put off by a man in the audience making ironical comments to his dog – "Very deep, isn't it, Dick?" – so that he walked out, affronted, amid jeers; preaching a sermon 'to a vast audience in a green marble hall. I could not find my MS and stood long in silence. In order to make things easier, Warre, who presided, kept sending footmen up to me to ask by what train I was going and whether I preferred tea or coffee. A masked cocotte danced up to me and powdered my face with a puff – but still I continued to fumble with my books and to accept my humiliation solemnly. When I *did* begin I was wholly inaudible.'

More often his dreams were wish-fulfilments, or a mixture of wish-fulfilments turning into inadequacy dreams. One might expect, in view of his suppression of his sexual instincts and his repugnance to intimate physical contact with others, that an outlet would be provided in dreams of sexual fantasy. Not many such dreams are recorded. In one, he makes love to a very pretty but hollow-eyed girl on a sofa in a tent, and is interrupted by the entrance of Leo Maxse. Nevertheless the sensation lingered with him, giving him 'an odd thrill of secret happiness' all through the day. Then again, at a dinner-party, he derives a certain satisfaction from pelting a décolleté female with greengages. He is thrilled by the spectacle of naked boys and girls playing football together, without embarrassment, on a beach. Hearing the barking of a dog at night-time, he discovers when he goes to investigate the exquisite naked figure of a boy or nymph swimming. A beautiful boy, dressed only in a tunic, standing on the staircase of a great house provokes 'the utmost seduction of every sense'. Certainly wish-fulfilment of a sexual nature appears in a dream about Geoffrey Madan in the autumn of 1915. 'Geoffrey in the dream did a little silent thing which moved me inexpressibly – I can't set it down – and then very sweetly apologised. I said: "Good Heavens, don't think that I didn't see what it meant, and the adorable kindness of it. I never have been so touched in my life by any kindness I have ever received. It was a surrender!" "Yes", he said, "it was a surrender: it was meant to be that. You are so good to me!"' Alas, the climax of the dream was that Arthur had a seizure, and a young doctor was summoned to examine him, diagnosing cancer of the thumb!

A second dream involving Geoffrey Madan ought here to be recorded because of the vivid recollection of the dialogue. The setting was an open-air party at Wellington College, when Arthur succumbed to Geoffrey Madan's insistence that he should take part in theatricals with him. Arthur played the role of an 'elderly enchanter, like Prospero, with a young and beautiful girl like Miranda'. It was dusk, Geoffrey Madan was in uniform, 'very slim and graceful'. Arthur performed after Madan had said "Just to please me". The following dialogue then took place:

P. Wilt hear a secret?
M. Ay, I love secrets.
P. I will tell it thee on a May morning. It is a charm! Wilt hear a tale?
M. A merry tale?
P. Nay, there are no merry tales.
M. A sad one, then?
P. Not sad neither. Merry and sad are for Gods, not men.
M. What tales else are there?
P. Real tales, girl!

M.   What is it to be real?
P.   To be empty. Things have no bottom in them. We fall through them
     into the void!

Most of the dreams of wish-fulfilment depict Arthur in some position
of extraordinary eminence: as Pope, or Prime Minister, Master of the
Rolls, Poet Laureate, a great Headmaster, or in the company of royalty
speaking on equal terms. Usually he is involved in some elaborate and
ridiculous ritual, with ecclesiastical processions, absurd uniforms,
grotesquely coloured hoods; as often as not, the solemn occasion ends
with him making a complete fool of himself, while supposing that he is
acting decorously, graciously and appearing rather grand. So, at Eton, he
processes gravely to the Vice-Provost's stall, discovering Edward Austen
Leigh and Luxmoore occupying it jointly. He turns them out with quiet
dignity and takes his place. 'I then sang a good many sacred solos to an
enraptured crowd, in a harsh but pleasing voice.'
A typical ceremony dream occurred in July 1915:

> We were to walk it seemed in the streets in a long procession – and I was to
> speak, preach, take the lead somewhere. I put on with affected indifference a
> cope of salmon-coloured silk, and we set off. I found J. W. Clark was to walk
> beside me in a surplice, and I could see a long procession wind away up a
> street crowded with people. J. W. C. was rather snappish, but I became
> more and more pleased and excited, and thought it looked better to walk
> slightly *bowed*, like a scholar, and then to simulate a little lameness, and then
> to put on a look of abstraction.
>   I did this for some time with ever-increasing pride, when someone,
> Luxmoore I believe, came up to me, and said in a low harsh voice 'Isn't it
> kinder to tell an old friend when he is making a real fool of himself?' I then
> looked round, and what with my limping and abstraction I had got far
> behind the procession, and everyone was laughing at me. But I was too
> happy to care, and I said to Luxmoore, 'I don't care what anyone thinks – *I*
> enjoy it!' However I managed to scramble on a bit faster and to regain the
> procession by taking little runs at intervals; and then I sate in a little stall, so
> tight that I couldn't get out, and the men on each side of me had to pull me –
> and I went to read aloud an illuminated parchment and went up pulpit
> stairs, but found myself in a tiny frowsy room instead with a small window
> looking on the church which I could not open. Then I saw that the
> parchment was only references to texts which I was to read, and I had no
> bible. ... so it went on, but I was shamelessly happy all the time, in my
> salmon-coloured cope.

Arthur believed that there was a relation between his dreams and his
depressions. He dreamt less when he was completely relaxed. Vivid,

elaborate, grotesque dreams usually took place when he was overworking his brain. His imagination could not rest. It was as if it ran riot during periods of exceptional creativity, and that his level of sleep was often a sort of limbo between sleeping and waking – a semi-consciousness. It was in such a state that he created poems in his sleep and remembered them accurately enough to write down in full on waking. Sometimes his perspective was a bit awry, and what he considered to be genius in his half-waking state turned out to be rather less than that in the cold light of day. Having been reading *Moth and Rust* by Mary Cholmondeley, he dreamt of a new creation from the same source which had been dedicated to Maggie. '"To M. B. Dross and Refuse from Airy Mary". This I thought to be exquisitely funny and characteristic at the time, and woke laughing. I still think it is funny, but not characteristic.'

He published one of his dream-poems – 'The Phoenix' – which was selected for the *Oxford Book of English Verse*. He records one or two more in his diaries. A clever little dream-satire, dated 9 January 1917, runs as follows:

A bold and cheerful company of ogres, ghosts and ghouls
Attacked and smashed to little bits the City of Tomfools.
The Tomfools sailed to Araby and raised another state
I can't say how refined it was, how noble and how great.
And now in High Tomfoolery, they're very fond of telling
What an almighty hash the ghosts made of their former dwelling.
They chant their deliverance, they write and preach and say
How good it was of God to take their former pride away.

In the course of his depressions, his dreams tended to become happier and more tranquil – peaceful landscapes, vast sweeps of scenery. The grotesque and frightening dreams, and sometimes the highly comic, tended to predominate in the period before a fit of depression, escalating in frequency before the actual breakdown. Just before the breakdown of 1907 Arthur had an exceptional number of graphic dreams, perhaps indicating nothing more than that his brain was racing with ideas and with images that he wanted to record in his diary or in his books. Returning from Skelwith Fold, for instance, in the autumn of 1906, where he had visited the Severns in Ruskin's house (Brantwood) at Coniston, he had a characteristically vivid dream with scene-changes of mounting absurdity. It started with the strange predicament of having to sleep in the same room as Ruskin and Mrs Arthur Severn. Arthur worried through the night how he could manage to get dressed without embarrassment, but found, in his dream, that he was actually fully dressed at the time. Then all of them – Ruskin, Mrs Severn, Arthur and countless visitors – executed a strange old English morris-dance, with Ruskin playing an instrument like a bassoon, dancing very slowly. 'We all moved about absurdly.' Ruskin then had a fit and collapsed on the sofa, from which vantage point he discoursed to the assembly 'for hour after hour'.

In the end, all we can say is that Arthur's temperament – restlessly seeking for images to amuse, to divert, to enchant, both sleeping and waking – was, like his father's, the temperament of the manic depressive. His sense of beauty would have been blunted if nature had made him any other way. Wherever he went, somewhere – now nearer, now further away – the black dog, the wild beast, padded the same road. He knew it was there even if he could not always see it or feel its presence. For two years he had had to wrestle with it on his back. Being the determinist that he was, he had little doubt that his suffering served some purpose. When he freed himself, at last, from its embrace, he came again into the full possession of his gifts and his zest for life and for friendship. What lessons – one might ask – had he learnt?

Chapter Eight

ON THE EDGE OF PARADISE

It is so strange to be always, as I seem to be, on the edge of
Paradise and never quite finding the way in.   (7 July 1910)

An intimate talk with Winstanley about romantic friendships.
I was elated with wine and good spirits, and talked
unadvisedly. But we agreed that to be a Don and not to care,
romantically, for the young men was a very chilly affair.
(November 1910)

The one, and perhaps the only, lesson that Arthur learnt from his nervous
collapse of 1907–9 was that solitude did not suit him and that he had
made a grievous mistake in seeking a refuge on the Silent Isle. 'I can no
longer bear to think of myself as banished to a village', he wrote in May
1910. 'The odd thing is that the life I seem to desire instinctively is not
the life which suits my spirits.' Something in the atmosphere of Hinton
Hall had induced morbidity, almost as if it had been haunted by evil
spirits. The people had been unfriendly and suspicious. He could never
feel quite the same about Fenland again. The fens now made him
dejected – 'so lonely and treeless, and I feel as if I had somehow *caught* my
illness there – very odd feeling – One knows that demons haunt low-lying
and marshy places.' He therefore put Hinton out to let, and R. V.
Laurence took it for a while. Interestingly, he came to feel the same way
about it, as E. W. Barnes told Arthur after visiting Laurence there. He
had himself conceived an intense dislike for the bedroom which both
Arthur and Laurence had occupied. 'The room had an atmosphere of
oppression and even of horror. . . . He said that Laurence disliked it, and
took another room.'

His love for Magdalene intensified, almost on the rebound. The Old
Lodge and its garden had languished unappreciated for almost two years,
and yet – Arthur wrote – 'I don't think there can be a sweeter corner in
the whole world.' The College was poor and needed raising and
beautifying. 'I have made just twenty thousand pounds by writing in four
years', Arthur calculated, 'and may surely throw a little about.'
Magdalene should be the beneficiary. If a deserving boy should require a

scholarship, Arthur would find the money. He had already paid out some £2000 in financing additions and embellishments to the Chapel, the Combination Room and the College gardens. He would now steadily, carefully and regularly provide for Magdalene financially, as circumstances required. It would be in fulfilment of a wish long expressed, before he had had any inkling of the fortune that he would gain from his literary endeavours. One thing was certain: King's should not benefit from his largesse.

> I *do* think that King's is a very *rude* place [he wrote in July 1910], like a great, clever, ill-bred, doctrinaire booby – and considering its huge endowments, it does very little for anything or anybody. It produces people genuinely interested in Sociology but not genuinely interested in other people, and this sort of scientific philanthropy is a stinking product, especially when it is done to parade one's own liberalism more than to help.

Insofar as he would be prepared to help the University by financial gifts, that would depend on his own personal whims and principles. He approved strongly of the belated decision to found a Chair of English Literature, which would have to be financed from private sources. He offered £500 on the spot – anonymously. 'I don't want to be supposed to be trying to get the post.' Indeed, this was not beyond the bounds of possibility. Gosse had excitedly told him of the foundation of a British Academy of Literature which would consist of the country's leading men of letters – perhaps 28 or 30 in number. In the first ballot, Arthur noted rather ruefully, 'I came out 32nd. ... I don't want an Academy, but if there is one, I should like to be in.' He need not have worried. He secured election. 'It is a little reward for work to find myself among them', he conceded, 'to be one of the 30 best-esteemed writers in England.' His lectures were still highly popular; and he had begun work again on a serious project, his study of Ruskin, to be delivered as a course of Cambridge lectures before publication. Now he was free of the disability that had incapacitated him, he accepted every opening for work that offered itself: membership of the Court of the Fishmongers' Company (1911); a governorship of the Perse School (1911) and of Soham Grammar School (1910); membership of the Teachers' Training Syndicate (1909), and of the Education Committee of the County Council (1910). He would be a recluse no longer.

To himself he privately acknowledged that he had learnt nothing, by way of self-amendment, from his illness. 'I fell back into the old, careless ways, greedy of pleasure'; and the same sort of pleasures, too: writing self-indulgent books, enjoying life for its spectatorial qualities, looking for attractive young men to enchant. Perhaps Cambridge had changed a little since he had last taken a good, appraising look at it. It certainly seemed to have become much less priggish. The favourite topic of conversation seemed to be 'Free Love'. The story was circulating that Jane Harrison was fiercely advocating 'free love' to her girls at Newham, so that S. H. Butcher was privately advising parents not to send their daughters there. Aunt Nora confirmed the story that H. G. Wells had run off with a young Newnhamite, who was already married to a socialist, and that apparently Mrs Wells had not been much affronted. Arthur found, a little to his surprise, that he was not much affronted either. He had once had a horror of promiscuity, but he was coming round to the opinion that it was a finer thing to indulge one's genuine inclination than to submit to the demands of convention or to the ugly enslavement of a loveless marriage. 'I am not sure that monogamy is not merely a social rule. The *one* valid argument to my mind against Free Love is that people don't stop loving each other at the same moment. Of course I am not praising promiscuity; but after all it is love which justifies carnal passion – and marriage intercourse without love seems to me a far viler thing because so much more shameless.'

He rather shook the ladies at Tremans by developing these ideas. 'If wedded love is pure, I do not see that unwedded love can be impure – either the whole impulse is bestial, or it is natural.' Divorce, therefore, was entirely permissible: 'the only way to get things straight is to heal horrors – a *bad* family life is as evil a thing as a good one is good'. He found himself rather admiring people who dared to elope with their forbidden loved one, provided of course they counted the cost and adhered to their decision. Why should not Professor Forsyth elope with Mrs Boyer, the wife of an F.R.S.? 'He has had enough of Board meetings and differential equations, and has dipped for real life. . . . I really can't think it sinful. It breaks the rules, of course – but if he has counted the cost, I approve.' In the improbable environment of a dinner with the Vice-Chancellor, Arthur found himself thinking such thoughts while talking to his neighbour, Margaret Eden, the daughter of the Bishop of Wakefield. She had turned to him and said that she yearned for the opportunity to be '*wild – really* wild, I mean', instead of endlessly talking with rural deans. He felt, for a moment, tempted to take her at her word.

He was not so sympathetic with Hugh Walpole, however, who seemed to be playing with other people's emotions in order to gain kudos in the literary world. Walpole stayed with Arthur in December 1909, and again in April 1910, and was full of his latest conquests. Henry James wrote to him twice a day. 'He seems to have conquered Gosse completely. He spends his Sundays in long walks with H. G. Wells. He dines every week with Max Beerbohm and R. Ross ... and this has befallen a not very clever young man of 23. Am I a little jealous? – no, I don't think so. But I am a little *bewildered*.' He had no high opinion of Hugh Walpole's abilities. 'I do not see any sign of intellectual power or perception or grasp or subtlety in his work or himself. ... I should call him curiously unperceptive. He does not, for instance, see what may vex or hurt or annoy people. I think he is rather tactless – though he is himself very sensitive. The strong points about him are his curiosity, his vitality, his eagerness, and the emotional fervour of his affections. But he seems to me in no way likely to be great as an artist.' His sojourn with Arthur was all too reminiscent of Ashbourne – talk, talk, talk about himself; and his emotional behaviour too reminiscent of those embarrassing few days at Hinton Hall. 'When we went to bed he surprised me by an unwonted demonstration of affection, which quite took me aback. But the fact that it moved me as little as it did shows how flaccid I am grown. Ten years ago it would have set me quivering with emotion – but not now!'

Whether it was because his passions had somehow dried up during his long illness or because he was peculiarly sensitive to emotionalism, it seemed to Arthur that Cambridge during the years that Rupert Brooke was an undergraduate at King's – the years of irresponsible manhood for a generation that would suffer grievously in the Great War only four or five years off – had never been so highly-charged with romantic talk and open, intensely emotional friendships. Arthur was amazed at the behaviour of the undergraduates at King's, in the Junior Combination Room, after a Feast at the end of the Michaelmas Term 1909. They acted drunkenly, tittered at Lowes Dickinson in his hearing, calling him 'Dirty Dick', and saying 'That's the Don who goes in for Free Love'. Was he being prudish?

> I dare say such Saturnalia do no harm. They sate, the undergrads, all massed together, interesting and attractive in many ways – the public fondling and caressing of each other, friends and lovers sitting with arms enlaced, cheeks even touching, struck me as curious, beautiful in a way, but rather dangerous.

Undergraduates were prepared to be very frank, too, about their emotional entanglements. He was a little surprised that one of his pupils,

Hopewell, should choose to come to discuss with him his relations with a small boy at Lancing, whom he had taken up 'to do him good'. 'These are very odd semi-sexual affairs', commented Arthur, 'full of the mystery and excitement of sex, yet with a sort of moral aspiration behind them. They are largely physical, I think. Hopewell is a very keen and virtuous creature. . . . I advised him to leave the thing alone at present.'

Dignity and decorum should, Arthur felt, always be maintained. He noted how his charming pupil, Miles, was quite evidently épris with another of his pupils, Hepburne. 'I could not help liking their romantic demeanour, and their little courtesies', he observed to himself, watching Miles' manner as Hepburne came into the room. How much more dignified than the foolish simpering of a guest at the Magdalene High Table, Charles Sayle, the eminent bibliophile, who would not stop talking about his undergraduate loves:

> Sayle rather horrified me. He is a great sentimentalist, falls in love with undergrads, pets them, worships them, flatters them. Some of them he tames and civilises – some he spoils. I mentioned Knappett [the Christ's Hospital freshman]. 'Isn't he a dear child', said S. This from a grey-haired bibliographer seemed silly. I like sentiment. I think it does both the lover and the beloved good; it always does young men good to be loved and admired; but it must not be effeminate. Later on, a new flame was mentioned, Don[ne] of Trinity [A. W. R. Don]. Salter spoke of him. 'Ah, you have discovered him', said Sayle. 'Don't steal him from me. He is *all my world* just now!' So it went on, and I hated to see a man so give himself away.

Returning out of his limbo, Arthur began to re-assess his own friendships. In a mild, uncommitted sort of way, he still toyed with the idea of finding himself a wife. He felt a little dewy-eyed at the sight of 'a charming and pretty suffragist, Kitty Margesson', sitting with her arm round her brother at a dinner at the Magdalene lodge. 'What would I not give to find myself a wife like that?', he mused. He was much attracted by one of the daughters of the Master of Jesus, a Miss Morgan, whom he met at a dinner-party – 'very pretty, but for a rather absurd head-dress of large rough ears of corn, stuck transversely in her hair. . . . If polygamy was the fashion, I should like to have such a girl as a subordinate wife. . . . She would be delightful if one was in certain moods.' He admitted that if he were left alone with her for a leisured hour, he might well 'ask her to marry me, knowing that it would be a mistake, and probably a very bad mistake'. Whenever he was with Cordelia Marshall, he acknowledged that there was no other woman with whom he could so easily relax. But the fact had to be faced, as he confessed in his diary after discussing the matter with Annie Marshall, 'I think I like women better the more they approximate to men.'

Some of his male friendships had withered during his illness. He could never quite forgive Shipley for cutting him, and began thereafter to regard him less as a friend than a figure of fun. He had become 'fat, haggard, rosy and demoralised. He drinks too much, and he talks about his disappointment [failure to gain a professorial chair] to everyone continuously.' Shipley told Arthur the whole sad story one night at a dinner at Christ's: 'that he had not thought about it 3 months ago – till he found he could hold a big class alert. They would sit on the floor and shirk their breakfasts to hear him. "I really can help and stimulate them." Then we had the whole story of the election, how the V.C. wouldn't vote, and Lister – fresh from a lunatic asylum – could not make up his mind, and Graham Kerr – "a man whom I have *made*" – voted against him etc. etc.' Arthur advised him not to talk about the matter, but to let it subside. There would be many other chances of advancement. Shipley thanked him and agreed.

> Then he left me, and I heard him telling the whole story over and over again, in the same words, with the same shrill melancholy cadences, interspersed with little gasps. It was pitiful – he looks like Falstaff blown out with sighing and grief.

A few nights later Arthur saw Shipley and Gaselee together, consuming two bottles of port between them. 'Poor dear S. began the ancient mariner story all over again: how the men would lose their breakfasts.... "Graham Kerr – a man whom I *made*" came floating to me from the cab, as he drove quivering away.' Arthur met one of Shipley's pupils the next day and asked casually about his lectures. 'One was quite enough for me' was the cheerful reply. Three months later, Shipley dined at Magdalene. The unbelievable happened. 'To my horror we had all the old lament about the Professorship. ... "The men would rather shirk their breakfasts than shirk me" ... "Kerr, a man whom I *made*" ... A sorry Jeremiad – one must never make public lamentations.' The description of Cambridge, provided by a guest at a meeting of the Foakes-Jackson dining-club, seemed not far short of the mark: 'a sad place, so many irresponsible young men and so many disappointed old men'.

The Lapsley friendship was fading too. He had moved out to live with a wealthy American friend at Ditton Hall, and Arthur had a strong suspicion that Percy Lubbock had taken his place in Lapsley's affections. Neither Mallory nor Edward Horner could cast quite the same spell as before. He became rather fidgeted by Mallory's dogmatism and the fierce, unlovely expression that came over him when defending an argument; and Balliol had contrived to reveal a side of Edward Horner's character that Arthur had not seen before: 'a luxurious, uncontrolled, greedy, showy element . . . which grates on me – his perpetual smoking, his wine-bibbing, his clothes, his absurd flat-topped hat all give me a sense of something half-sloppy, half-pretentious'. He somehow made Arthur feel rather provincial and bourgeois.

He was seeing less of his brother, Hugh, too, now that he had settled at Hare Street. The whole ménage there made Arthur feel profoundly uncomfortable: a dangerous and gossiping woman (Mrs Lindsey) who was obviously in love with Hugh; her little son (Ken Lindsey), to whom Hugh had totally lost his heart; a strange doctor (Dr Sessions) who had given up his practice for some unaccountable reason and had developed an interest in demonic possession; an old silent priest suffering from melancholia; and – in the midst of it all – Hugh, as dogmatic as ever, chain-smoking, cheerfully stealing from the outraged local incumbent the best part of his congregation, writing best-sellers of embarrassingly sentimental apologetic, and buying up land all round with the profits from his books. 'What these people don't realise', Arthur commented shrewdly, 'is that if Hugh gets bored with them, he will throw them all over tomorrow, because his dreams are like the dreams of a child, and *must* be instantly realised.'

New names now appear in Arthur's diary with increasing frequency: for a while, Father P. N. Waggett, an Anglo-Catholic friend of Lord Halifax, who was given dining-rights at Magdalene during his Cambridge ministry; more enduringly, D. A. Winstanley, historian, Fellow of Trinity, whom Arthur had first met in Lapsley's company in November 1906 – 'a heavy-looking person, and ugly, almost portentously so, but with inner geniality'; and the young Frank Salter, elected to a Magdalene Fellowship in November 1910 ('a most active-minded, wholesome, ingenuous creature – full of fire and pleasant impulses, I like him better every time I see him. If he were beautiful as well, he wd be too enchanting to live.'). With both Winstanley and Salter, Arthur could freely and relaxedly indulge his pleasure in discussing and speculating upon his fellow-men, their quirks and idiosyncrasies, and – above all – in comparing and assessing the fortunes of their respective romantic friendships. Although both men were much younger than Arthur, the bond between them was comradely rather than emotional. But their hearts beat, as it were, in time and their emotions were stirred by the same facets and physical qualities in young men. Arthur very soon established a rapport on such matters with Frank Salter. In April 1910 he took a walk with him through Chesterton and 'we talked over all our boys; and he confessed to being very sentimental – but it is all on the right lines'. In December, they talked again on the same subject during a walk by the river, comparing 'our own and other people's *affaires du coeur*. I said, and I believe it true, that it is an ill time with one when one's pulse does not beat a *little* faster when someone draws near. I did not ever think that I should feel this again in my life, but I *do* feel it now, not jealously nor foolishly, but with just a heightening of life and joy.' With Winstanley, a perfect understanding was struck up after the Pippin Audit Feast at Trinity in the same month. They had 'an intimate talk about romantic friendships. I was elated with wine and good spirits, and talked unadvisedly. But we agreed that to be a Don and not to care, romantically, for the young men was a very chilly affair.'

So all the love of youth had returned; and there was no dearth of enchanting young men to stir his heart, especially a group of Trinity men whom he came to meet through Winstanley and Salter. There was Robin Arbuthnot, a delightful Etonian and a fine athlete with all the qualities of ingenuous charm that Arthur found so irresistible. Equally charming was his close friend Jim Butler, 'shy and delightful – I never saw a sweeter face or a more perfect manner'. The third member of the group was Dennis Robertson, whose unaffected shyness concealed a curious melancholic streak very evident in the poems which he sent Arthur to read and comment upon. His shyness could be exasperating at times however. In February 1910 he took Dennis Robertson for a walk by the river for a very confidential talk.

> He had written me the most intimate letter, revealing the devastating emotions of his heart and soul, to which I had replied as kindly and straightforwardly as I knew how. And this little wretch meets me with the face of a baa-lamb, and is absolutely silent: takes up no subject; starts no hare; just murmurs politely, while I talk like a skip-jack on a thousand things – till weariness of the world and my life and my companion falls on me. .... What is the use of trying to make friends with the young, if they leave you to do *all* the talking?

The fourth young Trinity man was a Wykehamist, Archie Don, whom
Arthur met for the first time in May 1910 at lunch with Frank Salter –
'the beautiful and graceful Don[ne], who is all Sayle's world. I found a
very nice, frank, unaffected Wykehamist, not so much handsome as
attractive.' He met him again later that month. 'He certainly is a radiant
youth, so simple and responsive and humorous. I hope he won't get
spoilt. The worst of it is that in the presence of these young charmers, I
make desperate attempts to be amusing and get regarded as a voluble and
tiresome old Don, I fear.'

Freed from his crippling and souring depression, Arthur resumed his
life exactly where he had left off, almost as if the period of darkness had
never been. The atmosphere of Cambridge may have changed slightly;
there was a more highly-charged emotionalism; the rowdy set seemed a
little rowdier still; there were new fads and crazes, one of which was the
resuscitation of interest in psychical research, with dons going off in
parties to investigate the true mystery of *Edwin Drood*. Most of the
Cambridge personalities remained the same, however, only a few years
older. Montagu Butler still topped the list as the subject of the largest
number of Cambridge anecdotes. Arthur went to see him, at his request,
to discuss candidates for the Mastership of Wellington, on Bertram
Pollock's elevation to the see of Norwich. Butler had ten names for him
(and slightly to Arthur's chagrin his own was not among them). Alington,
Bowlby, Ford – each came up in turn; and with each candidate Butler
displayed his usual manner of 'infinite courtesy ("and then, as to his
delightful and gifted wife?")'. Arthur had no hesitation in pressing the
claims of W. W. Vaughan, Headmaster of Giggleswick.

A guest at the Trinity lodge described the experience of having
breakfast with Montagu Butler and his family:

> As soon as they had sate down to breakfast, after the Master's rich cries and
> entreaties for blessing, the Master took a piece of butter on a butter-knife
> and advanced round the table, saying 'We have a pretty custom here,
> initiated in the first days of my second marriage, that the proceedings should
> begin by my helping dear Momma to butter etc. etc.' He advanced with
> bland steps, taper fingers much trembling – but before he got half round,
> Mrs Butler was writhing in mouselike irritation, and the butter lump had
> fallen down the back of a guest's neck – so much for pretty customs and
> sentiment!

The politics of Cambridge – all pathetically parish-pump – interested
Arthur only in so far as they affected personalities. Stuart Donaldson had

been passed over for the Vice-Chancellorship on the ground that he took insufficient interest in university affairs. Lady Albinia took it rather more bitterly than Stuart; and although Arthur felt the slight for the College, he had to admit that the Master sometimes innocently displayed a quite exquisite lack of tact. Entertaining Rendall of Winchester, who had preached at evensong on 28 May 1910 (a very foolish sermon, giving the impression that 'Christ approved of horse-racing and disapproved of betting'), the Master brought up at dinner a subject most definitely to be avoided in the circumstances: 'I have been hearing a lot about the Headmastership of Harrow', he said to Rendall, 'and I gather that the choice of the Electors is not going to fall on you.'

Nor could Arthur take very seriously his new undertaking to serve on committees. He still regarded them as chiefly interesting for the opportunities they gave him to observe human kind at its most idiotic. It pleased him to attend the meetings of the Soham Governors in order to revel in the spectacle of its chairman with 'his mouth pursed up under his nose with an air of foolish consequence'; and to watch – at the Gresham's Council meetings – the old and very deaf Field Marshal Sir Evelyn Wood making 'no pretence of listening to the debates, though an odd machine like a camera with reflectors and fans and coils is rigged up in front of him'. As for the Teachers' Training Syndicate, he thought the whole proceedings absurd. 'How hopeless to teach people how to teach – like teaching people how to talk at dinner!' The only lasting conclusion he could subscribe to was 'what a damnable thing Education is, after all!'

The chief event in the world at large during 1910 was the death, in May, of Edward VII. It did not pass unnoticed in Arthur's diary. Indeed, he fumed at the absurd and ludicrous over-statements in the flood of eulogies that the King's death provoked.

> There are about five things to say, and they have been said about a hundred million times. He was not a high-minded man, but he had a British sense of fair play and of doing his job. He wanted everyone to be comfortable and friendly. He was fortunately not intellectual, and he had *no* refined tastes; but he was a 'good sort', and the kind of man that people like Henry Smith wd admire. That is all. .... The poor Queen has persuaded herself that her entire married life with Edward was perfect. She believes this instantly and for ever.

This must prove that people don't really believe in personal immortality. 'With what face should we meet the dear ones about whom we had lied so effusively and gushed so hypocritically?'

On 22 June, Arthur was privileged to enjoy a superb royal occasion: a levée at Buckingham Palace on the occasion of the presentation of a loyal address to George V by the Universities of Oxford and Cambridge. Arthur stuffed himself into his velvet court dress, rather proudly affixed his decoration, and arrayed himself in silk gown, bands, cap and hood. He then watched entranced. The Oxford delegation went first, looking 'rather feeble'. Lord Curzon led them in, 'like a very respectable butler, Warren in red, with his company smile, showing his teeth between his thick lips, Godley like a mouthing crane'. They were all led into the throne room. 'The King, looking very small ... like a perky little bird, sate on the edge of the chair, smiling nervously.' The Duke of Connaught was on his right, Winston Churchill on his left, 'bored, yawning, shifting about. ... Winston handed addresses to the King and took them away from him with entire unconcern, giving a familiar nod with his head – he looked a real cad!' Lord Rayleigh read the address, and the King replied. 'Such an odd, hoarse voice, as if roughened by weather, rather a vulgar accent.' Throughout the proceedings, Arthur noted 'the little sympathetic cries and moans with which the Master of Trinity punctuated both address and reply. Very characteristic of him.' Then came 'the ludicrous ceremony' of bowing out, and it was difficult for Arthur to restrain himself, especially at the sight of Henry Jackson 'straddling, stumbling, looking over his shoulders ... dreadfully absurd'. All in all, Arthur 'felt rather bewildered by it all, but decidedly amused'.

In July 1910 he took a longer holiday than usual in the Lakes. After a spell at Skelwith Fold he moved over to the Scale Hill Hotel at Loweswater. Cornish was his companion for the first few days; then the Marshalls, then his brother Hugh. Ross Todd and George Mallory came for the last few days. It was a time of great happiness. Todd told him 'you are simply a new man'. He enjoyed the solitary walks of the first few days, planting fetishes as the spirit moved him. Hugh fidgeted him a little by his dogmatism. He 'is not in the least interested in other people, except just in so far as they amuse him or enter into his plans. He is like a child, entirely absorbed in his own games. ... He would like to see everyone a R.C. ... If he found that God were not a sound R.C. he would try to convert him.'

He was not sure about Mallory at first. He thought his appearance a little affected 'with too much hair and not enough collar. He would be so much more attractive if he only were not so determined to dress unconventionally. Long hair cannot be comfortable. ... I think there is some root of vanity behind. I don't wonder. I should be vain if I were so gracious a creature.' When he saw him with his clothes off, however, bathing in Crummock Water, 'taking headers and racing in the sun', his heart fluttered as of old.

Arthur was exploring new territory. He climbed Pillar for the first time, doing the whole walk (from Gatesgarth to Looking Stead and down by the Black Sail) with Mallory in four hours. 'I never saw anyone show such ecstatic delight as Mallory in the presence of the mountains.' There were a few tiresome reminders of the holiday season. He was angered by a group of young men and girls coming down from Great Gable at the top of the Honister Pass, walking 'hand-in-hand' ('the taste for philandering in large troops seems to me unintelligible'). At the foot of Melbreak, by the church, a group was being photographed by a middle-aged man. Wanting Arthur and Mallory to pass, he shouted 'Look sharp!' and waved his hand. Arthur boiled with rage inside. 'This, I suppose, is democracy', he reflected. Walking by Buttermere, his spectatorial instinct seized control, and he peeped over the hedge round Hassness House, an alcoholics home. He had a twinge of ugly memory of his misery at Hampstead as he watched 'dolorous men in deck chairs, or playing small golf. It seemed to me an almost impossible horror, to live there under such circumstances, fighting a craving, with half-a-dozen other wretches.'

Disenchanted with the flat lands of the Fens, he felt again the call of the mountains. 'I should like to die out on a mountain', he declared, looking at the little white cross on the lower slopes of Fleetwith Pike, 'if only one could be buried up there too.' There was a peace about the Lakeland fells which 'settle down upon the mind. It comes partly from the fact that nothing has ever happened up on those grassy moors – nothing dramatic or human – just sheep feeding and flies buzzing for God knows how many hundred years.' And then the thought occurred to him: should he, perhaps, seek a retreat in that delectable country?

> What an ideal life one could live there if one had one's health and one's book and one's wife and one's walk. . . . The mountains loomed up over the low green hills of the foreground with their bracken and gnarled thorns – a great still Western glow burnt behind the smooth outline of Whinfell. The air full of the sound of streams. I wonder if I *could* live my vacations in this sweet valley with a few friends? I could not live alone, here or anywhere.

And that was the trouble – the old and poignant predicament. The most delectable spot in the world could become a prison if one were condemned to be alone. 'It is so strange to be always, as I seem to be, on the edge of Paradise and never quite finding the way in.'

* * * * *

It is the recurrent theme. As a younger man he had wanted 'to live on the edge of life'. Here, as in other things, his wish had been granted. Reflecting on his pilgrimage, if such could be called his journey through life, he had to admit that 'I found many pretty jewels by the way, but the pearl of price lay hid.' 'Yet, oh the place could I but find!' was the common lament of the disenchanted and the impatient; but this was hardly Arthur's problem. He knew where Paradise lay, but he could not find the door. In a very personal essay, entitled 'Herb Moly and Heartsease', intended as an allegory of his most intimate predicament (published in 1915, long after it had been composed), Arthur revealed how accurately he could diagnose the reasons for his failure to penetrate further than the periphery. It came down to an inability to achieve an enduring, genuine and committed personal relationship. He wanted – in a way – to love; but his understanding of love could go little further than 'falling in love'. And what one falls into one can as easily fall out of – the more so when the quest for such a relationship was really little more than a recreation or enticing pastime. For what had his friendships truly been? Unstable, unsteady; lacking 'any common aim, any real mutual concern'.

> They were nothing more than the enshrining of a fugitive charm, the tracking of some bright-eyed fawn or wild-haired dryad to its secret haunt, only to find the bird flown and the nest warm.

The hero of *Beside Still Waters* is, in truth, a pathetic figure. He was lofty about his friendships. 'The most shameful thing in the world seemed to him the ebbing away of vitality out of a relationship; and therefore he would not give pledges which he might be unable to redeem.' But this was a loftiness contrived to conceal a real inner deficiency – the inability to give himself wholly and to see a friendship in other than unequal or selfish terms. If that is the way one is made, then what is the most that one can hope for?

> He saw that he was condemned to pass through life, a smiling and courteous spectator of beauty and delight; but that, through a real and vital deficiency of soul, he could have no share in the inner and holier mysteries.

This is a profound analysis of a shallow level of living. But if one likes not what one sees of one's hopeless deficiencies and one's selfish motives (a common enough predicament), the fault may be repaired, or the strength found at least to try to work for self-amendment, through spiritual channels. If one's understanding of love is all awry, the cure may be vouchsafed through the gift of insight, however dim or imperfectly perceived, into the Love of God. How near did Arthur get to this perception?

Paradoxically he was almost too near to the religious world, or at least to the ecclesiastical world (not quite the same thing) to find the way that could have helped him. He was the son not so much of the manse as of the bishop's palace. He knew the life of the Anglican Church from the inside; he knew enough theology to regard it as the natural topic of conversation. It is only too possible to live too near the sacred mysteries of the altar to have any reverence for them left. Arthur delighted in the company of divines because he knew the way their minds worked. He could discern all the nuances of differing churchmanship; he could watch in his friends the constant tensions between the desire for humility and the lure of ambition. And in some ways, for the natural lover of the incongruous, the Church is the perfect field for spectatorial delights. Divinely instituted, it must necessarily be of the earth, earthy. Repository of truth and light, its message can easily be distorted into an ugly dogmatism, and human failings exhibited in a liturgical or ceremonial setting can seem the more comical and absurd when somehow dignified by the assumption of charismatic powers.

At least, so it seemed to someone of Arthur Benson's gifts, temperament and healthy disrespect. If one listed all the attitudes and dogmas which he could not accept, what would remain of his religious beliefs would form a somewhat tenuous corpus of theology. To begin with, he had no time for dogmatic and assured persons, people who claimed that they *knew* the answers and who were emphatic on matters which could only – by their very nature – be indefinite. Within his scale of religious monstrosities, the Evangelical was the worst of all. He was so assured of his own rectitude that he lived according to the text in *Job*: 'Let mine adversary be as the wicked, and he that riseth up against me as the ungodly.' Evangelicals 'mistrust everyone else's access to grace except on [their] own lines'. Roman Catholics came next in the order of disfavour, although he accorded them a grudging respect for what at least was apparent in some of them – their combination of 'Evangelical sternness' and 'easy Paganism', but 'the *middle tract*, half of superstition and half of indulgent tyranny, all of it slightly *dishonest*, is what I hate'.

He had little patience with ritualists. They lacked real vitality. 'It is all a case of fringes and phylacteries and faded doctrines. It is an upholstery movement, an aesthetic scum.'

What did this leave? Very little, in terms of what the clergy could offer. Middle-of-the-road Anglicanism had only a dim, aesthetic appeal for him in its cathedral services, provided the liturgy was dignified and correct and the music satisfying. For the most part its traditional worship was ludicrous. Matins at Horsted Keynes, for instance – 'I get no good out of such a service, I fear; no good at all. . . . To sit silent in rows, like sheep in pens, and to cry out suddenly at once, words that we are not thinking about, like ducks in a pool. How very odd it must seem to God that we should think that we please him so; and that he is in that frowsy and fusty building in a sense in which he is not in the elm-branches and the covert.' And why should people suppose that God would favour one form of worship any more than another? 'Yet devout Church people would dimly conceive of him as bending to listen with a moist and tender eye, while he put his hand up so to speak with a frown and a shake of the head at what was going on in the Baptist chapel.' The communion service or the Mass satisfied him less and less as he grew older. He was irritated by priestly gesticulations, 'harsh cries, quaint hoppings and scufflings, arms upheld, and then working away at cleaning up like a bootblack'. The whole theory of communion seemed to him to be wrong. It was like 'a drug or magical practice by which we can acquire holiness or virtue. . . . It's all a *symbol*, not a *means*.'

He believed in God. He had, in some ways, a profoundly religious mind – a consciousness of the spiritual, the sense of some transcendent force beyond and behind our lives. But he was totally unorthodox. 'Orthodoxy', he once said, 'seems the only position that is *not* true, because it is *bound* to alter. The only way of life seems to me to hold on to the few certainties, and never to hold on to anything that is *not* a certainty, but to welcome probabilities with interest.' Creeds and formulae were monstrously absurd. During the Christmas Day service at Horsted Keynes in 1906, Arthur found the service so dull that he fell to reading the Thirty-nine Articles with unusual care. In the end he reckoned he could assent to one and to portions of only four others. He found it exceedingly difficult to accept the divinity of Christ. His views on miracles came increasingly to accord with advanced modernist views. He could talk very nearly the same language as a man like Bethune-Baker, or E. W. Barnes. Reading Kirsopp Lake's *Stewardship of Faith* in 1916, he conceded that it was 'a very engrossing Modernist book. That is *exactly* what I feel about Xtianity.'

In matters of religion, Arthur knew very definitely what he did not like but only very nebulously what he did. Just before his illness of 1907, he discussed the question at length with Hugh. The certainty was that no church possessed the absolute monopoly of truth. There was probably *some* truth in all religions. Taking the statement of Tennyson – 'There's a providence that watches over us, and our individuality endures: that's my faith, and that's all my faith' – he decided that he could absolutely accept the first article. There is, indeed, a providence that watches over us. The second statement, however, he considered doubtful. He would prefer to say 'and our *life* endures'. How did one know the little that one *could* know about such things? By intuition, and by intuition alone.

In this Arthur was consistent. After his breakdown he developed his views – very much in accordance with this earlier *credo* – in his book *The Child of the Dawn*, published in 1912. It is an attempt at an eschatology, expressing his convictions now of three things: the providence that watches over us and determines the course of our lives; the fact of the 'personal immortality of the human soul'; and the rebirth or reincarnation of that soul after some period of purgation. The book begins with the description of the sensation of dying – pain, and a sense of falling; and then peace, which was a sort of 'conscious sleep'. Images cross the mind; recollections of the past; all while being peacefully aware that one has died. In time the mists part; and – in Arthur's fantasy – he becomes conscious of a presence beside him, which gradually and slowly materialises into his helper and counsellor, Amroth (a sort of guardian angel). A long period of enlightenment takes place, involving situations and relationships, with Amroth beside him at first, but later appearing as a helpmeet only at intervals. Heaven turns out to be a place of work and progress, where one learns the truth one is capable of apprehending but perhaps could not learn (because of physical or psychological impediments) in one's former life. Arthur discovers true love in his selfless relationship with Cynthia. He is allowed to see those whom he loved in life; and he meets Herbert Tatham again. He is shown the paradise that comes to those who want no more than what they delighted in during their mortal existence. The dogmatic and barren scholars dwell together in the 'paradise of thought' which turns out to be a sort of lunatic asylum.

Judgement comes through a real and terrifying trial: the scaling of

14 Archie Don
'*A radiant youth. I hope he won't get spoilt.*'

15 Geoffrey Madan
'*A perfect picture of youth and romance.*'

16 A.C.B. with Dadie Rylands, at Lamb House
'*It is irresistible to an elderly man to find a young man really eager to take the cake and wine I so assiduously hand round to reluctant recipients.*'

17/18 Travelling in Cornwall with Percy Lubbock, August 1923
  '*I have become definitely an elderly and hampered man.*'
  '*He's a charming companion usually, but he might have been the
  seigneur and I his secretary.*'

some perilous heights, conscious of alien forces lying in wait. When you reach the top, having passed the test, you find yourself looking down a sheer precipice, and there far below a great light burns. In the end, you leap; and it is a leap of pure faith, taken alone, unaided. Once the leap has been taken, there is no longer need for your helpmeet. The story ends with Amroth's departure, to be reborn as a crying infant in some mean dwelling in an industrial town. Arthur hears the cry of the new life before he, too, receives the summons to give up Cynthia, whom he loves, to return to the next stage of his pilgrimage on earth.

It is interesting to observe how Arthur theologised his own predicament. It was worked out in his mind during 1910. The name 'Amroth' stuck in his mind from a holiday with Gosse and Spencer Lyttelton at Tenby at the beginning of the year. He visited Amroth and St Issell's on 4 January. During the Loweswater holiday, one day as he was descending from High Stile, his thoughts turned to Tatham. 'What is he, where is he?' he reflected. 'I don't doubt that he *exists*, but I don't think he remembers me, or anything.' Already he had probably been born again and was – even then – some far-off infant 'whom I shall never see or know'.

Simply the theology amounted to this: 'It is He who hath made us, and not we ourselves' – the classic determinist text. What happens to us has been ordained; we might have to undergo chastening; certain events may lead to self-amendment. It may be His will that we remain incomplete persons throughout our lives. Perhaps, in some previous existence, we had other infirmities as well. Arthur believed that he had once been a canon of a cathedral, possibly at another time a farmer or a dalesman. At any rate, the period in paradise enables us to see the deficiencies in ourselves and gives us the opportunity to supply them, although we may, of course, fail the test. What we have learnt will then be tested further, to make us – presumably – more complete persons, when we are born again. Arthur, therefore, left his predicament in the hands of his Maker. If the fantasy of *The Child of the Dawn* is his own necessary process of amendment, as he conceived it, he discerned accurately enough how he should be judged. He needed to discover love; to achieve a perfect and unselfish relationship. But the fantasy also reveals one particular psychological barrier that he could not transcend, even in Heaven. Cynthia, his true love, has a sexless quality (so, too, has Amroth, who is an Ariel figure). Arthur and Cynthia long for a child and their wish is granted. An infant is deposited, during the night, on their doorstep; born 'out of our two hearts'. In just such a way did Arthur Hamilton, years before in the *Memoir*, crave for a son. He was a bachelor who loved the company of boys. His wish, too, was granted without the necessity of sexual experience. In Persia, he meets a strange Englishman living in exile with two very attractive young boys. Arthur Hamilton is asked to adopt one of them as his own.

The Ariel figure, then – the ideal of sexlessness – was not just a pleasing whim or fancy. It symbolised one of Arthur's very deepest problems: his repugnance for the way that nature had devised for the procreation and preservation of the species. His earthly paradise was the natural companionship of a youth or young man; he yearned for the relationship which he had never enjoyed with his own father, longing for a son of his own. But this he could never have. He could not marry; he could not countenance sexual intercourse, even though he was by no means immune to sexual arousal. So his personal relationships had to be pleasant diversions, and no more. Paradise could never be his. He must reside content 'on the edge'.

*   *   *   *   *

It was in no pathetic mood, however, that Arthur returned to Cambridge from the Loweswater holiday in the summer of 1910. He felt aggressively fit. Although he was enjoying several mild romantic friendships – Jim Butler, Archie Don, and a pleasant second-year Magdalene undergraduate from Malvern called Geoffrey Winterbottom who had rather caught his eye – he was not *sous la charme*. The romantic element in his relationship with Mallory had rather subsided. Anyway Mallory was off to Charterhouse in September to become a schoolmaster.

Indeed many long-standing friendships were rather put to the strain that summer. Arthur was in a somewhat waspish mood and found the emotional entanglements of others an irritation to him. Frank Salter had fallen for a sixteen-year-old Marlborough boy called Owen Morshead*. Arthur conceded that he was delightful, with a remarkable knowledge of 'double chants and church music', but could not relish his company all day long. Percy Lubbock had adopted Oliffe Richmond, guarding him 'as an angel might guard a boy', while the good Oliffe seemed 'as much bored as a boy might be with an angel'. When Howard Sturgis came to stay, and Percy and Oliffe Richmond visited them, Arthur was thoroughly put out by the over-charged atmosphere. Howard talked too much, Richmond

* Sir Owen Morshead, Librarian, Windsor Castle.

'sate regarding Howard with looks of love, while Percy simply worshipped'.

> The odd thing to see is the curious emotional flirtations that arise about Howard. He and Richmond must keep on making little overtures and whinneyings, like dogs and horses, about Xtian names etc. Then the simple Salter must be sent for, and Percy and Oliffe must be rallied on being jealous; then S. must arrive, and Howard be jealous. Then Salter goes, and Howard says that he bites his nails and has dirty hands. . . . Is not all this rather silly?

When it came to parting, Arthur was outraged at their behaviour. Howard gave Percy 'a long and loverlike kiss'. He 'apologised to me for sentimentality, and P. said that at emotional crises such behaviour must be excused. To me it is very distasteful. After all it is only a symbol, but I don't want that sort of symbol – perhaps I don't *really* want the thing symbolised. H. said afterwards that he wd have kissed me if he had dared. I am glad that he did not, tho' the fact that he could, rather relieves my perpetual sense of physical repulsiveness.'

And then there was Hugh Walpole, gushingly emotional as ever, full of his success with *Maradick* and making solemn plans about a book based on Epsom. If anything, he was worse than Howard. 'He told me of a friend of his, aet 23, who had such a passion for a friend, aet 21, that though hard-worked, poor and ill, he went down to Cardiff by night, not to call on him, but to see the house and gather leaves from the garden! This in my wildest days I cd never have done. It seems to me in a way noble, but silly?' Then he told Arthur of his own *amours*, which gave him a feeling of disgust:

> H.W. mentioned that he was written to by a clerical friend *every* day – about nothing in particular, golf, entertainments, gossip. I said it was a little *silly*. He resented this and said it was beautiful and touching. . . . He broke out into a strange rhapsody about his temperament, his sense of the sacredness of friendship, his affection for me, his difficulty in restraining sentimentality etc. etc. It left me cold, and worse, because it seemed to me savage and unrestrained. Neither could I understand what it was all *about*. It was somehow or other censuring me. . . . It is a sort of emotional sensuality. I was rather shocked and disgusted by the scene – it seemed so childish, and so remote from affection.

Hugh Walpole frankly worried him. 'I am not sure that his is not a girl's spirit got into a male body just as H.O.S. is a virile spirit in a rather feminine body. H.W. is just the sort of passionate, sentimental, impulsive, inconsistent, boyish creature a girl *would* be. He doesn't seem to me to value opinions on their own merit at all, but on the merit of the utterer.'

Arthur escaped to Tremans, and then to Savernake for a holiday with Gosse. This was not a success either and was the occasion of a fierce quarrel, precipitated apparently by Arthur's persistent and abrasive argumentativeness. As will be seen later, it led in time to a long and bitter estrangement. So the new academic year began with Arthur still in a waspish mood, gradually softening as the term progressed and as he became more and more conscious that a new romantic friendship was dawning. He saw a lot of Geoffrey Winterbottom during the term. At the end of November matters came to a head. 'I haven't felt so romantically inclined for years', he acknowledged, surveying this tall, well-built, good-looking young man, whom he had already found to be an easy talker with just the touch of ingenuousness that charmed him so much. 'But I shan't be silly.' Salter held a small dinner-party for Arthur and three undergraduates (Miles, Winterbottom and Hepburne), all of them in a relaxed mood:

> I did enjoy this evening enormously [Arthur wrote]. It was really delightful to find myself with these four, any of whom might have been my son, and to find (or think I found) no sort of gêne or stiffness in my company. We had an Xmas kind of dinner – pulled crackers, wore paper hats, told ghost stories. Then to my room for music. One or two others dropped in. I was pleased by Winterbottom securing the next place to me. In two crackers he and I pulled were two rings. He put one, quickly and smilingly, on my finger, and I put mine on his – and by this little absurd ceremony we seemed to plight a kind of troth. ... I found myself, when he was gone, thinking about him with curious persistence, and wishing that he were there.

The next day Geoffrey Winterbottom called on him and asked if he might write to him during the vacation. Arthur was deeply touched. During the next term he was determined not to spoil the relationship by pushing too hard, but he was entirely captivated. Returning, early in the term, from a performance of a Bach Mass at King's (which he didn't much care for – 'I am no good at serious music'), he 'got back ... fed up with music and to my delight the beloved W. came in. I am really almost foolishly romantic about this youth. ... I like his face and his radiant smile, and his elegant long limbs. The worst of it is that I am so anxious to please him that I overshoot the mark. But I don't want to be *silly* about all this, or to say silly things to him. Only it is delicious again to have the hope of meeting someone about whom one cares to see, and on seeing whom, one's heart gives a little flutter.'

The Lent Term of 1911 was a rather trying one for Arthur. Although he was enjoying writing *The Child of the Dawn*, he felt he was living somewhat dissolutely; accepting too many dinner invitations and smoking too much; he was also increasingly exasperated with Percy Lubbock who had developed an intense friendship with Lapsley and was practically living at Fen Ditton. But he played the relationship with Winterbottom very gently. During the Easter vacation, they went together with Frank Salter for a holiday at Burford in the Cotswolds, staying at a small country pub, The Lamb. At first Arthur felt rather shy of his young companion in their relaxed surroundings, but not for long. The holiday proved to be perhaps the happiest in his life.

> I don't know what sort of joyful nonsense occupies our tongues, but we discuss people freely, and chatter endlessly. I talk rather too much and tell too many stories. Salter is rather bluff and provocative; it is curious to find a man of his age so intensely conscious of righteousness and just judgement. W. is full of delight and laughter. His smiling eye and rich resonant voice and his bubbling laughter fill me with pleasure. Why, I don't quite know. I am quite unreasonably and unreasoningly happy. . . . When I compare this with Cleveden [with Gosse], the contrast is almost painful.

And so it went on: Salter and Winterbottom singing duets from Gilbert and Sullivan, cards in the evening; mornings of private occupation, Arthur writing about his picture of life after death, Salter trying to understand something about economics, Winterbottom reading Aristotle. They visited Northleach, Lechlade, Kelmscott – places he had been to before with Tatham, and yet now seeing everything in a new light. 'I don't quite know what has come over me. I see these beautiful places with a sort of detachment, and think of my dilettante enjoyment of them with a sort of contempt. Something seems to have come into my life; and just now it expresses itself in my feeling for this jolly boy who is with us, whom I do my best to amuse and please.'

They had a day alone together, when Salter went off to meet 'the imp Morshead, whom he adores'. They did not find themselves shy and tried 'to behave as Salter would wish'. Winterbottom told Arthur about his family and schooldays at Malvern. They spent the day at Asthall and then had a relaxed evening reading Browning together. Salter soon returned, bearing the young Morshead with him – 'a nice-looking rather sententious Marlborough boy who seemed quite at his ease'. The next day they went off in pairs on different expeditions. Winterbottom and Arthur walked to Leafield.

> Oh, dear – what a happy time this has been – like the dearest of all days. I hoped it would be happy, and it has been happier than anything! I have deliberately laid myself out to make W. care for me; and, caring myself, I think I have succeeded. We shall see!

Dennis Robertson, fresh from his triumph at winning the Craven, called in to see them; 'pale, youthful, cherubic, rather rabbitlike', collecting 'prizes as it were bread'. But Arthur had to confess 'we preferred, W. and I, being alone'.

The day of parting came, Arthur giving Winterbottom a little gold pin which he had intended as a birthday present for Fred: a memento of some blissful few days. Of course, Arthur recognised that this romance could 'only be just a little wave in his life, of unexpected friendship with an older man; and likely to be the last in mine'. It was, after all, to be his forty-ninth birthday in a week's time. 'I certainly never expected to feel like this about a boy again, and I am very grateful for anything so tender and serious.'

The experience could never be repeated. It couldn't be the same during term, Winterbottom's final term at Cambridge. Within a week, Arthur wrote sadly, 'I feel a little as if he was drifting away in this busy atmosphere.' He was busy enough himself: a paper to the Tabard Society, examining for the Winchester Reading Prize with Monty James, finding other young men – notably Archie Don – who wanted to claim his time. And on 5 May he had to hurry away to Tremans on hearing the not-unexpected news of the death of the beloved Beth who had never really recovered from a stroke some months before.

The family all came together again – apart from poor Maggie at Roehampton. Fred was full of stories about Marie Corelli; Hugh rushed over, elated with some private triumph which he soon allowed to become public. 'He gobbled a supper, blew a cigarette or two into clouds, and to bed; he tells me he is gazetted a Monsignor, and he is frankly delighted.' On the day of the funeral, they gathered in the hall, listening to the 'grating of wheels on the gravel, and the muffled tread of mutes, and the bumping of the poor coffin downstairs', and then followed the cortège to Horsted Keynes church. At the moment of the interment, Mary Benson tossed a little spray of orchids on to the lid of the coffin. Arthur's genuine sorrow – for he loved Beth as deeply as he had loved anyone in his life –

was to some extent assuaged by the little vignettes that caught his roving eye.

> I liked the look of a choirboy near me, with a wide-open, fearless eye, regarding the coffin and the trappings with serenity; but I noticed little else except the absurd grief of a red-nosed man in a frock coat, who kept looking into the grave as one might look into a cage of wild beasts, and retiring into a paroxysm of anguish – a nephew of Beth's, I believe, who might have seen her once in the last twenty years!

He returned to Cambridge in a rather testy mood. He had an unpleasant row with Gosse at the Royal Society of Literature. Most of his friends seemed under the weather, and Arthur convinced himself, in noting a certain numbness about the ankles, that he was suffering from locomotor ataxy and brooded for a while on his imminent demise. He was also finding Salter a trial: so dogmatic and possessive, trying to coerce others to accept his hotly-argued and absurdly limited views. Talking with Salter was 'like living in a street where you can't be sure you won't have some slops thrown on your head as you pass'.

The days were approaching for Geoffrey Winterbottom to go down. Arthur was determined at least to repay him for his friendship by settling all his debts. He sat next to him at the degree dinner. They went together to the station, as Arthur was leaving Cambridge too, for Skelwith Fold. 'I realised how strangely dear to me he was. He was as delightful as a son. His smiling face, his rich voice, his waved hand remained with me all day.' Indeed, it remained with him throughout his holiday. While the country was celebrating the Coronation, Arthur was pining for the company of the boy who had gone out of his life. They wrote to each other. 'I should like to write *every* day', Arthur admitted. '"He has given me medicines to make me love him" as Falstaff says.' They fixed up a holiday together at Cambridge, for three whole weeks during August. Then, Arthur conceded, it would have to end. Their paths would diverge; their experiences would differ. 'We shall have nothing to gossip about.' It was the perennial problem of such a relationship. To what can it lead? 'One has no aim in sight. That is where all friendship *must* stop short. I know he cares about me, but we can't spend our lives together, we can't work and live and face experience together. It can't be more than a serene and joyful sentiment, which one must guard from silliness or effusiveness, and just try to keep as a high sort of trust and sympathy.'

When August came, it was everything that Arthur had hoped – and feared. Some blissful days there were, during an idyllic summer, talking about the deepest problems of life: nocturnal expeditions, cycling out in the small hours to watch the coming of the dawn; sitting out late in the garden, smoking, during long summer evenings. But the boy got bored, while trying not to show it. There was too little active exercise to divert him, although he seemed 'content to moon about with me and read novels'. Arthur fantasised over ways of keeping him and prolonging the experience; imagined beforehand what the final day might bring in exchanges of sentiment; what they would do; what they would say.

What actually happened? Arthur had lumbago on the day of Geoffrey Winterbottom's departure; and on the last night they were too shy to talk about their feelings and spent the evening playing cards. Could one really have expected more? 'In these last days', Arthur wrote, 'I felt the curious unsubstantiality of unequal friendship. The essence of married love is the pledge, the facing the world together, the common interest, the joint house – and these are what really bind, not passion or sentiment. But this boy draws near me thus, so closely, and yet drifts away again – and never in all our lives shall we be so close again.' If there were some power to bind or cement a love as deep as this, Arthur reflected, 'one can't do it! If I could but have told him plainly what I felt – but Englishmen are awkward about this.' So the actual moment of departure came. 'Nothing could have been more hopelessly unemotional.' They said good-bye; and all the fantasies dissolved.

*　　*　　*　　*　　*

The summer of 1911 was charged with the mood of 'bitter-sweet'. Perfect weather in the first year of a new reign; bitter political contests; constitutional crises and ugly industrial unrest. Most of it passed Arthur by. He was not interested in politics. He was furious over the strike action, resenting the interference with his routine, but determined that good order should prevail. 'I had made up my mind not to be able to get food, but to live on dog-biscuit and sunflower seed', he wrote, when he heard that the railway strike had been called off.

In his own life, never had he come nearer to the heart of his own personal predicament. If love were the paradise he sought – a perfect relationship – he came nearer to discovering it, while becoming most poignantly aware of his inability to find the way in. He could not gain paradise, but at least he had come to know himself. Not only did he find the company of boys and young men irresistible, he also had the power to charm. It was not a sinister desire, nor a gross and unwholesome power

266

that he wielded. It is almost true to say that he was kind and open with all boys and all young men. Naturally enough, he had favourites; but he did not snub an undergraduate who needed his help or desired his company because he lacked the charm and physical attractiveness that made some of his pupils more congenial to him than others. He had time to help a clever but unappealing man like Richard Keable through his spiritual wrestlings, or to be patient (and personally very generous) with Bruce Dickens although he found him 'sour and chilly' ('how hopeless it is to get inside his prickles'). 'My particular testimony', Archbishop Ramsey has written, recalling his undergraduate days, 'is his thoughtful and careful kindness to young men who were *not* within his "romantic orbit".'

Take, for instance, the little gate-keeper who minded the railway crossing at Clayhithe. Arthur always had a word with him when he cycled that way. So, in June 1911, as Arthur stopped for the gate to be opened:

> The funny little boy at the gate said: 'So you have come to see me again? Will you buy a nice rose?' I bought two from a rose that grows over his boarded hut. I asked him what he did all day – he is there from 8 to 8. He said, 'I work in my little garden, I wash out my hut, I read a little.' 'So you have plenty to do?' 'Almost too much', he said, 'but it's hardly worth the money – and I can't get books to read.' He is a nice little boy – but what a trade to put him to – he can only be about 12.

The next time Arthur passed through Clayhithe, he noticed that there was something wrong with the boy's eyes. He chatted with him and discovered that his ambition was to become a greengrocer. He gave him 3/- to get some tools for his hut and some wood. He paid him two more visits to see the tools he had bought, and then to inspect some boxes he had made from the wood. Many years later – in January 1924 – when preaching at the Tabernacle in Barnwell, Arthur met him again: a spectacled clerk, still keeping up with his reading, and still using the tools which Arthur's money had bought for him.

Nevertheless, during 1911, Arthur came more frankly to recognise the sexual element in his attraction for the young male. It was physical beauty that really charmed him. 'What a pretty thing the human body is', he exclaimed in July 1911, when he had been watching people bathing in the heat not far from Clayhithe. 'I saw a fine radiant boy coming out of the water, looking like a little God. In 5 minutes he was clothed and shouting, a horrible cad!' Visiting Lancing in June, as the guest of Bowlby, he was overcome by the sight of the boys in the swimming-bath. 'There was a race going on . . . and I don't know when I have seen anything prettier in colour than the boys' bodies rushing through the tossing blue water. One handsome boy who stood intent, poised for a header, made a beautiful picture.' Just such a sight, at Byron's Pool, at the end of May, had stirred him deeply:

> The flash of the naked body of a bather, up by Byron's Pool, across the meadow grass and among the trees gave me an indescribable thrill of romance and desire. Winterbottom looked in, very gracious and smiling; and I nearly gave way to a somewhat sentimental impulse; but did not, and left the words unuttered. I have a strong feeling that one must not be silly in friendship – and yet one loses many beautiful things so; if only one could just be natural!

There was undoubtedly a longing that could not be fulfilled. There was some mysterious bond which linked him, time and time again, with the image of the unknown boy. On holiday at Carlisle in September, only a few days after his parting from Geoffrey Winterbottom, Arthur attended a Sunday service in the cathedral.

> I was much interested in the face of a thin, long-limbed boy who sate near us. Such a pure outline, with that sharp delicate line of cheek that shows some lack of vitality. He had fine soft eyes and long thin hands. He seemed listless, but the look in his face, rather sad, very sweet-tempered, very full of some sort of feeling, I couldn't quite determine what, thrilled me very strangely, with a sense of some relation, older than time, between us.

Only a few days before, watching a performance of Shaw's *Man and Superman* at the theatre at Carlisle, he had thought about Shaw's portrayal of the way in which women so relentlessly pursue their men. Then – 'I wonder why I have always preferred *men* to women. Some theosophist would say it was because I have the soul of a woman in the body of a man.'

But it was only a longing. Timidity prevented it finding stronger expression. Hearing his mother and Lucy Tait discussing an elopement that had taken place in the neighbourhood, Arthur confessed his admiration for the courage involved. He himself was 'too timid to run away with anyone. . . . I have never sacrificed anything to emotion.'

He had come to know himself; well enough, at least, not to fret too much when the promise of a sublime relationship had come to naught, and had been exposed as the pretty diversion which it had really been all the time. He said good-bye to Geoffrey Winterbottom, and was genuinely sorry. Within days he was looking out for some other 'bright-eyed fawn' to track. The tracking was so often the exciting part. It might still be Jim Butler or Archie Don; or a young baronet, aged 17, with attractive teeth and curls and a pretty, engaging smile, who was shortly coming up to Trinity Hall and whom he met while staying at Norwich with Bishop Pollock. 'I fell rather in love with him', he wrote, feeling annoyed that he was not coming to Magdalene. It might even be a young clergyman, called F. A. Simpson, just made Fellow of Trinity, whom he met in the Lake District when staying at Skelwith Fold: 'very youthful and engaging, with an innocent smile showing pearly teeth – a shock of black hair like fur – many shy motions, like closing his eyes, pressing his hands to his brow, starts and writhings'. He would make a hopeless schoolmaster, because he would be ragged, but he certainly knew a lot about Napoleon III and was a good acquisition for Cambridge history. And, 'as Annie said, he is "pettable" '. Arthur might not regard the quest as a diversion at the beginning. But such it would become. He had summed it up when he reflected on the final parting with Geoffrey Winterbottom. He needed 'to *care* as I have never cared'; but the fact had to be faced: 'I live on the outside of things.'

Chapter Nine

LITERARY LOG-ROLLING

Literary men are fittest for the common sink, as Carlyle said.
(February 1911)

'Praise me not much, neither find fault with me at all.'
(An appropriate motto for critics)

Paradise had a curious way of eluding him. It was rather like a mirage, seen at times tantalisingly close, but receding into the mists the moment one advanced towards it. Where, then, did one truly belong? Arthur had had his chance of high office and had fled from it. Understandably, at times, he coveted what might have been. How he would have enjoyed 'the pomps and vanities' – at least for a while. How it angered him to hear the hypocritical disclaimers of worthiness by those who succumbed to the lure. It was humbug in Lionel Ford, for instance, to pretend that the Headmastership of Harrow had not been sought, and that he had been pressed reluctantly by the 'dear people' at Repton. 'If he had been called to go to a place of less emolument, would it have seemed so cogent a call?' And why should Mrs Ryle be allowed to get away with such foolish and insincere rhetoric, when her husband was summoned from the see of Winchester to become the premier Dean in the land, in asking for prayers 'that they may be sustained by the Spirit of Grace through an anxious time' (i.e. 'moving house!') and 'that a wise and loving pastor may be sent to the Diocese' (i.e. that a 'suitable successor' should be found for the highly ambitious Herbert)? It did not make it any easier for Arthur that he had himself schemed and plotted to secure an undemanding life. 'I have got exactly what I want', he wrote in June 1910, 'yet I am discontented.' And there was nothing he could do, seemingly, to rectify the matter. He had got what his temperament deserved. 'I am quite unfit for any hard, regular, administrative work. ... Now I do nothing but scribble little articles and sit on little Boards, and do little bits of teaching.'

It might be easier to swallow if the pomps and vanities of Cambridge were enjoyed by men of pre-eminently superior gifts. 'I feel now that the mistake I made in coming up to Cambridge', he wrote in July 1911, 'was to feel that people here lived in an intellectual atmosphere. They do not! They live in affairs and gossip. They hate their work, I often think, and have few other interests. I believe my own intellectual temperature is higher than the average here.' If one wanted proof, the candidature for the Lady Margaret Professorship of Divinity was evidence enough. 'Bethune-Baker is very able, McNeile quite second-rate, Tennant a red-nosed philosopher, Brooke a cataloguer.' When he heard of Bethune-Baker's election, he acknowledged the success of a cousin in acquiring an income of £1200 a year 'and leisure and dignity, especially after the awful trials – an operation for the stone where no stone was, and his boy's death. But he is a prim, pessimistic, unhopeful, censorious little man, who was a hopeless failure with undergraduates. He is very learned, I think – but if he is the best they can get in the way of theologians, God help us all!'

'I don't *think* the grapes are sour', he wrote untruthfully, watching Monty James so unashamedly enjoying the dignity of his office, while responding to not a single educational challenge. Indeed he much preferred honest enjoyment of dignity, such as Archdeacon Cunningham displayed, rejoicing in his apron and gaiters, to timorous humbug. But he resented Cambridge's suspicion that a man who made money from his books could never be a scholar and the way in which rewards tended to be denied, almost contemptuously and deliberately, to the gifted teacher and popular lecturer. He pined for a scarlet gown, and privately sought the advice of J. R. Tanner, Chairman of the Faculty Board of History in 1913, suggesting that his biography of his father and the edition of the Queen Victoria Letters might constitute an adequate submission for the Litt.D. degree. Tanner thought otherwise. 'It would give the Degree Committee the peculiar pleasure which clever and unsuccessful men take in doing a spiteful thing, which they can represent to themselves as conscientious, and snubbing a clever man.' Arthur fumed. 'It is true of Cambridge, as has been said, that if an outsider comes and settles here he gets plenty of friendliness and as much *unpaid* work as he will do – but neither money nor honour. An outside reputation is *simply* a drawback.'

He had assuredly gained an outside reputation, bringing him both money and honour of a sort. The Queen Victoria Letters had brought in (as he had expected) gratifyingly substantial royalties. Five years after their publication, his annual royalties (from all his books) amounted to £3660. When he counted in his American sales, he reckoned at the end of 1911 that his reading public had risen to the figure of half-a-million. 'That's a big audience', he somewhat wonderingly conceded. And it seemed that they never tired of what he wrote, however repetitious, however trivial, however hastily conceived. This was not a situation to induce sound literary habits, to encourage him to cultivate the patience and care for the want of which the masterpiece that he yearned to write was never forthcoming. If anything, he wrote with increasing rapidity. Between April and November 1910 he calculated that he had written 184,000 words. More revealing, however, was his compulsion to write just as soon as an idea for a book or article had crossed his mind. To research a project was anathema to him. So, in April 1914, having read a life of Father Stanton, he wrote an article on his work and influence the moment that he had put the book down. 'Then I read Cottle's Coleridge, and hated Coleridge.' That very night an article on Coleridge was completed.

Writing was never a problem to him; finding the material to inspire a book or provoke an article was much more of a headache. Even Arthur recognised that there was a limit to the number of reflective books, enunciating the same philosophy, that he could produce, and in June 1912 Reginald Smith felt emboldened to advise him, for the sake of his literary reputation, to write rather less and to try to experiment with a different genre. This was easier said than done. Arthur had broken new ground in *The Leaves of the Tree*, but it had not enjoyed the success of his quasi-philosophical books, and while he had found the theme apt to his style, he had not himself gained personal satisfaction from writing it. 'This sort of *reminiscence* is what I can do best', he acknowledged, quite correctly in January 1911, '. . . but it is very little pleasure indeed to do it! It seems to me the sort of thing anyone can do or ought to be able to do. I want to criticise life, not to photograph it.' Ironically the genre which he most wanted to command – that of novel-writing – defeated him, although he was loath to admit defeat.

He could bring real people to life; he could not give flesh and blood to imaginary characters; nor could he handle drama or conceive dramatic plots. Visiting the Tate Gallery, some years back in 1906, he had felt this same deficiency in English painting.

> I came to the conclusion ... that the English can paint landscapes beautifully, because they love the country; but that they are vile painters of *genre* pictures, dramatic scenes, gatherings of people. They can paint good *portraits*, single figures. But when they paint a scene, it is all melodrama, not a bit like life. We are *not* a dramatic nation: we are stiff when we are natural, unemotional when we are moved. So that when artists make emotional

scenes (like the infamous 'Knox preaching before Mary Q. of Scots') it is all like a piece of very bad acting.

This was precisely the deficiency in his novels. As soon as his characters, almost all drawn from life to give them verisimilitude, move into action or open their mouths, they become wooden. All attempts to handle dialogue, even when based on actual conversations he could recall, fall flat. It was as if his imagination, which took fire when he contemplated actual people in real situations, lost all its inventiveness the moment that he passed into fiction. When Reginald Smith sent him back the manuscript of *The Orchard Pavilion* in April 1914, he inadvertently enclosed a copy of his reader's report. Arthur read it with interest. The book would undoubtedly sell because of the author's reputation, the report concluded, 'but it is vague in thought and commonplace like a Sunday afternoon in a country garden'. As a result, none of his novels brought him success. His readers rightly felt that he could have said the same things, and conveyed the same message, immeasurably more effectively if he had adhered to the genre he was used to. After a while Arthur gave up submitting them for publication, although he continued to labour under the delusion that one day he would be able to prove his critics wrong.

He had had to develop a very thick skin with critics, often enough conceding the validity of their strictures in 'sitting on me for my vapidity and commonplaceness and fluidity and lowness of literary aim'. He was quite amused when he read a description of *Thy Rod and thy Staff* as 'like a little girl saying how much worse her measles have been than her little brother's. That's rather clever and not untrue!' Part of it, however, was their jealousy and anger at his success. 'I wonder faintly why I am on the whole disliked and despised by reviewers', he wrote in March 1915, after a scathing review of his memoir of *Hugh*. 'I think they hate me for writing easily and frankly and for making money and for being popular. They think I lay my body on the sheet for them that go over.'

If he took solace in the adulation of his admirers, it was not because he respected their literary judgement. He was scrupulously courteous to them, replying to every letter he received, even maintaining continuous correspondence with the most tiresome and importunate widows and spinsters. As the years passed, the volume increased until the burden became well nigh intolerable. He received frequent offers of marriage; photographs of yearning, lonely hearts were sent to him with suggestions for assignations. 'Fancy her horror at finding a stout old buffer!' Arthur commented grimly after receiving one such missive. 'I must send her *my* photograph: that will complete the cure.' There was a foolish woman who counted Arthur among her 'three Angel Pets' (along with Arthur Balfour and Winnington Ingram). An American lady wrote to tell him she had christened her baby 'Cynthia' after Arthur's loved one in *The Child of the Dawn*. He was sent manuscripts by religious cranks, tight-lipped theosophists and 'infatuated poetesses'. An American schoolgirl wrote to him, offering a fee if he would write her a submission for a prize essay; another American lady wrote proudly to tell him that she had procured one of his buttons as a souvenir; he discovered that his signature in the Visitors' Book at the Teachers' Training College at Leeds had been snipped out and stolen overnight. Among his male fans were a machinist from Woolwich, a superintendent on the L.N.W.R., a fifteen-year-old schoolboy from Mill Hill, a retired ironmonger and the local greengrocer (a man called Pratt).

Usually he contrived never to meet his more importunate admirers face to face – Blanche Atkinson, Miss Allen or Maud Goldring. But sometimes fans arrived at Magdalene unannounced, and occasionally entrance was effected through devious means. A 'silly parson', who had come up to Cambridge to take a degree, called upon him, bringing in tow 'a golden-haired, simpering female' who adored Arthur's books. He was cornered with no chance of escape. 'It was impertinent', Arthur complained bitterly. 'A girl like a doll sate on a chair and stared at me.' He was most vulnerable, however, when he accepted outside engagements to lecture or to preach. These came with increasing frequency in the years just before the outbreak of war. Once he found that he could hold a massive audience he enjoyed these occasions. At the City Temple in 1911, with R. J. Campbell in the chair, he had a capacity audience of 800. He was invited again the following year and was told that a thousand had been somehow packed in, and he had to be protected on his exit, being 'pursued ... by a party of enthusiasts' all the way to King's Cross.

There – *en masse* – were the readers of his books; and Arthur confessed to feeling touched by their devotion: clerks, tradesmen, doctors, teachers, with their wives and daughters; lower middle-class professional families and educated working-class, revelling in the 'donnish and the aristocratic flavour' of his leisurely essays, 'the flavour picked up in episcopal palaces and county society and Eton and Cambridge', believing 'they have really found the charm of culture'. A lecture on Lewis Carroll at Whitefield's Tabernacle in January 1914 brought an audience of 1400,

19 Outside the Senate House, Cambridge, after an Honorary Degree
Ceremony on 13 March 1925
Front row : Daniel Davies, Bishop of Bangor (D.D.); the Vice-Chancellor
(Professor A. C. Seward, Master of Downing); James Loeb, Founder of
the Loeb Classical Library (LL.D.); Mrs Loeb. A.C.B. stands in the
back row, on the left, next to the Public Orator (T. R. Glover)
*'I confess that the sight of men in scarlet vexes me, because of the mad and
timid joy that flickers in their eye.'*

20 A.C.B. in the study of the Old Lodge, Magdalene
  'I am getting a pursy, puffing old fellow.'

as a result of which a lecturing agency tried to gain his services at the rate of £20 a night. At Kingsway Hall he lectured to an audience of 1200. In Birmingham, 1500 people were crowded into the Institute. On Ascension Day in 1915, he lectured at the Lyceum on Charlotte Bronte, discovering on the platform that the audience expected him to talk on George Gissing. Part of the pleasure of such occasions was the absurd surroundings and the incongruous context of these vast nonconformist preaching arenas – the only halls large enough to hold his audiences. At the Kingsway Hall, his lecture (on 'Leaders of Men') started with an organ piece, a sacred solo and some rousing hymns. On another occasion, at the King's Weigh House Chapel, after being entertained by three strange gnome-like men who plied him with food and wine, he lectured actually standing on a sort of altar 'with an odd kind of Gothic settee behind it, off a brass desk set in a box called "Communion Plate" – anything less *mystical* can't be conceived'. The audience was uproariously appreciative, possibly for the light relief it brought in times of war (it was November 1915). 'A young soldier, curly-haired and strong, listened open-mouthed and *roared* at my jokes, and I was much applauded. Then I went off, had sandwiches and coffee – devotees introduced, many compliments – and two of the good dwarfs took me to King's Cross, paid my taxi and gave me a cheque in an envelope.'

He might not be Head Master of Eton but he had certainly acquired fame and a very healthy income too. Nor was he cut off from the London literary world. His election to the Literary Society in 1907 and to the newly-formed Academy of Letters in 1910 gave him the opportunity, when he cared to take it, of mingling and talking with at least the literary establishment of the pre-war period, while keeping apart from the 'log-rolling' and backbiting of the fashionable literary set. This, too, was exactly what he had wanted and worked for. He had never really liked either the pace or the quality of life which his literary friends of earlier years had emulated as an essential part of literary success: a sort of upper-crust Bohemianism, intense, brittle and showy; all the characteristics of social behaviour that Arthur inwardly despised. He preferred his earnest bank-clerks and gnome-like civil servants to the George Wyndham and Harry Cust circle to which, for instance, Maurice Baring belonged, with their horrid orgies, tasteless extravagance, hobnobbing with Asquith, Cromer and Haldane and concluding their revels with 'eggs being fried in Max Beerbohm's hat'.

The Literary Society dinners were altogether more leisurely and placid affairs. They cost twelve shillings a time and were accordingly sumptuous occasions. One could be sure of interesting company – Sidney Colvin, Austin Dobson, Basil Champneys, John Murray, Randall Davidson, Spencer Walpole, Lord Crewe, Bernard Holland. Sometimes Balfour would come, if only for part of the evening, depending upon the timing of business in the House. At his second dinner, in April 1907, Balfour slipped in and took the seat next to Arthur half-way through the meal. Arthur immediately noticed the effect on Randall Davidson, who responding to Balfour's irresistible charm, did not take his eyes off him for the rest of the evening. Arthur had to concede unqualified admiration for Balfour's ease of manner and brilliant, yet unaffected, talk. He made a superb impromptu speech, all very charming and conversational. He talked readily about the politicians he had known: how Gladstone was naturally deficient in deep personal emotion; how little respect he personally had for Disraeli. 'Palmerston ... was really a desperate Tory all along, J. Russell whom he described as a "Don" with a smiling apology.' Back to Gladstone again, 'whose speeches and writings were alike, he said, hopelessly *dull* – the only things he could really do to perfection were – he said – to speak about the procedure of the House, and to make a speech at a wedding breakfast'.

The Academy of Letters was perhaps a more pretentious body; self-created, therefore self-inflating, having the dual function of fostering the arts and the purity of style of literature by public lectures and the award of prizes and medals. It also aimed to create an élite whose composition was determined by the very people who most valued professional élitism within the arts. It was not surprising that its early meetings were somewhat stormy. According to Gosse, both Rudyard Kipling and James Barrie refused to have anything to do with it on the advice of Anthony Hope; Bernard Shaw, H. G. Wells and Hilaire Belloc were rejected by the first committee, and nobody thought to put up the name of G. K. Chesterton. Sir George Trevelyan refused election, but ensured that his son was elected in his place. At the very first meeting of the Academy, in November 1910, attended by such figures as Sir Alfred Lyall, Robert Bridges, Maurice Hewlett, Gilbert Murray, Laurence Binyon, Austin Dobson, W. B. Yeats, G. W. Prothero, Edmund Gosse, proceedings began somewhat farcically. Everyone demurred coyly when it was suggested that they should take the chair – except Arthur who saw no reason for saying 'no'. It amused him, also, to think that the inaugural meeting of this august body should have its first minutes signed by him.

It was certainly a lively occasion. Mackail was very vociferous, becoming 'purple with emotion'; there was a heated controversy over George Trevelyan's resignation; Pember (the founder of the whole scheme) and Gosse fell out. 'R. Bridges was the glorious sight', however, 'the indulgent Father, making jokes, with his great tumbled thatch of hair.'

It was not a very auspicious beginning; and Arthur refused to take its proceedings very seriously. He accepted, with mild pleasure, the Professorship of English Fiction within the newly-styled Royal Society of Literature in May 1911 (along with Henry Newbolt and two others), fully appreciating that the honour was a somewhat hollow one; rather pretentious and ridiculous in a way, but – at least – 'a harmless compliment'. He was reasonably conscientious, too, in attending meetings and giving lectures. But his involvement was never much more than an amusing diversion. It pleased him, for instance, to have a hand – in alliance with Bernard Shaw (now a member) – in discomforting the old guard early in 1912, when Prothero was in the chair, by helping to secure the election of the men whose omission from the Academy rendered its pretensions derisory. That day saw the election of John Galsworthy, G. K. Chesterton, H. G. Wells, Arnold Bennett, John Masefield and Hilaire Belloc. When G.B.S. rose to nominate Chesterton, Gosse and Maurice Hewlett let out little cries of protest – 'Oh, Oh', and G.B.S.'s brogue thickened: 'I will just ask these gentlemen who have indulged in so unseemly an expression of their private prejudices', he said, 'whether they have ever really *read*, honestly and carefully, any of the works to which I allude.'

It was pleasant to be 'in the swim', as far as the literary world was concerned. But Arthur had no desire to be at the centre. He had to admit that some of the up-and-coming names were totally new to him. Who was 'De la Mare', the man whom Gosse pushed so hard for the award of a literary prize in the winter of 1911? Perhaps he was reminded of his impressions of the eminent American Wordsworth scholar, Lane Cooper, whom he had met in Cambridge only a few months earlier: 'the baffling thing about Americans is, if you ask them to tell you who is the *real* literary influence of America, they will reply "Silas P. Kitteridge" with no sense of incongruity'. Gradually it was borne in upon Arthur that, at least in *this* world, he was making something of a mark. How did the Literary Society, for instance, *really* regard him? Certainly not as a figure of renown. 'I am taken as a mild literary hack who turns out a lot of sentimental and rather mawkish books. I am simply accepted as a Don with a certain output of writing which men of taste don't read.' But at least he was recognised as a figure. People of eminence stopped to talk to him at the Athenaeum. If they were old and decrepit, like Edmond Warre, still Provost of Eton, he might be remembered for the wrong things ('Hard at work destroying Greek?', he had said on meeting Arthur in November 1910, 'with a bitter little smile', and then moving 'feebly away'). Never mind; he was acknowledged as much in London as he was in Cambridge. Lunching at the Athenaeum in late June 1912, the truth suddenly took hold of him. 'I had an odd sense, for the first time in my life, of being a personage – not a great personage at all, but a quite definite one, with my own standing and point of view.' Perhaps, after all, in a curious and individual way, he had arrived.

*   *   *   *   *

Within this literary world, most of Arthur's old friendships were waning or undergoing severe strain. He had seen little of Henry James, for instance, in recent years; although this was a friendship which could be renewed at will. They had so many mutual friends that they kept in touch by proxy, and whenever they actually met the old relationship resumed without consciousness of absence. Arthur was not an admirer of his work. Everything he wrote, subtle and beautiful as his exposition might be, seemed 'blurred in a luminous mist of words'. Yet it was this very opaqueness which his devotees regarded as oracular and profound. Percy Lubbock, Howard Sturgis and Hugh Walpole vied with each other in the extravagance of their adulation. Their attitude, Arthur complained, was 'like that of Kirkpatrick and Hort to the Greek Testament – bemused and credulous, and like Merlin overwrought and overworn'.

Meetings of the Royal Society of Literature brought them together at times. On 8 November 1911 they dined together after Arthur had delivered a paper. All the old Henry James charm was there – the characteristic caresses and gestures, the verbal convolutions, the love of literary gossip. But he was noticeably older and a little strained. He expatiated on Percy Lubbock's recent article on William Morris and how he had failed to reveal the bustling and noisy side of the man. 'In these things, my dear Arthur, we must always be *bloody*'; how Arnold Bennett confused him; and how H. G. Wells was for ever boring people with his intentions. 'Good God, what a waste of time! Go and do it, my dear man, get it done!' And then, dear Howard Sturgis: how he was ruled by 'The

Babe' and needed to be rescued from the prison he had made for himself at Qu'acre:

> If someone of strong-mindedness could say to him – 'Don't move from your corner, continue your – what shall I say, your sewing (a gesture), your work, your beautiful work (a laugh) and wait there till the cab is at the door to take you to your new surroundings', he would acquiesce – he would rejoice. Howard is absolutely unspoilt, absolutely simple. A small house in London, and solitude, or at least separation from encrusting influences – ... You will perceive that I allude to our unfortunate friend – perhaps that is too intimate a word – our associate (a laugh). ...

Then, what was to be done about Hugh Walpole and his craving for intimacies? Somebody ought to teach him the virtues of observation and discrimination.

Arthur himself had harder things to say about Hugh Walpole than that, if he had been so minded. Here was a literary friendship that had gone distinctly sour. Walpole had stayed with him for two nights in August 1911, in the midst of a heat-wave, so Arthur was far from his best. Hugh, however, was at his worst – full of solemn talk about himself and his new circle of friends, Maurice Hewlett, J.L. Garvin, John Galsworthy. Then 'he talked about Perrin and Traill with infinite solemnity'. Arthur had to recognise how very little they really had in common. 'He seems to me to be sinking out of literature into journalism – oh, dear, it's an odd thing this dying down of affection.'

In December he came to stay with Arthur again. It was to be for the last time.

> We dined alone and after dinner had an unpleasant talk about sexual matters. He has a strongly developed sexual instinct, but rather abnormally perverted. He seems to have found a solution in relations of some kind with someone. But this was all very mysterious to me, who the person is and what the relations are. From some things which he said I feared a nasty business. I don't like his way of talking about it – there seems something morbid and incontinent about it. These instincts are strange things, but I don't feel it decent to *talk* about them. I said feebly that people had the right to arrange their lives – but he took to pacing about and talking in a very wild and self-conscious way. I was both bored and disgusted. ... A wretched evening. I talked for six hours, listened to much ugly rant, and pumped up inanities. It seems neither useful nor pleasurable to waste time thus.

Perhaps Hugh Walpole realised that he had gone too far with Arthur in what he had said. At any rate they said good-bye 'without emotion'. 'He doesn't need me in any way, and he is pursuing his own line of life with entire self-satisfaction and energy.' Arthur asked Lapsley whether he thought he was being uncharitable. The reply was 'that H.W. seemed in talk, outlook, demeanour to be the apotheosis of the second-rate, and I think this is true'.

Thereafter he watched with interest Hugh Walpole's advance to popular success; remembering the young Emmanuel undergraduate who had come to him for advice and help to launch him on his literary career; recalling sometimes the protestations of everlasting devotion in Over churchyard. Travelling up to the Lakes in the summer of 1916, he read on the train his latest book on Conrad. What could he say? It was 'like a very small lump or pinch of Henry James dissolved in infinite quarts of not very fresh water, and then still further diluted. In one place he spins off a list of epoch-makers, not one of whose names is known to me. I suppose H.W. must increase and that I must decrease.'

The friendship of much longer-standing which suffered severest strain in the immediate pre-war years was his relationship with Edmund Gosse. As with so many of Arthur's companionable friendships, totally free from any element of romance, the *rapport* was cemented by certain common features in their make-up which brought about a natural *camaraderie*. They shared the same literary interests; they had many mutual friends. They had a similar sense of humour, delighting in the ridiculous and the incongruous. Gosse was essentially good company, when both were in the mood for foolish anecdotes. Typical, for instance, was Gosse's account, which amused Arthur so much, of the reception by the Court of Roumania of the news of Queen Victoria's death, related to them by Lord Wolseley. Immediately handkerchiefs were produced, and the Court all wept. But when Lord Wolseley went on to announce the accession of Edward VII, the handkerchiefs were stuffed away on the instant and the Court 'broke out into jubilation'.

In some ways they were almost too alike in temperament for comfort. Both liked to have their own way, and objected to being organised. Neither liked emphatic views when expressed by others than themselves. Both could be fidgety when bored and would therefore get on each other's nerves. In other respects they were wholly different. Gosse was a self-made man advancing in the world, via humble positions and the cultivation of patrons, in the face of opposition from a widowed father of extreme and rigid Evangelical views. Arthur was, by contrast, the son of a self-made man whose children were born to the purple. He had, it is true, his own insecurities, but they were of an entirely different origin and character from those of Gosse. Self-pitying sometimes, self-critical often, he could be ruthlessly critical of even his closest friends in the private pages of his diary; and when Gosse irritated him by his lack of taste, or his dogmatic manner, or by his fawning demeanour in the presence of the highly-born, Arthur did not spare him. The weeks that Gosse had spent in his company during his convalescence from his mental breakdown were forgotten at these moments. Indeed, this in itself tells its own tale. In his illness Arthur was submissive and dependent. He needed Gosse's company and made no objection to another ordering his life. In rude health he resented any reminder of the past and luxuriated in the recovery of his powers and of his independence.

It was therefore likely that there would be trouble during the first holiday that Gosse and Arthur took together after his recovery in 1910. And so it turned out. They were staying at Savernake during early September. Gosse was in a sultry mood from the start, lamenting the lack of any solid literary work and envying Arthur's capacity for romantic friendship with the young. They sparred together over politics during a visit to Sarum and Stonehenge, Gosse inveighing against democracy as the cause of all the present discontents. Arthur took a more liberal line, suspecting that what Gosse meant by liberty was 'that he be allowed to enjoy his life and his wealth exactly as he likes'.

The storm broke on the following day – 9 September – on a visit to Littlecote, the country house of the Pophams on the banks of the Kennet, and thence to Aldbourne and Upham, with a great earth-work called Lillington Castle. As they were exploring the earth-work, Gosse suddenly broke out into a fury and rounded upon Arthur.

> I must protest against the extremely insolent way in which you have contradicted everything I have said today [he began]. You have to be always right, whether you know anything about the subject or not.... It is insufferable. ... It is arrogance and incivility combined.

Arthur was so shaken by the violence of his words that he was rendered speechless. With as much dignity as he could muster he offered to abandon the holiday and return to Cambridge the following day. Gosse immediately became penitent. He had not meant to speak so. 'It is not true, not a word of it. ... I am ill and in pain.' They effected a sort of reconciliation, but – as Arthur realised – there were certain things which, once said, could never be unsaid. They certainly could not be forgotten. For him the whole holiday had been ruined.

Time passed, and the wound was partially healed. At the beginning of January 1911, Arthur joined Gosse with Ainger and Spencer Lyttelton for a holiday at Cleveden, staying at the Walton Park Hotel. It was not a success. Arthur found himself becoming more and more irritated by Gosse's manner towards him. He was accused of being provincial and humdrum in his writing. They quarrelled over E. M. Forster's *Howards End*, Arthur liking the book and Gosse dismissing it as 'vile, obscene' and 'decadent'. Arthur became fidgeted and annoyed at Gosse's efforts to be funny by deliberately mishearing 'what one has said and making a silly joke out of it. "I must have lost it, I greatly fear" becomes "I must have a great deal of beer" etc.' All 'the generous fibre' of his mind seemed to have shrivelled up, leaving only his 'animal instincts and the posé mannerisms'.

They visited the Eltons at Cleveden Court, and Gosse became insufferable in the presence of aristocracy 'on tip-toe with fingers pressed together', saying 'many arch things' and paying 'elaborate unanswerable compliments'. On the last night of the holiday Arthur nearly exploded in his exasperation. At dinner Gosse told him out loud to wipe his lips with his napkin because they were dirty ('it would have been offensive from a father to a boy of ten!'); he then took charge of the wine and served the others purely as he thought fit; finally, he was distressingly vulgar about querying items on the bill. Arthur left Cleveden thankful 'that this beastly holiday was over. . . . I never enjoyed a sojourn less.'

On 11 May a rupture took place in public. Gosse was taking the chair at the Royal Society of Literature and Arthur arrived at the meeting late, having been delayed at the Fishmongers' Court. As he entered the room Gosse said censoriously 'Now that Mr Benson has come, at the eleventh hour, we can perhaps get on with the business', and then, directly to Arthur as he stood at the door amazed, 'Have the goodness to sit down, rather quickly, and attend to what is being said.' Arthur was beside himself with rage at the indignity and the offensiveness of his attitude and fumed over it for days. A caustic correspondence ensued, Gosse infuriating Arthur by magnanimously forgiving him for taking offence.

It is surprising that the friendship survived – admittedly at a coolish temperature – this last exchange. But they tried to patch things up. They met again with Ainger and Spencer Lyttelton at Penzance in January 1912. But it was Cleveden all over again. Gosse took Arthur to task for taking more than his fair share of cream at lunch; he gave another demonstration of his winning ways with members of the House of Lords by his behaviour with the elderly Lord Courtney, which was 'almost like a barmaid's in its flirtatiousness. He gave the impression of sitting on Lord C's knees and pulling his old ears like a petted child.' Yet again they enacted a pantomime of reconciliation in a holiday at the Digby Hotel, Sherborne, in September 1912. The same vexations made it impossible for them to achieve a real *rapport*. But at least they made one outing together which they could both enjoy. This was a visit to Thomas Hardy at his home at Max Gate.

This was by no means the first time that Arthur had met Hardy, and he was to see more of him in the years to come when Hardy became an Honorary Fellow of Magdalene. But he had never talked with him at length. Once in the Athenaeum he had been witness to a wholly improbable conversation between Hardy and Henry James – a sort of triangular talk, with Arthur as interpreter, since neither of the literary masters could hear a word that the other was saying. 'I felt like Alice between the two Queens', Arthur recalled. But he had observed Hardy closely: 'a seamed, pale, shy, kindly face; which yet always to me has something inherently shabby and undistinguished about it; it is the face, not of a farmer or peasant, like old Carlyle, but of a village tradesman'.

At Max Gate, Hardy gave the impression of 'a retired half-pay officer from a not very smart regiment'. The house itself was mean and pretentious, with a strong smell of cooking as one came through the door. Rather coarse fare was served at lunch. Hardy – as host – was talkative but uncommunicative. Mrs Hardy was quite extraordinarily vague, and when told by Arthur that he was a Cambridge don, remarked rather helplessly 'Ah, I don't understand about that'. The third member of the household was 'a solid, plebeian, over-dressed niece', who had a passion to play croquet in the garden and, when this suggestion was scotched, lost all interest in the rest of the proceedings. They explored the garden after lunch, chiefly – it seemed – to afford Mrs Hardy the pleasure of pinching 'the pods of the *Noli me tangere* to see them writhe and coil up and shoot out the seeds. Mrs Hardy got entirely absorbed in this and went on ... with little jumps and elfin shrieks of pleasure.'

All in all the visit gave Arthur 'a rather melancholy impression'. Max Gate was 'airless and dark, like a house wrapped up and put away in a box; the crazy and fantastic wife, the stolid niece didn't seem the right background for the old rhapsodist in the evening of his days'. Mrs Hardy had taken Gosse aside to tell him that she and her husband were forever squabbling, and how – in a quarrel – she would beat him with a rolled-up newspaper. Hardy himself vouchsafed no confidences. He displayed 'the suspiciousness of the rustic, the idea that he must guard himself, not give himself away. .... There is something secret and inscrutable about him.' He was rather more confiding at Cambridge in the following year when he talked with Arthur over dinner at the Lodge. His first wife had died in the interval and Hardy was considering whether it might be thought indecent if he were to produce a volume of poetry. Turning to Arthur he said: 'It's natural to me to write poetry. I was never intended to be a prose-writer, still less a teller of tales. Still, one had got to live.'

This was actually the last holiday that Gosse and Arthur ever took together. An exchange of letters on their return confirmed the extent to which they had drifted apart. Arthur admitted to himself that he was far from guiltless. 'My fault is to cover up a very timid and diffident interior by a humour which has something unpleasant about it and by a silly sort of trifling which is very affected and insincere. .... The error lies in my theory that I am amiable *au fond*; and I am both selfish and intolerant.' But should one go on apologising for one's failures to a man 'who errs twenty times in these very ways for the once that I err?' Once the fact had been acknowledged, Arthur felt profound relief. Perhaps, looking back, he had never really been a willing partner in that friendship. At any rate, he felt strangely free again: 'no claims, no pettishness, no little slaps'. Another chapter of his life had been closed.

*   *   *   *   *

As the old friendships were dissolving, the circle of literary acquaintanceships was widening, largely through involvement in the Royal Society of Literature. Arthur had no great expectations that his generation would be remembered by posterity for their literary achievements. Perhaps five only would still be respected and read in fifty years time – Meredith, Swinburne, Kipling, Shaw and Chesterton. Probably knowing so many of them personally made one more sceptical about the claims of genius. Possibly W. B. Yeats was one, if the test of genius was one's lack of comprehension of his work. Arthur was impressed by his talk when he met him, although at a loss to understand his mysticism. As a result his own contribution to the dialogue rather shamed him in retrospect. 'I felt and talked like a boiled owl.' He went with Yeats and J. M. Synge to see the Irish National Theatre at work and was totally bemused. He gave up trying to follow the Yeats play: 'an absurd, wasted, mouldering-looking kind of woman, who chants her speeches instead of saying them, and turns out to be an allegory of Ireland. .... I thought the play only different from other plays in being slightly more absurd.' He thought Chesterton vastly over-rated on first acquaintance. After reading his *Heretics*, he 'thought it inflated, flashy stuff. No thought; nothing but glitter and paradox; like a meal of celery.' Pressed by Percy Lubbock to take Belloc more seriously, he accompanied him to Belloc's dilapidated cottage at Shipley in the summer of 1911. Arthur was horrified. The house was 'unutterably frowsy, mean, with vulgar accumulation of hideous objects, old and new'; and Belloc himself emerged from the shadows 'in slippers, very dishevelled, beery, smoky, unpleasant, with a shiny tail coat'. The whole atmosphere was that of a 'gypsy encampment'.

He invited both Belloc and Chesterton to the Pepys Dinner at Magdalene in the same year. It was a memorable occasion, especially at the end of the evening in Arthur's rooms, by which time both the celebrities had very obviously over-indulged:

> Belloc was now *hopelessly* drunk. He quarrelled with Mackail, who treated him drily, he burst into sudden laughter, he took a violent fancy to me and overwhelmed me with praise. He fell into instantaneous slumbers, he dropped his cigar. When I took Mackail away, Belloc came too, fell down my steps, entered the court at an involuntary run, dropped his cigar, which he seemed to have lighted at both ends – stopped every minute to pay me compliments with bows. He said he wanted to see Gaselee. 'I shall do very well with him' – but G. was gone to bed. So I took B. to Ramsey's rooms, and I left him bowing, with his heels together, saying he desired my further acquaintance – sported him in.

Arthur fell to reflecting upon the way in which different people reacted to an over-abundance of wine.

> Charles Sayle was tipsy! In Hall this took an Anacreontic turn. He said to Salter 'I'll give you a toast – Archie Don!' Percy affected not to understand. 'Ah, he's a sort of religion to *us*'. Later on, he took up his stand behind a bookcase, and when any man of eminence passed out, Sayle flew out in a tearful ecstasy, seized a limp hand in both of his and said 'Let me thank you, not in a personal capacity, but in the name of the University for your presence here tonight.' .... Thinking over the speeches, tho' Chesterton was clever, and Belloc fine, yet when the Master rose to make his little remarks, one felt the presence of something clean, straightforward and gentlemanly, as opposed to something rather dirty, stuffy, suspicious, second-rate. Belloc grumbling, coughing, scintillating, striving – dirty, unkempt, frowsy, was a thing of horror. Intellect is hardly purchased at this price. It was second-rate citizenship! Chesterton sweated so that when he shook hands and held

his cigar downwards, the sweat ran down and hissed at the point. Salter, fresh, crisp, clear-eyed, loud-voiced was a delicious contrast to all this pretentious, humbugging, stuffy quackery.

It was a sort of success – but literary men are fittest for the common sink, as Carlyle said.

One could criticise the life-style of Cambridge – the hot-house atmosphere, the petty jealousies, the resentment at success – but it was a cleaner, saner world than – for instance – the circle that his brother Fred had devised for himself. Only one of Fred's friends did Arthur really like, and that was the pathetically unsuccessful, but child-like, Philip Burne-Jones, who aspired to be a portrait painter in the family tradition. When he came to stay with Arthur at Cambridge in 1912 he had to confess his failure: an overdraft of £5000 and a year's professional earnings amounting to only four guineas. But most of Fred's friends were of the flashy, wealthy literary set who spent a large portion of each year in Venice. Percy Lubbock knew more of this group than Arthur and told him very much more than ever Fred would vouchsafe. There was a sort of Anglo-Venetian colony: 'Charles Williams in his Palazzo, Lady Radnor in her saloons – the silliness of it, the idleness, the sentimentality about bronzed gondoliers etc, with I dare say a nastier background. . . . It is this life which Fred leads so mysteriously and of which he says nothing. I wonder what it is all about.' Comparing his life with that of his brothers, Arthur unhesitatingly liked his own choice.

Percy Lubbock had made the definite choice for the other side. He had abandoned Cambridge for a literary career. In the late summer of 1911, he and Arthur took a holiday together in Yorkshire (near Northallerton) during the course of which one little mystery which had been troubling Arthur was cleared up. Percy and Oliffe Richmond, who at one stage had appeared to be in love with each other, had become estranged and abstracted. The truth was that they had both fallen in love with the same girl – Celia Newbolt. Percy's anxiety to accompany Arthur to Yorkshire was explained by the fact that Henry Newbolt and his family were staying at Mount Grace, one of the residences of Sir Hugh Bell, Lord-Lieutenant of the county, who lent the house to friends for periods in the summer while he was living at Rownton. Rather reluctantly Arthur accompanied Percy to stay with the Newbolts. He immediately appreciated how Percy's and Oliffe's hearts had been turned. When Celia entered the room, 'I saw in a minute what everyone meant. I don't think I have ever seen anything more utterly charming and sweet . . . anything more highly favoured among women ... since my life began.'

Poor Percy's romance did not prosper. In fact he nearly drove Arthur mad during the following term at Cambridge by asking himself to stay when he knew that the Newbolts were visiting Horace Darwin, and forcing Arthur to go with him to a performance of *The Magic Flute* purely so that he could feast his eyes on Celia sitting in the audience. 'He is ill and in love, and must be excused', Arthur magnanimously conceded.

While in Yorkshire, however, they went with the Newbolts to visit the Bells at Rownton. Here was another interesting literary group, most of whom Arthur had met before in Gosse's company. They were certainly well-endowed to indulge their tastes. The income of the Bells, for instance, was estimated at £60,000 p.a. Gertrude Bell, whom Arthur had last seen in 1908, was the complete antithesis of Celia Newbolt. She came out to meet them 'uglier than ever, all points and peaks and moustached – but so entirely frank and jolly, liking life and with a perfectly definite line'. There was a boy there (Maurice), apparently recently expelled from Eton, the aged Lady Bell and her sister ('a funny little old lady ... who winked and nodded, and told a story which she could not finish owing to hysterical laughter. She tried several times and at last abandoned it'). The following day Arthur had a long talk with Gertrude Bell, who had been detailed to pilot them for a walk ('Never have I had a worse guide'). Arthur commented on the ugliness of the Welsh, with faces 'like goats and parrots seen in spoons'. This amused Gertrude greatly. 'There', she said, 'that is a characteristic Benson remark. I like getting in touch with that again!' She turned the subject to Mary Benson, 'and I quoted Ethel Smyth's words "as good as God and as clever as the Devil". G.B. rallied me on the profanity of it and said "That's one comfort about all of you – You are not in the least like the children of Archbishops".'

The truth was that Arthur had a sort of love-hate for the literary world. He could not have coped with its pace and its passions in the 'log-rolling' atmosphere of London. But he enjoyed the company and conversation of literary people. In some ways his ideal would have been fulfilled if he could have gained literary honours within Cambridge itself; and the possibility of securing this came with the foundation of the Chair of English Literature (the King Edward VII Professorship) in 1910. He attended a meeting in June that year to discuss its aims and the type of man required to launch them. He found himself in entire disagreement with A. W. Ward, Master of Peterhouse, who was strongly in favour of an academic. He saw the Chair as a 'lectureless, erudite, research position

... to catch it for the pedants'. As speculation mounted, some (like Lubbock) argued for the foundation of a school of serious criticism; others (like Arthur himself) wanted 'a generous moving force' – such, perhaps, as himself? He was honest enough to reflect that the whole business 'will end for me by my not wanting it, but being angry with anyone else who may be offered it'. When he heard that the choice had fallen upon A. W. Verrall, his father's old pupil, he allowed his sense of family friendship to override his resentment at the selection of so eminent a classical scholar. 'That is a relief to me', he wrote: 'I don't want to give up the College work, nor do I want to devote myself to critical writing. Verrall will be a very stimulating lecturer, and the only thing against him is his crippled state. . . . I can help to hold up Moses' hands.'

Verrall's tenure of the Chair was to be very short-lived. He died in June 1912. The speculation and uncertainty began all over again. The new appointment was announced in October – Arthur Quiller-Couch, 'Q', a man not unknown to Arthur although they had never met. Newbolt, many years before, had spoken of his strange background – a mixture of fisherman and country doctor, with a wife 'of a lower class who is tiresome, very ugly, waxed moustache and very irritable'. Arthur was a little piqued at the news. 'I hear that Bradley and Ker refused', he wrote. 'Q.C. is at all events a *figure*: he is an amateur, of course. . . . If they were going to take an amateur, why not me?'

'Q' would have a difficult time at Cambridge, at least at first. He would suffer the penalty of public success – an extraordinary professional terminus for a man whose mother had been a lodging-house keeper at Oxford and who had been lifted up on the shoulders of Cassell through the success of *Deadman's Rock* (it was Newbolt again who passed these details to Arthur). The arbiters of Cambridge society – notably Lady Albinia – rapidly suspected that he was not quite a gentleman because of his cavalier disregard of social invitations; and Arthur rather agreed. He was 'amiable but somehow common. I don't like his dress nor the scent of drink and smoke he diffuses. He looks like a racing tout.' When he persuaded him to dine at Magdalene and succeeded in making him relax, he changed his mind somewhat. 'He wants to do his best, and he's a good fellow', he conceded. He was interested, and rather flattered, to see 'Q' one day sitting among his lecture audience; but it nettled him to receive no word of praise at the end. 'Q's only comment was 'Browning was a bit of a grocer in real life!' Arthur chewed that one over. He added, when he recorded the comment, 'What is Q.C.?'

Equally difficult to imagine as a figure of literary eminence was the new Kennedy Professor of Latin, A. E. Housman. At their first meeting Arthur rather disliked him. He was a quaint figure with 'odd champagne bottle shoulders', who would sport in the streets of Cambridge 'a funny little round cap like a teacake'. He could be vulgar and acrid in conversation, delighting in saying 'little bitter icy things about people', and he had a disturbing habit of correcting other peoples' stories by disputing details. 'He inspires a sort of terror and I have no doubt would not be displeased to know it. I thought of Conway Morgan's definition of a gentleman as a man who never unintentionally made himself offensive – and how a mild donnish voice said, "you mean *intentionally?*"' Arthur came, in time, rather to enjoy his company, especially when he discovered that Housman's caustic manner was really only a front to cover up his shyness at social occasions. But 'that this funny little prim, fussy, particular, conventional man, with his little digs and pokes and ironies should have written *The Shropshire Lad* is inconceivable. I thought of the cherry blossom poem today and wondered where it had all gone.' Many years later – in February 1925 – Housman explained the riddle to Arthur himself. His first poems had been the product of a deep personal attachment which had lasted fifteen years. For him, poetry originated only 'in a depressed and sickly mood'. He was totally unable to write when well. 'I never found H. so human and engaging in my life', Arthur commented. 'The frost all gone and a very simple soul left.' Not for the first time he discovered that it was rash to judge a person too harshly on first appearance.

*   *   *   *   *

Friendships might wax or wane, but the pattern of Arthur's life, his aspirations and frustrations, remained much the same. Geoffrey Winterbottom visited him still at Cambridge until he left for employment in Burma in the summer of 1912; but the close relationship had ended, as they both knew it must. Gradually Arthur advanced to positions of greater consequence within the corridors of power, although he still maintained his chosen peripheral stance. He became a member of the Press Syndicate in November 1911 – 'the centre of all Cambridge jobbery', Arthur commented. 'It will mean much work, but I like to be included. ... It means that I have after eight years a really recognised position here. Very unexpected.' He was appointed to the Oxford and Cambridge Board, a useful vantage point from which to snipe at the classicists and also to observe dons and headmasters at close quarters. It was in connection with the setting-up of a school's leaving examination, controlled by the two universities, that Arthur paid a private visit to Lord Haldane, at his house in Queen Anne's Gate, in February 1912. Haldane was then Secretary of State for War, and was interested in the impact of a national examination system on army entry and the desirable age for admission to Woolwich or Sandhurst.

Again Arthur conceded a pleasurable sense of self-importance. Haldane was very frank with him, although totally non-committal. As they walked, after lunch, to the War Office in Whitehall, he remarked to Arthur that his days as a Minister were numbered. 'We shall soon be out. We have been in quite long enough.' As they parted Arthur reflected on the importance of personal influence. 'Odd that I should have worked at education for so long, and yet I think I may have done more by today's talk for the whole affair than by all my thirty years of teaching. I am not insensible to the pleasure of taking my problem to one of the biggest men in the country and having real and serious attention paid it.' Perhaps, in little ways, he was even influencing big decisions. The Press had certainly much to be grateful for in his using his position on the Joint Board to persuade his Oxford colleagues that it would be in their common interest for the Oxford and Cambridge presses to combine in the printing of the Bible – a very major decision, as it turned out.

If he ever were to have any influence, he reflected, he ought to be exercising it now. In March 1912, he wrote in his diary:

> I am close on fifty, and I suppose the best part of my life is gone; but I have some vitality left, I can write, I can teach. I might with good luck have twenty more years of activity. But one might always die, the idea of which is insupportable; and I might have another illness. I am not at all likely to marry, or to have any more romantic adventures. But I think I am more interested in affairs and people than ever, and I am very anxious to help in the cause of common sense, work and peace. I am still mildly ambitious. . . .
> I also feel very strongly the duality of my nature: a strong, stupid slow-moving old nature underneath, which goes blindly and bluntly on its way – and a quick, perceptive, ingenious, inquisitive nature above, living in brain and eyes, which has no permanence. That will die, I think, with all its memories; but the other will pass silently and stubbornly on its way, and reappear again, I don't doubt. That is almost all that I believe.

He had certainly not reconciled himself to the abandonment of romantic adventures. It was not so much that he missed Geoffrey Winterbottom. He craved for a new emotional excitement and the thrill of pursuit; and the longing irked him the more because all his friends seemed preoccupied with entanglements which only served to accentuate his own isolation.

Percy Lubbock was still dreaming hopelessly of Celia Newbolt. Oliffe Richmond, with whom Arthur took a holiday at Ashbourne, had returned to his infatuation with the youngsters of the King's Choir School, and – what was worse – had been making a shamefully hypocritical fuss about the behaviour of a King's undergraduate, MacMichael, who shared the same propensity.

> MacM. seems to have behaved like a sentimental ass, pursuing two of these boys to their homes in Suffolk and Norfolk, calling at the vicarages, scraping acquaintance, and then getting his mother to invite them to tea, and going to King's day after day to ogle them and speak to them. He is in with a set of similar donkeys. It does not necessarily mean vicious tendencies, but it seems an abnormal kind of flirtation. I don't think there is any real harm in him. But the odd thing is that O.R. who has exactly the same abnormal tendency makes a prodigious fuss about this, lectures MacM., and bothers every one of the Cambridge authorities – as tho' he was resenting intrusion, on high moral grounds, into a Seraglio of his own.

Was it *morally* wrong to have a flirtation with a King's choirboy? Arthur found this a difficult question to answer. It really depended upon motives and emotions which others were in no position to judge; perhaps, also, upon the *mores* of any particular society at any particular time. This occurred to him on a visit to the Leys School, to give a lecture, at the end of January 1912. He was very much struck by a curious incident at the conclusion of his lecture, as the boys were leaving the Hall.

> An odd thing in the seats quite near me. A pretty red-haired boy of about 12 was standing up on the seat, when a very handsome and charming boy of about 15 came up and clasped his arms round him with a look of intense affection, and so stood holding him, while the little boy stroked the big boy's hair and cheek. This close to me and the Headmaster. If I had seen that at Eton I should have been very anxious – but the boys close by made no comment and didn't even look surprised; and the publicity of it seemed to free it from any morbid sentiment.

It was all rather touching, natural, unaffected. Why, then, should anybody be outraged? And was there not something idiotic in the scale of values – Arthur thought – when the College authorities dealt very sternly with MacMichael for his behaviour with the choirboys, and yet would take correspondingly lighter measures with an undergraduate who had a flirtation with his landlord's daughter? After all, the potential risk to the girl was far greater. It was a puzzling world, and Arthur was rather relieved that he had no disciplinary role or responsibility to discharge within it.

Oliffe Richmond, however, was a different matter. He was indulging in ridiculous self-deception. Arthur decided to talk with him very frankly when he heard him complaining about the short-sightedness of the College in not appointing him a Tutor, maintaining that he took a genuine personal interest in the young men. What is the real truth, Arthur asked?

> He takes a strong sexual kind of interest in the attractive men, and nothing else. . . .[He is] obsessed with a sort of perverted eroticism for anything young and fair. . . . It is the combination of sensuous motive with a kind of lofty priggishness, only paralleled by Farrar's school stories, about using influence and directing other minds and hearts which is so impenetrable.

As for the choirboys, 'O.R. has a morbid predilection for *boys* – it is a sort of sexuality, an erotic mania, though wholly pure and good. . . . I don't think I ever saw anyone so indignant, so silly, and so entirely self-deceived. I told him today that it *was* a sexual perversion and that he must drop it.'

Possibly Arthur, too, was self-deceived; and the advice, so strongly expressed, would perhaps have come better from someone less prone himself to romantic male attachments. But he certainly did not perceive any element of hypocrisy in his condemnation. He could find open fault with Richmond because of his lack of decorum combined with a strident, self-pitying attempt to claim a righteous motive. For this reason he was less censorious in his remarks about Charles Sayle, whose sentimental attachment to Archie Don was at least honest and unashamed. Arthur visited Sayle at his house in August 1912 and described it in his diary.

> It's an odd house, a kind of pussy-cat place. There are many books, the rooms are small but pleasant – and there are many photographs of children, boys, youths – all the object of Sayle's innocent adoration. There is something a little silly about it, but still it's a definite life on a definite method. Sayle is not concerned with what is thought of him and goes his own way in a cosy, old-maidish, sentimental way, full of adorations, without passion.

It was easier to be critical of others when one was not oneself *sous la charme*. Arthur was fidgeted by a sense of emptiness in his emotional life. No one had been found to take Winterbottom's place. A visit from George Mallory stirred none of the old feelings. His world was

Charterhouse now; 'and I gather from him that he has some emotional affairs in hand with boys'. Their own little romance was a thing of the past. While Arthur looked rather vaguely and pathetically round for suitable successors, his other friends seemed happily preoccupied with their own *affaires du coeur*. Frank Salter had taken up with a young Fellow of Trinity Hall, a fervent nonconformist by the name of Angus. Winstanley appeared to have captured the heart of the young Lord Doune (a Trinity undergraduate) and invited Arthur to lunch with him and Dennis Robertson, rather obviously to show him off. Arthur was impressed: 'An enchanting youth . . . like the son of Archestratus . . . I fell quite in love with him, but I suppose I shall never see him again.' He mused over the inexplicable chemistry that determines physical attraction:

> A creature like this fills one with strange and vague emotions, and a desire to please and interest him. I suppose that something sexual is mixed up in it; but if so it translates itself into very emotional regions, and is as if one had seen an angel. I can't believe that it all arises, this sort of grace and sweetness, from a mere aim on God's part to get the race propagated.

But this was Winstanley's prize; and Arthur could not quite bring himself to indulge in the adulation of those so conspicuously highly-favoured that they drew to themselves a whole circle of prostrate admirers – Rupert Brooke, for instance; or Archie Don; or all those whom Lapsley deliberately gathered together to sup with him one night – 'the pets, epigoni, "nice" people, "treats" to the number of twenty men', whom Winstanley pressed Arthur to join. '*How* I should have loathed it', Arthur wrote, declining the invitation. That was not the atmosphere in which romance was engendered. He preferred to track the solitary fawn.

But there seemed none suitable or responsive to hand. He had several private tête-à-têtes with Rupert Brooke, sometimes in romantic settings, sitting in the garden in the gathering dusk, but he never felt remotely tempted to sentimentalise. Quite apart from the 'tied-up voice' and 'awkward hands and feet', his affected dress was an irritation. 'I should have liked him better if he hadn't worn a very low-necked deep blue shirt, and a great flaming tie. . . . He would have been more attractive to me with cropped hair and in evening dress.' He found Archie Don much better company, and could wholly relax with him, trying out on each other imitations of notable Cambridge characters – Shipley, E. W. Barnes and Stuart Donaldson. But he was not in love with him. He worked mildly on Jim Butler, finding him 'wonderfully delightful and charming – so very modest and simple'. On a ride to Newmarket together in August 1912, Arthur recognised a genuine advance in their relationship. 'I felt much drawn to him, and crossed the line from acquaintance to affection.' But by then it was too late for anything deeper to develop between them. Butler's time at Cambridge was coming to an end and he would see him but rarely again.

A more hopeful prospect was a young freshman from Lancing, called Fixsen. Arthur conducted his 'viva' for the scholarship examination in January 1912 and was entranced. He invited him to lunch the following day. Once he came into residence, however, the incipient romance was quickly scotched. 'Why do I always lose all interest in *ordinands*?', Arthur bemoaned in his diary after lunching Fixsen a second time. 'They seem to me to put heart and mind into a kind of box and adopt an ugly convention.' He did not give him up all at once, but it was no use. 'He's a nice boy', he wrote in February 1913, 'but not the beloved youth for whom I am always on the look out. The more I miss Geoffrey, the more I see what an extraordinary power of unselfish affection he had. . . . He did really reach out to me, and that is rare.'

1912, in fact, had not been a very happy year for Arthur. It seemed that he had learned nothing new in his writing. He returned to the old genre in *Joyous Gard* which he dashed off in the course of a fortnight. He conceded that he had been fidgety and ill-tempered. But one pleasing piece of recognition had come to him within the College. A. G. Peskett, President of Magdalene (in effect, Vice-Master), retired at the end of the academic year; and Stuart Donaldson, who at last himself received recognition by his election to the Vice-Chancellorship for 1913 and 1914, needed a deputy who would be very active in College affairs. He approached Arthur with the invitation to become President in October 1912. The only aspect of the post that failed to attract him was the supervision of the College servants; otherwise it suited him to perfection. 'It is a fitting crown for me', he wrote. 'A little sinecure, with a high-sounding name – glory without usefulness – just what I have always desired.'

He had fears that A. S. Ramsey, the senior fellow, would be greatly put out. As it transpired, the College meeting which saw a complete reshuffling of all the College offices confirmed the Master's wish without demur. Ramsey was appointed Tutor and Bursar; Talbot Peel became Steward; Vernon Jones was made Assistant Tutor and Stephen Gaselee Praelector. 'All the difficulties about the new appointments seem to have melted away', Arthur noted with satisfaction. 'We all licked our chops.'

As the year drew to its close he took stock as was his wont. Although he had become President of Magdalene, he had somehow become immersed in University committees and intrigues. It was the old Eton 'scurry' all over again. Furthermore 'I have tended to alienate and vex my friends. I have squabbled with Hugh Walpole and Gosse – not to be made up. I have rubbed up Percy and Salter. I have nearly squabbled with Gaselee and Donald. Meantime I have made no *new* friends at all, and it is clear that I must somehow regain my former amiability.' His writings had made little impression. He had become 'largely a journalist and this won't do'. In *The Times* annual survey of the year's publications, neither *The Child of the Dawn* nor *Thy Rod and thy Staff* received a mention. Hugh Walpole's latest novel did, however. There was a warning here somewhere. All he could really count on the credit side was his entry into the inner ring of Cambridge affairs. There was a certain satisfaction, for a while, in plotting with R. V. Laurence and young Will Spens ways and means of ousting the Radical doctrinaires. But, in his heart, he pined for close companionship. The malaise could be simply explained. 'I am not épris with anyone.'

Chapter Ten

BITTER-SWEET

Oh, so you think you are enjoying yourself, do you?
(March 1913)
I am always still searching for something which I cannot find
– more peace, strength and certainty.   (December 1913)

The malaise continued until the summer of 1913. Arthur sought in vain a congenial young friend. The friendships of longer standing seemed to be weakening. Percy Lubbock had eyes only for Celia Newbolt; and – on hearing of her engagement to Ralph Furse – decided to leave the country and bury his grief in Venice. Lapsley seemed to have hardened in his dogmatism, so that Arthur found himself trying to avoid his company. Neither Archie Don nor F. A. Simpson seemed to respond to his blandishments; Archie Don became rather bored by them and Simpson was 'a charming creature, but reserved'. Frank Salter, too, had proved a real disappointment. In the first place he had severely reduced Arthur's teaching, claiming the historians for straight Tripos supervisions and not disguising his scepticism over the efficacy and value of giving them general essays and trying to teach them how to write. Secondly, he had become foolishly involved in tiresome missionary camps to which he would repair with vulnerable undergraduates in the vacations. 'It seems to me incredibly distasteful', Arthur wrote. 'They sleep in tents, they have many addresses and prayer-meetings – they are undenominational, and are filled with Christian buoyancy of a boisterous kind – such godly mirth!'

He felt fretful and out of sorts. In June he received a summons to present himself before the Surveyor of Taxes at Cambridge, and immediately anticipated a prison sentence and financial ruin for failing (as he supposed) to declare his American royalties on his tax return. When the dreaded moment came, however, he discovered that all that was in question was the fluctuating annual figures for his literary earnings; and when he confessed his suppression of his American income he was told that tax had already been deducted at source. All this seemed to convince him of his inherent timidity and ineffectiveness.

My own real failing is that I have never been in vital touch with anyone – never either fought anyone, or kissed anyone! Like Dmitri Rundine, I can neither be soldier or lover – and this not out of any principle, but out of a timid and rather fastidious solitariness. ... I have great perception and a love of beauty but I can't finish or perfect anything, and so a sort of ineffectiveness is very legible in all I do.

He found it impossible to relax and enjoy the successes he had gained. Even at Tremans he was fidgeted. None of the family seemed well. Fred had had a serious operation for an internal tumour and – since his recovery – had set up house for the summer at a villa in Capri, which he shared with a friend, John Ellingham Brooks, whom Arthur found distasteful. Hugh, at Hare Street, was grossly overtaxing himself with preaching engagements and confided to Arthur that he had taken to whisky for the worst reasons ('not for drinky but for drunky'), and doubted that he would live to be fifty. Arthur himself was putting on far too much weight. He was sixteen and a half stone, when he weighed himself in August, and Ross Todd had given him 'some shrewd advice'. He had steeled himself to visit Maggie at the Priory at Roehampton and had been allowed to take her out for short journeys and visits to churches and museums. These were always rather harrowing occasions. Her condition was clearly hopeless, although in the early summer of 1913 she was moved from the Priory to become a resident patient of a Dr Barton and his wife who lived in Wimbledon. Arthur discussed the situation with his mother later that summer. Her spirits, he noted in his diary, 'are wonderful, in spite of what she suffers. We are a tough lot, I think, below our sensibilities. But the knowledge of Maggie's weakness, and how certainly derived it was from papa, and my own tendencies make it clear to me *why* we are coming, as a stock, to an end – and I don't think it would be *right* to prolong it.'

He visited Maggie at Wimbledon in August and took her for a walk over the golf course. What began as a quiet, but tense, stroll ended in a sort of nightmare. Maggie suddenly insisted that Arthur should leave her. She wanted to be alone; she had no intention of returning to Dr Barton's house. Arthur feared that she was carrying a knife. Fortunately the golf course was enclosed within a barbed-wire fence, and he was able to call for help. A cab was summoned and, by careful talking and wheedling, Maggie was eventually persuaded to board it. The effect on Arthur's nerves was longer lasting than he supposed at the time. He feared that it might induce a return of intense depression; and it certainly clouded his holiday with Oliffe Richmond at Ludlow at the end of the month. 'The scene at Wimbledon has left its traces', he noted at the conclusion of an outing to Stokesey Castle, when his appreciation of its beauty had been overshadowed by black and ominous apprehensions. He seemed to see omens everywhere that summer: a pheasant asleep in a hole; a partridge lying at his feet; a wild duck with its brood flapping suddenly across his path. On one day of mounting sulkiness at Tremans, when the Maycocks had called on them at an inconvenient moment and Arthur was in no mood to indulge in small talk, he took himself off into the garden and mooched about peevishly until they departed. In exasperation he sat down with a heavy sigh on a garden seat. It broke and he ended in a heap on the grass. It was that sort of summer!

Earlier that month, however, there had been a blissful interlude which brought with it hopes of delights to come. On Saturday, 8 August, a young Balliol undergraduate, King's Scholar of Eton, called Geoffrey Madan, had come to Magdalene to spend the week-end with him. The assignation had come about through an exchange of letters while Madan was still at Eton. He had sent Arthur a pamphlet he had written on Herodotus. Arthur recognised the boy's classical ability; but, more than that, there was something about the tone of the letter which attracted him. Having encountered his father, who was Bodley's Librarian at Oxford, Arthur ventured to suggest that they should meet.

> A tall, handsome, well-dressed, rather self-conscious boy, with a slight outward cast of eye, a little like my old pupil King, came forward, very much self-possessed, and shook hands. He seems half shy, half loquacious: has many interests; but has that rather confusing and disconcerting sort of Etonian politeness – I had it strongly at his age – which ends in a sort of pretentiousness, a claim to know more than one does know about everything mentioned, not for self-satisfaction but out of real *civility*.

Arthur took him into Hall to dine. 'Only Gaselee there, who played up most vigorously, and we had a nice evening. He is a beautiful fellow to look at. By day he is a little touched by the anaemic eruptiveness of youth – but by the dim light of combination room, his fine and sweet expression comes out. He is ingenuous, simple, clever: he has that sort of youthful shyness which is not diffidence so much as deference – "the sweet and sudden passion of youth for greatness in an elder". ... I sate for sometime and talked; and felt an old and unfamiliar glow – how silly it is at my age to fall in love at first sight again, and behave like a sportive walrus.'

All the little arts and wiles of a mild seduction were brought into play: a tour round the colleges, a visit to Ely, the procuring from Monty James of an invitation for both of them to dine at King's; and all the time Arthur strained to enchant him, feeling somewhat 'like a seal playing with a kitten'. But he was careful not to swamp him all at once. On their parting he gave him a copy of *From a College Window*, which Madan described as 'nice' ('the *mot propre*', Arthur agreed, '. . . I'm not a writer, so much as an improvisatore'). In return, the boy was to send him some of his poems. A letter of thanks arrived on the Tuesday morning.

> I feel like Amos when the Lord showed him the dish of summer fruit, or like a flower hummed over by a bee. It is rather absurd in a stout man of fifty to fall in love with a boy of 18 thus – for this is what I have done! But it shows that I am rather juvenile in mind; it has been the same all my life; and now I must put out all my best magic to captivate M. I think he cares about literature in the same sort of way that I do. I have an interesting note from Luxmoore about Madan – I consulted him. He says he is able, self-conscious, modest, affectionate. That is enough for me; and my experience has always been that if one cares enough one can always provoke affection back – even if one weighs sixteen stone and looks like the cornet-player of a German Band.

This was all that Arthur needed to restore his good humour and revive his powers. He went off to Norwich to stay with Bishop Pollock and to address a conference of diocesan curates in a state of near elation. 'Many people would have thought this very tepid fun', he mused, 'the nice, close, comfortable clerical fug is horrible to them. It's very different to a son of Aaron!' He was amused to hear that an elderly parson had been taken to the operating-table clutching a copy of *The Thread of Gold*. He delighted in the sight of Bishop Pollock in bed with phlebitis, wearing a Cambridge Blue blazer ('a touch of vanity?') and in watching his expression as Mrs Pollock announced very solemnly that the Bishop had been restored to life by prayer.

> 'It's the simple truth, Mr Benson. The doctors said "We can do no more – we are powerless." But prayer prevailed!' The Bishop looked uncomfortable and hastily changed the subject.

His sense of beauty had returned too. In Hugh's company, while they were both staying at Tremans, he went for an outing to Seaford. They stopped the car at a spot in the Cuckmere valley on the Eastbourne road and walked to the beach through yellowed grass. The sea was at low tide. Hugh bathed while Arthur luxuriated in the beauty and the sunshine.

'The picture strangely completed by a young and shapely man, quite naked, strolling to the cliff base, a few yards away, and sitting there in a most graceful pose, reading in a little book – a curiously pagan finish? ... I fell into a dreamful, half-hypnotised state, among all these blissful sights and sounds.'

When he returned to Cambridge for the new academic year he had a presentiment of some significant event to come. 'I hope not death', he wrote. 'I don't want to die.' Whatever it was to be, it would affect – he believed – his inner life. 'I feel as if a door was to be opened, and as if I were about to be *shown* the inner life.' The only events of immediate consequence were his finding himself on yet another committee – a gathering of divines, for the most part, to meet regularly at Church House in London to revise the Prayer Book Psalter – and the news with which Stuart Donaldson greeted him, that he had been ordered by his doctor to resign the Vice-Chancellorship forthwith because of a serious heart condition. Monty James was therefore to become Vice-Chancellor at a moment's notice.

There, in a matter of days, was the good Monty walking breezily through the streets of Cambridge in top hat and bands. Arthur sat under his chairmanship for the first time at the meeting of the Syndics of the Press.

M[onty] very grand in bands and silk gown, and rather proud to show himself in the streets. It was odd to think how we walked together 30 years ago as undergrads. He is the bigger man – Provost and V.C. I better known, perhaps, and richer. But this is very unlike what might have been supposed. I think it would have been expected that I should have been more ambitious, less likely to make a literary success and certainly unlikely to make money. He wd have been supposed likely to be Professor and a scholar of note.

A week or so later, he was dining at the King's lodge with a varied gathering of worthies – the Dean of Wells, the Tanners, Lord Curzon. Arthur again reflected on the curious destiny that had shaped the lives of his Eton contemporaries.

Curzon looked pale – he is fat, lame, *respectable* looking, like a great butler. His head is spherical, his body is spherical. I could not have believed that so handsome a boy as he was, and so eminent a man as he is, could look so awfully commonplace.

He indulged in Eton stories 'inartistically exaggerated'. His voice 'is mobile, youthful, and beautiful in cadence and timbre, but with a certain pedantry and donnishness. He pronounces all his "a's" flat (pass, bath, as in flat).'

> It is odd to see Curzon at Monty's and to think ai ~ut old times. Curzon's a failure, on the whole. He has had *every* advantage – uirth, industry, ability, ambition, money (someone else's made by money-lending!), but he hasn't done much: he wasn't a success in India; he will never hold *high* office again, I think. His health is bad. But it is a very commonplace mind, priggish, donnish. If he *hadn't* had birth and rank, he wd have been an Oxford professor, I think – not much liked, but rather feared. That's what he really *is*.
>
> Then there's the Dean of Wells. That's a failure too – dressed up, in his big house, deplorably idle and useless, a mere Abbé, with nothing done, and certainly not preaching the Gospel, but smoking Virginian cigarettes.
>
> Then there's me – I'm a failure too, partly from a lack of moral courage and partly from an original lack of perseverance. So I certainly have missed chances of distinction, and not made the most of my gifts.
>
> Monty is *not* a failure. He doesn't like his work, but he does it well. Yet of the four I think in many ways I was the best equipped with the kind of advantage which made for success, except for having no self-confidence.

But he was happy again, he had in all honesty to admit. He enjoyed standing in for Stuart Donaldson as Master while he was away for practically the whole of the term under doctor's orders. With the prospect of Geoffrey Madan coming to stay with him just before Christmas, he could take aesthetic pleasure in handsome undergraduates again without the agonising self-pity of the unloved; and the stupid little committees in London proved quite entertaining diversions. He tried to avoid Gosse at the meetings of the R.S.L., but was not always successful. It was clear that Gosse wanted a repentant reconciliation, but Arthur was not to be taken in by his 'bows and smiles' whenever he caught his eye, or his ostentatious reception of Arthur's speech on behalf of W. R. Inge, at a meeting to elect new members, when he 'clapped me as if he were scaring birds'. And the Psalter Revision Committee, chaired by the Bishop of Chester, proved quite as absurd a gathering as he had anticipated. Everybody disliked the Dean of Ely and voted against every suggestion he made. Professor Nairne was simply 'fatuous', invoking in support of his own renderings the simple faith of the simple woodmen who composed his parish. Mackail could be relied upon to puncture all Nairne's flights of fancy. When they came to consider the words 'I said in my haste, all men are liars', Mackail recalled the comments of a minister who had drily observed to his congregation, 'David might well have said it at leisure.'

Geoffrey Madan duly came to stay again. The days passed more blissfully than Arthur had dared to hope. He talked freely about himself and his impressions of Eton and Balliol: how he had become fascinated by the Greek language and had turned to a study of Byzantine Greek, rendering the whole of St Luke into Byzantine hexameters; how he had developed a sort of contemptuous affection for Hugh Macnaghten; how Edward Lyttelton had become popular with the boys for his friendliness, but how deplorably bad and muddled he was as a teacher. And then his contemporaries at Balliol: 'the foolish Ronnie Knox, with his 39 buttons on his cassock to represent the 39 Articles etc.'. They passed on to religion and their views on Nietzsche. Arthur had rarely met a boy so ready to share his feelings and his enthusiasms.

> As I write [he recalled in his diary] I watch him sit in a chair, with a book, but not reading – his big eyes turned to the fire, his smooth cheeks and hair and long hands – a perfect picture of youth and romance. I like the way in which at intervals he thanks me, very simply and sweetly, for being kind to him. I grow very fond of him and would like to make him care for me.

He took him to Clayhithe; to Haslingfield; to look up fetishes and to tell him about them. He showed him off to more of his friends, noticing with satisfaction Lapsley's jealousy ('Where did you get that enchanting creature from?', he whispered to Arthur at the conclusion of dinner). And then, to cap it all, the boy agreed to prolong his stay by three days, and the enchantment continued. At the end, Arthur bought him a pencil-case as a memento and travelled with him back to London.

> At K.C., he was really, I felt, rather *moved*. I saw him into a taxi, and then he slipped from my sight. He goes off smiling into the world. ... It's an odd thing that an elderly buffer like me, with all my syndicates and nonsense, should yet be so sentimental. I wonder what mystery of temperament and sex lies behind it!

Would it last? The year 1914 would see the answer to that question. As for the year that was passing, Arthur reflected on New Year's Eve, the malaise of the early months had faded into oblivion. It 'has been a much-abused year; but it has been good to me'.

*   *   *   *   *

The year 1914 saw events of more significance in the history of the world than the blossoming friendship between Arthur Benson and Geoffrey Madan. But until the great cataclysm came at the beginning of August, the diary supplies hardly a hint of troubles in the outside world. Indeed Arthur rarely alluded to political affairs unless they directly impinged upon his life. He would grouse over industrial troubles when he was incommoded by a strike; he might spare a glance at some particular absurdity of the suffragettes if he sensed the shaping of some choice vignette. On the road past Thirlmere, for instance, he noticed one rainy afternoon a despondent group of 'gloomy suffragettes, who are supposed to be *walking* to London, holding meetings as they go; but seven stout ladies with coloured scarves in a waggonette was all we saw of them'. As for the possibility of European war, he could not countenance it. Listening to A. J. Mason declaiming against the Turks and the troubles in the Balkans, Arthur refused to be aroused. 'I personally am against war in any guise', he commented. 'I think it an anachronism in civilised nations, like duelling.' The mounting tension in Ireland only served to convince him that Lloyd-George was a bully and a 'vile demagogue'. He noted in June 'the Archduke Franz Ferdinand and his wife killed at Sarajevo' but drew no conclusions from the event. As far as politics went, he was more interested in Waggett's account of a row between Margot Asquith and Lady Londonderry in the Women's Gallery in the House of Commons when they abused M.P.'s 'like two fishwives'. When complaint was made to the Speaker, he pronounced sadly 'Alas, I am so much occupied with restraining the demons below that I can't intervene with the angels above.'

This fateful year, then, ran its course until the late summer with Arthur as deeply engrossed as ever in his own little affairs and strategems. He was certainly dreaming more than usual: highly dramatic inadequacy dreams and fantastic episodes involving esoteric ceremonies and processions, a sure sign of tension and overwork. In one such dream of seemingly endless processions, he found himself the focus of the ceremonial. 'Oh, the things I wore and carried. I was called the *Evarch* . . . I remember. It ended by a huge congregation in a modern Gothic Hall, singing hymns – a curious metre with an emphatic time. When all was over a verger came to me and said he thought they would be pleased if I thanked them. I did so, in a very silvery voice, and most touchingly.' In another, he found himself dining with the King, who entertained his guests with imitations of Lord Esher, Balfour and Lloyd-George. On the spur of the moment he decided to make Arthur Prime Minister, and he was despatched on the instant to the House of Commons. Then the dream passed into nightmare as he tried to find the entrance to the

Chamber, looking through endless rooms, stables and lofts, and climbing up metal ladders, hearing a crucial debate in progress, and – at one moment – peering down on the proceedings from a small window near the roof.

Cambridge itself exhibited its own particular brand of almost calculated insouciance – at least the circles at Cambridge in which Arthur moved. Perhaps with hindsight one can discern a heightened intensity, born of suppressed apprehensions, so that romantic friendships seemed to become just that little bit more over-charged, the figures of fun that little bit more ludicrous, the intrigues more trivial and the atmosphere of debate consequently more bitter. The young men who needed to be loved had to be wooed more quickly, before perhaps it was too late (as some subconscious thought might urge). So Winstanley's pursuit of the young rowing blue, Clarence Buxton, and his excitement over the pert and brilliant Romney Sedgwick, became an undergraduate joke. Lapsley retold the gossip somewhat ungraciously to Arthur at a Trinity dinner. 'He ate and drank too much', Arthur commented. 'He amused me by saying that two undergraduates going to call on Winstanley bet each other a luncheon that W. would mention Clarence Buxton within two minutes, accurately timed – He did so in 15 seconds.'

Some of the jokes had a touch of irony about them, granted the knowledge of things to come. A. E. Shipley (now Master of Christ's), for instance, had in his grossness become to Arthur very much a figure of fun; and his old habit of repetitive lamentation had certainly not improved with the years. Having made the remark in the Athenaeum that he was going off to Germany in the summer 'to live for a few days in a well-governed country', he fancied to himself that he had perpetrated rather a pleasing *bon mot*, so that every time Shipley was seen during the Easter term in converse with another, the words 'in a well-governed country' huskily and hoarsely uttered were heard by passers-by. Almost it seemed as if everybody was caricaturing himself. At the Pepys Dinner at Magdalene that year, the guests invited were chiefly eminent musicians. Arthur met C. H. Lloyd of Eton again, more 'bird-witted' than ever; and Arnold Dolmetsch – always a comic turn – was almost embarrassingly absurd: 'the *most* hideous figure I have ever seen in dusky frizzled wig, fallen almost *green* features – and such a tiny creature with feeble hands – an almost *frenzied* poseur'. Later in the evening he gave a little recital in the gallery with 'a child of nine, D's daughter, who sang songs like a Punchinello or Ventriloquist'.

One Cambridge figure remained, however, serenely the same – Montague Butler, Master of Trinity, even though, according to his doctors, he had really no right to be still alive. Arthur dined with him in January 1914 and was told all about his 'chest constriction and breathlessness' and was shown his tonic tabloids which his doctor had given him, together with instructions about never dining out or speaking in public. In Hall, however, 'he was very civil and entertaining, told endless stories in beautiful old-fashioned style, laughed much and showed no signs whatever of age or fatigue. He told me that when Uncle Henry came to see him to tell him he was doomed, they knelt and prayed together. During the latter part of dinner he constantly held my hand, patting and fondling it, which was very touching and sweet.'

Certainly the intrigues and issues at Cambridge, and in Magdalene in particular, could hardly have been more petty in these opening months of 1914. There were endless discussions in the Oxford and Cambridge Board over the future of compulsory Greek. Arthur found himself in attendance at a conference of headmasters who had been invited to state their views. He studied them carefully, many of them old friends: Lionel Ford, Edward Lyttelton, A. A. David, Frank Fletcher. Did he feel the slightest pang? 'Altogether, they gave me the sense of thoroughly tired, over-driven men, beset by routine and small problems and anxieties, with no time for looking into them .... The sense of *exhausted* men was strong upon me. I did not envy them.' But Magdalene had its small problems and anxieties of its own. In May 1914, a fierce row broke out amongst the Fellows over the high-handed action of Lady Albinia in insisting on the right of the Donaldson children to play tennis on the Fellows' court. Gaselee and Salter became so angry, and Lady Albinia so obdurate (she took away the reservations book to keep at the lodge) that Arthur genuinely feared a major College crisis. He himself was so disgusted by the acrimony ('the tone of the servants' hall and I am not going to be the under-butler any longer') that he threatened to resign the Presidentship. In the end, by visiting each Fellow individually and by diplomatic representations to the Master, he was able to secure peace.

Faced with this challenge – absurdly parish-pump as it was – Arthur responded sensitively and sensibly. Rather foolishly, earlier in the year, he had refused a challenge which might have given him the opportunity to produce some really serious work. He turned down an invitation to give the Clark Lectures at Trinity. 'I haven't time to write them', he complained, 'and I don't believe in literature – moreover here have I been *ten* years and they have never offered it to me until I am become a personage.' This was a feeble excuse, hardly redeemed by the insubstantial offerings he produced for his publishers during that year – *The Orchard Pavilion, The Happy Threshold, Where no Fear was*, and a lamentable edition of some unpublished Emily Bronte poems. Indeed, during these months, as Arthur was caricaturing others, he seemed almost to be caricaturing himself. He was full of typical little enterprises to satisfy his whims and fancies. He had bought up land on Grange Road and was building a house largely to his own design ('Howlands'). He had secured the woodwork of an eighteenth-century church in Rotterdam, recently renovated, which he decided to offer to Selwyn College for the panelling of their Hall. He was busy with plans for buying up all the old houses opposite Magdalene with a view to the building of a new residential block. But, above all, he was once again *sous la charme*.

When this mood was upon him he could be fickle over old friendships and more casual relationships. The news of George Mallory's engagement was recorded quite dispassionately. That little affair was long over. Percy Lubbock, in his Venetian adventures, had linked up with a Mrs Wharton, a rich invalid with a passion for literature who had separated from 'a tipsy husband'; and she, Percy and Lapsley were planning to go off to Algeria together for an expedition. Arthur found this wholly incomprehensible. Hugh Walpole tried to renew diplomatic relations. But Arthur had no wish to be reminded of the past. 'His commonness and sexuality bore me', he wrote. 'While I could be of use, while he depended on me, there was a charm, but now there is none, and I don't want this cheap sentiment poured over my feet and dried by his hair. H. Walpole and Gosse were the two people who made violent friends with me – laid violent hands on me – and it has been a failure in both cases; and indeed in both cases a real relief to have the association terminated.' Even the younger men, due to leave Cambridge that June, caused no real flutterings in Arthur's heart. 'I can't get up any emotion this year about people going down. . . . I care for Don, but for few others. I can't hold many people in my heart.'

To be accurate, with his friendship with Geoffrey Madan prospering, he could really hold only one person in his heart. By February that year, he had made a significant advance to Christian name terms. In the same month he had visited him at Oxford while staying with R. W. Livingstone to give a lecture at Corpus. They had then arranged that Madan should join Arthur for a few days' holiday at Broadway over Easter. The holiday began with Winstanley as Arthur's sole companion, staying at the Lygon Arms in the same rooms he had occupied with Tatham ten years before. Winstanley proved an ideal companion. 'These tête-à-tête sojourns are always more or less like a honeymoon', Arthur wrote. 'We make fun over our friends and it's all easy and pleasant.' They discussed why they should fall victim to the charms of the same sort of young man (Lord Doune, as a case in point); they composed parodies together in the course of their walks, taking – for instance – a song of Chesterton's as the metre and producing this:

> And Laurence would often say to Barnes, as they sate together to dine
> 'I don't care much where the water goes, if it doesn't get into the wine.'

Then they would invent absurd examination questions, Winstanley offering – over breakfast one morning – '10. "The flight into Egypt was dictated by the pressure of economic conditions." Comment on this.'

Winstanley departed to give way to Madan on 28 March. They soon discovered they could relax completely in each other's company alone. They enjoyed the same card games. They delighted in playing with words, Geoffrey Madan causing amazement by his facility at Greek, rendering two lines of Tennyson – thrown out at him by Arthur – into two fine spondaic hexameters with only a moment's thought. They spent an idyllic day at Bredon Hill and planted a fetish together – a cache of coins in a limestone boulder – just as if they were two children. 'I have never known anything quite like this before', Arthur recorded. 'Let me say frankly that I doubt if I have ever in my life felt so much in love with a human being as I felt today, nor come so near to one who seemed to me to realise more closely what I mean by beauty, grace and charm.'

There followed another blissful day at Little Malvern.

> Well, these two days will I think be long memorable to me. I don't see how I can forget them. I can't indeed recall any days of deeper and sweeter significance for years. As I write, someone begins to play softly and gently in the drawing-room, and the music takes me on its wings and flies with me into a strange region of loveliness and desire – one may say it is all a sort of imaginative intoxication; but it is as real, more real indeed than many dull and occupied days.

Madan agreed to accompany Arthur to Tremans for a prolongation of the holiday. The journey to London together was a joy. They were hardly intruded upon in their first-class compartment; and Arthur sensed the *rapport* with his companion. They did not talk much, but would occasionally 'intercept a smile'. On their arrival at Tremans, Madan was a little shy at meeting the others but soon relaxed. And then – to Arthur's horror – the boy became witness to a moment of nightmare. A telegram arrived from Dr Barton at Wimbledon to say that Maggie had unaccountably disappeared. Hardly had it arrived before they heard a knock on the door – and Maggie walked in.

It was a test of all their nerves. Geoffrey Maden had to have all his things taken out of Maggie's room. Dr Barton had to be speedily contacted. Meanwhile Maggie insisted on going round the house. She ignored Beatrice Layman, who had been so long a close friend; she would say nothing to Ryman, the gardener. In Mary Benson's room she found the whip she had used for her own self-chastisement before she had been taken to Wivelsfield. She flung accusations at her mother; she begged not to be sent away. At last (about midnight) Dr Barton arrived with Maggie's nurse, and together they removed her into a cab. The strain had been horrific; and what somehow made it worse was the evident fact that Maggie's intellect was as sharp as ever 'but the emotions . . . all atrophied or perverted'.

Geoffrey Madan had coped with the crisis superbly. 'The contrast between him, with his young and beautiful face, so full of animation and tenderness, and poor Maggie's dark and wizened features was rather awful', Arthur noted. Their short time together at Tremans had been, to some extent, blighted too. Madan left the following morning. The matter could not be left like that. Arthur decided to take a step he had rarely even contemplated before. He wrote a letter of open affection and waited in trepidation for the reply. 'I have generally made the mistake of holding myself in, when I have cared, and I think I am old enough to speak my mind! So I sent it, and we shall see!' Nothing convinced Arthur more of the delicacy and sensitivity of his young companion than the reply which he received two days later. His letter said 'neither too much nor too little – but that he could – he thought – and would respond. When I think how I should have helplessly blundered over such a letter at his age, I am amazed at the tact of it, and the little touch of stiffness too, which I like, because it has a virginal quality.' It had been right, then, for him to write. In the past, 'my caution has lost me much richness'.

Inevitably he suffered a touch of reaction after this. The 'beloved Geoffrey' visited him in Cambridge later in April, an unexpected call on his way to Norwich. They discussed together their lack of understanding of the ways of the opposite sex, 'the disappearance of their rationality into a tunnel of sex, as he said, from 15 to 50, and emerging so helpless and immature'. But their relationship was difficult, if not impossible, to maintain at a distance. In May, Madan confessed to Arthur in a letter that he had 'fallen in love with Cyril Asquith'. 'My nose will soon be out of joint', Arthur observed ruefully. 'I feel foolishly jealous – but can't compete.' Like Edward Horner years ago, he was moving away into a circle that would be bound to attract him and which was wholly alien to Arthur's tastes. The next news was that he was spending the early summer in the company of the Berensons in Florence. He would not see him again until the middle of August.

It was the old, old, story. 'But oh, the very reason why I love them is because they die.' For the few sweet moments, one must pay the price of disenchantment and ultimately bitterness. Even while one exulted in a beautiful experience or a relaxed relationship or contemplation of some sublime trick of nature, there nagged at the back of one's mind the little demon with his mocking question, 'Oh, you think you are enjoying yourself, do you?' And, even now, as August approached and Madan was to stay with him at Cambridge out of term, all the plans and hopes were to be dashed by circumstances wholly beyond his control. Not until 30 July did Arthur recognise what was about to happen, and only then because Percy Lubbock, recently back from Italy, impressed upon him the full seriousness of the situation.

> The news is very gloomy [Arthur acknowledged on the following day] and it seems as if we might be plunged in war for simply nothing at all, and when no direct interests are involved. There's an awful fatality about it, and none of our statesmen seem able to do *anything*. I can't believe that Germany is prepared to take on Russia, France, England, Holland and Belgium all at once – and possibly Roumania too.

By this stage, everybody was alerted, and the mood changed from hour to hour. Arthur refused an invitation on Saturday, 1 August, to join Norman Angell's Neutrality Committee. The following morning he agreed to sign a peace protest drawn up by A. S. Ramsey, begging the government not to be 'egged' into war. Later on the same day, the news came that Germany had declared war on Russia and France. 'A sort of *madness*', Arthur wrote in his diary. 'I would hang the Emperor if I could, and I would hang Garvin, the inflammatory writer in the *Observer*. It's true we can't avoid war if France is invaded – it would be neither honourable nor prudent – but Garvin speaks as though we must arm and ride off as if to a crusade. I agree with Hugh that *if* war comes,

I hope Germany will be beaten into a pulp, for embroiling everyone.'

On the Bank Holiday Monday Arthur went to London for – of all things! – a meeting of the Psalter Revision Committee. Everywhere he noted people 'very grave and silent'. There were territorials bivouacing in Dean's Yard; a silent crowd gathered in Downing Street. On his way back he saw the Cabinet coming away from the Prime Minister's. 'A few handkerchiefs waved – not a large crowd – and a little applause – but no sort of *demonstration*.' He spent the evening with Monty James (who had returned to Cambridge as Vice-Chancellor to deal with an emergency situation) and they tried to take their minds off the crisis by playing cards.

On Tuesday, 4 August, after a cycle ride with Monty, they returned to Cambridge to hear the news. 'So the fat is in the fire', Arthur wrote. 'I have a feeling that Germany has taken on too heavy odds – yet so did Frederick the Great! God doesn't squash pride, only the carelessness of futile pride.' He noted that *The Times* had listed him a pacifist. That was not true. 'I'm not a Pacifist any more – at least I think our intervention now more a *police* intervention, to preserve an unprovoking nation against gross bullying.'

Within days, it seemed, Cambridge had become something approaching an armed camp. Monty had summoned a meeting of the Heads of Houses, over which he presided with great calmness. He was given powers to offer University buildings for war purposes in case of emergency. Trinity, King's, Jesus and Downing were immediately to prepare to act as military hospitals. Midsummer Common and Coldham's Common became cavalry camps; there were soldiers everywhere; military wagons rumbled along the streets; field officers in cars with maps on their knees flashed by; cyclists with rifles on their backs passed silently through the night. Into this unfamiliar Cambridge, Geoffrey Madan arrived, having had a hair-raising trip across Europe. He arrived, and left soon after. This was not the holiday that either Arthur or he had expected. Even Arthur had to admit that it was a relief to see him go. 'This vile war just breaks off the *spontaneous* efflux of all delight, so that I am heavy and mournful.' Besides, everyone had to ask himself what part he might be expected to play in the events that were to come.

*   *   *   *   *

The first part that Arthur had to play, apart from standing in for Stuart Donaldson at the meeting of the Heads of Houses, was to write two more stanzas, to suit the occasion, for 'Land of Hope and Glory'. His second task, having done all that was possible to advise such of his young men as were up in Cambridge for the Long Vacation, was to see how events had been taken at Tremans. His arrival there coincided with the news of the fall of Namur. Fred and Hugh were already in residence and in a very 'snappish' state. As the news from France worsened every day, Randall Davidson and Edie arrived to stay.

The Archbishop was in a state of great depression, being 'entirely a man of peace'. He certainly succeeded in fidgeting everybody. He could not decide whether he ought to be in London, at the King's beck and call; he was always wanting to be driven to Hayward's Heath so that he could receive the latest news by telephone; he would then groan aloud as each bulletin came in, wringing his hands in despair. Arthur was frankly thankful to see him go.

> The more I think about the Abp's behaviour [he wrote], the more furious I am with him. I'm a bit of a coward myself, but he went about yesterday looking like a fish in an aquarium, returned again and again to the subject, culled out all the darkest bits of news, wouldn't eat or drink, made not the smallest attempt to encourage anyone, and indeed pushed us down, as with a punt-pole, into irreclaimable gloom. ... I feel really rather *ashamed* of him. His flight to London yesterday was as though he felt he might any minute be summoned to the front with a blunderbuss. Perhaps moderate Anglicanism is rather a tepid beverage in cases of spiritual frostbite.

The whole country was in a strange and rather ugly mood, veering between dignified calmness and hysterical war fever. On the whole people acted true to type. Prothero, for instance, became immediately 'insolent and domineering', condemning all those who had signed the Cambridge petition for neutrality in a letter 'partly in the style of a Prussian officer and partly of a Commission Agent'. There were ugly stories of victimisation of people accused of being pro-German. C. C. Perry, German master at Eton, was seen pathetically walking the streets, waving a Union Jack and saying to every soldier he met 'Splendid fellows, God bless you!' Arthur himself had to suffer for writing an article in the *Church Family Newspaper* warning readers not to accept hearsay evidence on the extent of German atrocities. The *Daily Express* demanded an apology, referring to him as 'Mister, nor Herr'. The editor of the *Cambridge Daily News* warned him of the danger of a public demonstration against him unless he made some unequivocal recantation. All in all, the tone of his books – the lack of robustness and virility – suggested a leaning towards pacifism. 'I represent rather an unpopular figure', Arthur had to admit; 'the superior, well-endowed, leisurely don, who despises the rough and tumble of the world and lives in an elegant seclusion.' This was a curious irony, considering that the country, in its moments of most strident patriotism, chose Arthur's lyric for what became virtually a new national anthem.

His female admirers, of course, sought to protect him. One (Madame de Nottbeck) wrote in anxiety from America in case so eminent a spokesman for the English way of life should be called to a position of 'high military command'. Another (Mrs Boedakker of Locust Grove, Connecticut) offered him immediate sanctuary for the whole duration of the war. One of the most fatuous requests, however, came from on high and was addressed to all the writers of distinction in the country. The Government were concerned about the extent of German propaganda in America and wanted a united effort from British writers to counteract it. A conference was accordingly summoned in London at the beginning of September. They met at Wellington House, Buckingham Gate.

> I found the meeting assembling in an upstairs room [Arthur recorded], very hot with a circular table. The chair taken by Masterman, soft, worried, mild. Acland (F.O.) on his right, ugly and gaunt, Schuster on his left, small and anxious. It was an extraordinary gathering. Galsworthy, cool, bald and solemn; Conan Doyle, strong, solid and good-humoured; R. Bridges a glorious sight, wavy hair, black coat, huge red tie, light trousers, white socks, patent leather shoes; he sat in a tilted chair, looking at his ease, calmly indifferent, every now and then craning his head backwards out of an open window. Zangwill, hideously ugly with long teeth, a mixture of negro and Jew; Hall Caine with long hair, high white collar, dressed like a Victorian statesman; Wells – fat, brown and perky, very smart; Chesterton enormous, streaming with sweat, his hair dripping; Hugh next him looking hot; Hardy very old and faded; Trevelyan very dark and gloomy, G. Murray very bald and mild, Barrie small and insignificant. Arnold Bennett very pert and looking every inch a cad, Newbolt cool and anxious. . . . Hewlett, like a little rat, very curt in talk – I sat between them – Archer like a groom – and a good many others whom I didn't know.

The chairman ventilated the problem, with Acland's and Schuster's help. 'Trevelyan produced a manifesto, very unwillingly and rudely, and read it. It was moderate in tone and was applauded. . . . Zangwill made an interminable speech about the Jews and their importance as journalists', pressing for a petition to the Csar for their liberty. H. G. Wells, in a cockney accent, spoke for acting individually. 'Chesterton spoke humorously – he was ready to write pamphlets, he said, which would appeal even to Americans. Doyle suggested an agency for placing articles.' All in all, Arthur (who held his peace) confessed that Chesterton came out best of all. He rather liked him. 'He reminded me oddly of Rupert Brooke – he was so jocund and pleasant.'

It is not surprising that Arthur felt totally at a loss during these months. His younger friends were full of plans for active involvement. Some were already at the front. Geoffrey Madan had successfully applied for a commission. 'I was made to be of use in peace', Arthur lamented. 'I am useless in war . . . I feel today an embarrassed loiterer on the fringe of life.' Even when he escaped to the peaceful and untroubled haven of Skelwith Fold he was haunted by a sense of guilt. On a beautiful early autumn day, at Arnside, when the papers were full of the German advance on Antwerp, Arthur contemplated the seemingly endless stretch of sands over to Morecambe, a jackdaw pecking round a public fountain, the broken line of low cliffs with their little copses, freshets bubbling up under rocks – the sort of scene that made one in love with the world – and had to confess that he was 'half-ashamed of so much beauty and enjoyment in these sorrowful times'.

Cambridge was hardly better. Winstanley was wretched company; he seemed 'ravaged by anxiety. He could speak of nothing but the war and Clarence Buxton.' The only thing that seemed totally untouched by the times, and proceeded on its bland, oblivious way, was the Psalter Revision Committee. One of the members recalled, in a moment of light relief, how a parson of his acquaintance had ventured to call a tiresome boy 'a little humbug', and how his father had then called upon him brandishing a stick. The Dean of Ely shook his head sanctimoniously. 'Ah, I fear he must have mistaken it for a far more objectionable word, which I regret to say is not uncommonly used by the more heedless of the less privileged classes.' He had unwittingly delivered himself into his opponents' hands, because they all pressed him to tell them what the objectionable word could possibly have been. The Dean shook his head 'solemnly and importantly'. He had heard the word too often to be in doubt. The Dean of Wells looked shocked. 'Why, Dean, what bad company you must keep!' The Dean of Ely went crimson.

In the middle of October, Arthur received bad news of Hugh which sent him post-haste to Salford. He had been half expecting it. At Skelwith Fold, Hugh had been staying with the Marshalls and had complained of breathlessness and acute chest pains, extending down both his arms. The local doctor had dismissed the trouble as indigestion. At Tremans, a month before, he had spoken frankly to Arthur about his expectations of an early death (he had been told so by a soothsayer). He was living recklessly, laughing off appalling calumnies about him from his former associate Frederick Rolfe, smoking thirty-five cigarettes a day, taking on endless commitments. He had fallen ill while preaching at Salford Cathedral. Ross Todd had been sent for and diagnosed 'a sort of neuralgia or "false angina"'. There was no actual heart disease. The chest pains had become agonising, however; a bed was made up for him in the Bishop's study; and within a few days pneumonia had set in.

When Arthur arrived, he was advised to sleep in the same house, Hugh's condition being described as 'touch and go'. He asked the doctor if the situation could have been avoided. 'Not by him', was the reply. 'He went his own way – and we must live our lives according to our temperaments. Monsignor could not sit with folded hands.' Arthur talked with Hugh for a while. 'I don't feel like dying at all', he said. The following day (Sunday) Arthur was sent for at Hugh's request.

> Hugh was sitting up in bed – a chair had been placed beside him . . . with a cushion so that he might lean upon it. He was pale, and breathing very fast – but he did not seem in pain. He hardly coughed at all. When I came in he fixed his eyes on me, and said 'This is the end!' [Canon] Sharrock was there with a red stole over his coat and a book. The nurse was wiping Hugh's brow and cheeks. Sharrock began to read prayers. I knelt down near the bed. Hugh joined in the prayers – crossed himself once or twice very faintly. Then he said 'One moment!' – and to me, 'My love to them all!'
>
> The big room was brightly lit, and something boiled over on the hearth. The nurse went to the fireplace and returned. Once Hugh said 'Make certain I am dead.' Then he said to the nurse 'Is it any good resisting . . . making an effort?' She said quietly 'No, Monsignor, it is no good.' He closed his eyes at this, and his breath came quicker. Then he opened his eyes, and seeing I was looking at him he said gently 'Don't look at me, Arthur', and to the nurse 'Stand between me and him.' The nurse moved round and I saw his face no longer. Then at one point he said 'I commend my soul to God, to Mary and Joseph.' Sharrock went on quietly reading. Twice Hugh drew up his hands to his chest – but there was no struggle. I heard him moan a little very faintly, but more like one who was tired out than in pain – and the nurse kept feeling his pulse. I heard his breath no longer, and she said 'It is over'. Then I saw his face, fallen forwards, the under lip dropped, very pale and helpless, but looking very young. The nurse laid his head back on the pillow. I kissed his hand which was warm and firm.

Arrangements then had to be made for his funeral at Hare Street. They 'robed Hugh in biretta and cassock, and he looked very natural indeed, just as if he was asleep, or like an alabaster statue. I gave directions to the doctor to make certain of death.' Mary Benson arrived. The coffin was despatched by the midnight train. Cardinal Bourne agreed to officiate. All the Hare Street household were gathered together when Hugh's body arrived.

> The intense attachment to Hugh among all these people is wonderful [Arthur wrote]. He was somehow very lonely with it all. He charmed people, but he did not need them. I don't think he needed anyone – and he kept all his friends separate. He went on his way, and much of his planning and designing was a kind of refreshing *game*, energetically played. But one must not be sentimental. He would have hated that.

Arthur had loved Hugh best of all his family, excepting only his mother. He saw his faults only too clearly – his selfishness, his love of complete independence, his almost shameless exploitation of his talents to further whatever cause he embraced, his dogmatism, the core of hardness within him belied by the boyish appearance and the sentimental tone of his books. Indeed he discerned the faults so clearly because they were in fact very largely his own. He could love Hugh in a way which he could never feel about Fred. He had no doubt that Fred would always prove a better friend to him in times of trouble (he had reason to know too). Hugh would never put himself out if it caused him inconvenience. It was Fred and Arthur who found the money to pay for Maggie's expenses with Dr Barton at Wimbledon. Left to Hugh, an appeal for financial assistance on Maggie's behalf would receive the response 'Back to the Priory!'

Hugh and Arthur might frequently quarrel; but they could also be completely relaxed in each other's company. They could laugh at each other's stories. They could take enjoyment in the same things. There were aspects of Hugh which Arthur could not wholly understand, but he understood him better than most of his co-religionists and infinitely better than the host of foolish women who swamped him with sentimental letters, pouring in by every post in the days after Hugh's death. To one he was a 'mystical recluse'; to another, he had become 'an angel in paradise, hovering over her as she prayed' ('I can imagine into what helpless convulsions of laughter Hugh would have gone on hearing this'); to another (Mrs Agnes Lewis), their spiritual union was such that she claimed the right to be buried beside him to demonstrate a kinship as between 'Joseph and Mary'. Poor Hugh! Arthur sympathised, because his own life was tormented by the presumptions of his female admirers. Little did they realise that Hugh 'never had the slightest touch of sexual passion. He liked friends, and he loved children; but he shrank from women.' This, too, was not a bad description of himself.

For months Arthur was involved with the aftermath of Hugh's death – the funeral at Hare Street; the answering of hundreds of letters of condolence; the sorting out of his effects; the transfer of his property to the Westminster Diocese; the selection of a fitting biographer of his life. On this last question Arthur had definite views. He would himself write a 'memoir' of Hugh (and he set about it immediately – it was published in 1915). But he could not write the official biography. He agreed to the selection of a Jesuit, Father C. C. Martindale. They had long talks together, and Arthur wondered – not for the first time – at the extraordinary character of some of the Romanists whom Hugh had known. There seemed to be a touch of Rolfe about Martindale. He had been sacked from Harrow by Welldon for 'bullying'. He had become a Jesuit (and then a master at Stonyhurst) for the sake of the discipline.

> He is naturally *pagan*, *sensual*, epicurean in all ways. This I should have gathered from his looks: he dwells seductively on all appetites. I suppose this instinct became partially 'sublimated' – but I am sure it is all there, horribly suppressed and imprisoned.

He told Arthur that his close friendship with boys was the only thing that kept him alive. 'But even so it mostly turns to "confidences", that is to say confessions, morbid strippings of the soul, spiritual and emotional "nudities". .... It isn't wicked or evil, but it's unclean because it is all choked and boiling and secret. ... I shan't easily forget his sunken face, his pallor, the bald skull, the closed eyes, how he turned and shifted in my chair from side to side, how he *yawned*.'

At least Martindale would understand the side of Hugh which Arthur's temperament could never penetrate – his influence as a spiritual director. His penitents would recall how Hugh demanded absolute submissiveness. How could this be, mused Arthur? 'Why should one believe that Hugh's advice was like an oracle of God?' To Arthur, Hugh was the volatile, irresponsible, puckish, lovable younger brother – essentially a boy who refused to grow up. In May 1915, after sorting through more of his effects at Hare Street, he stood by his graveside and thought for a while in silence.

> The love I bear him is a very real thing; and I felt today how I *missed* him – and how much more I would have seen of him if I had guessed either how he loved me or that he would leave us.

As is so often the case, reflections such as these come when it is too late; too late, at least, to act upon them.

* * * * *

Gradually the country, and Cambridge in particular, adapted itself to war. And although Arthur grieved at the draining of Cambridge of its real life-blood – the young men going off to the wars – he gradually adapted himself too. He had a sad but affectionate parting with Geoffrey Madan, who came up to show himself off in the uniform of a second-lieutenant. He was full of the extraordinary life-style of the Asquiths, with whom he had been staying: the household incredibly vague, the meals huge and fortuitous. 'The Prime', as Asquith was called, 'very merry and gross, not much occupied, playing Bridge and drinking whisky and soda.' His chair would be surrounded with corks of soda-water bottles; his talk would be very rapid and brilliant, treating Kitchener as a bit of a joke ('The Oriental'), but showing unfeigned admiration for Winston Churchill. 'Dining with Cyril Asquith, they had each drunk twelve Benedictines, in a match.'

On 21 December, Arthur met Madan at the Royal Bath Hotel, Southampton, before he left for the front. 'We simply told little stories and did not speak of the state of our affections.' No one at Cambridge could quite take his place. The nearest candidate in a depleted college was an undergraduate called Gordon, with whom Arthur had been cultivating a mild friendship for over a year. The boy had volunteered the moment that war was declared but had been found medically unfit. 'He is a very beautiful creature, in face as well as in character', Arthur wrote in November. 'This dreadful trial of having to stay at home instead of getting a commission – it *is* a trial in a family of soldiers – has improved him greatly; and he has a serenity of mind and heart which pleases me greatly. I have grown much attached to him.' Thwarted in his wishes to fight, Gordon took an assistant-mastership at Lancing, but kept in touch with Arthur and visited him from time to time. In the Christmas vacation he came for a short stay and to have 'an intimate and affectionate talk'. They travelled together to Ely, Arthur seeing him off at the station. 'A sympathetic inspector asked if I had been seeing my son off to the front, and detected a personal likeness, to say nothing of my paternal solicitude.'

Waggett was away at the front; Salter went off to Salisbury to train for the Rifle Brigade; Lapsley went off to France to nurse his brilliant pupil, Geoffrey Hopley, who had been mortally wounded; Percy Lubbock was working with the Red Cross. The first fatality of someone whom Arthur had known well was the death of Rupert Brooke early in 1915. Arthur was amazed at 'the growth of the legend before one's eyes'. Gaselee's brother had said, when he heard the news, 'perhaps the cruellest stroke of the war!' Edward Horner came to visit him later in the year, having been badly shot up and having lost a kidney. Archie Don had already seen action and was hating every minute of it. He heard news of Geoffrey Winterbottom, but of an entirely different kind. He had become engaged to be married. 'He says it doesn't mean an end of friendship', Arthur noted. 'No, but it means an end of companionship – that can't be helped.' Another voice from the past was that of Arthur Grimble, writing very Stevensonian prose from the Pacific Islands. 'He can't write really well in the epistolary style', Arthur commented, '... but I like his enthusiasm and his fine words, and his description of coral islands is good. ... He was an odd mixture of cricketer and aesthete.'

Cambridge itself was full of military activity – Tommies drilling in Nevile's Court at Trinity; fusiliers being taught how to salute in the front court of King's; a party of officers billeted at Magdalene, with the Reading Room and Lecture Room taken over for their use. Billeting numbers could be seen chalked up on house doors on Cambridge streets; hundreds of horses were picketed along the railings on Midsummer Common. 'All the things that I care for are lost sight of', Arthur lamented. And the senior members who remained behind were, many of them, hardly a credit to the University's reputation.

> Pigou flaunting the flag of peace and being wished further than I need repeat. Shipley in a letter to the *Morning Post* says that he wants to be in the limelight. This from Shipley who is regarded here as a limelighter, pure and simple. Is it that he doesn't know, or that he thinks other people don't know, or mere bluff? Cunningham makes violent anti-peace speeches, and is hissed and hooted as a disgrace to the university. I must keep out of all this. I have no taste for martyrdom. ... I must do all I can on positive and quiet lines.

The noblest response, however, came from the stately and aged Master of Trinity. Butler could be seen from time to time 'taking out convalescent soldiers to drive – he sitting, discoursing on Pitt and Chatham, with a fine, tremulous hand upraised – they sitting on the edge of the seat, rather proud but shy and stupefied – not quite knowing if he was a man or a woman ... pleased to have gone once, but determined never to go again.'

There were moments when Arthur felt he would like himself to escape from this strangely transformed Cambridge. When he slipped off to Tremans for Christmas, he found Fred there, irritating everybody profoundly with his inside gossip about the war 'from mysterious unnamed people, in high official positions, who only confide in Fred'. One could not escape the braying jingoism of the newspapers, everlastingly thundering nonsense about every young man coming forward to fight for his country. 'If the nation was really the sort of people typified by the newspapers, they would not be worth perpetuating or fighting for.' The average Jingo, once the war was over, would be seen toasting and foolishly praising the dead, 'complacent about his having deserved to get what they died to win'. St. Loe Strachey in the *Spectator* was the worst specimen of all, positively 'gloating over conscription'. He allowed himself to forget that '*real* tyranny is the bullying of a minority', rather like compulsory games at school, recalling his own misery as a non-cricketer at Eton. That sort of attitude 'might have done coarse and self-satisfied louts, who bossed the show, good to be mocked, but it only made me, who was naturally timid and diffident, entirely unadventurous'.

The Church came out pretty badly too. Ought one, for instance, to pray for victory? He found himself at variance with Stuart Donaldson on this, having heard him preach an ineffective sermon on intercessory prayer.

> I can't get in line with this! If God means us to suffer, we shall suffer. Either He cannot or will not avert the war. If he cannot, it must be only aggravating to be prayed to – if he will not, why ask him? It seems to me it is so entirely anthropomorphic – and yet not anthropomorphic enough. If I were almighty and meant to send war, the prayers of individuals would be no more than the chirping of sparrows. I can imagine doing everything to stop it, and everything to ameliorate it, except feebly sitting still and asking God to stop it. It can't be only a device to teach men to pray. Who would want to arouse such feeble bleatings? ... The only prayer worth praying is 'Show me Thy Will, and help me to endorse it with decent courage – and *don't* spare me, if you have any good intentions towards me.'
>
> This is all very crude – but the idea of getting on a force of prayer seems to me simply to degrade God into a tyrant. If he is a tyrant, he can coerce me, but he cannot make me either love or respect him. If I love him, I can trust him.

But the most shaming exhibition within the Church came from the clergy who preached the doctrine of hate. The worst culprit was Michael Furse, Bishop of Pretoria, who wrote a letter to *The Times* describing Germany as the 'Devil Incarnate'.

> This from a stockbroker, or a general merchant [Arthur wrote] would have been gross but pardonable – but from a Bishop! M.F. was always the sort of man who slapped everyone on the back and told them what they ought to be doing – but M.F. in the guise of Jeremiah is awful. The letter is on the side of Caiaphas – not of Christ. He calls the nation to be organised. If it would organise him out of a Bishopric into a bleaching factory, where he would be muzzled all day, it might be of use.

Arthur adapted his life-style very little. He continued to deliver popular lectures. He went on writing the same type of books, completing – during 1915 – *Father Payne* as well as his memoir of *Hugh*. He accustomed himself to lunching alone, without the company of undergraduates, and discovered that this gave him greater opportunity to write. There was a sprinkling of junior men in residence – two very able scholars, for instance, Bruce Dickens and I. A. Richards. The handsome Romney Sedgwick was still at Trinity, but Arthur noted that his sharp cutting-edge had been somewhat blunted from having been left behind from the war. Winstanley had discovered another Buxton to warm his heart – Clarence's younger brother, Jocelyn. For the first time in his life, Arthur went off for an Easter holiday, to Kingscote, alone. He was to be joined later by Oliffe Richmond, who had gone off to be a Professor at Cardiff. Actually he enjoyed the experience of solitary walking and exploration. It was a discovery: 'I like the hermit life. . . . I shall be sorry when Oliffe comes.'

When Oliffe arrived, full of obscure researches into Freemasonry and Pythagoreanism, they were swiftly reminded of the omnipresence of war-fever. They were suspected of being spies. A policeman had noticed them walking the countryside with maps and asking questions of passers-by. A report had circulated of two escaped German officers from a prison-camp in Denbighshire. To their amazement they were confronted by a cluster of people round Chapman in the car and found the policeman not at all easy to convince. That night an inspector arrived to interview them in their hotel.

So war had come; and early expectations that it would end quickly were gradually dashed. Arthur appreciated, as he returned from Kingscote for the Easter term of 1915, that he had really nothing to offer. 'I am not sure that I am doing anything very *real*.' Then again: 'It is not my hour! I seem to have nothing just now to think about, except futile and helpless perplexities, and the sense of death striking down so many fresh lives.' Still, he was curiously free from depression. 'It's no use being too tragic or serious about it', he wrote. 'The good evoked doesn't seem to me to justify the war – and, once over, I shall never think of it again.' No more characteristic remark, in the face of something genuinely unpleasant, could Arthur have ever made!

Chapter Eleven

THE HEIGHTS AND THE DEPTHS

Strange gifts – a fortune, a Mastership ... a sign that I have
had my say?   (1 January 1916)

The Truth is that I have never faced life, never seen that it is
harsh and strong; and now I have turned a corner, as I
sauntered and sentimentalised, and find the great creature
facing me, with flaming eyes and lashing tail.
                                                      (February 1918)

The very day after he had returned to Cambridge after his Easter break
(25 April 1915), feeling very poignantly the inadequacy of his present
mode of life, Arthur found in his post a letter from America making
the most astounding proposition that he had ever either received or
contemplated. For a period of years he had been receiving letters from an
immensely wealthy American lady by the name of Madame de Nottbeck.
She was herself an Astor, who had inherited a fortune and had married a
very rich man. Arthur had been scrupulous in replying to her letters –
indeed, he rarely failed to answer any letters from his host of admiring
readers – but had, it seems, regarded Mme de Nottbeck in a rather
different light from the mass of his importunate female correspondents.
She did not gush; she did not make claims upon him; she seemed to enter
sensitively not only into the thoughts behind his books but also into his
private plans and aspirations at Cambridge.

Only a month before, Arthur had inveighed to Geoffrey Madan against
the intolerable demands made upon him by his female public ('I'm a good
deal driven just now ..., persecuted by these d----d women. ... The
typical woman is horrible.') He did not, however, include Mme de
Nottbeck in this condemnation. And then – totally unsolicited – came the
letter in question, temperately expressed and carefully considered,
containing her offer. She wished to pass to Arthur, as a free gift without
any conditions, the sum of 200,000 dollars (£40,000) for him to use in any
way he liked. 'I don't think any writer ever had a more extraordinary
offer', Arthur reflected. Of course he would have to say 'no'. 'It isn't to be
thought of.'

The Heights and the Depths

Mme de Nottbeck had expected this reply; and the offer was renewed on three more occasions during the following month. At least there was no doubt about the seriousness of the proposal. Arthur supposed that he might have accepted the gift as a legacy, but could not bring himself to be beholden to any benefactor. He would have to go on declining. Further letters came in June. The money was of no consequence to the de Nottbeck family. If Arthur did not accept, it would otherwise be unused. At last – on 25 June – while holidaying at Skelwith Fold, Arthur made a decision. He wrote to Mme de Nottbeck as follows:

> I have left unanswered 3 of your kind letters, not because I have not been much moved by their kindness and generosity, but because I had a week full of business when it seemed quite impossible to think over anything quietly and carefully. On Monday I came away to this house (Skelwith Fold) which is like a second home to me, belonging to a cousin of mine. From the window of the little room where I write, I can see nothing but woods and mountains; and I have had long rambles by the sea and among secluded valleys, and much thought as well. ...
>
> Yet I find it very difficult to decide. I can't explain my feeling. It is a sense that all I have hitherto possessed has been earned by my own hard work, by teaching and by writing. I have more than enough to live upon; and I have a sense that the great gift which you offer me is in a way unearned.
>
> I can't say that it wd not give me pleasure. It gives me intense pleasure even to think that you have wished to offer it to me; and I feel very deeply what you say, that I have given something to you by my writings and why should not you have the pleasure of giving something in return. It would enable me also to indulge what I can honestly say is my greatest pleasure – the pleasure of giving and helping – of doing this in larger measure than I have ever been able to do by myself. That you should continue to offer it me after I have more than once refused it touches me, if I may say so, by its motherliness; and I feel it churlish to go on putting an unreasonable unwillingness of my own in the way of your kindness.
>
> If then I may be sure of two things – that the gift has the full and open approval of your family and relations, of those I mean who have so to speak a right to be consulted; if I injure and impoverish no one now or in prospect; and if I may feel free to use it as I think fit in any gifts or for any purposes, then I will accept it in the same simple friendliness as you offer it to me.
>
> But you must not speak of its being accompanied by your own silence and as you say 'disappearance'. Your continued kindness and confidence has been much valued by me: it is a comfort to know that someone listens to one and believes in one and I shall desire to remain in communication with you, if you will allow it, to tell you what I am doing and how I have used the power you entrust me with.
>
> There is one more thing – it is hard to say what will be my feeling about it,

as time goes on. Will you promise that if I find it in any way an overshadowing or undeserved burden, you will let me either restore it to you or let us agree on some purpose to which it may be devoted? If you can reassure me on these points, I will refuse no longer – and I will only add this – that I feel your kindness very deeply and am full of wonder at the goodness of the world as thus exemplified.

Very sincerely yours, A.C.B.

There was some further correspondence. At first the lawyers in New York queried the gift and made some difficulty. This was quickly ironed out, and the first instalment of £4000 was paid to Arthur towards the end of July. In the following month, Arthur reviewed his financial position:

I calculate that I made £20,000 and spent £20,000 at Eton – in twenty years. In the next 12 I have made £30,000 and spent £10,000. Now I have a gift of £40,000. So that I shall have £80,000 of capital, with a possibility of inheriting £20,000 more – a great fortune.

It took a little getting used to. His first reaction was to discount it; or, at least, to put such a windfall into perspective beside the grimness of the times and the more lasting achievements that a man might aspire to. 'I don't want it!' he wrote. 'What do I want? It is hard to say. My fame, such as it is, is of a very tame and bourgeois quality – and yet I have a sense of something ahead of me.'

Almost immediately he began to indulge the pleasure of giving, if only very modestly at first. Vernon Jones, ever since his marriage, had been in financial difficulties. Arthur sent him a cheque for £50. Ramsey was lamenting the loss of his tutorial fees because of the war. Arthur gave him £100 as compensation. He had already made many gifts to the College: to finance fellowships and exhibitions; for substantial additions and renovations to the Chapel, the Hall and the College gardens. The largest expenditure he had incurred was over the development and extension of the Old Lodge. Even before the de Nottbeck windfall, Arthur offered to put up £4000 to assist with the purchase of the properties opposite Magdalene, the College paying him an annuity of 5%. In October 1915, he offered the College a loan of £5000 for the Magdalene Street development at half the rate of interest ($2\frac{1}{2}\%$) that they would have been charged by the bank. He also offered to finance a bye-fellowship from the rent of his house in Grange Road. In December he drew up a new will. Magdalene was to be the largest beneficiary, receiving the sum of £35,000.

'I have a sense of something still ahead of me', he had written. But what? When he heard of the death of the Master of Downing in June, he allowed himself to think that he might be approached. But he viewed the possibility without enthusiasm. Stuart Donaldson, in very uncertain health, had already sounded Arthur's views on the Magdalene Mastership in February. In the course of a walk, 'he asked me if I would take the Mastership here. I don't know! I don't want that sort of life. I think official life is good for me – it keeps me out of brooding and morbidity. I don't really believe I have very long to live. I think I have used myself up! I must just do what I can. I think I have been very tenderly used by God – given just the sort of work I could do and made as happy as possible. But I think I am nearly at the end of my tether. I expect I have done most of my work. I should like to write one more book – a beautiful book.'

He dismissed the thought from his mind. His immediate concern was how to spend the summer months. Although he had passed from comfortable circumstances to affluence, he had not the slightest intention of changing his habits and way of life. He had become a comparatively wealthy man by not being spendthrift; his only expensive indulgences were his taste for designing houses or altering properties (very modestly exercised, in actual fact) and his pleasure in his car. When his chauffeur, Chapman, decided to enlist, however, in November 1915, he had no hesitation in 'putting down' his car for the duration. He liked comfort but rather despised luxury. He enjoyed the presence, and sometimes the casual company of his long-standing servants (the Huntings most of all), and – when he went on holiday – he would invariably take Hunting and Chapman with him. They knew his quirks and his whims. Hotel servants, or any new employee, would fidget him.

With the news, from Ross Todd, that Maggie was not expected to last out the year – she had dropsy and a bad heart condition following an operation – he decided to adhere to his normal procedure, spending late August at Tremans followed by a spell at Skelwith Fold. He was determined, however, to avoid coinciding his visit with Randall Davidson's annual sojourn at Tremans, with memories of his dreary company a year before. When they had left he would take their place, with Geoffrey Madan joining him for his 'leave'. He was therefore much put out, on his arrival at Horsted Keynes, to see the Archbishop's car parked outside the station. Randall had been taken ill and was confined to bed at Tremans; the car was waiting for the doctor. Unforeseen circumstances seemed to have a habit of upsetting his spells at Tremans with Geoffrey Madan. With the Archbishop laid low, a stream of visitors came to consult him on his sick-bed – Bishop Pollock, A. A. David (to be offered the bishopric of Newcastle) and the Archbishop's chaplain, G. K. A. Bell.

As it turned out, Arthur rather enjoyed the holiday. He was certainly brought into the thick of political and ecclesiastical gossip; and his opinion of the country's leading statesmen was hardly heightened by the experience. Perhaps it was an omen that he found himself in close proximity to Winston Churchill at the Athenaeum just before leaving for Tremans. He certainly did not like what he saw.

> I had not realised what a horrid little fellow he was – like some sort of *maggot*. His head is big, he stoops. He has thin nervous limp sort of hands. He looks like a drug-taker, or at least as if there was something wrong to be ashamed of. He went off in great high polished hat. I happened to be next him also in the lavatory and I hated the way he washed. He seemed self-conscious even there and on edge – indeed as if he were on fire within. Since I saw Lord Fisher (at Gresham's Speech Day), I have not seen so little likeable a man.

It was not surprising that since Geoffrey Madan had just been staying with the Asquiths the Prime Minister should become the subject of discussion. Madan was frankly amazed at Asquith's consumption of alcohol, especially the amount of brandy he could consume at lunch. He would pad and shuffle about the household, never turning his head but moving his whole back and shoulders when he needed to look round. He would never do any work after 6 p.m. He seemed 'entirely lazy and greedy and indifferent to public events'; and yet – when anything had to be said – 'he could say it better than anyone else'. Randall agreed. 'Asquith could pull himself together after really drinking too much in a wonderful way – but was becoming egregiously flirtatious with young girls – his pet just now being a daughter of Lord Sheffield's.' He had also become more and more dependent upon his secretaries and liked to be surrounded by Wykehamists (hence the favours extended to Burge).

Arthur liked Bell, whom he soon discovered to be something of an expert on modern literature: 'A rather interesting man, bright-eyed and snub-nosed'; but, as they talked together on a walk to Lindfield, he began to feel himself distinctly *passé*. Whatever did Bell mean by describing Hugh Walpole as belonging to the '*Cinematograph* school'? Randall was still at Tremans when Arthur returned from Skelwith Fold. This time Gordon had joined them as Arthur's guest. The Archbishop was even more expansive, now that he was allowed to have dinner with them downstairs. He began to talk about the King – how 'cheerful and noisy' a conversationalist he was, although (because of the war) he refused to do any entertaining. He would spend the day reading every newspaper he could lay his hands on. He recalled how rude and direct Edward VII could be, especially at the expense of the Duke of Clarence. 'Eddy, you are a d----d fool', he snapped at him when the Duke of Clarence had ventured to ask Lord Spencer, then leading the Liberals in the House of Lords, if he were a Tory. Altogether Randall stayed five weeks at Tremans before the doctors would allow him to return to London. Before he left, Arthur rendered one service to a close Cambridge friend. He obtained Randall's agreement to press Asquith to offer E. W. Barnes the Mastership of the Temple.

Arthur returned to Cambridge for the new academic year, celebrating with Monty his release from the Vice-Chancellorship. He had every expectation of a quiet and uneventful term. On Sunday, 24 October, however, during a service in Chapel, Stuart Donaldson had a stroke, sinking down by the credence with a groan, his left side completely paralysed. It soon became clear that he was dying. He had a relapse three days later, and died at midnight on 28 October.

> I have known him for 37 years [Arthur wrote in his diary], and for 30 years I have been his colleague and close friend. Before his marriage I lived more in his company than in anyone's. He was always the same, transparently good, sincere, straightforward – spoke his mind but gave no offence. Incapable of any meanness or diplomacy – kind rather than sympathetic – not perceptive but entirely sweet-tempered. A happy and successful life, and his married life the happiest of all, much due to Lady A. He was the best of husbands and fathers. He had gained much influence here of a quiet kind, and made an excellent Master by being fearless and just and genial. He had few faults, and none that mattered.

Inevitably Arthur's mind went back to the old days at Dunskey. 'I don't want it all back again, nor do I mourn over the ending of pleasant days. I have a curious sense that we must go forward. But ... I think of Dunskey, the odd grey house in the woods, with the curious, damp, big rooms so sparsely furnished. How we used to range about the moors shooting and fishing – the pleasant winter days spent there, shooting in the glen, with the evening closing in early. The long summer days, with such big varied parties and all sorts of fun – and the stroll in the dusk, among the wind-swept woods, and the sun going down – the sense of being at *home* there and all the affection and sweetness of it.'

Speculation over the Mastership began at once. Monty James was the first to raise Arthur's name in his hearing. It was felt, however, that Lord Braybrooke might insist on a clergyman (possibly Sydney James). On the night before the funeral, Arthur slipped into the Chapel quietly to pay his respects. It was dark, but for the flickering of the six candles around the coffin.

> I had a sense of happiness [he recalled]. It was strange to think of Stuart lying there – but I don't think of him as there, and I had no feeling of darkness or dismay, only just the sense that it was all over, and that the new must rise out of the old, both for him and for us. It was strange to think that in all probability I shall lie there some day just so. For whatever happens I shall probably live the rest of my life here, and that my coffin will rest there.

The next few days were far from easy. As soon as speculation began to mount in earnest, Arthur knew that he wanted to be Master and that he would be deeply hurt if anyone else were appointed. Stephen Gaselee, who had suggested that the office should be sequestrated until the end of the war, assured him that he would drop the proposal if Arthur would accept appointment. Lady Albinia told him that she had made known to Lord Braybrooke Stuart's own wish. It was expected that Lord Braybrooke would consult the Fellows, and when no word came from Audley End, after the passing of a few days, Arthur became jumpy.

> If I am not even consulted, it will be a great slight [he wrote]. I have worked here 11 years, gratis, done my best for the College, and spent over £10,000. I have lent £5000 more, and am just giving them a house worth £2500. If a Master is appointed over my head, I shall certainly resign my position here and take to University work. . . . What I can't submit to is being turned over to a new Master, like part of the stock of the place, a cow whose duty it is to produce milk.

He need not have worried. On 11 November, a letter from Lord Braybrooke arrived, offering him the Mastership. Arthur accepted by return. To his delight he learned from Gaselee that he was now entitled to supplicate for a doctor's degree *jure dignitatis*. He decided at once that he would take the LL.D. He jumped on his bicycle and rode out to Haslingfield and Harston, his head spinning with excitement.

> I am ashamed to record that I thought more of my own honour and glory than of any good I could do or influence I can wield. That must take its chance – but I am very grateful to God for giving me a not impossible task to perform, and one so congenial. I am almost *exactly* the age that papa was when he went to Canterbury.

By the time he had returned he had already settled on the vital dispositions. Ramsey should be President. Gaselee should become Dean.

Congratulations poured in. He had two hundred and fifty letters, following a flood of telegrams, the day after the announcement appeared in the press. Another one hundred and fifty came the next day – 'the Cardinal, the Abp, 5 Deans, all Heads of Houses, Hardy, Bryce, T. Barlow, Lord Guthrie, Marie Corelli! – All this kindness is very refreshing and I feel myself out in the sun. If only the jam wouldn't come first and the pill later!' He made a speedy visit to Tremans, stopping at the Athenaeum for lunch (being greeted by the Archbishop and others as 'Master'). Mary Benson was overcome with delight for him and solomnly kissed his hand. He then returned to discuss all the financial arrangements with Talbot Peel. He would accept only £150 of his salary for expenses. The salaries of Ramsey and Jones were to be raised by £100 and £50 respectively out of the salary set aside for the Master; the remainder should go back into the College. 'My income apart from this is fully £5000.' He then went to his tailor to be measured for the LL.D. robes.

Within five months his circumstances had wholly changed. He had acquired a massive fortune; he had gained the position which – in his heart of hearts – he had truly coveted ever since his first sight of Magdalene in the autumn of 1904. He had even got his scarlet gown as well. '1915 has brought me strange gifts', he recorded in his diary, 'a fortune, a Mastership.' It would not have been Arthur, however, if he had not allowed some melancholic twinge to intrude upon his happiness. 'I ought not to be ungrateful ... but at present I am mostly conscious of having lost my freedom. .... Is the fortune a sign that all money motives are removed, and the Mastership a sign that I have had my say? I have always held that an honorary degree means the end of a man's influence on thought.'

*   *   *   *   *

He had had a touch of depression at the end of the year when he was taking stock of his new situation. It was in part reaction; partly also sheer fatigue from the volume of letters he had had to cope with. 'My letters, from mild and egotistical old ladies, clad in stuffy clothes, wearing brooches, are worth writing in a way, as an act of kindness – but not worth spending force upon. I have about 12 spinsters who write once a week, several of them Hugh's pets, yet I can't bring myself not to answer – and so it goes on day by day.' He was grieved, too, at Geoffrey Madan's departure for Salonika. This friendship had survived the experience of the smart set and they were exchanging letters at a rate of one a week. A new friendship had been nicely maturing with an engaging young Salopian, David Loveday; but he was commissioned in the Oxfordshire Regiment towards the end of the year, although loathing the idea of the war. Arthur watched him depart with deep regret. 'We could have been friends', he wrote. '. . . I hope he will come back.'

The pattern of his life hardly changed at all with his new responsibility. He had, after all, stood in for Donaldson on many occasions and it was no new experience for him to take the chair at Governing Body meetings. He decided not to move from the Old Lodge, a decision heartily approved by Lady Braybrooke who had been waging a battle with Lady Albinia ever since 1904 over the upkeep of the graves of her dogs in the Fellows' garden (she was the widow of Stuart Donaldson's predecessor as Master). She made a brisk visit to Arthur in January 1916; satisfied herself that he would keep an eye on the state of the graves, and hopped away happily into her brougham 'looking like an old good-natured witch, in her brown wig, and eyes gleaming out of a seamed and rubicund face. She is rather a jolly old girl! She must be over 80!'

Despite a succession of inadequacy dreams at the beginning of 1916, he unashamedly enjoyed his new position. He delighted in presiding at High Table; at 'the feeling of being the unquestioned boss of the very modest show'; he took pleasure in the company of the officers quartered at Magdalene and the deference they showed to him. Inevitably his committee work increased. On top of the Press Syndicate and his other boards and committees, he now found himself attending the meetings of College representatives and Scholarship Managers – 'the most frozen of all meetings, everyone horribly afraid of everyone else and nervous about giving the College away'. In the Michaelmas Term 1916 he was elected to the Council of the Senate, beating Shipley by seven votes. 'It is pleasant to belong to the innermost oligarchy', he reflected. Outside the University, he had become Chairman of Soham Grammar School, Vice-Chairman of the Gresham's Council, and was still very active on the Fishmongers' Court and on the Perse Governing Body. In October 1916 he was elected an Alderman of the Cambridge Town Council. He grumbled at times at the futile way in which so many hours of his days during term had to pass. But he still valued these occasions for their spectatorial blessings. At a meeting of the Pass Examinations Syndicate, the members were required each to make a study of the procedures at other universities and to report back. It was quite clear, when they next met, that some had done their homework rather badly: Shipley, for instance, who gave 'a short hoarse ill-prepared statement about Welsh universities – no facts or figures. He said that as a matter of fact most men in Wales took honours. This was fiercely challenged by Keynes who said that almost all were Passmen. "That may be so", said Shipley feebly.'

He enjoyed University occasions – the honorary degree ceremonies, the great receptions. Some dreams come true, after all; and he could process solemnly, in scarlet gown, a buffer among buffers, being watched by puzzled sightseers and pointed out as one of the accepted Cambridge worthies. He was treated with the greatest deference at Council meetings and on municipal committees. 'They like having the Master of a College among them, and are mildly gratified by my company', he noted after attending a meeting of the Roads and Bridges Committee. 'It is very hard to remember that I am a person of standing and note here. I feel so very obscure and so dependent upon personal goodwill.' One could always switch off during dull debates, or play disrespectful word games with a congenial neighbour (as he would sometimes do with Hugh-Smith at the Fishmongers, compiling lists of their colleagues according to their 'decency' or 'indecency'). Some of the University receptions produced ludicrous vignettes – a dinner at Queens', for instance (Fitzpatrick being Vice-Chancellor) to honour some visiting French professors, providing the pleasurable sight 'of the Master of Sidney [Charles Smith], translucent with inner fires, suffused with blood, like a soul in hell, wondering where he had got to and what the strangers were saying'.

Even outside Cambridge, one was conscious of a new respect. When he went to Tremans for Christmas, the sexton at Horsted Keynes church approached him with the remark 'There's been a deal about you in the papers. I don't understand it, but they say that you have got promotion in your school.' Randall Davidson, who was back again as a family guest, was noticeably more respectful to him in his manner, and became unusually confiding about his own personal background: how he had sustained a shooting accident as a boy and how his academic prospects had been ruined as a result; how he gained the attention of Archbishop Tait through his travels with Craufurd, his son. It helped, of course, to be 'twice connected by marriage'. The household at Tremans was a little more conscious of his dignity too (not Fred, however, recently flushed with his new triumph, *David Blaise*, and affecting a total ignorance of University affairs). So a gentle Nemesis overtook Arthur while staying there in the summer.

> I talked rather solemnly and importantly about myself and my singular, though modest, virtues and gifts, and went to bed feeling rather noble, head in air – but slipped on the top of the stairs, gave my bad shin a tremendous knock, found my sock full of blood and spent an hour in cursing and bandaging.

It was still a very abnormal Cambridge – only a handful of young men in residence. Occasionally Arthur had to upbraid both Bruce Dickens and I. A. Richards for abusing their scholarships by presuming to act like 'bloods' while the bloods were away at the wars. He would advise the conscientious non–combatants about their cases before the Tribunal. As ever, he was very anxious to secure the best possible entry for Magdalene; and at his first election of scholars he gave the College an additional £200 p.a. to bring their list to twelve scholarships and exhibitions. In the following year, he rejoinced to see the superior quality of the Magdalene award-holders to the larger quantity secured by Queens'; and Walter Durnford pleased him further by congratulating him on the impressive standard of the Magdalene list. With the money from his Grange Road property, B. L. Manning was elected to a bye-fellowship; and a further gift of £150 for seven years enabled Magdalene to appoint a Kingsley Lecturer in Science.

Not all the youthful beauty had disappeared from Cambridge. Nor did his new dignity mean that Arthur could no longer succumb to boyish charm. He was much taken with a young officer from Beaumont College, by the name of Hoare – 'full of charm and beauty – with that half-hoarse, half-childish voice, and an indefinable prettiness of manner which is most alluring. He sate ... with listless grace and expected to be courted. He seemed ill, but aroused a curious pleasure, every movement, tone, and gesture provokingly attractive. The sort of boy of whom people become passionately fond – yet I don't see why. It's just an instance of personal charm upsetting all human arrangements and precautions.' There was also a young Australian called McPhillaney, whom Arthur greatly liked and asked frequently to lunch with him. He, however, had been spotted by the indefatigable Charles Sayle. McPhillaney admitted ruefully to Arthur that 'Sayle's sentimentality late in the evening, with the light low, was rather a horror to him.'

On the whole, Arthur relied for relaxation on the company of his longer-standing friends, liking nothing better – as was his wont – than a tête-à-tête discussion of the quirks and foibles of their mutual friends and colleagues. So, with F. A. Simpson, they would ponder over Lapsley and Monty James, agreeing on the following propositions: (1) that Lapsley 'had *no* comprehension of English life or tone'; (2) that Lapsley 'had been much helped in mind and body by his sick nursing'; and (3) that Monty James 'was a very charming, dignified and idle person'. With Lapsley, Arthur discussed the sexual connotations of *David Blaise*.

> I always feel uncomfortable with L. on sexual problems. He seems to have formulae without emotions – and I am forced to recognise that for me the real sexual problem does not exist. I mean that my relations with women and men alike are of a dispassionate kind, without jealousy or desire. I don't want to claim or to be claimed. I want nothing but cordial camaraderie – and thus a whole range of problems mean nothing to me.

This was not quite the whole truth; but nearly so. When he met Percy Lubbock, they talked about the changing ideals of the younger generation, Percy noting that young men were 'giving up discussions and metaphysical thought, and living rhythmically with bare feet on the summer grass. . . . The intellectual young man was quite out of fashion.' With Oliffe Richmond and Frank Salter (briefly returned from the wars) on holiday together at Broadway over Easter, the atmosphere was altogether more light-hearted. They composed limericks and discussed the mysterious love-life of Monty James.

It all helped to take one's mind off the ugliness of the war and the tension of the great battle being fought around Verdun. But as the months passed, it became impossible not to count the cost in terms of the generation over whom Arthur and his friends had watched or romanced. Rupert Brooke was dead. Julian and Billy Grenfell had both been killed in the early summer of 1915. In April 1916 Arthur heard that Geoffrey Madan had been wounded (to his profound relief the wound was only a slight one). In the summer of 1916 came the news of the death of Archie Don. Jocelyn Buxton was killed a few months later. Edward Horner was horribly wounded again and died in 1917. How could one go on bearing this carnage? Charles Sayle, for instance, went almost maudlin in his grief: all his friends dead; all killed; he wished that he himself might die in his sleep. Arthur, on the other hand, seemed almost brutally realistic in his refusal to sentimentalise about the tragic passing of the young Apollos. He read Lady Desborough's family chronicle, written after the death of her two sons; it made him angry rather than sorrowful:

> They were much beloved, and would both of them have been, I *think*, fine men – but there seems to be a touch of greediness and self-assertion about them both. Julian had a touch of morbidity, piety, want of balance. His hunger for *sport* rather terrible. Billy was very clever, but idle and dissolute. The book with all its talk of 'golden boys' didn't wholly please me.

He was equally realistic about Rupert Brooke. Henry James, shortly before his own death, following a stroke ('it's come – it's come at last – the distinguished thing', he had said as he was smitten) had written a preface for the collection of Rupert Brooke letters. In different ways Arthur had been fond of them both. But he could not swallow unmerited adulation.

> What nonsense it is, to be sure. H.J. hadn't much to say except that R.B. was a cheerful and high-spirited boy who lived in many ways a normal life, enjoyed himself, was not spoilt, and then wrote some fine bits of poetry. All this is presented in long, vague, sentences, very confusing and Johnsonian, with an occasional scrap of slang let in. It *isn't* good writing – of that I am sure. Then come a lot of jolly, ordinary, sensible, wholesome, rather funny letters of travel by R.B. After all H.J.'s pontification, dim with incense-smoke, stately, mysterious, R.B.'s robust letters are almost a shock. It is as if one went up to receive a sacrament in a great dark church, and were greeted by shouts of laughter and a shower of chocolate creams.

One does not honour the dead by sanctifying them; nor does it mean that one may not be sorrowful oneself because one rejects the extravagant eulogies of others. Arthur felt the losses of these years keenly. One death, however, in May 1916, came as a blessed release – that of Maggie. 'There is nothing to mourn for', Arthur admitted. 'It was a heavenly deliverance.' As he thought of her tormented life, while attending the very quiet funeral at Addington, he felt more convinced than ever before of the reality of life after death. 'Mortality is not a cruel thing; it is a fact, but a little fact.' At the very end of the year came the truly tragic news of Reginald Smith's suicide. He had thrown himself from his office window in a state of desperate depression. 'He made my fortune', Arthur acknowledged, 'and was endlessly good and careful and kind, the most dutiful and generous of men.'

Certainly there were moments when Arthur's detestation of the war, and the havoc it had wrought, came explosively to the surface. 'It is all deeply horrible to me', he wrote. Almost everybody had been in some way coarsened by it.

He was horrified to hear Owen Morshead, back from the front with an M.C. and expectations of becoming Brigade Major, airing his views' 'about the rightness of shooting a coward, which seemed to me *vile*. He also said that whatever a man believed to be right, was right. What a crude little view! ... I thought him charming but childish.' He felt a deep sympathy for a gentle pacifist like Goldsworthy Lowes Dickinson, who was ostracised and reviled, 'so undeserved by one who has always sought for peace and beauty'. The worst offenders were those too old to fight who presumed to denounce and deride the 'shirkers'. 'Elderly non-combatants denouncing shirkers seem to me a generation of vipers indeed – fit for hell, and wholly unfit for heaven.' A poem by Owen Seaman in *Punch*, inviting young soldiers returning to Oxford and Cambridge to 'duck' the youthful dons who had shirked the war made him feel quite sick. 'I hate bullying', he wrote, 'and there are none.'

> I very much mistrust the howling patriots, even more than I mistrust the 'shirkers'. ... I feel that timid individualism is *possibly* better than the kind of corporateness which consists in flinging others' lives and others' hearts into darkness. ... If there is such a thing as Hell, I feel that Northcliffe is safe of a place there, because his arrogance must be burned out of him, if he is to be fit to continue. But the 'shirker' wants something put into him, and no one ought to be punished for a defect. ... I am not sure that *coercion* is not perhaps the basest of all the devices of evil.

People, in their natural weakness, become the playthings of shameless impostors. Travelling back to Cambridge one night in July 1916, he caught sight of Horatio Bottomley in the restaurant car:

> I recognised the type at once. He is a strongly built stout man, with a plump preacher's hand and pulpit gestures. The knuckles are merely dimples lower than the surface. Blue eyes, a big half-pious half-sensual mouth, of the Roman Ecclesiastic type – an important and self-conscious manner – a great resonant voice which filled the whole car with its rumbling, like a gong. He ate a great deal, drank champagne and brandy and smoked cigars – had a pretty girl with him with whom he flirted. His articles just now are full of hideous piety, implying that he is on familiar private terms with God. 'Oh God, surely thou hast made a mistake – why send away our hero Kitchener from us when our need was sorest? Is it for our sins? No, I believe that thou art merciful. ...' and so on. He read one of these vile effusions aloud. He is the everlasting *performer* type, who is now a quack doctor, now an actor, now an M.P., now a priest.

The war made some people quite intolerably self-important. It gave them an excuse to be officious and superior, so that they would presume to

335

act in ways wholly unacceptable in normal times. Take the philosopher McTaggart, for instance:

> On coming out of Hall [one night in January 1917] met the officious donkey McTaggart in a sort of military cap, prowling about. He said he was 'looking at our lights' as a special constable. This is the role which suits a pragmatical busybody like McT. to go about not really to safeguard the state, but to make himself unpleasantly felt. If he summons us, I will deliver my opinion freely about him, as a sneaking informer. This is what happens to the philosopher who wants to pose as a practical man. His only idea of doing it is to be a fat sneak.

Arthur never forgot the incident; and never forgave him for hectoring the servants in the presence of the Master. When he heard of McTaggart's death in January 1925, he wrote in his diary: 'He was a singular figure – fat, red, winking – always friendly with me, except when during the war, he marched into Magdalene and demanded . . . to inspect lights. . . . A vain man, vain of his singularity, and exploited it.'

It was almost as if the war brought out the hardness in Arthur's character, so that he became scoffingly dismissive of sentimentalism and the natural human foibles that tend to come to the surface in times of crisis. How *could* Burge write of Archie Don that as a boy 'he vowed himself like a Gamaliel to social service and consecrated it at the altar of the Lord'? 'This is all stuff. A.D. took up social service because he was so much interested in other people; and as for the altar he went to Communion because his mother wished it.' Earnest moral reformers who saw the war as a call to the nation to rebuild society upon the principles of Christ were indulging in 'diluted moonshine'. Oliver Lodge's account of his communications with his son, after his death at Ypres, which he published as an inspiration to others evoked from Arthur a snort of contempt.

> It seems to me that if the other world is like that it is a very cramped and ugly place. Spirits seem to lose all humour and delicacy and freshness, and to become a sort of muddled gabbling hacks – like a yard of fowls. All freedom and vividness lost. They talk like shy and stupid children. I don't believe a word of it.

The war never touched Arthur on his rawest spot; and perhaps a sort of Nemesis lay in wait for him for this very reason. If he could not sympathise with human weakness, he must be shown how weak human nature can actually be. But throughout 1916 Arthur seemed to be at the top of his powers. Monty James sounded him on the possibility of his becoming Vice-Chancellor if the Master of St Catharine's should turn it down. He was delighted to be told by Romney Sedgwick that 'I was the *easiest* talker he knew – not a high distinction in Cambridge', Arthur rather wickedly added. Dining with the Family one night, he was paid by his neighbour, Langley, a unique compliment. 'Benson', he said, 'I have no doubt that you are one of the most impressive men in Cambridge.' Arthur laughed this off and corrected him. 'You mean *solid*?' he said. 'No', replied Langley, 'I mean impressive. I have long thought so and tonight I suddenly see that it *is* so.' It helped, of course, when other people recognised you as Rabbi. The Mastership had given him the confidence that he had for so long lacked. Arthur acknowledged this. 'A Mastership has one result: one is criticised for what one says, but no one disputes one's right to say it.'

So assured did he feel that he decided to lay a bogey now over ten years old. He would revisit Eton.

    *   *   *   *   *

The first of three visits over the next twelve months or so was in April 1916, when he heard that his old friend Frank Cornish was dying. It was an idyllic day in early Spring. Memories flooded back, and something of the old love-hate. 'I had *some* happiness there as a boy', he recalled, 'but no experience. And as a master some experience and not much happiness. But it isn't my native air. . . . I was never big enough to embrace and overlap Eton. . . . I was always a little afraid of it and its mockery, without ever respecting its ideals. I was glad to get away; now that I go back after a gap, I see its pretty paces and ornaments. It bounds along like a greyhound, it has no *virtues*, only some instincts.' There indeed was Frank Cornish, so little changed at first sight, so obviously an invalid nearing death when one observed the little things that made him different as the day passed on. Mrs Cornish was more hectic than ever in her talk, with a touch of hardness that might have been a mask to conceal her true feelings. On occasions the mask would slip. Arthur spoke of Frank's tenacity and his 'combatancy in his own handling of life'. 'She looked at me penetratingly and said "Yes, that is true – Frank was that".'

He saw Luxmoore, Ainger, Rawlins. There was already speculation as to Cornish's successor as Vice-Provost. Would Hugh Macnaghten succeed him? The news had broken, too, that Edward Lyttelton had sent in his resignation. Arthur had a brief glimpse of him as he was leaving – a white-haired woodman wielding an axe, Gladstone-style, on Poet's

Walk. Not untypical, Arthur thought, that he should choose to do this exercise in public.

Did the thought cross his mind that it might be his turn this time? One or two friends suggested it. Arthur dismissed the idea at once. Alington was the obvious successor. He had visited him at Shrewsbury only recently, on affairs of the Millington Trust (the Master of Magdalene being ex-officio a trustee), and had noted how 'the place flourishes under his hand'. He had also sounded David Loveday, who had reported that Alington was engaging in a quiet mood, although he 'disliked him as a teacher, loathed him as a parson'. He had, for instance, a very familiar way in the pulpit ('and then that dumpy and fussy old lady, the mother of James and John, came bundling in ... etc'). Arthur summed him up as follows:

> Alington has a touch of genius and is full of courage; he is not, as they say, quite a gentleman, and he has some of Creighton's cynicism. But he has much character and fearlessness, and is ambitious enough to run a show well. A. poses as unconventional, but I think he is very conventional in his ambitions, and just understands the value of stimulating curiosity. I should fear him as an adversary rather than respect him as an opponent.

He visited Eton again later in the year for Cornish's funeral, and again in February 1917 when Alington was securely in residence – 'very restless', overflowing 'with jerky amusing talk, asking endless questions and not much concerned about the answers'. He sat on the floor, his head reclining against the sofa, as he sparkled with 'witty rhymes' and 'brisk stories'. But the visit was memorable to Arthur for another reason. Warre, still Provost, but a very sick man, had heard of his coming and sent word that he wished to see him. Arthur was taken in charge by a 'solid nurse' who led him to a large low bedroom on the upper floor of the Provost's lodgings.

> In a bed, propped up with pillows, he half-lay half-sate. It was a terrible sight. His complexion still sanguine and the face fuller than formerly. But his head hung helplessly down on his left breast – his eyes were closed and his lips compressed. His big hands were crossed on the counterpane. My name was mentioned and he unclasped his hands which trembled much, and grasped mine – and I felt the old silky softness of his palm, which used to surprise me. He spoke very low at first and said he was deaf. ... He talked a little about old days and about Papa, and about his sons, and gradually I became aware that he was there, just the same in mind and heart, only with something else as well, a grand sort of patience, much-enduring and serene, and a greater tenderness I thought.

He said how happy he was with Alington, and how kind he was 'and not the least of his kindness is the bringing of you here today – I wanted to see you; and it is so long since we met!' Then he began to be weary and I saw I must go. So I said to him that I wanted to say how grateful I had always been to him for all his goodness and kindness to me; and he said 'Oh, don't speak of that – we are old friends.' Then he said 'God bless you, God bless you – Come and see me again someday', and raised his trembling old hand in blessing. As I went out, he said again very faintly 'God bless you, my dear boy.'

I was infinitely and deeply touched, and could not help shedding tears. The nurse saw I was moved and said 'You must not think of the Provost as unhappy. He goes out every day and enjoys that; his appetite is good, and he lives there quite happily – he remembers the old times and enjoys seeing a few people.' I went down, and found Mrs Warre in the sitting-room, looking quite youthful, and pleased to see me. She spoke vivaciously of several people – I am not sure she knew who I was. She winked and nodded a good deal in the old way. 'Yes, the Provost is quite an invalid now.' It seemed as if she hardly knew that he had been her husband, only a man distressingly ill in her house.

The young men were being killed; the old men were slowly dying. Only a month before, Arthur had been at the Trinity Lodge for the final adjudication of the Chancellor's English Medal. Two figures that belonged more properly to the nineteenth century were present for that occasion – Henry Jackson and Montagu Butler. It was the sight of Butler that moved him.

The Master received us in gown and cassock [Arthur recalled]. Such a really beautiful sight, his gracious smile, his fatherly look at me, his white hair. He looked well and serene, but he was much troubled by breathlessness. 'I puff and blow in so singular a manner', he said. The butler gave him coffee, pouring it into a saucer. . . . The great portraits round the room glimmered richly – Thompson, Wordsworth and Whewell, and I seemed to see Gods ascending out of the earth. The Master (who was not on our Board) sate apart at a table and waited. He closed his eyes, he seemed to be slowly consuming some species of lozenge: his face was brightly lighted up – and I think I had never seen so lovely a picture of paternal age and dignified courtesy. Sometimes he shook his head, or smiled to himself, and sometimes his lips moved and I thought he was praying. It was entirely beautiful: and I do not know why but it came strongly into my head that I should never see him again: he was at the end of his course, and living in happy memory and certain hope.

Actually Arthur was to see both Warre and Butler briefly again in the course of the next few months, but never again thereafter. As 1917 came in, the war news worsened and more of his friends were called away to other concerns. Marcus Dimsdale was teaching at Winchester; Winstanley went off to Egypt to work in Intelligence, 'arresting spies'. Arthur revived his friendship with R. V. Laurence, now Bursar of Trinity. His most frequent companions were Monty James, Lapsley and Laurence – just as it had been some ten years before. Geoffrey Madan, on sick leave, visited him often, but Arthur felt that their relationship had changed. 'I feel I would rather be alone. ... He is affectionate and entertaining, but he makes me exert myself, like a young wife and an elderly husband, and I feel now fit for slippered ease. It isn't the young disciple and the old teacher, but the young Fortunatus and the elderly Polonius; and I am not a worshipper [at] the shrine of youth, like Sayle. I have my own rather emphatic life, and want to lead it undisturbed.'

On the whole he remained in reasonably good humour. The committees and the syndicates began to get rather on his nerves, and he nourished a deep distaste for those of his colleagues who deluded themselves that university administration was a serious business. There was Mollison, Master of Clare, for instance, 'who loves business for its own sake and speaks acutely and tediously on every point, foreseeing every contingency'. ' "Have you a copy of the Ordinances?" ', he would ask. 'This book he fingers reverently, like the Bible.' At a meeting of the Syndics in May 1917 Arthur nearly despaired. 'The dreadful fact is that dons, if they get together and talk, think they are doing something. It is like the spirit brooding over the abyss. Mollison gibbered, and Cunningham in a skull cap lowed like, not a cow, but a herd of cows.' His women admirers were also giving him a very bad time. One (Miss Allen) threatened to come and see him and asked him to share her cottage with her at Broadway; another (Maud Goldring) kept offering him her services as an unpaid secretary to help him with his correspondence. 'These letters are really only the signals of a woman desiring a mate', Arthur growled.

In the early summer of 1917 there were hardly any indications of the blow that was soon to fall. He was dreaming very vividly: grotesque scenes of ugly accidents or imminent disasters, often involving Maggie, with himself as a helpless spectator. 'This is not healthy dreaming', he admitted. It reminded him, rather ominously, of an earlier period in his life. 'I am rather drifting back into dreams, as in 1905 when it was a danger signal', he wrote in April 1917. 'But how is one to put the stopper on?' It was perhaps an ill-advised decision to take on the sorting of Maggie's papers and letters and to embark upon the writing of her life.

Arthur had a horror of Maggie's illness, and all the circumstances attending it. He was playing with fire in brooding upon the collapse of her sanity, and the strange, almost sinister, effect upon her of the death of their father. Outwardly, however, Arthur was as full of vitality and humour as ever, and it was only the excessive heat of that summer which appeared to get him down, making him feel – to use his own phrase – 'highly explosive'.

Towards the end of June 1917 he visited Eton yet again. It was almost as if the intervening years away had never been. There was Ainger playing croquet, his regular evening occupation in the summer; there were Marten, Goodhart and George Lyttelton exchanging Eton talk with him over dinner. It was admittedly odd to see Alington entering Chapel in state on the following morning, although the entry itself was characteristic: 'too self-conscious in slowness, but *he* seemed to enjoy it'. There was an outing with Ainger in the afternoon, going to old familiar places – Dorney and Hunterscombe and Britwell, and thence to the beeches. 'Every field and tree and house entirely dear and familiar.' They had tea at Macro's, the old tea-house, before walking through the beech-woods. On their way back Ainger took one of his unorthodox short-cuts by trespassing through Stoke Park. He met Walter Parratt and Lloyd again. He went over to Luxmoore's garden, there to encounter a quite unforgettable vignette as he crossed the stream over the narrow bridge to the island:

> Oh, the joyful place of streams! Four or five cool and clear channels coming down among the Tangier islands, covered with willows and tall waterplants. ... A steep bank with steps, the light filtering softly in through grey willow leaves – the cool, fresh stream spinning round a curve in fine loops and pools, all green and shadowy, and three handsome boys disporting themselves in the water. Luxmoore called them out and I held a sort of levée – the three naked, half-dried, graceful youths, quite at their ease, chattering as they dressed – Colquhoun, Bowlby (son of Henry) and Smith (son of H. Bab. Smith) – I liked this pretty episode.

As Arthur took his leave, his heart went out to his old friend Ainger, with whom he had rather lost touch in recent years. Of the many old colleagues he had met, Ainger 'wears the best of all. . . . I seem to have had a wild sort of waltz or cotillon through Eton: but it's a happy place. It seems to me happier than I remember it.'

From Eton he went on to Tremans. He was at once troubled by severe headaches and had a series of bad nights. Percy Lubbock came to stay and they found themselves bickering from the start. They were both in a critical mood, indulging in lofty literary judgements and disagreeing on almost every point. Arthur wrote angrily in his diary, after a thoroughly unpleasant exchange between them during a walk to Latchetts:

> I think that our friendship has come to a natural end. He takes the wind out of my sails by his heavy and cold judgements. 'Who is able to abide his frost?' – and he much resents any irony or criticism or attempt to rebel. . . . The moment that two friends get into this state, they had better frankly part company, and I will not subject myself again to such rudeness as I got this afternoon. I saw him go for the first time not only without regret, but with real and frank relief.

From the beginning of July, while Lapsley was staying at Tremans, the old attacks of crippling depression returned, at first in short acute bouts, accompanied by nausea – just like 'a breath from Hell'. It reminded Arthur too painfully of his agonies of ten years before. 'The misery of this wretched shadow is that it is often so long in closing upon one. In 1907 it took 6 months to get firm hold, but then I had had a severe shock.' On the evening of 4 July, 'I had an access of horror and wretchedness so *awful* that I became aware that I was becoming actually insane, as Maggie did.' The next day he arranged for an appointment with Ross Todd for 7 July. It was all that he could do to survive the period of waiting. On the afternoon of 6 July, while walking by East Mascalls to Paxhill, he stopped by a patch of woodland where the road takes a bend opposite Paxhill Lodge, and sat down with his head in his hands 'as utterly crushed with misery and despair as I have ever been in my life'. When he returned home, he wrote a prayer, signed and dated it, and hid it in a bedroom drawer.

The nightmare had come again. At first Todd was inclined to dismiss the whole thing as exhaustion through over-work, and the recollection of old symptoms which had led him to exaggerate his condition. He exhorted Arthur to struggle on and not to give way. Throughout July the battle continued. He consulted a specialist called Wingate. He began to take bromide. At odd moments the clouds would break and he would delude himself into thinking that all would be well. He returned to Cambridge and tried to be as normal as possible. The nights were the worst – when the brain seemed feverishly active and to race uncontrollably until he felt that his head would burst. So, on the night of 8 July:

I made up tunes, poetry, prose, the thoughts diving and darting about, really hardly under control: very painful in a way, but I wasn't at all depressed; but as I got sleepier, at each dip into sleep, a thousand curious images darted into my mind – one only which I describe – a large green bottle, hanging in space, by a series of linked chains. No meaning whatever. There was no terror or agitation about these; suddenly without any warning an awful access of horror and despair, so that I wondered if my end was come.

Two nights later he woke in the early hours in a state of 'moaning nightmare'. The sudden attacks would come, from time to time, during the day. Cycling along Huntingdon Road, on the afternoon of 11 July, the 'black dog' came at him again.

Is it possible to suffer more? I suppose so. But I feel that in an ordinary year of health all my sufferings put together hardly equal five minutes of this. If simply to have suffered, body and mind, is great, then I am enormous! Yet the ludicrous thought was lurking in my mind that no one who passed a stout, rather bronzed, ill-dressed man on a bike going very slowly, had the smallest idea that they saw a martyr at the stake!

He could still write about his symptoms with a touch of detachment; but as the situation worsened, and the attacks became more frequent, so the diary entries became more sporadic. He had consultations with Todd and Wingate together. Despite their assurances, he could see that they were worried. They counselled him to persevere, but Arthur himself was convinced that his brain had become addled through over-work; and yet the only relief he could find was to work his brain relentlessly. In his heart he knew he must soon collapse and that his 'whole elaborate little world' was in the process of crumbling into dust. He made preparations for the inevitable, writing out his resignation of the Mastership, making directions about his effects, and placing them in a little safe in his kneehole writing-table. The actual collapse was protracted until the middle of August. On 13 August he composed his own epitaph: 'a rhetorician without passion, a quietist without peace'. He would struggle no longer. Let the doctors decide his fate. On Saturday, 18 August:

Todd arrives, to take me, I expect, to Ascot. .... Never have I experienced such pain which yet isn't pain. But it is clear to me that I am very ill. .... What it means to sit here, the soft wind rustling, butterflies poising on the buddleia, apples dangling, the garden I love beyond, the life I love all about, and have this horror over me can't be even faintly guessed. Yet a man may live so for years; and I seem built for long life. It separates me from everything and everybody. Affection fades before it – its only life is to say: 'I should love this and do that, if the pain were away.'

This was his last entry until January 1918.

＊　　＊　　＊　　＊　　＊

On 18 August 1917, Todd took Arthur away by car to St Michael's, Ascot, a nursing home for the mentally sick, where he was placed under the care of Dr Crouch. Hardly a word passed between them during the journey. Arthur tried to read some Nietzsche (*The Joyful Wisdom*); he could scarcely bear to look out of the window, especially as they passed by the pine-woods and rhododendron bushes that told him they were passing near Wellington. On reception, he was given a small white-papered, red-curtained room within the house, with all the necessary arrangements near to hand so that he could live apart from all other patients for a while. It was like a 'little cell', but for the obvious invalid conveniences, and the setting of his prison amidst spacious gardens of trim lawns, woodlands and shrubberies. For weeks he lay under sedation, from time to time hearing distant sounds to remind him of humanity – a conversation from the balcony on a room adjoining; golf being played by patients on the lawn below.

He could recall, months later, a series of hallucinations. His first was a chain of horrors arising from his certainty of imminent financial ruin:

> I thought I had spent all Mme de Nottbeck's gift, and that my own money was so fallen in value that it would hardly pay my debts. A few direct questions to the Bank would have settled it, but I hadn't the courage and tried to find out indirectly. Then I thought I must be declared bankrupt, and then began to agonise over income-tax returns and the mishandling of family Trusts. I will put down plainly what I thought. I believed that it would begin with bankruptcy and that all the money for which I am Trustee would be swallowed up and my best friends beggared. That M.B., the Bishop of Wakefield and I would be criminally prosecuted for malversation of funds. That all the Magdalene dons would be ruined, and that it would be one of the most awful scandals ever known. That it would ruin Cambridge, and that when the Nottbeck story came out, it would cause a rupture of Anglo-American relations, and that the Germans would win the war. I had visions of the Old Lodge being sacked and burnt and myself lynched.

The next hallucination was an intensification of his self-loathing. 'I thought I emitted a horrible smell – this was partly true – and that everyone in the house knew it and could hardly pass my room, and that everything I touched was infected by it.' This conviction took longer to shake off. As Dr Crouch began to wean him back into some form of social life – by allowing him to take short walks with his nurse, and to encourage him to take lunch occasionally with him at his house – so Arthur was rendered the more wretched by his fear that people were talking about him and shunning him when they decently could. 'I lost weight and looked ghastly and I thought that everyone who passed my door was talking about me with horror and disgust. The whole thing was like a dreadful nightmare day and night.'

Gradually this stage passed. He came to make tentative advances to other patients: a strange collection of elderly men, some very wealthy, some obviously permanent residents, many of them Jews. He started to form a companionship for walks with a Mr Mackay, formerly an art-expert in the firm of Colnaghi. He became almost pathetically attached to his nurses – Nurse Allen and then Nurse Barnes. Each day passed according to a precise routine. He woke regularly at 6 a.m. and waited for the cup of tea which was brought to patients at 7. When he had recovered from the total breakdown of the first few weeks, he was allowed to receive letters and to read the papers which came at 8.15. He breakfasted at 9. At 10.30 he rose for a bath, and then was allowed out to walk in the grounds and play golf. He would lunch at the Doctor's house (Shepherd's Corner) on most days and take another walk in the afternoon. After tea he had a session with the masseur before returning to his room to write letters or to play cards or a boardgame. He was given dinner in his room, after which he would play a game of draughts or backgammon before being settled for the night at 10.

Occasionally he allowed himself to think of the world outside and the pitiful existence to which ill-fortune had sentenced him. The feeling of guilt was so intense that he could not face the prospect of visitors. He was being punished for a wasted life; for taking a foolish pride in futile and trivial work, becoming a sort of Mr Chadband, satisfied with the admiration of the second-rate; above all, he had called upon himself a bitter chastisement for his failure to learn the lessons of his last illness. He had got precisely what he deserved. It was as if God were saying to him: 'As you will not interest yourself in the great movements of the world or do anything to help, you shall be put in a comfortable cage, and have something at all events to be sorry for.' He had been warned. He had now only himself to blame. One day he heard one of the patients quoting a passage from *Julius Caesar*. The lines seemed to bite into his very soul:

The Heights and the Depths

Men at some time are masters of their fates:
The fault, dear Brutus, is not in our stars,
But in ourselves, that we are underlings.

The shuffling walks with melancholy companions; the indignity of being pummelled by an over-rough masseur; the shameful confinement and yet, too, the terror of being evicted from one's prison into reality – were these the penalties one had to pay for acquiring wealth and honour so vulgarly and cheaply? Occasionally one's torment was intensified by glimpses of one's former life, which brought back nagging memories of joyful independence and the companionship of healthy and vibrant young life. One afternoon, as he pottered aimlessly outside the grounds, he saw George Lyttelton flash by on a bike, cycling purposefully to Sandhurst. 'His energy and solidity brought home to me the tragedy of my position.' On another afternoon, the sudden awareness of the delicious scent of a mezereon bush brought back a flood of happy memories, which turned sour on the instant as he recognised that his punishment, although deserved, was far from chastening. He was still learning nothing for his edification. 'I can't repent', he wrote. 'My deep wish is to be well, that I may go back to my mezereons and little phrases. The truth is that I have never faced life, never seen that it is harsh and strong; and now I have turned a corner, as I sauntered and sentimentalised, and find the great creature facing me, with flaming eyes and lashing tail.'

The only treatment that he received for his neurasthenic condition appeared to be rest, confinement, sedatives and massage. It seemed to have some salutary effect, however, because he was well enough during the early months of 1918 to resume his diary and to give some account of his life and thoughts. He even reached the stage of envisaging some eventual release. Reading *Pilgrim's Progress*, he took heart from the experience of 'Doubting Castle' and 'how the Giant beat the two pilgrims daily, and how Xtian suddenly broke out into the words "What a fool am I to lie here in a stinking dungeon when I have a key in my bosom, called Promise, which can unlock all doors!"' As Spring came, however, he suffered a relapse. The entries became infrequent and almost all were cries of dereliction and despair. An entry for 15 June 1918 proved to be the last for nearly two years.

We can be sure of one thing. On 18 June 1918 Arthur would have heard the news of his mother's death at Tremans. It was very sudden. As Fred recalled, at the beginning of the month she had been as indomitably cheerful as ever, responding to his suggestion that he should spend a week with her at short notice with a characteristic reply – 'Oh, Fred: a whole week! Lovely! Come to your foolish but ever loving Ma.' She had been interested in all his doings, blithely optimistic about the future, and had seen him off with the usual 'family ritual of departure, with wild wavings of hands as the car turned sharply round at the angle of the house'. Two days later she died peacefully in bed, as she settled for sleep on a Saturday night.

The total blankness of Arthur's diary over this period tells its own story. Months of abject depression followed. His mother – the rock on whom they all depended, the person whom he loved, in his heart of hearts, most of all in the world – had died. The family home just ceased to be. Fred presided over its dispersal. Arthur, the senior of the family, was locked away in another world – not even a spectator any more; just the helpless and hopeless recipient of news from far-off places, about remote people whom once he had loved. The world moved on. The war came to an end; and hardly an echo of the national rejoicings reached the ears of a crushed and pathetic invalid, bowed down by the weight of the futility and hollowness of his success. The longer he remained a patient at St Michael's, as he gradually – during 1919 – surfaced into a sort of life, the more dependent he became upon the security of its routine. To rescue him from lapsing into chronic invalidism, Ross Todd resolved to bring him back, by stages, into the outside world again. It was two years, however, since his admission to the nursing-home before he made the first experiment. Towards the end of 1919 and during the early part of 1920, Arthur was persuaded to take lodgings in Hastings with a companion. A former friend of Hugh's, a struggling, sickly Roman Catholic writer by the name of Virgo, whom Arthur had tried to help after Hugh's death, offered to live with him. Arthur's memories of the experience were hardly flattering to his helpmeet. There was more than a touch of Frederick Rolfe about Virgo. He belonged to a world which Arthur could not enter temperamentally and which he distrusted and rather despised – the combination of sacerdotalism and Italianate sensualism soured by seedy unsuccess. He had felt this very strongly on his first meeting with Virgo, 'something very fine about him, yet also strangely shadowed by sex and by a certain perversion which is unpleasant to me. Though he is pure and temperate and incapable of evil, yet there is a sentiment about him which is not wholesome.'

Three months he spent with Virgo at Hastings. Looking back on those dismal days, he shuddered at the slightest reminder of them: walks along the sea-front, with Virgo slipping off into every public-house they passed; a particular view of high grey houses on the cliff top 'which caught the earliest sunrise and which I used to watch in the awful early hours from my bed hearing Virgo snore next door'. Fred would visit them from time to time, and Arthur would fight against tears at his going, like a home-sick schoolboy, convinced that he would never see him again. Nevertheless, through careful guidance and the co-operation of the Magdalene Fellows, a slow and gradual process of weaning back to life and work began. Todd had pressed the Fellows not to accept Arthur's frequent pleas to be allowed to resign, and they had agreed without demur. The College was flourishing and things were going smoothly. The first experiment was to contrive an issue which would compel Arthur to return to Magdalene to preside as Master and to spend at least one night in Cambridge. Todd and Ramsey conspired together early in 1920, and a debate was engineered in the Governing Body on the question of the possible expansion of the College and future policy with regard to numbers. Arthur agreed to attend. A. S. Ramsey went over with Todd to the Master's study to have his first sight of him after a gap of nearly two and a half years. 'It was a shock', he wrote, 'to find him only a shadow of his former self. But though he could only be persuaded to stay the one night, the visit served its purpose.' A few months later, Todd pressed Arthur to make his base in Cambridge once again.

For two months (April and May 1920) Arthur even ventured to write some jottings in a diary once again. But every entry tells of unrelenting torment. 'I get worse every day', he lamented. 'There is not a single ray of light or hope, and yet I have to live on.' He was placed in the hands of a Dr Prideaux, who applied a form of psychiatric treatment, forcing him to concentrate his mind on all the aspects of his life which he most wanted to forget. Arthur described the experience as 'most agonising'. Nevertheless he somehow held on. He needed constant companionship; he had to take several spells away. Percy Lubbock and Fred took turns in staying with him. Increasingly his visits took him to Lamb House at Rye, where Henry James had lived and which Fred had secured on a tenancy for a part of each year. Eventually Arthur shared the tenancy with Fred so that he could use Lamb House as his holiday base to take the place of Tremans.

But he could not face living alone, and the work he could undertake was – for a long while – only desultory. During 1921 one of his closest companions was David Loveday who, after a spell as an assistant-master at Malvern, was preparing for Orders. He would accompany Arthur on cycle-rides in the afternoon and play endless games of jacobi, bezique or chess in the evenings.

> I want to thank you very much for all your constant and friendly companionship [Arthur wrote to him in June 1921, when Loveday had gone home for a break]. I am well aware that it is often a dreary business, for I can't throw off this perpetual depression – but that makes me all the more grateful to you. I am afraid that things haven't improved in this respect as much as I had hoped. I can do more in some ways, but it is always a great effort and I get a good deal exhausted.

He was, however, mixing again in society and going through the motions of being Master of the College. When Loveday was away (he became chaplain of Aldenham in 1922), B. L. Manning sometimes stepped in to take his place. Although no sparkle or zest seemed recoverable, and no will to write, Arthur began in the opening months of 1922 to work on some translations of Greek epigrams and lyrics which he eventually published under the title *The Reed of Pan*. But he remained locked in melancholic introspection, hardly noticing the emergence of post-war Cambridge and the passing of so many figures that he had known. Montagu Butler was dead; Ainger and Howard Sturgis had both died during his isolation at St Michael's; Monty James had gone off to become Provost of Eton, and Walter Durnford had taken his place at King's. Geoffrey Madan was married.

What sort of existence was this? Certainly not worth recording in a diary. He had no one to live for; he felt an incubus to his friends; the old romantic impulse was gone; the world offered no savour of beauty, no suggestion of love. One day was very like any other. The companions might change between Fred, Percy, Loveday or Manning, but it was a case of walking or cycling, looking blankly at scenes that once had inspired, sometimes sensing the faintest echo of an old emotion; and then the endless letters (they did not cease) and the evening games, spun out to pass away the time. He was becoming aware, too, of the infirmities of advancing age – increasing weight, swellings in the legs, the oncoming symptoms of painful neuritis.

Actually, however, as his physical condition deteriorated so his mental anguish seemed to diminish in inverse proportion. Arthur did not concede that he was getting better, but his doctors – both Todd and his Cambridge physician, Dr Jones – were convinced of it. They came to the conclusion that Arthur could only achieve full recovery if he were placed in a position without instant medical help at hand. He had become too psychologically dependent upon his doctors. In August 1922, therefore, they despatched Arthur for a holiday to Blakeney in Norfolk, with Fred as his companion, telling him beforehand that they would themselves be away and unable to attend on him until October. Arthur was both unconvinced and angry. Reluctantly he agreed to go.

It is significant, perhaps, that he had resumed his diary earlier that month. It does not make for happy reading. It is cantankerous and sour. 'I haven't had a happy hour for 5 years', he moaned. He had suffered 1862 consecutive days of abject misery. As the days passed, his anger mounted. 'The only good that five years of doctors and the spending of many hundreds of pounds has done me is that they have reassured me a little – but no treatment they have given me has made me anything but worse.' He spotted Dr Cooke (his oculist whom he had consulted for his headaches) on holiday with his family and sought at once to engage his sympathetic attention. All he got in response was a cheery wave, as his party passed hastily on. This was 'stuffy and selfish beyond words', Arthur fumed. 'He charges me very keenly as it is for his visits while all he has done for me is to damage my eyes by the glasses he prescribes, and to alarm me by his gloomy prognostications.'

In early September he began to panic as Fred made preparations to leave him. Percy Lubbock, with the Huntings, was due to take his place. But the indifference of his doctors to his pleas for help seemed callous and unprofessional. 'Here I sit devouring my soul, with no one to consult and feeling insanity slowly closing in upon me. It is simply incredible to me that two experts should leave a man in this condition simply to sink or swim.' He began to contemplate suicide, rather – one feels – in his desire to prove them wrong. He was convinced that he was the victim of a conspiracy and that Percy Lubbock had been made a party to the plan. Telegrams angrily summoning Todd and Jones were blandly ignored. Jones sent a wire back: 'Am quite confident so will not come.' At the end of September Percy left him, congratulating him on his evident return to better spirits. This was too much. Arthur wrote sadly in his diary:

> I can't say what P. has been to me all through this bad time. He has made great and constant sacrifices, for he loves cheerfulness and variety – while I have been the most overwhelmingly dreary of companions. He began by giving up six months of his company to me, and at intervals ever since. It has been a great misery that instead of improving and becoming more genial, I have sunk steadily deeper into depression. P. has *tried* to make me move on

and to keep me up to the mark. What surprises me is that he hasn't seen my slow decline. Indeed he speaks now as if my recovery were assured. He will be paid I hope for all this tender care. I don't know what I should have done without him. Bless him a hundred times.

Back in Cambridge, at the beginning of October, at last Todd and Jones consented to see him. He was so much better, they assured him, that he could safely extend his social engagements. They suggested that he should start dining with the Family again. It was months before Arthur conceded that they might be right. He saw the term through; he spent Christmas at Lamb House with Fred as company. 'I felt it sad that the old family life had come down to this, two moderately successful men – no children; F. in much discomfort (from rheumatism), and I in the nethermost pit.' 1923 began with Arthur in the same mood. Lots of old friends made contact with him. Gosse sent him new year greetings (the long illness had healed the breach, it seems). Morshead, Gordon and Salter all came to see him on the first day of the Lent Term. To all intents and purposes, it was like old times. Despite his fears, he made a speech at a dinner for the Old Members' Association; he attended the Library Syndicate. At a dinner of the Family with Anderson (Master of Caius) as host, he laughed and chatted with Durnford, J. J. Thomson, A. E. Housman, R. V. Laurence, Winstanley and Langley as of old. 'It was *really* pleasant', he had to acknowledge. 'I told a lot of stories etc. Thomson's laughter crashed and reverberated.'

At first the sense of respite was intermittent. Good days were followed by black days. Not until early March did Arthur dare to admit in his diary 'it is incredible to me that this depression seems *really* vanishing'. On the following evening, dining with Winstanley, he met the young George Rylands for the first time, of whom he had heard Winstanley speak in rhapsodies. An old excitement stirred in him. 'I ate, drank, talked and smoked too much.' He knew that he had made an impression on the undergraduate. And another compulsion was coming over him: the urge to write; to try some essays of a reminiscent type, sketches of his family life, little biographies of friends who had passed away during the war years. He started work on both *Trefoil* and *Memories and Friends*. One evening, after being beaten soundly by Fred at chess, he discovered to his amazement that he didn't feel annoyed and crushed.

There was no doubt about it. The doctors had been right after all. He was cured. On 12 April he took a decisive step, cancelling the power of attorney which Crouch had compelled him to sign in 1917. Two weeks later he had a bonfire – scattering upon it with a feeling of rapture and wild relief whole bundles of letters, valedictions to his friends written against the day when his reason totally collapsed. Against every expectation – happiness, humour, love of life, ambition, the desire for romance – all the best things in life – had come back to him. He would now redeem the wasted years, if not to make them holy, at least to make them lively, productive and – in so far as it was seemly in an elderly man of sixty-one – reasonably spiced with fun.

Chapter Twelve

INDIAN SUMMER

I have cared for this boy more than I have done for anyone for years.... But the Head of a College can hardly hope to inspire undergrads with romantic passion.   (June 1925)

We thought how hard it was to think of any people who were both happy and also radiated happiness. He disconcerted me by saying I was one.   (March 1925)

It is characteristic of the manic depressive that he can do nothing by halves. Emerging from a state akin to living death, Arthur Benson bounced back into life with all his powers renewed, delighting as ever in the incongruous and the absurd, hungry as ever for the companionship of radiant, ingenuous youth. There was a whole new world to observe, to savour and to record: Cambridge of the early twenties, populated by old friends in new situations and a new generation of undergraduates in the old familiar setting; there were a whole host of books to be written, perhaps the one beautiful book which still eluded him, yet ever waiting upon his creation; there was the College, fuller than it had ever been, and his patient, long-suffering colleagues, whom he would immediately reward with a substantial gift. £1500 towards a new Reading Room might seem an appropriate start.

The day after Todd and Jones had pronounced him cured, there appeared a diary entry for that evening which fully confirmed their findings: a typical description of dining with a tiresome neighbour – a Brigadier-General who couldn't stop reminiscing about the war – in which the details of his vexatiousness escalated with the pleasure of chronicling them. Arthur was pinioned to his seat by the General's heavy hand upon his knee, so that he could not shift his chair from the direct heat of a roasting fire. He could neither move nor reach his wine.

Then he upset my coffee over my coat, so that I smelt like a marsh. I could not reach the ash-tray so got sprinkled with my cigarette ash and then found that he was knocking off his cigar-ash over my trousers. I gave a faint signal at last, and rose dizzy, sick, hot, covered with ash like old Father Xmas, and smelling like a midden.

353

Arthur was back to his old form all right. David Loveday turned up from Aldenham three days later, and they rejoiced together in the pompous absurdities of Michael Furse, now Bishop of St Albans, and how he had given an address at the Confirmation at Aldenham, preening before the boys in his cope and mitre, beginning his charge 'Well, boys, I'm here in this get-up that you may see for once what a real Bp ought to look like.' St Clair Donaldson, now Bishop of Salisbury, was a much more agreeable prelate. Arthur had the satisfaction in early May of admitting him to an honorary Fellowship and proposing his health in Hall, talking animatedly with him into the evening 'like two Eton boys again'.

What changes had time wrought upon his friends and colleagues? During the summer of 1923, they came about him – so it seemed – like a pageant of the past. There was George Mallory, now a married man and anxious to gain the post of Secretary of the Local Lectures Syndicate: he had changed for the worse, and had become over-serious, talking endlessly about the League of Nations as if it really mattered, and entirely without sparkle. Then there was Edmund Gosse, with whom Arthur dined in July: definitely a change for the better. Their talk together was 'like the uninterrupted continuance of the old relation, not like a reconciliation', so that Arthur could not understand why the rupture had ever taken place. 'I think I was in a very morbid state of inner irritability, probably drifting fast into illness – and G. was trying and irritable too; but it was mainly my fault, I confess.' Lapsley was assuredly on the downward path, mainly through over-seriousness. They walked together, as of old, but Arthur felt no sense of real companionship. 'I don't think he likes me quite as well in my exuberant health as he did when I was sick and in prison and he visited me', he concluded. The same – alas! – was true of the faithful Percy who, once he had seen Arthur restored to health, took up with an elegant young painter called Adrian Graham and had no eyes for anyone else.

Much as Arthur felt indebted to Percy, he gave him no sympathy in this absurd romance. All Percy's critical senses seemed dulled by his adoration of this young and – as Arthur believed – not very talented artist. But he agreed to allow Adrian Graham to paint his portrait. When he saw the result his reaction was somewhat violent:

> What did I see? A copper-coloured, humped-back ruffian, all hunched up in a chair with long ape-like hands, glaring at things in general. The face not a moulded thing, but a torso struck out by smashing blows of a hammer. The

354

head the worst type of dolichocephalism. The background a suspicious-looking copper pot. I never saw so horrible a presentment. If any man ever looked like that he might at least have the decency not to be painted. P.L. in a tone of mild deprecation begged me to think it was a perfect likeness, noble in character. He seems to me in dealing with this young man, whom he likes, to be almost besotted! He speaks as if the picture were the work of the only man in the world who saw clearly and had the courage to present it. One by one my friends pronounced it a gross and hideous libel. . . . It looks like a rueful fevered man, a sort of baffled sensualist, full of a bitter and resentful endurance – while to add to his natural beastliness, he seems to have been half-baked or roasted before a hot fire, till he has acquired a cracked and vitrified sort of mask, glazed like porcelain, indurated and calcined, the bony structure morbidly visible. It must certainly be destroyed. The deformity of it is disgusting.

He vouchsafed his opinions to the proud artist who confessed that he was 'a little disappointed'. Arthur did not actually destroy it. After Cockerell had burst into a fit of laughter on seeing it, he had it confined to a garret. Percy demonstrated his loyalty to his 'shepherd boy' by offering himself as a subject. Arthur was still not impressed. 'His new picture of P. represents him as fat, white, sardonic, grinning and leering against a background of Scotch firs – Why?' For a while, and not by any means for the first time in their long relationship, Arthur and Percy became somewhat estranged. Percy accused him of unreasonable contentious-ness, a sure sign of his recovery to full health. Arthur shook his head in bewilderment. 'When I said I always felt lamb-like, and with the meekness of the worm that never turns, trotting sheepishly to the slaughter, he laughed derisively. Of course it is obvious that I am in some way more disagreeable when I am well.'

Other friends Arthur saw less of because they had married: Stephen Gaselee, Geoffrey Madan, even (to his surprise) Frank Salter. He thought that marriage would improve Salter. 'He is getting peevish and self-centred and damaged by these incessant friendships with not very intelligent undergraduates. He reads nothing and only gossips about the place.' He also approved Salter's choice – 'a little boyish-looking demoiselle'. He was frankly amazed, however, when Bruce Dickens came to tell him that he was engaged to be married to the very pretty daughter of Professor Grierson. 'D. is lucky', he sighed. 'His manners are partly dry, partly ingratiating – but I find it difficult to conceive of him as a *lover.*' In that same summer, two old Eton pupils came to pay their respects, now as staid married men: Edward Ryle, whom Arthur found 'elderly-looking and bald', painfully uninteresting and 'wholly self-absorbed', and Caryl Lyttelton, 'once a very pretty and wistful boy ... now a rather sad and gentle ecclesiastic'. The world, indeed, had moved on, taking a whole generation with it, in the years of his pathetic exile.

But some people had not changed. Shipley, for instance, had just steadily deteriorated. Arthur had him to lunch with the young I. A. Richards in May. It was not a success. 'Shipley was terrible. Immensely fat and wheezy, with a strangled voice and very indistinct. He rambled on most discursively and tried to be amusing ... a rueful close to a career.' Could one see anything in him of 'the little neat bright-eyed man' whose friendship Arthur had so much valued in his early days at the Old Granary? 'He went away, quite globular, quivering like a jelly. Richards never got a word in.' On the whole the fraternity of the Family had changed very little. R. V. Laurence's appetite for gastronomic pleasures was unabated ('there's an Epicurean stoicism about L. that I like', Arthur admitted); Housman was as precise, formal and enigmatic as ever ('He is a man with whom I can never be at ease; his judgements seem to me narrow and arid, and occasionally rather immature'); Winstanley had found new 'pets' within the highly-born circles of Eton and King's, who took the place of the Buxton brothers and Lord Doune. The *inamorato* of the moment was the elegant Vincent Yorke ('Winstanley turns to a youth', Arthur commented, 'like a sunflower to the sun').

Arthur himself returned to his former pursuits. He was greeted warmly by the Fishmongers again and was soon back on the Court. One of his first tasks for them was to compose a Latin inscription for a presentation to Owen Hugh-Smith. 'Very good, very funny, I am sure', General Blewett commented to Arthur after the ceremony. '*Owenus* – Latin for Owen, hey? Very funny! What a clever fellow you are!' Then there were all the syndicates and university committees who welcomed him back. Arthur recovered his enjoyment of dignified university occasions now that he could indulge again his pleasure in irreverent and disrespectful observation of eminent worthies in close proximity: Lord Grey at an honourary degree ceremony – 'like a seed-eating bird with pendulous throat'; a Library Committee at Emmanuel – 'a dull affair, like the grunting of pigs'; a University reception for a conference of eminent international chemists – 'a sort of shoddy Pentecost'. Within the College he could begin once again to play a decisive role, engineering the election of the young men he wanted both as scholars and as Fellows, taking great pleasure in securing the election to bye-fellowships of Francis Turner and Fairfax Scott in June 1923.

And he was writing prolifically. In the same month (June 1923), three articles of his appeared in different magazines; *Trefoil* was proceeding apace. In July he received an invitation from Princess Marie Louise to edit 'The Book of the Queen's Dolls' House' in collaboration with E. V. Lucas (then the Editor of *Punch*), intended as a guide-book to explain and promote the nation-wide exhibition of Sir Edward Lutyens' fantastically elaborate creation in miniature, which Arthur first viewed in the architect's house in Mansfield Street, pronouncing the whole scheme as 'ineradicably silly'. It had been a long time since he had received a royal commission and he did not refuse. In August he dined with Princess Marie Louise at the Carlton Restaurant to discuss the project with Lucas and Lutyens. It was not an occasion that gave him pleasure. He did not take much to Lucas ('a bluff, good-natured, common sort of man') and thought Lutyens 'rather facetious and jocose'. The Princess arrived incognito, 'not unhandsome, but with rolling eyes, and much royal *nodding*, intended to reassure; and head too large. A special table in corner. The crowds of silent, well-dressed people, the silvery blaze of light, the music, the troops of waiters all rather horrible to me – the whole place simmered with wealth and luxury.' Geoffrey Madan who – as ever – seemed remarkably well-informed about the domestic life of famous people, filled Arthur in with details of Marie Louise's private life, telling him about 'her disastrous marriage to a real blackguard', planned by the Kaiser, and her consequent miseries, culminating in her husband running off with his chauffeur.

At the end of August Arthur took a genuine holiday – the first since his long illness – with Percy Lubbock for company, at Falmouth. Madame de Nottbeck had insisted on the break. She was still sending him gifts of money, either specifically for Magdalene or for himself. At the beginning of the month a cheque for £200 had arrived with instructions for him to spend it in relaxation by the sea. Perhaps it was all the talk about the royal Dolls' House, and memories of his recent evening with Marie Louise, that caused his subconscious to conjure up perhaps the most ludicrous dream that he recorded throughout all his diaries:

> I was to lunch with the King and Queen, but on coming into a large saloon where I was to meet them, they had gone into lunch. A huge hall with many people. The Q. waved her hand to me, and the K. beckoned me to a small side-table where he had turned down a chair. He said, 'You see I have kept you a place. The Q. wanted to send up to you, but I said we wouldn't disturb you at your writing.' Then after a little he said, 'Do you ever reflect that I am

the only King who has ever inherited *all* the virtues and *none* of the faults of his ancestors. I have the robustness of the Normans, the activity of the Plantagenets, the romance of the Stewarts, the common sense of the Guelphs.' Then he said, 'I want you to look at the roof of my mouth. That will show you. That is how you tell a well-bred spaniel.' He turned to me, threw his head back and opened his mouth – but I cd see nothing except that it was of enormous extent, cavernous and dark. I said I couldn't see, and he called an attendant, who brought an electric torch. Then I saw it was as black as jet. I thanked him, and he said, 'I particularly wish you to look at the roof of the Queen's mouth – do so afterwards.' I said I could hardly do that, but he said 'Tell her I wished you to do so.' Events followed which I can't recollect, but I was eventually in a small sitting-room with the Queen, who said 'Mind, it is only because the K. desires it that I show you my mouth.' She threw her head back, and it was an enormous cavity of a dark purple, as if enamelled. I said, 'It's very remarkable', and she said with a smile, 'You are right. You are about the only person to whom we have ever shown our mouths!' This did not appear either strange or ludicrous – only a solemn privilege.

Arthur enjoyed the holiday on the whole. Lameness prevented him from walking much (Todd explained the infirmities of his legs as a combination of eczema and gout), but he had frequent expeditions by launch and by car; revisiting Truro, meeting the old gardener at Lis Escop, who was the garden-boy when the Benson family lived there and addressed Arthur as 'Your Lordship', presuming him to have the same title as his father. He and Percy spent a day at Fowey with Quiller-Couch, lunching sumptuously off red mullet, eggs and lamb, seeing their literary colleague for the first time in his natural habitat. At Fowey 'Q' was 'quite a little potentate'; Commodore of the Yacht Club, Chairman of the Harbour Commission and owner of much of the land and hillside round the harbour. 'No one would have known, as Percy said, that it was a meeting of three literary men. One felt that Q is slightly ashamed of literature, and proud of local influence and county prominence.'

So back to Cambridge for a new academic year. As controversy raged over the appointment of a new University Librarian (between Gaselee, A. M. Scholfield and Charles Sayle, with Arundell Esdaile – to Arthur's surprise – as an outside runner), he noted for the first time the number of new figures who were emerging into prominence. On the whole they did not please him. Lapsley invited him to dinner on 9 October to meet George Santayana, Kenneth Pickthorn and E. F. Collingwood, who – with A. E. Housman – were his other guests. Arthur described the gathering:

Santayana a soft, swimming-eyed philosopher – discussed 'reality' and 'existence'. Told me of his odd life drifting about among hotels. *Housman* fairly genial. But *why* is he regarded as a desirable guest? Pure snobbishness. He can occasionally be persuaded to talk, but he sits prim and grim, and casts a chill over the talk – no *ease*, nor is his wit very good.

Pickthorn and Collingwood the young type. They take no trouble to be civil, smile contemptuously, condemn everything. Why should they not say or do or write something brilliant? I have no patience with this inert consciousness of brilliance, and derision of elderly civility. Lapsley a fair host, too anxious about food and service – a little lengthy in over-dramatised talk. I did not enjoy it much.

A few days later Arthur found himself, in entertaining John Clapham (the economic historian) to dinner, even less enamoured of the sententious and respectable academic 'climber' who was clearly on a higher rung of the ladder and made little secret of his ultimate ambitions. Clapham was 'rather loud, egotistical, indiscreet. Disturbed at Pigou's fatuous worship of an undergrad. They are always together. The undergrad reads the lessons in the chapel, and Pigou, who *never* attends, appears in his place and the undergrads giggle.' But Clapham had become the self-appointed monitor of Cambridge morals. 'He browbeats undergrads and is not popular with his colleagues – the eternal righteousness of Nonconformists. The strong Protestant type is very unpleasant in ordinary life, though it may be the moral backbone of the country. A man like Clapham needs culture and art, not a varnish of them, but to live a little in such things and to care about them. A man like that knows nothing of the possible beauties of life.'

Clapham's strictures (which Arthur was perfectly capable of echoing in his private comments about Pigou or Winstanley) touched, of course, a rather raw spot. Arthur was still by no means immune to the seductive charms of clean-limbed and good-looking undergraduates. For five years he had been denied the thrill of tracking down some 'bright-eyed fawn' and the joy of conquest when one's blandishments received their – admittedly ephemeral – rewards. He wanted to be loved again; cosseted a little, perhaps. A pang of heart-hunger came over him on the Windermere train in June 1923, when he found himself sitting next to a charming and handsome American boy. As the boy nodded off to sleep, his head gradually sank on to Arthur's shoulder. He hardly dared to move in case the boy should wake up and a rare moment of bliss should pass. Suddenly the boy's father saw what had happened and lashed out at his son with a rolled-up newspaper, upbraiding him for his bad manners in incommoding travellers. Arthur sighed sadly to himself. 'I didn't mind his innocent contact.'

He had resumed his practice of entertaining undergraduates regularly to lunch; and the generation of the early twenties provided him with some interesting young companions: Guy Pentreath (years later to become Headmaster of Cheltenham College); J. M. Blakiston (whose younger brother, Noel, still at Eton, had been strongly recommended to Arthur for his charm by David Loveday); a Fettesian called Francis Ogilvy who was making a name in the A.D.C.; a 'pleasant Bluecoat boy' called George Seaton; the younger of A. S. Ramsey's sons, Michael, not so academically brilliant as his brother Frank (who became a Fellow of King's in 1924) but destined to achieve fame and distinction in the Church of England beyond any other of Arthur's Magdalene pupils. Arthur found Michael Ramsey a friendly boy, but 'slightly priggish'. Years of close acquaintance with his father had never resulted in a relaxed relationship between them; and to be entertained by the family was always something of a strain. Arthur took lunch with them in October 1923:

> Curious how the amenities are neglected. The drive is like a sea-beach, the shrubs sprawl, dead leaves pile up, flowers straggle. The house is bare and unbeautiful. It was something of an ordeal. R. genial but a little frozen. Mrs R. very voluble and emphatic, Frank solid and *very* clever, Michael a distressing object, so sharp-faced, dull-eyed, spotted – Bridget charming and long-limbed, and Margery (6) really pretty. But this silent circle was alarming and I grew nervous in drawing-room after.

But none of these, nor any other Magdalene undergraduate, was the golden boy for whom Arthur pined. During 1923, and throughout 1924, one figure alone dominated his heart and thoughts and dreams, and that was the young Kingsman and Etonian whom Arthur had met at Winstanley's, at the dinner-party of 13 March 1923: George Rylands. As with all his other *grandes passions*, Arthur knew at once that he was under the spell. He immediately put out all his powers to enchant him in return.

*   *   *   *   *

It began with an invitation to dine on 28 April, with Winstanley as the other guest. Arthur's first sensations were confirmed: 'Rylands a most charming, handsome, eager, unaffected boy (President of A.D.C.), gracefully puritanical. A lovable creature altogether.' On the following evening he asked Dennis Robertson to dine to find out as much as

360

possible about him. He then compared notes with Winstanley on a cycle ride. On 24 May he asked Rylands to dine with him alone. This would be the first big test. Would he open up? Could they talk relaxedly together without the help of another? In the event, it turned out more of a success than Arthur had dared to hope.

> The delightful Rylands, with his curly head of golden hair, dined with me; told me all about the wretchedness of Eton in the war – anti-militarism in College. He seemed to have very few friends there, yet I should have thought he would have been run after. Told me about the brilliant, friendless, dependent Egerton – a sad story.

At that point their talk was interrupted, to Arthur's intense annoyance, by a message from the A.D.C., asking Rylands to deal with a situation immediately. Arthur waited impatiently until he returned. They went on talking till 11 p.m. 'He is in great doubt – wants to teach and write, but is offered a partnership in the great Rylands firm, with unlimited wealth ahead. He has a fine beautiful rather austere character, I think. His shyness makes him formidable. I enjoyed every minute of our talk.'

Arthur knew that he must not rush the relationship. He contented himself with an invitation to tea on 13 June, when he pressed him to let him see something of his writing. This would provide an excuse for further meetings at the beginning of the Michaelmas Term. They dined together early in October, and Arthur felt that the relationship had advanced. 'A charming creature with his thick golden hair and delight in anything amusing. . . . When he went, he helped me gracefully out of my chair: a beloved youth with a lively mind and much ingenuous beauty.' Later that month they met again for dinner with Winstanley as host. Arthur studied the boy carefully all evening.

> He is not handsome exactly [he wrote] but very charming and attractive. Features dull even heavy – but a childish look, and his eyes have a dancing smile when he is amused – his hair thick and wavy, like pale gold. He is not popular, thought haughty – he likes older people better. But it is a beautiful nature – with much humour, puritanical austerity, perhaps impatient – very enthusiastic about books. We had a strange intimate talk – about being in trouble, and speaking to other people about troubles, whether it helped us or not. We all took different views, but all talked the same language. I have seldom had a more intimate talk. They did not know the experience of a thing simply too bad to talk about. I can talk about most things, but there is a line past which I can't go. I left at 12.0 Winst. walked with Rylands to King's. I thought *W*. a *little* jealous tonight. He is devoted to R. I have not seen this before.

On the next day Rylands accompanied Arthur for an afternoon outing. They were driven to Swaffham and Reach, and then walked by the fen to Bottisham. Arthur enjoyed every moment, noting how his young companion helped him over stiles, showing no impatience at the leisurely pace of the older man. 'We were at ease together and I think he was happy.' Thereafter their meetings became more frequent. They had a blissful outing to Whittlesford together on 13 November, followed by tea in Rylands' rooms in Bodley's building. 'I do not want to get épris over this delightful youth', Arthur commented, not altogether truthfully. 'But his real pleasure in one's society, his appreciation, his quick and sympathetic perception gives me an immense delight and *tendresse*. I would do much to please and help him in any way. And it is delicious at my age to have an *affaire du coeur* and to feel that something young and ardent cares for one's battered relics.' When he met Rylands next at Winstanley's, with Bridgman (the son of the Home Secretary) as the other guest, an incident occurred which bathed the whole evening in a radiant light. Bridgman was too full of himself, and Rylands changed his seat to come and sit by Arthur so that they could talk quietly together. 'It dawned on me', Arthur wrote, 'how much I had fallen in love with him, so to speak – the old flame.' By the end of the month, to his delight, Rylands accepted his invitation to stay with him after Christmas at Rye.

1923, a year which had opened – for Arthur – in a mood of black despair, drew to its close with a consciousness of a deeper happiness than he could ever recall. Everything seemed to glow with humour and love of life. It is true that he was lame and becoming as 'pursy' and infirm as the old men whom he loved to describe so unflatteringly in his diary. He was now over eighteen stone. In his dreams, the ludicrous and hilarious elements predominated. In November he had yet another extraordinary dream about royalty:

Lunching with King and Queen. I gave imitations of the Royal Family which were well received. The King's eyes very bloodshot, voice very loud. I walked with him along a street. 'There's the police station! Ha, ha! We all know what *that* means. There's the cemetery – cremation in my dominions is not obligatory, though advisable. I am told I have a remarkable facial resemblance to the late Dr Pusey!' A footman arrives – we were now on a terrace. 'I am to tell your Majesty that Her Majesty is waiting in the carriage.' K. to footman 'I prefer to walk!' To me – 'That's the way to treat women!' – pause – 'You are a bachelor, Benson?' 'Yes, sir', 'Remain one, Ha, ha!' 'You are a writer, Benson?' 'Yes, sir', 'These remarks of mine would make good copy!' This all written down on waking.

In his romance Arthur came to behave unashamedly like a man in love, even though the boy who had won his heart was unaware of the depth of emotion he had aroused. In the Court of King's, while Arthur was conversing one afternoon with W. H. Macaulay, he caught sight of Rylands flashing past 'looking delightful'. Arthur broke off the talk as soon as he decently could and set off in somewhat laboured pursuit. But he failed to track him down, and returned to Magdalene 'rather dull'. The next night he attended a Feast at King's and had to make a speech. The whole evening was transformed for him by the sight of Rylands' 'golden head at the B.A. table', while he was in full flow. The following day, Rylands came to spend the afternoon with him 'and greeted me delightfully'.

> Am I foolish about this boy? He is an impulsive creature, and has been over sociable: but he isn't spoilt, and has a strong puritan fibre, and much zeal for literature in the background. But what is irresistible to me is that he likes and seeks my company.

They walked in the spitting rain down the old green Roman road to the deserted railway.

> I chattered unashamed, 'You know *nothing*!' – a phrase I shall long remember, and his delightful laugh. He has a pleasant confiding way of laying his hand on one's arm – all absurdly pleasant to an elderly man conscious of physical unattractiveness. In fact I enjoyed the afternoon incredibly, completely bewitched.

They returned to have tea in Rylands' rooms. They talked about Adrian Graham and his portrait of Steven Runciman. As they walked to the gate together, they bumped into John Clapham 'who looked sternly at us'. Arthur cared not a scrap for what he thought.

He decided that he would write Rylands a long letter, it being the end of term. Alas, there came no reply. 'Rylands severely silent', Arthur wrote in frustration. 'I *could* not have left such a letter as I have written him unanswered at any time of my life – it's incredible!' He comforted himself with the reflection that at least he had been sent a book, with a 'fond inscription'. On 1 January 1924, however, the boy came to stay with him at Lamb House and all resentment was forgotten. He arrived at seven in the evening 'radiant ... in elegant attire – plump and young and smiling, his golden hair a little dimmed by travel. It is irresistible to an elderly man to find a young man really ... eager to take the cake and wine I so assiduously hand round to reluctant recipients.' They had a game of piquet and retired to bed early. Arthur lay awake staring at the ceiling, taking comfort in the fact that 'Phaedrus was not far away'. How could he entertain him – fond as he was of a world that meant nothing to the older man, the glittering world of dancing, parties and fashionable women? They had an outing to Winchelsea, where Rylands nearly got trapped in some quicksands; they spent a day at Canterbury with the Davidsons. They were shown round the Cathedral, and Arthur had a little private talk with Randall during which he effectively secured for his old King's contemporary, J. L. White-Thompson, the bishopric of Ely. They were three golden days, but so soon over. When they said good-bye, the boy was off in a flash 'leaping down the street'.

Arthur had other guests to stay – Francis Ogilvy and Bernard Manning – but they could not fill the gap. When he returned to Cambridge he found himself feeling strangely self-conscious in Rylands' presence. Worse than that, he became aware that he had rivals to contend with, as Lapsley rather unkindly and ungraciously pointed out. At least Rylands was prepared to confide in him about it, as became clear after a dinner together at the end of January.

> I knew at first sight there was something wrong. He had lost flesh, and his eyes had a curious look. . . . He was suffering from great depression. He had had this on and off for two years. He told me all the familiar things. He wanted to break away, to leave Cambridge. He couldn't bear all the claims made on him by Winstanley and Dennis Robertson etc. etc. They expected him to be always cheerful. He said he sate all day in his rooms and worked, and had a nervous terror of even the bedmaker coming in. I encouraged him to talk. He is living among people who don't know what it all means. He is anxious about his degree, his exams. He finds *home* trying and the constant claim for sympathy. 'They don't know that I have grown up – they don't know what I really am.' He has been living, I see, on nervous reserves, feeling things acutely, launching out into adventures. Many people have fallen in love with him, I perceive. He told me how he stood with E.P. – how he went and stayed two nights with her in town (very rash) – and I don't quite know what his relations with women may have been. But he was so anxious and bewildered and troubled that it went to my heart. I told him I knew every step of the road – and that the feeling of self-reproach etc *always* came in these states. I don't know if I did any good. . . . I made him promise to consult me, not to take any rash decisions. . . . I never cared for him so much before as in this helplessness.

In one sense this drew them closer together; in another – because Arthur was sensitive to the need to relax the pressure on the boy – it drew them apart. He found himself becoming intensely resentful of

Winstanley and Dennis Robertson. 'I don't want to be another of the earnest satellites like W. and R. who pursue him and make him dance for their amusement.' And yet the boy was quite genuinely tender and responsive. 'He leans his shoulder against me and puts his arm round me as he talks. . . . I don't pet or cherish him – it is his own idea.'

What did he hope from this friendship, so necessarily short-lived? What could be the end thereof? There were moments when he knew, in his heart of hearts, that Rylands let him down lightly by inventing plausible excuses for terminating a conversation or an engagement; that he could hardly compete (in his shop-window, at least) with the seductive charms of Ida (Joan) Sandwich, with whom a rival relationship seemed to be forming; and that when he was beguiled into the 'Bloomsbury Group' by the 'Lucas folk', that world would offer far more excitements and challenges to a young man than anything he could provide from his stores. Sebastian Sprott, a promising young psychologist from Clare and a fellow-Apostle with F. L. Lucas and Rylands, told Arthur something of the Bloomsbury *mise-en-scène* and filled him with alarm. 'Rylands is to join the Hogarth Press and to live with them (Lytton Strachey, Clive Bell, Leonard and Virginia Woolf). He gave me an unsavoury account. They seem to live with each other rather promiscuously, expected to have love-affairs and yet not to be sentimental. It gave me a feeling of very pedantic wit and bird-like morals.'

Nor did he particularly admire in his new friend the qualities which others so rapturously applauded. He watched him act the title-role in the *Duchess of Malfi* in March 1924 with stiff and stony disapproval. He thought the play detestable – 'the whole thing . . . *sickening* and not redeemed by any art or beauty. . . . I could hardly believe that this sad, stately woman was the young man who had been walking with me in the fields all the afternoon.' He discussed the play with Francis Ogilvy afterwards only to discover that he, too, was much 'épris about Rylands now', although he was severely critical of his idol and his habit of collecting people 'like specimens' only to 'throw them aside – no real affection'.

But none of this made him love him any the less. During the Easter vacation they met again at Lamb House for three blissful days. The friendship had now advanced sufficiently for Arthur to call him 'Dadie'. He was secretly pleased to learn that Ida Sandwich had been discarded. Now, then, was the moment to be entirely frank about his own feelings. On an outing to Camber, Arthur opened his heart:

D. in high spirits dancing, frolicking, gathering shells. I never saw him so merry. I told him very simply how much I thought of him and how happy he made me. He took it sedately, but was surprised. But somehow it brought us together. As he stood in his blue clothes, pearly stockings, slouched hat, with his scarf blowing – with his blue eyes looking out to sea and a touch of gold in his hair I thought I had never seen so beautiful and gracious a youth.

They walked together arm-in-arm. That evening Dadie confessed to Arthur in return that he had now lost all sense of fear in their relationship. 'A new sort of ease had fallen on us.' Whatever happened, whatever considerations of tact, decorum and responsibility might seem to require, one fact could not be escaped: 'This boy has taken me captive.'

The mood of rapture continued well into the following term. They wrote frequently to each other ('I would like to have him always by me and write to him every day', Arthur confessed). On a walk along the Pilgrim's Way, to Wimpole and Kington Wood, 'I took his arm, and he manifested a sort of childish pleasure in it all – very touching to me. In fact the whole walk was strangely delightful – a conspiracy of "Time and place and the loved one all together". . . . I find him irresistible, and spoil him to his heart's content. He came back to tea, and as we drove, leaned his head on my shoulder like a child.'

As the summer advanced, Arthur's eczema on his feet became very much more troublesome; as Tripos approached, Dadie Rylands became more preoccupied with immediate concerns. At any rate, the relationship seemed to become a little cooler from this point. By June, Arthur had become fretful and irritable and was beginning to find fault, as he had so often done before, with those whom he loved best. As soon as the mood of ecstatic romance passed, a sense of harsh reality struck him. He had made the old mistake yet again: failure to recognise the impossibility of forming a genuine and lasting alliance with someone far younger than oneself. He received the news of Dadie's 'starred First' with great satisfaction, however, and determined to be dignified and sensible over saying good-bye. He had been told of the emotional scenes with Dennis Robertson. He had taken '*six* successive leave-takings' with Dadie, and seemed 'half-crazy. They don't *say* anything. D.R. sits and moans and his head rolls on his shoulders.' At least he would not be like that.

> We did not have a sentimental scene at all. He looked very happy and serene, and I gave him a little seal with the motto from the Song, *nec flumina obruent.* But I don't know what will come of this. I have cared for this boy more than I have done for anyone for years. . . . But the Head of a College can hardly

hope to inspire undergrads with romantic passion. ... I did my best to amuse him, and he went off simply and gently enough without any adieux.

He would see him again; their friendship would endure; but the intensity could never be recaptured. As a *grande passion*, the affair was over.

*   *   *   *   *

One might reasonably suppose (did one not know him better) that in the midst of his emotional entanglements, Arthur might have been more sympathetic to those of his own friends in the same predicament. But this was not his way. While, in a candid mood, he could admit that the faults one most derided in others were the faults most manifest in oneself, this did not restrain him from castigation and mockery of those who made an exhibition of themselves in their search for romantic relationships. Howard Sturgis, G. T. Lapsley, Frank Salter, Oliffe Richmond, A. C. Pigou, D. A. Winstanley, Dennis Robertson, Charlie Sayle – all, at one time or another, had their knuckles rapped for falling victim to the seductive charms of boyish beauty. At the height of his emotional relationship with Dadie Rylands, Arthur was especially angry with Percy Lubbock over his infatuation for Adrian Graham. Both he and Lapsley, in a walk together, deplored Percy's fall from grace. Lapsley, very unkindly, observed that Percy 'had for once met someone in whom he was more interested than himself'. Arthur criticised him for his lack of taste and discrimination.

> Howard Sturgis loved the Babe and H. James loved Hugh Walpole – but neither H.S. nor H.J. were ever under any illusions whatever as to the Babe's or H. Walpole's intellect or character or superiority. It is a horrible dethronement of Percy's inflexible power of valuation. Percy writes to me lamely, as if palely smiling – but I feel that he has cast me off, or drifted away. If only the Beloved were not so common, perky, calculating a youth.

Was it some sort of moral failing that threw one so off balance? Indeed, was the sensation in some way unnatural or abnormal? Arthur consulted Ross Todd on the problem, ostensibly on Percy's behalf. Todd was both sympathetic and realistic. A friendship of this sort, he said, 'is bound to end in disillusionment and quoted some similar cases. He says it is "paternal" rather than sexual in origin and comes from suppression. ... We had a long discussion about these masculine devotions and passions, so boycotted and misunderstood by "sensible" people. He says they are not in the least abnormal, though can become so. ... I noted the fact that I had had 104 undergrads to lunch this term, besides lunching with several of them. This Todd said with a smile might be regarded as quite abnormal.'

At the end of the year Arthur talked the matter over with both Fred and Geoffrey Madan. Had one's whole attitude to sex been wrong? Did the problem go back to shortcomings in one's own upbringing? As Arthur admitted to Madan, 'I think . . . I have suffered by being brought up to regard all sexual relations as being rather detestable in their very nature: a thing *per se* to be ashamed of.'

Perhaps one tends to discover the deepest truths about oneself when it is too late radically to change; or too late to contemplate the cure. Nevertheless, intense as this last close relationship was, neither in its fulfilment nor in its severance did it leave the trace of a scar. 'I don't think I have had a single hour of depression', Arthur wrote at the end of the year. He had had ailments in plenty; his weight had risen to nineteen stone; but he had enjoyed every aspect of a fully active life which he had thought, in the days of his illness, he would never experience again. He was more conscious than ever before that both he and his contemporaries were well entrenched in bufferdom, if not yet quite senile. Monty James, who visited him from time to time, had become distinctly 'pursy and elderly'; Walter Durnford, he noted, 'seems now an old man'. Talking with the Master of St John's (Sir Robert Forsyth Smith), whom Arthur had grown rather to like, he realised that within the perspectives and time-scale of Cambridge he was still a comparative youngster.

> He told me about Liveing, who had moved at 97 to the University Arms, and is held in high honour there. Still comes to Hall. Liveing said that Bonney had injured his health by mountain climbing and that he never thought his constitution a strong one. Bonney died at 89. Liveing had to be excluded from house, because when B. was bed-ridden and delirious, Liveing was always pressing him not to give way to invalid habits but to come out for a brisk walk. Bonney celebrated his 89th birthday by a seven course dinner in bed.

He had devised for himself the routine of a reasonably leisurely and elderly man. Because he went late to bed and slept very fitfully, he always lay in late of a morning. He was called at 7.30, but was usually found reading. At 8.30 the barber, Reed, came to shave him, and he breakfasted in bed. He wrote letters in bed until 10.30. Thereafter he was ready to attend to College business; to lunch undergraduates; to take the car to set him down for his chosen walk and to collect him in time for tea. As usual, he wrote regularly between tea and dinner. He was lecturing still, and accepting invitations to deliver papers or to preach.

He attended the Fishmongers' meetings regularly, and – in April 1924 – accepted the position of Renter Warden. He also began attending Literary Society meetings and dinners again. But, on the whole, his companions were either his pre-war Cambridge friends or under-graduates. He became somewhat more kindly disposed towards King's than he had been and dined more often at the High Table, feeling – as Head of a House – no longer the sense of being snubbed. Of the Fellows of King's, apart from 'Goldie' and Mann (still organist), he would seek out the company of Maynard Keynes. 'I always like him', he wrote. 'He is not formidable and talks with ease and good temper about everything that turns up. He is an interesting fellow. Made his name after the war as a financial expert. Has written a famous book, made his own fortune, and made money for King's. He is bursar and a director of companies. He is freely said to live with the famous Russian danseuse (Lopokova) but no one seems to care. He is much in the Bloomsbury set.'

He himself had become enormously rich. In June 1924, he totted up his assets.

> I find today that my securities are worth over £98,000 – what a fortune! and how little difference it makes except that one can give unheeded gifts. What with cash and money out I have over £100,000. I always desired wealth, but never dreamed I should have such a fortune – and this after *lavish* pouring out of money here. Half of this is my own making – half Mme de Nottbeck's gift.

Still money was coming from America. He had only to express a need or a wish in a letter and his distant benefactress responded: the offer of a new car with a chauffeur; a cheque for £300 out of the blue to enjoy a 'wasteful holiday'; in April 1925, a further huge gift of £20,000 – a joint donation from her husband and herself. 'It is like a romance', Arthur wrote, 'and it fills my mind with affection for the dear donor, who has brought so much sunlight about my path of late and asks so little.' His assets rose to £120,000.

With his vast fortune, on the one hand, and his tiresome physical infirmities on the other, Arthur pictured himself as a 'mixture of Dives and Lazarus, covered with sores and with all useless conveniences'. But it was pleasant to be able effortlessly to pay off all George Rylands' debts for him (Winstanley contributed £100 as well) and to lavish money on the

College very much as the whim took him. After all, it was very difficult to gainsay the Master of the College when his wishes were reinforced by the financial capacity to execute them. Some of the Fellows, for instance, were none too enthusiastic about the purchase of an altar-cross for the Chapel. Arthur, rather gleefully, had his way, consulting the more sensitive of his colleagues about appropriate designs. As they turned the pages of a catalogue together, 'whenever we came to a crucifix, Peel drew in his breath sharply and winced, Ramsey turned it over as if he had opened an improper book'.

It seemed as if there was nothing that money could not buy. He liked mountains; he had become increasingly attached to the Lake District. Why should he not own the highest mountain in England? Gordon Wordsworth put the idea into Arthur's mind and suggested that Lord Leconfield might be prepared to sell Scafell to the two of them as joint owners. In September 1924 they lunched with Lord Leconfield at Cockermouth and discussed the proposition, poring over maps with his agent afterwards.

> 'Half is my freehold, half my manor [Lord Leconfield observed]. I can't think why you should want to *buy* – You can go anywhere, do anything already. I have no rights but mineral and shooting rights; and there isn't an ounce of anything but soft stone, nor any sign of life. If I weren't transparently honest, I would not tell you all this. Half of it is common, and you can't buy out the commoners. Still if you have money to throw away and like to buy rights which you enjoy already, well and good!' Gordon [Wordsworth] said it was a question of sentiment. 'Where does *my* sentiment come in? I rather like owning it – and I have given the Scafell Pikes to the Trust.' He said he would consider an offer for all above the 2000 foot contour. I told him I was a N.T. Trustee. 'Then you have already more rights than I have.'

He could not buy the Pike, the highest point of the Scafell range; but he could be co-purchaser of its highly dramatic neighbour. The Rock and Fell Club were indignant, demanding an option to purchase if Leconfield wanted to sell and accusing Arthur of 'vulgar self-advertisement'. George Trevelyan took his side and encouraged him to go ahead. As soon as the purchase was announced Arthur was approached by other parties seeking to dispose of places of national interest. Would he be interested, for instance, in buying Porchester Castle?

He could indulge his whims; he could survey with justifiable satisfaction the rising prestige of the College. Magdalene personalities were undoubtedly making their impact upon the university. Although, as a schoolmaster, he had inveighed consistently against the absurd lack of proportion in the adulation at athletes, he came to think rather differently when the prestige of the College rested on his own shoulders. He allowed himself to be taken to Fenner's to watch athletic matches, priding himself on the achievements of Lord Burghley in the hurdles; he allowed the cricket Blue, E. W. Dawson, to have leave-of-absence to play for Leicestershire during full term, taking exception to A. S. Ramsey's lack of imagination and inflexibility. 'Ramsey is rather absurd about it all', he wrote; 'fears we shall lose our reputation for strictness if we give him any rope. He won't see that to have a thoroughly good and delightful boy here, in the Cambr XI is worth more than any repute for strictness. He won't or can't face facts.' In the following year, he unashamedly rejoiced that Magdalene had secured the Presidency of the Union (in Michael Ramsey) as well as three athletics Blues. 'Very good for the place and makes me proud of the boys.'

Arthur – it must be said to his credit – did not live in the past. He did not lament the passing of the pre-war generation; and although he was critical of the younger dons, he was as responsive as ever he had been to the needs and enthusiasms of the undergraduates of the early twenties. A sad letter from Luxmoore at Eton, deploring the frivolity and irreligion of post-war youth, provoked from Arthur a forthright defence. 'These young men are more pagan in some ways', he admitted. 'At least they have thrown over all the lumber of religion – but they are much more civilised.' Occasionally, however, his mind was forced to dwell nostalgically on past memories. In June 1924, when he was feeling very low in health and confined to bed as a remedy for his sore and swollen legs, he received the news that George Mallory had been killed on Mount Everest. 'This entirely knocked me over', he wrote. 'It is so utterly tragic. I think people have a right to risk their lives – but this is his *third* expedition, and he had a wife and 2 children – and after all it is only a *feat*. He has been a very dear friend ever since he became my pupil here in 1905, and I have known him in all moods and stages. He had become much gentler and more tolerant of late.' It grieved him especially that he could not deliver the address at the memorial service in the College Chapel on the following Sunday. He wrote what he felt was fitting and arranged for Ramsey to deputise for him. From his bed he heard the hymns being sung in the Chapel – 'and I not there' – 'but I am tired and acquiesce in anything'.

More evocative of the passing of an epoch was the death, in the following month, of Charles Sayle. Arthur was fit enough to attend his funeral at St Bene'ts. Somehow the era of intense romantic friendships, of Rupert Brooke and Archie Don – those who had once been 'all Sayle's world' – demanded a more fitting memorial.

> The coffin brought into the Church with a purple pall. A fussy old vicar for ever peering out from a pillar and signalling with his cap. . . . Sayle was very particular about funerals and liked pomp. But this was a melancholy fiasco. He should have had a big company of bright boys (whom he loved best) to take him to his last resting-place, weeping for him and yet prepared to forget. Instead he had a band of undistinguished mourners and a crowd of rather dilapidated dons. . . . It was horrible to think of S. cold and frozen in his box and his harmless, courteous, kindly innocent life over. He was always good to me; but there seemed *nothing* behind his little varnish of self-importance – no thought, no style, no enthusiasm, no loyalty even. As long as he had a pretty boy to pet, it mattered little. 'He's almost a religion to us', as he said of Archie Don. He had no faith and yet no negation of faith – a very gentle, empty soul.

Sayle really belonged to a Cambridge that died during the first World War – a Cambridge of 'books, music and beautiful young men'. Arthur could never quite make up his mind about him. 'What his emotions led to, I don't know. There was something tepid about it. But he was full of kindness and real courtesy. . . . He knew his own mind and lived his own life – and it wasn't a vulgar one.'

So Sayle had died – as had most of the young men whom he had loved. Arthur could write of it all with humour, pathos and detachment. He did not pause to ask himself whether the world that was passing was in reality the world to which he himself temperamentally belonged; nor did he consider the extent to which his description of Sayle might have been applied to himself. In the summer of 1924 Arthur was in one of his vigorous, critical and caustic moods. He was angry with Dadie Rylands for not answering letters ('the little idyll will all fade out . . . the glow has faded'); he was totally unsentimental in his appraisal of Lord Esher, when invited to compose an obituary for *The Times* ('It is hard to express Esher's inner emptiness and selfishness and his general amateurishness, all concealed under so suave and courtly a demeanour'). He was frankly annoyed at Mallory's mother's attempts to over-rate the influence of the excellent, but limited, George upon his generation. She had become 'strangely exaltée over his death', he wrote. 'She seems to be stirring the situation with both hands, like a stewpot over a fire.' In disrespectful converse with Winstanley, they sought for the appropriate epigram to describe the grotesque self-centredness of Percy Lubbock, whose affair with Adrian Graham seemed to be wearing distinctly thin. They settled for Winstanley's suggestion: 'If he had been one of the Twelve Apostles he would have been the first to leave the Last Supper and the last to arrive at the Tomb.'

He was, in fact, in excellent form. He had just completed two of the best books he ever wrote; a third in the same genre (a memoir of his mother) was in preparation. He was never more wickedly observant of the faults and foibles of his colleagues and friends. The world of the twenties was no new age to Arthur. The war, and the private nightmare that followed, had been but a parenthesis – a disturbing one, admittedly – both in his own and in Cambridge life. Not for a moment did it enter his head that he might himself have only a few more months to live.

*   *   *   *   *

A danger sign, if he had interpreted it aright, occurred on 19 July 1924. While being driven by taxi to Fleam's Dyke with Maurice Baring as his companion for an intended walk, 'a violent attack of burning pain came on'. It passed; and they took their walk. Arthur consulted Dr Jones on return who – much to his annoyance – persuaded him to take an aspirin. He awoke the next morning 'with the filthy taste of drugs and with a narcotised brain. I *hate* drugs and would rather have any pain.' Apart from his increasing weight and the troublesome sores on his legs, however, he was incommoded no more for several months. He spent the late summer at Rye with various companions – David Loveday, Bernard Manning, Owen Morshead, Dadie Rylands. As soon as Rylands was with him again, all the recriminations evaporated on the instant. 'No one has ever made so free with me', Arthur commented. 'He pats one's shoulder, puts his hand through one's arm and behaves as a son might.' Arthur even tried out Sebastian Sprott as a holiday companion, but was not greatly taken. He wore his hair too long ('that ugly mane which falls on his eyes *cannot* be comfortable and looks much affected') and was too precious in his mannerisms. Arthur thought him 'aesthetic and heterodox and possibly hermaphrodite. He must once have been a beautiful young man.'

In September, with a certain trepidation, he made a sentimental journey to Horsted Keynes to see Tremans once again. He looked up Lucy Tait; they visited Marshall, the Bensons' coachman, who was dying of cancer. They stood by Beth's grave.

> So down the lane to TREMANS – a new lawn tennis court – but *all just* the
> same. Kind and patient, as though it welcomed me. The garden a little
> neglected. The accursed Mrs Hardy has pulled the dovecote in the orchard
> down. How well I remember my first sight of it in 1899! The stables
> enlarged, some greenhouses. But all my nightmare dreams vanished and I
> felt I could live there – the whole place, every corner, full of presences and
> pictures and scenes. It is more my home than any place.

As he returned to Rye, he reflected on his earlier apprehensions. 'We
need never be afraid of memories', he wrote, 'they spill their bitterness, as
a stream drops its silt.'

The new academic year at Cambridge began with discussions in the
Governing Body about the purchase of a College hostel; and Arthur, with
Talbot Peel, went over to the Old Brewery on the following day to make
an inspection. There were the freshmen to inspect, too – and Arthur's eye
roved round their number to find Noel Blakiston, about whom he had
heard so much from David Loveday. His first sight of him was actually at
the ceremony for the admission of the new scholars, and Arthur was so
preoccupied with Blakiston's physical comeliness that he admitted him to
a Fellowship by mistake. Shortly afterwards he invited him to accompany
him to a performance of *Ruddigore*. Definitely promising, he thought: 'A
dark-eyed creature whom Loveday told me would be stand-offish. But I
find him most forthcoming and delightful.' An invitation to stay at Lamb
House after Christmas was soon extended. In quick succession, Geoffrey
Madan, Dadie Rylands and Noel Blakiston were his guests there. With
Geoffrey Madan, Arthur felt that they had reached the parting of the
ways. He had become dogmatic and tiresomely narrow in his concept of
beauty. Dadie Rylands was as charming as ever ('Compared to him G.M.
feels a little like an iceberg'). As for Noel Blakiston – 'This young man,
who is very nice to me without being shy or submissive, stirs something
in my heart.'

Early in the new year, Arthur attended what turned out to be his last
royal occasion: the service for the dedication of the ancient episcopal
throne of Norwich Cathedral, attended by the Queen. It was just the sort
of ceremony that Arthur loved. He was put out, initially, by a tiresome
neighbour, 'a great stout sad lady ... enveloped in furs, smelling of myrrh
and cassia, and herself strongly scented, so that it seemed like an
embalmed corpse.' But there were splendid processions, with
improbable dignitaries and self-conscious civic persons to enliven him,
exciting his disrespectful descriptive powers to the full. 'Old Canon

Aitken, Bishop of Thetford, like a good-humoured baboon' took the prize. Arthur studied the Queen carefully. She 'looked cold, shy, ill-pleased. It is a curiously rigid face, and the mouth (when singing) very grim. She held up a double eye-glass and followed service very closely.' He talked with her afterwards and she was exceedingly forthcoming in her opinions, delivered between short, nervous puffs at a cigarette. They found themselves in agreement over Lord Northcliffe. 'A dreadful man', the Queen said, 'Quite unbalanced. The King and I thought we must really stop taking in *The Times*.' The civic party were then presented 'They were led up to the Queen one by one, making all sorts of grotesque contortions. I was much struck by the way the rather dowdy lady, in a brown baggy gown, worked away with a certain dignity, pertinaciously and good-humouredly, saying or trying to say something civil to everyone, though it was evidently not congenial. . . . A foolish woman said to me, "How gracious she is – every inch a Queen." Now that was *exactly* what she was not. She had no majesty of mien, or ease or stateliness. She looked a hard-worked and rather tired woman, plainly dressed, doing her best to be civil to nervous people.'

As the Lent Term progressed, Arthur was profoundly irritated by a particular issue of University politics. There was a debate in the Senate House over the practice of granting doctorates *jure dignitatis* to bishops, deans and heads of houses, the outcome of which was a successful vote by the *non-placets* securing the abolition of the conferment of such degrees in the future. Arthur took this as a personal snub and protested at once to the Vice-Chancellor, informing him that he would forthwith resign his degree of Doctor of Laws. 'I don't want to give up my doctorate and its little glories – but better that than hold one under false pretences.' The Vice-Chancellor, after advice, pointed out that a degree could not be resigned. It could only be removed for the commission of felony. But Arthur would not let it be. He enquired into the possibility of a special grace to deprive him of the LL.D. degree as an individual submission. He discussed the matter with the other Heads. Walter Durnford blandly told him that he knew that he himself hadn't earned his doctorate for any conceivable academic distinction, but he had certainly no intention of giving it up. Fitzpatrick claimed that his own particular doctorate had been fully deserved because of his responsibility as Vice-Chancellor during the War. Arthur's pique gradually subsided, but he felt that he would never again feel quite the same pride in putting on his scarlet gown. He consulted Laurence over the possibility of a Litt.D. on the merits of his published work, but received little or no encouragement.

His spirits rose again at the prospect of Noel Blakiston staying with him for a few days at Rye over Easter. Shortly before the end of term, however, on the train to London (to attend a meeting of the Fishmongers), he was again troubled by a totally unexpected attack of violent pain. It is true that he had not been feeling well for the previous week; but the attack was worse than anything he had ever experienced before; a sort of 'violent cramp in left side. I thought I should faint. I was deadly pale and the sweat pouring down. I never felt such pain. It passed off.' The following night, when Sebastian Sprott was dining with him, he had a similar attack. Arthur gave the matter no further thought once he had recovered. Dadie Rylands visited him the next day, and all else was forgotten. They discussed 'happiness'. 'We thought how hard it was to think of any people who were both happy and also radiated happiness. He disconcerted me by saying I was one.'

The second holiday with Noel Blakiston saw a real advance in their relationship. On the day after they arrived at Rye together, the talk became intimate. It was Blakiston who raised the topic of Platonic love. 'I aired my belief that one must submit to conventions and human arrangements unless one felt one *ought* to break with them.' There seemed about the boy a complete lack of 'prudishness and false shame'. He gave imitations of the 'dreary Chitty' at Eton and his 'talks on serious matters'. After dinner, when they had entertained the Vicar, 'we sate and talked over a dying fire. ... N. seemed a little tired, and in dress clothes looked very beautiful with large eyes and rather pettishly-folded lips. He seems happy here.' Other visitors followed – Cordelia Marshall, Francis Turner, Owen Morshead, Fred; Arthur was much occupied in writing *The House of Menerdue*. He reflected on the approach of his sixty-third birthday:

> I liked Noel Blakiston's visit *very much* – he was charming. The rest of my visitors very nice. ... But I haven't been enough alone. ... I am not ambitious. I don't at all want to be V.C. nor much to be Prime Warden. I don't foresee any other possible work ahead, except *perhaps* the Provostship of King's. ... My health and spirits are good – but I weigh nearly 20 stone and am very stiff and lame.

Before he left for Cambridge two little incidents occurred. The first was the curious behaviour of his gardener, Spicer. Just as Sharpe had known – way back in September 1907 – when Arthur had left Hinton Hall for Windermere, that he would never again return to live there, so Spicer showed a quite inordinate grief at the prospect of his going, almost as if he knew that they would never meet again. The second was a little whimsical act, which gave him a thrill of pleasure. It was in Bixley Wood near Beckley, where he was walking with Fred.

> Met 3 delightful little Sutton boys, wheeling the youngest in a box – the eldest charming and confiding. I asked if they were taking the youngest away to sell him and what he was worth.

He appraised the youngster carefully and offered his companions threepence. It was almost the last financial transaction of his life, and in itself exquisitely symbolical: to make as if to buy himself a little boy.

*   *   *   *   *

A host of engagements awaited him at Cambridge: several preachments, a lecture at the Royal Society of Literature, several visits to London on Fishmonger Pensioner business. He had a short reminder of an old friendship which had gone very sour, in attending a lecture by Hugh Walpole in the Senate House. It was not until the beginning of June that he noted in his diary that he was feeling ill, with occasional shivering fits and the aches and pains suggestive of a high temperature. On Friday 5 June he woke in the middle of the night 'in violent pain on left side of chest. I meditated dying in dignity like Dr Arnold. But after an hour it bettered.'

His doctors thought he might have pleurisy and kept him in bed. Arthur certainly did not rest. He wrote twenty-one letters and began to sketch out the plan of a novel. He wrote up his diary on Monday, 8 June, following a visit from A. S. Ramsey who had retold him some gossip.

> R. told me a story of Mrs Weekes, wife of Master of Sidney, a dusky rolling-eyed hag (there is no other word for it) who is said to like to hold undergrads' hands and influence them. She is supposed to have said to one of them archly 'I know your disrespectful phrase, when you come to see my husband, about "keeping a Master". I hope when you come to see me, you don't describe it as "keeping a Mistress".' She is a good and active woman, but of low origin, a hospital nurse, I think.

This was Arthur Benson's final diary entry. On 10 June, while his bed was being made and he was sitting in an arm-chair in his study, he suffered a severe heart attack. He was kept there – it being thought unsafe to move him – until 12 June. He recovered consciousness and asked Hunting to arrange for Ramsey to see him. 'I found him [Ramsey recalled] sitting in the chair, where he had been all night, looking very much altered, very weak and exhausted. He had been opening and reading a pile of letters. .... He was only able to speak in a whisper.' His anxiety was that Ramsey should attend to two testimonials which he had been asked to supply by that morning's post. 'His parting words as I left the room were, "We mustn't let people down!" That was the last time I saw him.'

On Monday, 15 June, his mind began to wander, and it was soon obvious that he was past recovery. 'Late in the evening of Tuesday, June 16, a message was sent round that he was sinking. Most of the Fellows came into College, impelled by the wish to be near him, and sat sadly together; and about twenty minutes after midnight they learned that he was no more.'

If he had had the power to do so, this compulsive chronicler would have described his sensations to the very end. Only he could know how near he was to the actuality when he attempted to chart the passage out of the world of time into the sphere of timelessness in *The Child of the Dawn*. It would have been a falling out of turmoil and pain into a sort of conscious sleep. He would have been carried along as by a 'moving tide, glad to rest, not wondering or hoping, not fearing or expecting anything – just there, and at peace'.

RETROSPECT

My idea of Heaven is a terrace with a view.
(September 1924)
It is like looking out of a tower in the mist ... an impossibly
beautiful world, thousands of feet below.   (June 1906)

Only a fortnight before he died Arthur Benson wrote to Geoffrey Madan
in a somewhat introspective vein. Madan had used the phrase 'first-rate'
in describing the genius of the great Orientalist, Sir William Jones.
Arthur reflected on the phrase:

> I doubt if one can *become* first-rate. ... A small percentage of people have
> germs of first-rateness, which don't always ripen owing to surroundings
> being unfavourable. But it can't be done by taking thought. I for instance
> am a good case of an essentially second rate person who has had every
> opportunity to be first rate, except the power to do so.

Not everybody has the courage to admit that they can rise no higher
than the second-rate; and it is, perhaps, one of Arthur's charms that he
was so engagingly self-critical, and – although an inveterate grumbler and
sensitive to slights – never claimed for himself more than he deserved, or
represented himself in his private writings as an unappreciated genius.
He recognised very honestly that even the best of his writings rarely rose
above the second-rate; he could never find the theme to match such
powers as he had; he was doomed, by a deficiency in inventiveness,
everlastingly to serve up 'sauce without meat'. He was not a scholar, yet
spent the larger part of his life among scholars, very few of whom he
would allow to be labelled 'first-rate'. The greatest gift he possessed –
that of a teacher – he tended to underrate.

But the consciousness of second-rateness goes far deeper than that. He
believed that he consistently failed to realise his true potential through
natural timidity: a fear of being hurt, of becoming involved, of taking
responsibility which might circumscribe his liberty. Arthur knew himself
only too well. The tragedy was that the very deficiency he discerned in
himself was precisely the impediment which prevented him from doing

379

anything about it. He was too cautious and timid to undertake commitment: but *because* he was so cautious and timid he could not make the resolution to supply the defect. Indeed, because self-knowledge was never accompanied by self-amendment, despite the chastening effect of depressive illness, he could never truly appreciate the extent of his loss. He accepted his powers as second-rate, and thereby he restricted his objectives to the second-best.

One of the essays which he used regularly to set his undergraduate pupils was the subject: 'The Best Thing in the World'. Very few, he believed, supplied the right answer. The commonest answer was 'Health'. Arthur did not agree. Surely the best we can aspire to is 'anything which gets us away from our private claims and ambitions and grievances and makes us interested in life'. It is the answer we should expect him to supply. But applied subjectively to himself, it is certainly the wrong answer. It is almost true to say that the error it contains provides the primary clue to Arthur's unsatisfied and incomplete life. He was interested in people, scenes, natural phenomena, buildings, simple vignettes of normal people going about their daily business; but he was interested in them chiefly as spectatorial objects, as things which he could view, savour and describe. Their pleasure to him was essentially aesthetic. They fed his love of the interplay of contrasting forces – the simple and the grotesque, the normal and the strange, tragedy and farce. 'Interest in Life' is all very fine; but one cannot actually live a full life until one is prepared to abandon the spectatorial role, to descend into the arena and become actively involved.

One of his favourite aphorisms was the observation ascribed to Goethe: 'Of that which a man desires in his youth, he shall have enough in his age.' He recognised that life had been almost cruelly good to him in enabling him to realise ambition after ambition one by one: fame (of a sort); power; a great deal of independence; considerable wealth. He had more than enough of all these things by his middle-age. But he knew that he was still dissatisfied. If he defined Paradise in these terms, he had certainly gained the paradise of his fantasies. And yet all he had gained was the territorial vantage-point from which he could view Paradise, never Paradise itself. It might be argued that whatever heaven or hell might turn out to be, they constitute for each individual that final resting-place for which his soul craves. Where our heart is, there shall our paradise be found. And if the fulfilment of life is the granting of our youthful desires, the Paradise beyond may be *a fortiori* some eternal bestowal of the good things we have yearned to acquire. There were moments when Arthur seemed to learn so little from life that his chosen Paradise appears to be merely an extension of his earthly ambitions.

He dreamt of the Day of Judgement once – in characteristically absurd terms. He was lined up in a corridor outside an office in a building like the Foreign Office. Hugh was in the queue ahead of him, and Marshall (the Tremans coachman) on his other side, waiting to follow him in. Hugh was summoned and came out in awful misery. 'It's been all wrong!' he wailed as he tottered down the passage. Then it was Arthur's turn. He was asked a few questions by a brisk man behind a desk, who then sat back and blasted him with a most scathing indictment of his indolence, selfishness and self-centredness. Arthur waited for Marshall to emerge. His interview was shorter, and he came out rubbing his hands. 'It's all right and I always thought it would be', he said, 'That's a sensible person!'

If Arthur were doomed to a scathing judgement, perhaps the worst punishment he could be subjected to would be the Paradise that he thought he wanted for himself. How did he describe it? Shortly before he died he put it like this: 'My idea of Heaven is a terrace with a view . . ., with the people I like sitting silent or talking or reading, listening to music – and some solitude as well.' Years before, he had compared his view of literature with that of G. T. Lapsley, and had given a similar picture of his ideal. 'With me, it is like looking out of a tower in the mist – the mist parts and breaks. I see something I take to be a shrub at the tower's foot – suddenly the senses swim, and I see that it is a forest, in an impossibly beautiful world, thousands of feet below.'

The 'beautiful world' is always 'thousands of feet below'. One looks down upon it and views to one's heart's content. It is the sublime experience of the compulsive *voyeur*: to see and not be seen; to view innumerable and endless private things without interruption or discovery. Only one further requirement would be pressing: an abundance of paper, pen and ink, because all these things would have to be described.

And this is where the life faltered, and perhaps failed. It would be foolish to suppose that it was ineffective. Too many people, through generations of his pupils, owed too much to him and his personal kindness for such a judgement to be countenanced. Too many people took real pleasure from his books, and were rendered the happier through the reading of them. Nor was his life a discontented one, even though there were stretches of blank misery when the things he found most beautiful turned to ashes in his mouth. But still he failed as a person to live a fulfilled life because he valued his independence too highly and could not achieve a lasting intimacy with any other human being. Always he protected himself from the danger of being entrapped in a relationship. In the end, however much he pined for love, he had to be free.

The septuagenarian, General Blewett, one of his colleagues of the Court of Fishmongers, once murmured to Arthur in the course of a boring discussion that the one regret he felt in his old age was that he had not *sinned* more as a young man. Sometimes Arthur felt the same. As he grew older, he envied those who were prepared to take risks, especially for love. He had no sexual life; all his sexual instincts had to be sublimated, mainly – he thought – through his timidity, which itself sprang from his upbringing. His fear of a sexual relationship made him shun all women who might in any way become a threat to him, and made all his relationships with young men rather pathetic inconsequential romances which terminated almost as soon as they developed into intimacies. Friendship had to be undemanding for Arthur. He could not, and would not, accept the demands.

Perhaps this was pure selfishness? Arthur could be very harsh with himself on this score. He read with fascination a passage from George Tyrrell:

> I don't think you understand how absolutely, indeed culpably, little I have ever cared about my own present or future peace, except as a condition of helpfulness to others.

Arthur commented:

> I put this down because it so strangely represents the exact and precise opposite of my own frame of mind, and is the origin of all my hollowness and feebleness of spirit. I have never cared about helpfulness to others except as a condition of my own present and future peace.

This is not the epitaph which ought to stand for posterity, true as it is of Arthur Benson in certain moods. He liked his comforts; he cherished his own precious routine. But he was never mean in his actions; he loathed all forms of cruelty; he never attempted to impose or force his views on others; he was endlessly courteous and kind, even to those whom he personally disliked or enjoyed deriding in the pages of his diary. Although the Paradise to suit his temperament would have been an Ariel-like existence 'flying all over the world ... just simply looking at things', he believed in fact (it was one of the few positive religious convictions to which he constantly adhered) that the after-life v ould be a process, or a sequence, of self-amendment. Life seen *sub specie aeternitatis* was essentially a journey. At any particular stage of the journey, one might have to make the best of the rather puny equipment with which one had been supplied. But other chances would come.

There was one motto which he treasured more reverently than the aphorism of Goethe, because it spoke directly and most keenly to his greatest need, however little in his life he succeeded in filling it. It was the motto of the Duchess of Sutherland, written on the title-page of her keepsake. Arthur copied it into his diary. This described life as a journey, too, but one made possible by the sense of never being alone.

> 'Let me take your hand for love, and sing you a song', said the other traveller. 'The journey is a hard journey, but if we hold together in the morning and in the evening, what matter if in the hours between there is sorrow?'

'Is not that beautiful?', he wrote.

It was far too beautiful, it must be admitted, for Arthur to live up to in his life; but, given the conviction that the journey does not terminate with death, who knows what might not be achieved in the end?

SOURCES AND BIBLIOGRAPHY

The principal source of this book is the diary of A. C. Benson, housed in a specially-constructed crate in the Old Library of Magdalene College, Cambridge. After Arthur Benson's death, two people only saw its contents – E. F. Benson, who refers to it in *Final Edition*, and Percy Lubbock who made a fascinating, but necessarily innocuous, selection from it in his book, *The Diary of Arthur Christopher Benson*, published by Hutchinson in 1927. Since their deaths, the whole contents have been read only by Dr Walter Hamilton, who was Master of Magdalene at the time when the period of embargo (fifty years) expired, and by myself.

Probably ninety-five per cent of the quotations in this book have been taken from this diary. It has therefore seemed unnecessary to supply footnotes and references. These would have overloaded the book and undoubtedly raised its published price. A typescript of my text, with full references, has been lodged in the Old Library at Magdalene, so that every reference can be checked by those wishing to consult the sources. I have also compiled an index to the diaries which I have given to Magdalene College, both as an aid to future researchers and as a mark of my gratitude to the College.

The whole collection amounts to 180 volumes, of which Volume 6 is missing. Since Percy Lubbock undoubtedly used this volume, covering the period from January to August 1901, one can only assume that Lubbock either mislaid it or for some reason thought it better suppressed. The diaries vary in size. The longest (Volume 3) is 562 pages; the shortest (Volume 169) is 21 (numbered by sheets, written on each side). Volume 180 (15 sheets; 30 pages) is unfinished. The total number of pages (although they are mostly numbered by sheets) is, by my calculation, 24,518. Since the dimensions of the diaries are not standard, it is difficult to supply an average number of words per page. If we were to take 200 words as the average (probably an under-estimate), the total number of words amounts to a little under five million.

In general, the legibility is exceptionally good. Only Volume 1 presents a few difficulties, where the early entries are written in a tiny script and some of the pages are in pencil. There are remarkably few erasures. A few names have been scored out. Occasionally Percy Lubbock has annotated the text with pencilled comments, usually when questioning the accuracy of statements made.

The scope and coverage of the diaries may be briefly tabulated as follows:

YEAR	VOLUME NUMBERS	MAJOR EVENTS
1884–1897	1	Miscellaneous entries, mainly depressions. Death of Abp. Benson.
1897–Aug. 98	2	Eton.
1898–1899	3	*Life of E. W. Benson.*
1899–1900	4	*Fasti Etonenses.*
1900–Jan. 01	5	Eton. Death of Queen Victoria.
1901	6–10	Eton.
1902	10–22	Elgar conducts 'Ode'.
1903	22–44	Eton fire. Hugh Benson becomes R.C. Resigns Eton. *Hill of Trouble.* Begins *Q.V. Letters.*
1904	44–64	Old Granary, Mustians. *House of Quiet*; *Rossetti.* Fellow of Magd.
1905	64–77	*Upton Letters*; *Thread of Gold.* Meets H. Walpole.
1906	77–88	Hinton Hall. *From a College Window.* Meets G. Mallory
1907	88–98	*Beside Still Waters*; *Q.V. Letters.* Awarded C.V.O. Breakdown.
1908	99–104	1st breakdown.
1909	104–109	1st breakdown. Death of Tatham.
1910	109–117	Meets G. Winterbottom. *Silent Isle.*
1911	118–127	*Leaves of the Tree.* Death of Beth.
1912	127–135	*Child of the Dawn*; *Thy Rod and Staff.* President of Magd.
1913	135–142	*Along the Road*; *Joyous Gard*; *Watersprings.* Meets G. Madan.
1914	142–150	*Where no Fear Was*; *Orchard Pavilion.* Death of Hugh. War.
1915	150–157	*Hugh*; *Father Payne.* De Nottbeck offer. Master of Magd. LL.D.
1916	157–163	*Meanwhile*; Death of Maggie (*Life & Letters*). Revisits Eton.
1917	163–166	2nd breakdown in August.
1918	167	St. Michael's, Ascot (breakdown).

YEAR	VOLUME NUMBERS	MAJOR EVENTS
1922	168	With E. F. Benson at Blakeney (breakdown). *Reed of Pan*.
1923	169–173	*Trefoil*. Meets G. Rylands.
1924	173–178	*Memories and Friends*; *Chris Gascoyne*. Death of Mallory. Meets N. Blakiston.
1925	178–180	*House of Menerdue*. Illness and death.

ADDITIONAL MS SOURCES

1. 7 miscellaneous volumes of jottings, housed with the diaries at Magdalene.
2. The letters of A. C. Benson to Geoffrey Madan. The originals are in a cardboard box in the Old Library at Magdalene; there are also 3 volumes of typescript copies.
3. Collection of 'Bensoniana', bequeathed to Magdalene by Mr W. Poyser.
4. A few letters from individual correspondents (e.g. the letters of Benson to the Revd. Richard Keable).
5. The letters of A. C. Benson to David Loveday (kindly lent to me by the Rt. Revd. David Loveday, of Wardington, Banbury).
6. The letters of A. C. Benson to Dr E. W. Barnes (kindly lent to me by Sir John Barnes, of Hurstpierpoint).
7. Memorandum of Mr A. S. Ramsey, President and Bursar of Magdalene (kindly lent to me by the Rt. Revd. and Rt. Hon. Lord Ramsey of Canterbury).

PUBLISHED WORKS

A. WORKS OF A. C. BENSON
(*given in chronological order of publication*)

1886 *Memoirs of Arthur Hamilton, B.A., of Trinity College, Cambridge, extracted from his letters and diaries, with reminiscences of his conversation, by his friend, CHRISTOPHER CARR of the same College* (Kegan Paul).

1887 *William Laud, sometime Archbishop of Canterbury. A Study* (Kegan Paul).

1890 (with H. F. W. Tatham), *Men of Might. Studies of Great Characters* (Edward Arnold).

1892 *Le Cahier Jaune. Poems*, privately printed, Eton.

1893 *Poems* (John Lane).

1895 *Lyrics* (John Lane).

1896 *Essays* (Heinemann).

1897 *Lord Vyet and other Poems* (John Lane, Bodley Head).

1899 *Fasti Etonenses. A Biographical History of Eton* (Eton, Ingalton Drake).
       Life of Edward White Benson, sometime Archbishop of Canterbury, 2 vols.
          (Macmillan).

1900 *The Professor and other Poems* (John Lane).

1902 *The Schoolmaster. A Commentary upon the aims and methods of an assistant-
          master in a Public School* (John Murray).

1903 *The Myrtle Bough. A Vale*, privately printed, Eton.
       The Hill of Trouble, and other stories (Isbister).
       Selections from J. G. Whittier.

1904 *Alfred Tennyson* (Methuen).
       The House of Quiet. An Autobiography (John Murray).
       The Isles of Sunset, and other stories (Isbister).
       The Olive Bough, privately printed, Eton.
       Rossetti (English Men of Letters, Macmillan).

1905 *Peace, and other Poems* (John Lane).
       Edward Fitzgerald (English Men of Letters, Macmillan).
       The Upton Letters (Smith, Elder).
       The Thread of Gold (John Murray).

1906 *Walter Pater* (English Men of Letters, Macmillan).
       From a College Window (Smith, Elder).

1907 *The Letters of One. A Study in Limitations by 'Charles Hare Plunkett'*
          (Smith, Elder).
       (with Viscount Esher). *The Letters of Queen Victoria. A Selection from Her
          Majesty's Correspondence 1837–1861*, 3 vols. (John Murray).
       The Altar Fire (Smith, Elder).
       Hymns and Carols, privately printed, Eton.
       Beside Still Waters (Smith, Elder).

1908 *At Large* (Smith, Elder).

1909 *The Gate of Death. A Diary* (John Murray).

1910 *The Silent Isle* (Smith, Elder).

1911 *Ruskin. A Study in Personality* (Smith, Elder).
       The Leaves of the Tree (Smith, Elder).
       Paul the Minstrel, and other stories (Smith, Elder).

1912 *Thy Rod and thy Staff* (Smith, Elder).
       The Child of the Dawn (Smith, Elder).

Sources and Bibliography

1913 *Along the Road* (James Nisbet).
Joyous Gard (John Murray).
Watersprings. A Novel (Smith, Elder).
1914 *Where no Fear was* (Smith, Elder).
The Orchard Pavilion (Smith, Elder).
1915 *Escape, and other Essays* (Smith, Elder).
Father Payne (Smith, Elder).
Hugh. Memoir of a Brother (Smith, Elder).
(editor), *Bronte Poems. Selections from the Poetry of Charlotte, Emily, Anne and Branwell Bronte* (John Murray).
1916 *Meanwhile. A Packet of War Letters by 'H.L.G.'* (John Murray).
1917 *Life and Letters of Maggie Benson* (John Murray).
1918 (editor), *Cambridge Essays on Education* (Cambridge University Press).
1922 *The Reed of Pan. English Renderings of Greek Epigrams and Lyrics* (John Murray).
1923 *The Trefoil. Wellington College, Lincoln and Truro* (John Murray).
1924 *Memories and Friends* (John Murray).
Chris Gascoyne. An Experiment in Solitude, from the diaries of John Trevor (John Murray).
1925 *The House of Menerdue* (Heinemann).
'The Art of the Biographer', privately printed.
1926 (posthumous), *The Canon* (Heinemann).
(posthumous), *Rambles and Reflections* (John Murray).
1927 (posthumous), *Cressage* (Heinemann).

B. Other Works

This list includes only those books which have actually been quoted in my text or which have supplied information unavailable from other sources. Place of publication is London unless otherwise stated.

Askwith, Betty, *Two Victorian Families*, 1971.
The Lytteltons. A Family Chronicle of the Nineteenth Century, 1975.
Asquith, Margot, *Autobiography*, 1920.
Battiscombe, Georgina, *Reluctant Pioneer. The Life of Elizabeth Wordsworth*, 1978.
Beerbohm, Max, *A Christmas Garland*, 1912.
Benson, E. F., *Our Family Affairs, 1867–1896*, 1920.
Mother, 1925.
As We Were. A Victorian Peep-Show, 1930.
Final Edition. Informal Autobiography, 1940.

Sources and Bibliography

Benson, M. E., *At Sundry Times and in Divers Manners*, 2 vols., 1891.

Blakiston, Noel (editor), *A Romantic Friendship. The Letters of Cyril Connolly to Noel Blakiston*, 1975.

Charteris, Evan, *The Life and Letters of Sir Edmund Gosse*, 1931.

Esher, Reginald Viscount, *Ionicus*, 1923.

Fletcher, C. R. L., *Edmond Warre*, 1922.

Forster, E. M., *Goldsworthy Lowes Dickinson*, 1934.

Furbank, P. N., *E. M. Forster. A Life. The Growth of the Novelist*, 1977.

Hart-Davis, Rupert, *Hugh Walpole. A Biography*, 1952.

    (editor), *The Lyttelton–Hart-Davis Letters. Correspondence of George Lyttelton and Rupert Hart-Davis, 1955–6*, 1978.

Howarth, T. E. B., *Cambridge between Two Wars*, 1978.

James, M. R., *Eton and King's. Recollections, mostly trivial*, 1926.

Jones, L. E., *A Victorian Boyhood*, 1955.

Lubbock, Percy (editor), *The Diary of Arthur Christopher Benson*, 1927.

Martindale, C. C., *The Life of Monsignor Robert Hugh Benson*, 2 vols, 1916.

Mosley, Nicholas, *Julian Grenfell. His Life and the times of his death, 1888–1915*, 1976.

Newsome, David, *Godliness and Good Learning. Four Studies on a Victorian Ideal*, 1961.

Rothblatt, Sheldon, *The Revolution of the Dons. Cambridge and Society in Victorian England*, New York, 1968.

Ryle, E. H. (editor), *Arthur Christopher Benson, as seen by some friends*, 1925.

Sayle, Charles (editor), *Archibald Don. A Memoir*, 1918.

Sidgwick, A. and E. M., *Henry Sidgwick. A Memoir*, 1906.

Young, Percy, *Elgar, O. M., A Study of a Musician*, 1955.

INDEX

Index

Index

Index

Index

397

Index

399

Index

Index

Index

Index

Index